THE UNIVERSITY OF WINCHESTER

Walt Whitman once described New York City as "the great place of the western continent, the heart, the brain, the focus, the main spring, the pinnacle, the extremity, the no more beyond, of the New World." From its origins as a Dutch trading post called New Amsterdam to its embodiment of modernity at the turn of the twentieth century, New York has always held a special place in America's national mythology, a gateway to the USA and its premier cultural center. Illustrated and featuring a chronology and guide to further reading, this Companion explores a wide range of writing by and about New Yorkers, from early poetry and plays to modern punk rock. It sheds new light on the work of Whitman, Melville, Wharton, O'Neill, Ginsberg, and a host of other authors who have contributed to the city's – and America's – rich literary history.

CYRUS R. K. PATELL and BRYAN WATERMAN are Associate Professors of English at New York University.

A complete list of books in the series is at the back of this book

THE CAMBRIDGE
COMPANION TO
THE LITERATURE
OF NEW YORK

EDITED BY
CYRUS R. K. PATELL
AND
BRYAN WATERMAN

CAMBRIDGE
UNIVERSITY PRESS

CAMBRIDGE UNIVERSITY PRESS
Cambridge, New York, Melbourne, Madrid, Cape Town, Singapore,
São Paulo, Delhi, Tokyo, Mexico City

Cambridge University Press
The Edinburgh Building, Cambridge CB2 8RU, UK

Published in the United States of America by Cambridge University Press, New York

www.cambridge.org
Information on this title: www.cambridge.org/9780521735551

First published 2010
Reprinted 2011

Printed in the United Kingdom at the University Press, Cambridge

A catalogue record for this publication is available from the British Library

Library of Congress Cataloguing in Publication data
The Cambridge companion to the literature of New York / [edited by]
Cyrus R. K. Patell, Bryan Waterman.
p.   cm. – (Cambridge companions to literature)
ISBN 978-0-521-51471-2 (Hardback)
1. American literature–New York (State)–New York–History and criticism.   2. Authors,
American–Homes and haunts–New York (State)–New York.   3. New York
(N.Y.)–In literature.   4. New York (N.Y.)–Intellectual life.   5. Literature and
society.   I. Patell, Cyrus R. K.   II. Waterman, Bryan, 1970–   III. Title.
IV. Series.
PS255.N5C35   2010
810.9'97471–dc22
2009052176

ISBN 978-0-521-51471-2 Hardback
ISBN 978-0-521-73555-1 Paperback

CONTENTS

List of illustrations   *page* vii
Notes on contributors   ix
Acknowledgments   xiii
Chronology   xiv

Introduction   1
CYRUS R. K. PATELL

1 From British outpost to American metropolis   10
ROBERT LAWSON-PEEBLES

2 Dutch New York from Irving to Wharton   27
ELIZABETH L. BRADLEY

3 The city on stage   42
BRYAN WATERMAN

4 Melville, at sea in the city   58
THOMAS AUGST

5 Whitman's urbanism   76
LYTLE SHAW

6 The early literature of New York's moneyed class   90
CALEB CRAIN

7 Writing Brooklyn   109
MARTHA NADELL

8 New York and the novel of manners   121
SARAH WILSON

9   Immigrants, politics, and the popular cultures of tolerance   134
ERIC HOMBERGER

10   Performing Greenwich Village bohemianism   146
MELISSA BRADSHAW

11   African American literary movements   160
THULANI DAVIS

12   New York's cultures of print   176
TRYSH TRAVIS

13   From poetry to punk in the East Village   189
DANIEL KANE

14   Staging lesbian and gay New York   202
ROBIN BERNSTEIN

15   Emergent ethnic literatures   218
CYRUS R. K. PATELL

Epilogue: Nostalgia and counter-nostalgia in New York City writing
BRYAN WATERMAN   232

Further reading   241
Index   244

ILLUSTRATIONS

Figure 1   "A description of the towne of Mannados or New
            Amsterdam as it was in September 1661." By
            permission of the British Library.   12
Figure 2   Drawing of Diedrich Knickerbocker by Felix
            O. C. Darley for the 1849 edition of *A History of
            New York*. By permission of the New York
            Public Library.   28
Figure 3   John Searle, *Interior of the Park Theater*, watercolor,
            1822. By permission of the New-York
            Historical Society.   47
Figure 4   F. S. Chanfrau as Mose in *A Glance at New York*,
            1848. Courtesy of the Library of Congress, Prints and
            Photographs Division, Washington, DC.   50
Figure 5   "Bird's-eye view of New York City with Battery Park
            in the Foreground," 1851. Courtesy of the Library
            of Congress, Prints and Photographs Division,
            Washington, DC.   59
Figure 6   Walt Whitman. Steel engraving by Samuel Hollyer
            from a lost daguerreotype by Gabriel Harrison.
            Courtesy of the Library of Congress, Prints and
            Photographs Division, Washington, DC.   77
Figure 7   Allen Ginsberg, New York City, Fall 1953. © Allen
            Ginsberg/CORBIS. Used by permission.   80
Figure 8   Frontispiece from Charles Astor Bristed's *The Upper
            Ten Thousand* (1852). Courtesy of The Fales Library &
            Special Collections, New York University.   95
Figure 9   Frontispiece from Matthew Hale Smith's *Sunshine
            and Shadow in New York* (1868). By permission of
            the New York Public Library.   96

Figure 10   Photograph of the Brooklyn Bridge, 1934. Courtesy of
             the Library of Congress, Prints and Photographs
             Division, Washington, DC.   111
Figure 11   Publicity photo of Edna St. Vincent Millay, 1914.
             Courtesy of the Library of Congress Prints and
             Photographs Division, Washington, DC.   154
Figure 12   Silent protest parade on Fifth Avenue, New York
             City, July 28, 1917. By permission of the New York
             Public Library.   164
Figure 13   Gerard Malanga and Patti Smith. Flyer for a poetry
             reading at St. Mark's Church in-the-Bowery,
             New York City, 1971. By permission of Gerard
             Malanga Private Collection.   191
Figure 14   A scene from the Split Britches' play, *Upwardly
             Mobile Home*, 1984. Photograph by Eva Weiss. Used
             by permission.   206
Figure 15   The Five Lesbian Brothers performing *Brave Smiles*
             at the WOW Café in 1992. Photograph by Dona Ann
             McAdams. Used by permission.   207

CONTRIBUTORS

THOMAS AUGST is Associate Professor of English at New York University. His scholarship explores the historical and social contexts of reading, writing, and speaking, seeking to interpret how literary institutions and practices have shaped the moral life of modern liberalism. He is the author of *The Clerk's Tale: Young Men and Moral Life in Nineteenth-Century America* (2003), and the co-editor of *Institutions of Reading: The Social Life of Libraries in the United States* (2007).

ROBIN BERNSTEIN, originally from Coney Island, Brooklyn, is an interdisciplinary scholar of US theater, performance, and literature. She teaches at Harvard University, where she is an Assistant Professor with a joint appointment in the Program of Studies of Women, Gender, and Sexuality and the Program in History and Literature. The editor of *Cast Out: Queer Lives in Theater* (2006), she is currently completing a book manuscript titled *Racial Innocence: Performing Childhood and Race from "Uncle Tom's Cabin" to the New Negro Movement*. She has published articles on the playwrights Anna Deavere Smith, Lorraine Hansberry, Angelina Weld Grimké, and on the children's author Louise Fitzhugh.

ELIZABETH L. BRADLEY is Deputy Director of the Cullman Center for Scholars and Writers at the New York Public Library. She is the author of *Knickerbocker: The Myth Behind New York* (2009), and edited the Penguin Classics edition of *A History of New York*, by Washington Irving (2008). Her work on New York City history and culture has been published in *Bookforum* and *The New-York Journal of American History*, and she is a contributor to the *Encyclopedia of New York City*.

MELISSA BRADSHAW is Assistant Professor of Women's and Gender Studies at DePaul University. Her research focuses on personality, publicity, and flamboyant excess in early twentieth-century literary culture. She co-edited *Selected Poems of Amy Lowell* (2002) and *Amy Lowell, American Modern* (2004), and is currently completing a book manuscript on Lowell.

CALEB CRAIN is the author of *American Sympathy: Men, Friendship, and Literature in the New Nation* (2001). He lives in Brooklyn and has written for *The New Yorker*, the *New York Review of Books*, and the *London Review of Books*.

THULANI DAVIS'S most recent book, *My Confederate Kinfolk* (2007) explores her black and white ancestors' lives around the time of the Civil War. Her other works include two novels, *1959* (1992) and *Maker of Saints* (1996), several plays, PBS documentaries, opera libretti, and the scripts for the films *Paid in Full* and *Maker of Saints*. A past recipient of a Lila Wallace-Readers Digest Writers' Award, a PEW Foundation National Theatre Artist Residency, and a Charles H. Revson Fellowship on the Future of New York City, she is a 1993 Grammy winner and has taught at Barnard College, Princeton University, and NYU's Tisch School of the Arts.

ERIC HOMBERGER, Emeritus Professor of American Studies at the University of East Anglia, Norwich, UK, is the author of four books about New York City: *The Historical Atlas of New York City* (2005), *Scenes from the Life of a City: Corruption and Conscience in Old New York* (1994), *Mrs Astor's New York: Money and Social Power in a Gilded Age* (2002), and *New York City: A Cultural and Literary Companion* (2003).

DANIEL KANE is Senior Lecturer in American Literature at the University of Sussex. He is the author of *We Saw the Light: Conversations Between the New American Cinema and Poetry* (2009), *Ostentation of Peacocks* (2009), *All Poets Welcome: The Lower East Side Poetry Scene in the 1960s* (2003), *What Is Poetry: Conversations with the American Avant-Garde* (2003) and, as editor and contributor, *Don't Ever Get Famous: Essays on New York School Writing after the "New York School"* (2006).

ROBERT LAWSON-PEEBLES held posts at Oxford, Princeton, and Aberdeen before moving to the University of Exeter, England, where he is now Leverhulme Emeritus Fellow and Honorary University Fellow. He has published on transatlantic cultural relations from Viking settlement onwards. His publications include *Landscape and Written Expression in Revolutionary America* (Cambridge, 1988, reprinted 2008), *Views of American Landscapes* (Cambridge, 1989, reprinted 2008), *Modern American Landscapes* (1995), *Approaches to the American Musical* (1996), and *American Literature before 1880* (2003). Work in progress includes a biography of Benjamin Franklin and a book on the impact of jazz in Britain.

MARTHA JANE NADELL is Associate Professor of English at Brooklyn College of The City University of New York. She is the author of *Enter the New Negroes: Images of Race in American Culture* (2004) as well as a number of articles about race, modernism, and the literary and visual culture of the Harlem Renaissance. She is at work on a literary and cultural history of Brooklyn.

CYRUS R. K. PATELL was born and raised on Manhattan's Upper West Side. He is Associate Professor of English at New York University and the author of *Negative Liberties: Morrison, Pynchon, and the Problem of Liberal Ideology* (2001) and *U.S. Multicultural Literatures: An Introduction to Emergent Writing after 1940* (forthcoming). He is collaborating with Bryan Waterman on a cultural history of New York City.

LYTLE SHAW is Associate Professor of English at New York University. He has recently published art catalog essays on Robert Smithson, Zoe Leonard, and Gerard Byrne as well as the book *Frank O'Hara: The Poetics of Coterie* (2006). His *Specimen Box: The Art of Institutional Frames* is forthcoming in 2010, and he is currently completing *Fieldworks: From Place to Site in Postwar Poetry*.

TRYSH TRAVIS is Assistant Professor in the Center for Women's Studies and Gender Research at the University of Florida, where she teaches contemporary US cultural and literary history with an emphasis on the gendered history of the book.

BRYAN WATERMAN is Associate Professor of English and American Literature at New York University. The author of *Republic of Intellect: The Friendly Club of New York City and the Making of American Literature* (2007), he has also published on topics relating to eighteenth- and nineteenth-century American writing in *The William and Mary Quarterly*, *Early American Literature*, *American Literary History*, and the online quarterly *Common-place*. He is currently collaborating with Cyrus R. K. Patell on a cultural history of New York City.

SARAH WILSON is Assistant Professor in the Department of English at the University of Toronto. She is the author of *Melting-Pot Modernism* (forthcoming).

ACKNOWLEDGMENTS

We are grateful to the Humanities Initiative at New York University for its support of our research into the literature and culture of New York City. Special thanks are due to Jane Tylus and Asya Berger.

Publication of this volume has been aided by a grant from the Stein Fund of the Department of English at New York University.

We are grateful to Betsy Bradley, Marvin Taylor, and Mike Kelly for helping us to research and obtain permissions for illustrations in this volume. We owe special debts of gratitude to Kristen Doyle Highland, who prepared the chronology for this volume; to Allison C. Green, who assisted with the index; and to Caroline Howlett, for editorial assistance.

Thanks to Alex Roe, director of the Metropolitan Playhouse in New York City, whose commitment to early American drama has inspired us and helped us to think through aspects of our research.

We are grateful to the teaching assistants who have worked with us in our *Writing New York* lecture course at NYU: Heather Alumbaugh, Brendan Beirne, Kyung-Sook Boo, James Brooke-Smith, Emily Cone-Miller, Laura Fisher, Adrienne Ghaly, Meghan Hammond, Stephanie Hsu, Spencer Keralis, Alyson Kiesel, Carmelo Larose, Jessie Morgan-Owens, Megan Obourn, Rachel Rosen, Catherine Savini, Jonathan Shaw, and Lenora Warren. We've learned a lot from you.

Without the love and support of our families, this volume would never have happened. Thank you Stephanie, Deborah, Anna, Molly, Charlie, Liam, and Caleb – we owe you big time!

Finally, this volume is dedicated to the students who have studied and enjoyed New York's literatures with us over the years.

CHRONOLOGY

1524   Italian explorer Giovanni da Verrazano, searching for the Northwest Passage, sails into New York Harbor.

1609   Henry Hudson, sponsored by the Dutch East India Company, explores and charts the Manhattan Harbor.

1621   The Dutch West India Company is chartered for the purposes of business profit and the protection of Dutch interests.

1625   Belgian and Dutch settlers found New Amsterdam on the southern end of Manhattan as a trading post and defensive position guarding Dutch business interests on the Hudson River.

1624–30   Nicolaes van Wassenaer publishes his news journal, *Historisch Verhael*, twice yearly.

1628   The *Letter of Reverend Jonas Michaëlius* describes New Amsterdam in the 1620s.

1638   First ferry service connects Manhattan and present-day Brooklyn.

1643   Exiled Puritan minister Anne Hutchinson is killed in Native American hostilities in New Netherland, in the present-day Bronx.

1650   Adrian van der Donck, *Remonstrance of New Netherland*, criticizes Governor Peter Stuyvesant's policies.

1653   New Amsterdam is granted its own charter, ending control of the Dutch West India Company; Stuyvesant orders construction of a palisade wall, later named Wall Street with the demolition of the wall in 1699.

1654   Stuyvesant attempts to prevent twenty-three Sephardic Jews from entering New Amsterdam, but is rebuked by the West India Company.

1657   The Flushing Remonstrance protests Stuyvesant's ban on Quaker worship and argues for religious tolerance in the colony.

1659   Jacob Steendam, "The Complaint of New Amsterdam"; "The Praise of New Netherland" (1662).

1664	The Duke of York captures New Amsterdam for the British crown, renaming the colony New York; the Dutch briefly regain the colony in 1673, before permanently ceding it to the English in 1674.
1670	Daniel Denton, *A Brief Description of New-York*.
1697	Trinity Church is established for Anglican worship; three different buildings, built in 1698, 1790, and 1846, would occupy the site at Wall Street and Broadway.
1711	Slave market opens at Wall Street and East River.
1712	Twenty-three slaves rebel, setting fire to homes and attacking white colonists.
1725	William Bradford publishes the first New York newspaper, the *New York Gazette*.
1731	First public library opens in City Hall; smallpox epidemic kills over 500 colonists.
1733	Newspaper publisher John Peter Zenger, on trial for seditious libel, is exonerated in a defense establishing freedom of the press.
1741	Slaves and poor whites accused of plotting rebellion are faced with mass arrests, executions, and deportations in an investigation led by judge Daniel Horsmanden, who publishes a trial narrative.
1750	Charlotte Lennox, *Harriot Stuart*.
1754	Charter is granted for King's College, renamed Columbia College in 1784, Columbia University in 1896.
1763	*Rivington's New-York Gazetteer* is first published.
1767	John Street Theater opens.
1775–83	American Revolution; Manhattan is occupied by the British army from 1776 to 1783.
1776	A large fire on the southern end of Manhattan destroys over 400 buildings, including Trinity Church.
1785	The *New York Daily Advertiser*, the city's first daily, is published.
1785–90	New York City serves as the national capital.
1787	Royall Tyler's *The Contrast*, performed at the John Street Theater, is the first American play to be produced by a professional company and the first to make New York City its setting.
1789	George Washington is inaugurated president at Federal Hall on Wall Street.
1790	Charlotte Lennox, *Euphemia*.
1792	New York Stock Exchange is founded on lower Wall Street.

1794	The American edition of Susanna Rowson's *Charlotte Temple, A Tale of Truth* is published; a tombstone engraved with the protagonist's name would appear in Trinity Churchyard in the early nineteenth century.
1798	The Park Theatre is founded.
1804	The New-York Historical Society is founded.
1807	Washington Irving, William Irving, and James Kirke Paulding, *Salmagundi*; Samuel Latham Mitchill, *The Picture of New York*.
1809	Washington Irving, *History of New York*.
1811	Commissioners' Plan of 1811 establishes a grid plan of development from 14th Street north to Washington Heights in Manhattan.
1812–15	War with Britain.
1813	Harper and Brothers Publishing House is founded.
1816	John Lambert, *Travels*.
1819	Walter Whitman is born on May 31 in Long Island; Herman Melville is born August 1 in New York City.
1820	The Mercantile Library is founded.
1825	Erie Canal opens between Buffalo on Lake Erie and Albany on the upper Hudson River, spurring tremendous commercial growth in New York City; the *New York Daily Advertiser* (1817–36) is the first American paper to install a steam-driven cylinder press.
1826	Bowery Theater opens.
1827	New York abolishes slavery; the *Freedom's Journal*, the first black newspaper in the United States, is founded.
1828	James Fenimore Cooper, *Notions of the Americans*; Philip Hone, businessman and mayor of New York from 1826–27, begins his diary and records mid-nineteenth-century New York life until his death in 1851; J. K. Paulding, *The New Mirror for Travellers*.
1829	Coney Island House opens, establishing Coney Island's status as a seaside resort; Andrew Jackson is inaugurated president; Basil Hall, *Travels*.
1832	T. D. Rice, a native New Yorker, performs his song "Jump Jim Crow" at the American Theatre on the corner of Canal Street and the Bowery. Minstrel troupes would be organized in the 1840s and remain a popular performance form for decades; New York University, established the year before, admits its first student.
1833	The *Knickerbocker Magazine* is founded and continues monthly publication until 1865; the *New York Sun*, the first penny press newspaper, is issued; construction begins on the Custom House

on Wall Street – today's Federal Hall; J. K. Paulding, *The Lion of the West*.

1834   Anti-abolition riots target African American and abolitionist homes, businesses, and churches; City of Brooklyn is incorporated.

1835   George Templeton Strong begins the 2,250-page diary that he will continue until 1875; fire destroys over 700 buildings in downtown Manhattan; Alexis de Tocqueville, *Democracy in America*.

1837   Financial Panic of 1837 begins in New York City when all banks cease payment in gold and silver coins.

1839   Brooklyn street plan establishes a grid system.

1841   Horace Greeley founds the *New York Tribune*; P. T. Barnum establishes Barnum's American Museum at Ann Street and Broadway; David Valentine begins serial publication of *Manuals of the Corporation of the City of New York*.

1842   Walt Whitman, *Franklin Evans, or the Inebriate*; Charles Dickens, *American Notes*.

1845   Anna Cora Mowatt's comedy *Fashion* opens at the Park Theatre; the New York-based Young America movement attracts and promotes writers such as Nathaniel Hawthorne, Herman Melville, and Walt Whitman, and remains influential into the 1850s.

1845–55 The Irish Famine propels over 1.5 million Irish immigrants across the Atlantic, many of whom settle in New York City.

1846   Edgar Allen Poe, "The Literati of New York City," in *Godey's Lady's Book*; Herman Melville's debut novel, *Typee*; Edmund O'Callaghan, *History of New Netherland; or, New York Under the Dutch*; E. Porter Belden unveils his popular urban panorama of New York at the Minerva Room on Broadway; publishing house Charles Scribner's Sons is founded.

1847   The Free Academy is founded, eventually becoming City College.

1848   Benjamin A. Baker's comedy *A Glance at New York* opens at the Olympic Theater on Broadway at Hester Street; Ned Buntline (E. Z. C. Judson), *The Mysteries and Miseries of New York: A Story of Real Life*.

1849   George F. Thompson, *New York Life: or, The Mysteries of Upper-Tendom Revealed*; George G. Foster, *New York in Slices*; Astor Place Riot erupts at the Astor Place Opera House; the Astor Library opens its doors.

1850   George G. Foster, *New York by Gaslight*; George Lippard, *The Empire City; or, New York by Night and Day*; P. T. Barnum stages William Henry Smith's temperance melodrama *The Drunkard* at his American Museum.

1851   Herman Melville, *Moby-Dick*; the *New York Daily Times* begins publishing.

1852   Herman Melville, *Pierre*; Charles Astor Bristed, *The Upper Ten Thousand*; John Vose, *Fresh Leaves from the Diary of a Broadway Dandy*. Harriet Beecher Stowe publishes *Uncle Tom's Cabin*; stage adaptations will run in New York for decades.

1853   Herman Melville, "Bartleby, the Scrivener: A Story of Wall Street" in *Putnam's Magazine*; Charles Loring Brace founds the Children's Aid Society; New York hosts the World's Fair, called the Exhibition of the Industry of All Nations.

1855   Walt Whitman publishes the first edition of *Leaves of Grass*; expanded and revised editions appear in 1856, 1860, 1867, 1870, 1881, and 1891–92 ("death-bed edition"); Fanny Fern (Sara Payson Willis), *Ruth Hall*; Evert and George Duyckinck publish the *Cyclopedia of American Literature*; Brooklyn annexes Williamsburg and Bushwick, becoming the third-most-populous American city.

1857   Dion Boucicault's play *The Poor of New York* opens at Wallack's Theater on the corner of Broome Street and Broadway; Frederick Law Olmsted and Calvert Vaux win the commission to design Central Park; residents in this 760-acre area in northern Manhattan are evicted, including the free black residents of Seneca Village.

1861–65   The Civil War.

1862   Theodore Winthrop, *Cecil Dreeme*.

1863   Emancipation Proclamation takes effect January 1. Precipitated by increasing racial and class tensions, the New York City Draft Riots erupt and consume the city for five days in July, violently targeting and forcing from the city hundreds of black residents before being quelled by federal troops.

1865   *Anthology of New Netherland, or Translations from the Early Dutch Poets of New York, with Memoirs of their Lives*, edited by Henry Cruse Murphy, is published; President Lincoln is assassinated; Walt Whitman, *Drum-Taps*.

1867   Augustin Daly's melodramatic *Under the Gaslight*, performed at the New York Theater (Broadway at Waverly Place), introduces the sensational tied-to-the-train-track-rescue device; *Harper's Bazaar* is founded.

1868   Horatio Alger, *Ragged Dick.*

1872   James D. McCabe, *Lights and Shadows of New York Life.*

1873   New York City annexes Harlem.

1880   The Metropolitan Museum of Art opens in Central Park.

1881   Henry James, *Washington Square.*

1882   Chinese Exclusion Act is passed, first race-based restriction on immigration in US history (repealed 1943).

1883   Brooklyn Bridge, under construction since 1870, is opened; Emma Lazarus, "The New Colossus," later engraved inside the Statue of Liberty.

1886   The Statue of Liberty is presented to the United States by France.

1890   William Dean Howells, *A Hazard of New Fortunes.*

1891   Jacob Riis, *How the Other Half Lives.*

1892   The first Ellis Island Immigration Station opens; the area is used at various times as New York's primary immigration portal, a detention facility, and a hospital over the next half-century until its closure in 1954.

1893   Stephen Crane, *Maggie: A Girl of the Streets.*

1895   A group of Tin Pan Alley music houses, traditionally located on West 28th Street between Fifth and Sixth Avenues, form The Music Publishers Association of the United States; William Randolph Hearst buys the *New York Morning Journal* and engages in a circulation war with Joseph Pulitzer's *New York World*, introducing yellow journalism.

1896   Abraham Cahan, *Yekl.*

1898   The modern-day five boroughs of New York are created with the consolidation of Brooklyn, Queens, Staten Island, the Bronx, and Manhattan.

1900   Theodore Dreiser, *Sister Carrie.*

1901   Herman Knickerbocker Vielé, *The Last of the Knickerbockers.*

1902   Paul Laurence Dunbar, *The Sport of the Gods.*

1903   W. E. B. Du Bois, *The Souls of Black Folk.*

1904   Manhattan opens its first underground subway operating between City Hall and Harlem; Times Square is named for the relocation of the *New York Times*.

1905   Edith Wharton, *The House of Mirth.*

1907   Henry James, *The American Scene.*

1909   *Narratives of New Netherland, 1609–1664*, edited by John Franklin Jameson; Clyde Fitch's posthumously staged *The City* opens at the Lyric Theatre on 42nd Street; the newly founded

National Association for the Advancement of Colored People holds its first conference in New York City.

1911 Floyd Dell and Max Eastman publish *The Masses*; the New York Public Library, a combination of the Astor and Lenox libraries consolidated in 1895, opens its doors; fire guts the Triangle Shirtwaist factory in Washington Square, resulting in 146 worker deaths and leading to fire safety reforms.

1912 James Weldon Johnson, *The Autobiography of an Ex-Colored Man*.

1913 Ebbets Field in Brooklyn opens as the home of the Brooklyn Dodgers; demolished in 1960.

1914–18 First World War; United States enters the war in 1917.

1915 Djuna Barnes, "Paprika Johnson"; Alfred A. Knopf's publishing house is founded.

1916 The Provincetown Players establish their theater in Greenwich Village; important early playwrights include Eugene O'Neill and Susan Glaspell.

1917 Abraham Cahan, *The Rise of David Levinsky*; Djuna Barnes, "The Terrorists"; Edna St. Vincent Millay arrives in Greenwich Village; riots in East St. Louis provoke African American citizens to stage a silent protest march down Fifth Avenue, which helps to launch the Harlem Renaissance; the Jones Act grants US citizenship to Puerto Ricans.

1917–21 First Red Scare.

1918 *The Dial*, a transcendentalist magazine in 1840s' Boston and political organ in 1880s' Chicago, moves to New York and becomes an important publisher of modernist literature.

1919 Emma Goldman, Alexander Berkman, and 247 other radicals deported during Red Scare; Dorothy Parker, Harold Ross, Alexander Woollcott, and others form the Algonquin Round Table, a daily lunch of literary luminaries.

1920 Edith Wharton, *The Age of Innocence*; Anzia Yezierska, *Hungry Hearts*; Edna St. Vincent Millay, *A Few Figs from Thistles*; the Volstead Act initiates Prohibition.

1921 Eugene O'Neill's *Anna Christie* debuts at Vanderbilt Theatre on 48th Street; the Port of New York Authority is created.

1921–24 Restrictive immigration quotas favor western and northern European countries, while limiting immigration from southern and eastern Europe and entirely excluding Asian immigrants.

1922 Claude McKay, *Harlem Shadows*; Eugene O'Neill's play *The Hairy Ape* is performed at the Provincetown Playhouse; Anne

Nichols's play *Abie's Irish Rose* premieres on Broadway; *Reader's Digest* is first issued from a basement room under a speakeasy in Greenwich Village.

1923   Theodore Dreiser, *The Color of a Great City*; *Time* magazine is founded.

1924   Edith Wharton, *Old New York*; Richard Simon and M. Lincoln Schuster found their publishing house.

1925   F. Scott Fitzgerald, *The Great Gatsby*; Alain Locke edits *The New Negro*; Anzia Yezierska, *Bread Givers*; Harold Wallace Ross and Jane Grant found *The New Yorker* magazine; Bennett Cerf and Donald Klopfer found Random House.

1926   Langston Hughes, *The Negro Artist and the Racial Mountain*; Michael Gold publishes *The New Masses*.

1927   Herbert Asbury, *Gangs of New York*; *The Jazz Singer*, based on Samson Raphaelson's short story "Day of Atonement," is released by Warner Brothers, as the first full-length motion picture with synchronized dialogue sequences.

1928   Claude McKay, *Home to Harlem*.

1929   Nella Larsen, *Passing*; Countee Cullen, *The Black Christ and Other Poems*.

1929–39 The Stock Market crash in October 1929 ushers in the world-wide Great Depression by 1932.

1930   Hart Crane, *The Bridge*; Michael Gold, *Jews Without Money*.

1931   The Empire State Building is completed.

1932   Damon Runyon, *Guys and Dolls*.

1933   Edith Wharton, *A Backward Glance*; *Esquire* begins publication.

1934   Daniel Fuchs, *Summer in Williamsburg*; Henry Roth, *Call It Sleep*; the *Partisan Review* begins publication; the Apollo Theater opens.

1937   Djuna Barnes, *Nightwood*; Zora Neale Hurston, *Their Eyes Were Watching God*.

1939–40 Flushing Meadows in Queens hosts the New York World's Fair; the site is again used for the New York World's Fair in 1964–65.

1939–45 Second World War; United States enters the war following Pearl Harbor in 1941.

1943   Betty Smith, *A Tree Grows in Brooklyn*.

1945   F. Scott Fitzgerald's "My Lost City" is published in Edmund Wilson's *The Crack-Up*.

1946   The Rockefeller family donates $8,500,000 to purchase land along the East River for the United Nations headquarters.

1947	African American baseball player Jackie Robinson joins the Brooklyn Dodgers.
1947–57	Second Red Scare.
1948	Lin Yutang, *Chinatown Family*; E. B. White's essay "Here is New York" appears in *Holiday* magazine and in book form the following year.
1949	Arthur Miller's play *Death of a Salesman* premieres on Broadway.
1951	J. D. Salinger, *The Catcher in the Rye*; Alfred Kazin, *A Walker in the City*; Jack Kerouac writes *On the Road*, published in 1957, over three weeks in a Manhattan apartment.
1952	Ralph Ellison, *Invisible Man*.
1955	Arthur Miller's play *A View from the Bridge* premieres at the Coronet Theater; Ed Fancher, Dan Wolf, and Norman Mailer found the *Village Voice*.
1955–68	Civil Rights Movement.
1956	Allan Ginsberg, *Howl and Other Poems*.
1957	Charlie Chaplin releases *A King in New York*; Frank O'Hara, *Meditations in an Emergency*.
1958	Truman Capote, *Breakfast at Tiffany's*.
1959	William Burroughs, *Naked Lunch*; Paule Marshall, *Brown Girl, Brownstones*.
1961	City University of New York established; Louis Chu, *Eat a Bowl of Tea*; Lewis Mumford, *The City in History*.
1962	Louis Auchincloss, *Portrait in Brownstone*; Andy Warhol's first New York solo Pop exhibit is held at the Stable Gallery.
1964	Hubert Selby, *Last Exit to Brooklyn*; Frank O'Hara, *Lunch Poems*; the acquittal of a white police officer in the death of a young black Harlem resident ignites one of the first major race riots in the United States.
1965	Sol Yurick, *The Warriors*; Ed Sanders, Tuli Kupferberg, and Ken Weaver form The Fugs and release their album *The Village Fugs – Ballads and Songs of Contemporary Protest, Points of View and General Dissatisfaction*; the Immigration and Nationality Act of 1965 abolishes the national-origin quota system established in 1924.
1966	Robert Ludlam forms the Ridiculous Theatrical Company after splitting from Ron Tavel and John Vaccaro's avant-garde theatre troupe Playhouse of the Ridiculous; the Poetry Project is founded at St. Mark's Church in-the-Bowery; Andy Warhol opens the Electric Circus featuring The Velvet Underground and

the "Exploding Plastic Inevitable" at 23 St. Mark's Place in the East Village.

1967   Piri Thomas, *Down These Mean Streets*.

1968   The Fillmore East (rock-music venue) opens on Second Avenue at Sixth Street in the East Village.

1969   The Stonewall riots erupt in Greenwich Village; the first Gay Pride marches occur the following year in New York and Los Angeles.

1970–73   The World Trade Center, begun in 1966 and consisting of twin skyscrapers and five other buildings on 16 acres in lower Manhattan, is opened.

1973   Richard Hell and Tom Verlaine (together under the pseudonym "Theresa Stern"), *Wanna Go Out?*; John Ashbery, *Three Poems*; music club CBGB is founded on the Bowery at Bleecker Street, becoming a major venue for punk music (closed 2006); Miguel Algarín founds The Nuyorican Poets Cafe; Don DeLillo, *Great Jones Street*; Nicholasa Mohr, *Nilda*.

1974   Miguel Piñero's play *Short Eyes* premieres at the Public Theater.

1975   Patti Smith releases her album *Horses*; E. L. Doctorow, *Ragtime*; Kenneth Koch, *The Art of Love: Poems*; Woody Allen, *Without Feathers*; *Daily News* publishes the "Ford to City: Drop Dead" front page during the city's financial crisis.

1976   Ellis Island is opened to the public and undergoes restoration over the next twenty years.

1977   Richard Hell & The Voidoids release their album *Blank Generation*.

1979   Woody Allen, *Manhattan* (film).

1982   Lewis Mumford, *Sketches from Life: The Autobiography of Lewis Mumford*.

1984   Stephen Brook, *New York Days, New York Nights*.

1985–86   Paul Auster, *The New York Trilogy*.

1985   Larry Kramer's *The Normal Heart* opens at the Public Theater; E. L. Doctorow, *World's Fair*.

1987   Tom Wolfe, *The Bonfire of the Vanities*.

1989   Spike Lee, *Do the Right Thing* (film).

1990   Oscar Hijuelos, *The Mambo Kings Play Songs of Love*.

1991   Don DeLillo, *Mao II*; Bret Easton Ellis, *American Psycho*.

1992–94   Tony Kushner's play *Angels in America*, first staged on Broadway in 1993.

1993   Tower One of the World Trade Center is bombed in a terrorist attack.

1995   Chang-rae Lee, *Native Speaker*.

1999   Jonathan Lethem, *Motherless Brooklyn*.

2000   Michael Chabon, *The Amazing Adventures of Kavalier & Clay*.

2001   World Trade Center towers collapse in a terrorist attack.

2002   Jonathan Safran Foer, *Everything is Illuminated*; Truman Capote, *A House on the Heights*; Bob Holman founds the Bowery Poetry Club.

2003   Jonathan Lethem, *The Fortress of Solitude*; Colson Whitehead, *The Colossus of New York*.

2004   Art Spiegelman, *In the Shadow of No Towers*; Tony Harris and Brian Vaughan launch the comic book *Ex Machina*.

2005   Paul Auster, *The Brooklyn Follies*; Michael Cunningham, *Specimen Days*; Jonathan Safran Foer, *Extremely Loud and Incredibly Close*.

2008   Lin-Manuel Miranda's musical *In The Heights* premieres on Broadway; Richard Price, *Lush Life*.

CYRUS R. K. PATELL

Introduction

Now Dick had listened to all this conversation. Being an enterprising young man, he thought he saw a chance for a speculation, and determined to avail himself of it.

Accordingly he stepped up to the two just as Frank's uncle was about leaving, and said, "I know all about the city, sir; I'll show him around, if you want me to."

The gentleman looked a little curiously at the ragged figure before him.

"So you are a city boy, are you?"

"Yes, sir," said Dick, "I've lived here ever since I was a baby."

"And you know all about the public buildings, I suppose?"

"Yes, sir."

"And the Central Park?"

"Yes, sir. I know my way all round."

The gentleman looked thoughtful.

"I don't know what to say, Frank," he remarked after a while. "It is rather a novel proposal. He isn't exactly the sort of guide I would have picked out for you. Still he looks honest. He has an open face, and I think can be depended upon."

"I wish he wasn't so ragged and dirty," said Frank, who felt a little shy about being seen with such a companion.

Horatio Alger, Jr., *Ragged Dick*.[1]

What is it that the Kander and Ebb song says about New York City? "If I can make it there, / I'd make it anywhere." From its origins as a Dutch mercantile center to its modern incarnation as the financial center of the United States and a target for the terrorists of 9/11, New York, as the song suggests, has held a special place in the country's national mythology.

In "New York, New York" (1977), the singer wears "vagabond shoes" and "long[s] to stray," to "wake up in the city / That doesn't sleep" so that his "little town blues" will "melt" away.[2] Fred Ebb's lyrics draw on the rags-to-riches mythology made famous in Horatio Alger, Jr.'s bestselling novel *Ragged Dick, or, Street Life in New York with the Boot-Blacks* (1868), which traces young Richard Hunter's rise from a vagabond boot-black to a respectable, upwardly mobile clerk with a penchant for learning. What does young Dick have going for him as the novel opens? Pluck, conscience, a streak of altruism, and the ability to recognize an opportunity: Dick thinks of his encounter with Mr. Whitney and his nephew Frank as "a chance for a speculation." What sets Dick's story of upward mobility in motion, however, is his ability to use the local knowledge that he possesses – his street smarts – to guide Frank around the city. Dick knows "all about the city," "all about the public buildings" and "the Central Park." Frank regards him skeptically at first: "'I wish he wasn't so ragged and dirty,' said Frank, who felt a little shy about being seen with such a companion." But Dick turns out to be a very good companion indeed and, as Frank puts it afterward, "a capital guide." Dressed in some "half worn" clothes that Frank no longer needs, Dick shows Frank around the island of Manhattan: the two boys wander from Chatham Square up Broadway to Madison Square and then Fifth Avenue, all the way up to the still-unfinished Central Park. By the end of the tour, which lasts a "few hours," Dick has formed a "strong attachment" to Frank and promises to stay in touch. When Frank sends him a letter from boarding school, Dick writes back, promising to "go round" with Frank next time he's in the city: "There's lots of things you didn't see when you was here before."[3]

This *Cambridge Companion to the Literature of New York* presents you with a series of "capital guides," opinionated companions who will show you around some of the different eras, enclaves, genres, and ideas that mark the city's literary and cultural history. (But by no means all of them: the city's literary history is too rich and complex to be surveyed completely in a book such as this, so don't *kvetch* too much if you find that some familiar figure has been omitted or given short shrift. Or, rather, *kvetch* all you want: complaining, after all, is one of New York's great cultural traditions.)

Taking you on a temporal as well as a geographical tour of the city, our guides treat their subjects as if each were a neighborhood, pointing out its distinctive landmarks and offering glimpses into its particular wealth of local knowledge. This tactic is fitting, because New York is still the city of neighborhoods that E. B. White described in his extended essay *Here is New York*, first published in *Holiday* magazine in 1948 and then in book form the following year. Although it is less and less true that "many a New Yorker spends a lifetime within the confines of an area smaller than a country village," the sense of neighborhood that White identified remains strong. Local knowledge offers comfort when you're in your neighborhood, but can make you feel subtly ill at ease when you're away from it: "Let [a New Yorker] walk two blocks from his corner and he is in a strange land and will feel uneasy till he gets back."[4] Even diehard New Yorkers, it seems, can use a tour guide when they're off in some unfamiliar part of the city, though most would be loath to admit it.

It is, however, precisely that sense of uneasiness that drives the literature and culture of New York City. Its greatest writers and artists have tended to be explorers, moving beyond their comfortable neighborhoods, embracing rather than shrinking from the experience of difference. Some have attributed this to the city's Dutch past. Kenneth T. Jackson and David S. Dunbar, the editors of the anthology *Empire City*, put it this way: "Unlike Boston, which was founded as a kind of religious experiment, New Amsterdam was founded for the purpose of making money." Commenting on an account of New Amsterdam included in Nicolaes van Wassenaer's *Historisch Verhael* [Historical Account], they note that "the countinghouse, not the church, was the most important building in town."[5] This emphasis on making money sets in place a logic of exchange, which begins with the exchange of money and goods, but expands to include the exchange of cultures and practices as the city itself grows and expands.

In his introduction to the anthology *Writing New York*, Philip Lopate postulates that "there is such a thing as 'New York writing,' and that it goes beyond the coincidence of many superb authors having resided and worked in the city." According to Lopate, "New York writing flows from the rhythm and mode of being that this singular place imposes on everyone who lives in it or even visits it at length ... [New York] began as a cosmopolitan, international port, a walking city with a vital street life and a housing shortage, and stayed that way. The more the metropolis grew, the more it attracted writers."[6] Arising from the rich variety of experiences to be found on the streets and in the neighborhoods of the city, New York writing dramatizes the ways in which difference – whether it is based on culture, ethnicity, race, gender, sexuality, or class – is not a problem to be solved, but rather an opportunity for individual and cultural growth.

The intellectual historian Thomas Bender has suggested that New York sometimes seems un-American because of its emphasis on difference. "It is puzzling but true," writes Bender, "that the outlook associated with New York's cosmopolitan experience has been unable to establish itself as an American standard." Often, Bender argues, "American history – and the meaning of America – has been framed as a political and cultural dialectic" between Puritan New England and Jeffersonian Virginia: "In spite of the narrowness and purity of the Puritan dream of a 'city upon a hill' and of agrarian Jeffersonianism, these myths have come to be associated with the essential America, evoking the virtues of the small town and the agricultural frontier." As Bender notes, Puritanism and Jeffersonianism are very different ideologies: "one is religious, the other secular; one hierarchical, the other egalitarian; one town-oriented, the other rural; one reminiscent of the medieval worldview, the other drawing upon the Enlightenment." But in Bender's analysis, despite their differences in outlook, what Puritanism and Jeffersonianism share is this: "both reject the idea of difference. Neither can give positive cultural or political value to heterogeneity or conflict. Each in its own way is xenophobic, and that distances both of them from the conditions of modern life, especially as represented by the historic cosmopolitanism of New York and, increasingly, other cities in the United States."[7] As the epitome of US urban culture, New York can sometimes seem like the most un-American place in the country, a residue perhaps from the time when, as Eric Homberger points out in his chapter on New York's immigrant cultures at the turn into the twentieth century, New York was "the most 'foreign' of American cities": in 1910, over 40 percent of the city's population was born abroad.

New York's cosmopolitanism arises from the points of contact among its different neighborhoods and among the cultures and subcultures they represent. It arises from acts of literal crossing from one neighborhood into another, whether for work or for play, and in zones where neighborhoods abut one another or even overlap. It arises from conversations across cultural (and sometimes even linguistic) boundaries. New York's history is marked by what the philosopher Kwame Anthony Appiah calls "cosmopolitan contamination." Cultures, in Appiah's account, never tend toward purity: they tend toward change, toward mixing and miscegenation, toward an "endless process of imitation and revision."[8] Cultures are all about "conversation across boundaries." Such conversations, Appiah writes, "can be delightful, or just vexing: what they mainly are, though, is inevitable."[9] New York's history demonstrates, however, that if cultures tend toward mixing, the process of cosmopolitan change is never easy, and sometimes it is violent. The close proximity in which New York's different peoples have been forced to live with one another has often had the effect of producing a kind of cultural retrenchment and an insistence on cultural purity. What we see in many of the writings that the *Cambridge Companion* investigates is a dramatization of the vicissitudes of cosmopolitan contamination and, more often than not, a sense of why it is important to embrace, rather than resist, difference.

In comparison to Puritan Boston, the New Amsterdam described by Russell Shorto and others seems almost modern with its ethnic diversity, multiculturalism, and (at least theoretical) emphasis on religious tolerance.[10] By the 1640s, although there were fewer than one thousand residents in New Amsterdam, there were eighteen different languages being spoken there. The dominant language, of course, was not English, but Dutch. Indeed, the fact that the earliest narratives about New Amsterdam are all written in Dutch helps to explain why so many American literary histories have centered their accounts on New England.

Typical approaches to the history of American writing still tend to unfold by emphasizing the importance of Boston and Philadelphia to the emerging national culture, with occasional detours south to Jefferson's Virginia. Most college survey courses in US literature undervalue New York's contribution to American literary history: they commonly begin with some Native American creation stories and Columbus's letters, before launching into Puritanism and a procession of New England writers, leavened by one Philadelphia writer (Charles Brockden Brown) and two New Yorkers (Washington Irving and Walt Whitman) – three, if you include Herman Melville. New York receives little attention as a literary center even, curiously, in courses that include the turn into the twentieth century, when New York was clearly the site at which the national cultural mythology was being produced by new mass media and by the publishing industry. One of the goals of this *Cambridge Companion* is to suggest what a reconfigured US literary history might look like if its center of gravity were shifted southward from Boston to New York.

One impediment to the full realization of this goal lies in the paucity of literary materials from New Amsterdam accessible to modern readers. Current anthologies of both US literature and New York writing tend to pay little attention to Dutch New York, because most of the available materials are written in Dutch and have not been translated. Since 1974, the New Netherland Project, directed by Charles Gehring and based in Albany, has been translating and publishing documents held by the New York State Library and the New York State Archives, with approximately twenty-four volumes anticipated when the project is complete.[11] Literary texts, however, are another story. The intrepid reader who wishes to investigate New Amsterdam's literary writing must venture to the library to find *Narratives of New Netherland, 1609–1664,* published in 1909, and *Anthology of New Netherland, or Translations from the Early Dutch Poets of New York, with Memoirs of their Lives,* originally published in 1865 and reprinted in 1969. Literary New Amsterdam was a coterie culture, in which poets like Henricus Selyns and Jacob Steendam wrote in Dutch for one another and for occasions like weddings and funerals. Some of their work was published in Dutch in Amsterdam. The case of Selyns's work is instructive: his poems have been carefully preserved in a bound manuscript in the New-York Historical Society, still undigitized and untranslated as this volume goes to press. The Society's catalog offers this description of the manuscript: "Undated manuscript volume of poems by Henricus Selyns, comprising approximately 200 epitaphs, and nuptial, birthday, and other congratulatory odes of a personal character and chiefly dedicated to the author's contemporaries in Holland, New York, and the West Indies. Most are in Dutch, but also included are several in Latin, and one in Greek." The situation (as Elizabeth L. Bradley notes in her contribution to this volume) that first inspired Washington Irving to write his *History of New York* (1809) – a lack of knowledge about New York's Dutch past – remains a problem for literary historians today.

Our *Companion*, therefore, examines the Dutch past as it is reconstructed through Irving's eyes: Bradley's chapter traces the rise of the idea of the Knickerbocker, from its first appearance in Irving's burlesque history to its later manifestations in New York's popular culture and novels of manners. Chronologically, however, we begin in British New York, with Robert Lawson-Peebles's account of gastronomical motifs in early writing about New York. "The epic that is New York was founded in conquest," Lawson-Peebles tells us, and is "then transformed into the capacious corporeality that would be celebrated by Whitman." The chapters that follow guide us through a variety of different New Yorks. Bryan Waterman treats nineteenth-century New York as a metatheatrical space, in which "New York audiences of various stripes flocked to see representations of themselves on stage" and sometimes became the primary spectacle presented in the theater. Thomas Augst traces New York's impact on Herman Melville's writing and highlights the Young America movement's attempts "to move the nation's literary capital from Boston to New York, while at the same time proclaiming the revolutionary power of literature to promote an 'original' national consciousness," with New York serving as its "stronghold." Lytle Shaw articulates the principles of Whitman's "urbanism" and traces his legacy in the work of Allen Ginsberg and other twentieth-century poets, while Martha Nadell situates Whitman as the originator of a tradition of Brooklyn writing that "complements and complicates" the literary history of New York City as whole.

Likewise, Caleb Crain's account of writing about New York's "high-life" and Sarah Wilson's analysis of New York's novels of manners both complement and complicate the story of upper-class New York established by Bradley's treatment of the Knickerbocker mythology. Crain treats little-known novels about New York's "overclass," a world exemplified by the writings of Charles Astor Bristed, in which "wealthy New Yorkers were dyeing their moustaches and elaborating rules about cocktails while Henry James was still in short pants." Wilson complicates the story of the novel of manners from James to Edith Wharton by situating works of Lower East Side realism in its midst. Eric Homberger deepens our understanding of immigrant New York at the turn into the twentieth century by viewing it through the lens of the successful stage play *Abie's Irish Rose*. New York's ethnic literatures reappear in Cyrus R. K. Patell's examination of the dynamics of emergent literatures that offer a challenge to the kind of reading promoted by late twentieth-century multiculturalism and exemplified by the controversy over the choice of Chang-rae Lee's novel *Native Speaker* (1995) for New York's abortive "One Book, One City" program in 2002. Patell also shows how the evolution of the idea of the "Nuyorican" serves as a late twentieth-century case study of the kind of cultural mixing embodied by New York's literatures.

Our other chapters devoted to the twentieth century focus on some of the city's famous literary enclaves. Melissa Bradshaw takes us on a tour of Greenwich Village bohemianism, orienting her story around Edna St. Vincent Millay and Djuna Barnes as much as around Eugene O'Neill or the Provincetown Players. Thulani Davis demonstrates the impact on African American writing of Harlem's transformation from Black Mecca to urban ghetto. Daniel Kane offers a reinvigorating take on New York's Lower East Side poetry scene by highlighting its links to punk rock. Robin Bernstein looks at lesbian and gay New York through the prism of the theater scene. And Trysh Travis's account of New York's print cultures traverses these different enclaves, moving from the commercial to the bohemian, from the middlebrow to the avant-garde. What emerges from all these chapters is a set of distinctive, sometimes idiosyncratic, accounts of overlapping scenes, some connected geographically, some connected through time. Each chapter will introduce you to a particular archive of local knowledge, but we hope that from the specific details we examine something like an abiding portrait of New York and its literary cultures will begin to emerge.

E. B. White's *Here is New York* is often taken to present that kind of abiding portrait. That's what Hillary Clinton believed when she cited it during a debate with her challenger Rick Lazio during her campaign in the fall of 2000 to become one of New York's US senators. But when you read White's essay you are surprised by the specificity of his references – the book is full of once-recognizable names that now beg for footnotes – as well as by the way so many of his general statements about the city and its culture still ring true. That's one of White's points: in his foreword to the book version of his essay, he suggests that "the reader will find certain observations to be no longer true of the city, owing to the passage of time and the swing of the pendulum." So much, White tells us, has changed in just a year: "The heat has broken, the boom has broken, and New York is not quite so feverish now as when the piece was written." And yet, he argues, "the essential fever of New York has not changed in any particular, and I have not tried to make revisions in the hope of bringing the thing down to date." Living before the advent of the internet, White playfully suggests that "to bring New York down to date, a man would have to be published with the speed of light – and not even Harper is that quick" (17). Of course, the internet now allows us to publish with something akin to the speed of light, but White's point about the constantly shifting cityscape is no less true.

There are darker ways in which White's essay is marked by the historical moment in which it was written:

> The subtlest change in New York is something people don't speak much about but that is in everyone's mind. The city, for the first time in its long history, is destructible. A single flight of planes no bigger than a wedge of geese can quickly end this island fantasy, burn the towers, crumble the bridges, turn the underground passages into lethal chambers, cremate the millions. The intimation of mortality is part of New York now: in the sound of jets overhead, in the black headlines of the latest edition.

White's prose suggests that the dropping of the bomb changed everything, that New York would never be the same now that it "must live with the stubborn fact of annihilation." White's contemplation of "the destroying planes" seems uncanny in the wake of 9/11, which White did not live to see. Those of us who did live through it are often tempted to point to that day as the day that changed everything. Adam Gopnik, the *New Yorker* writer who might be considered White's heir as a chronicler of New York, wrote, only days after 9/11: "We have heard the jets now, and we will probably never be able to regard the city with quite the same exasperated, ironic affection we had for it before."

Perhaps. But just a little more than five years later, Gopnik admits in a *New Yorker* article entitled "Gothamitis" that 9/11 "turned out to change almost nothing in the city's interplay of money and manners." He goes on to *kvetch* about gentrification, arguing that "for the first time in Manhattan's history, it has no bohemian frontier."[12]

Maybe he's right. Or maybe we just haven't found the tour guide who can show us the way to the latest incarnation of bohemia in New York. If the tour guides we've assembled in this *Companion* tell us anything, it's that New York's writers have always found new sites within the city's neighborhoods and cultures to stake their various claims.

NOTES

1. Horatio Alger, Jr., *Ragged Dick, or Street Life in New York with the Boot-Blacks* (1868; Philadelphia: John C. Weston Co., 1910), pp. 33–34.
2. John Kander wrote the music and Fred Ebb the lyrics for the song "New York, New York," which was featured in Martin Scorsese's 1977 film of the same name. The song was performed by one of the film's stars, Liza Minnelli, but

it later became one of Frank Sinatra's signature songs. Sinatra changed the lyrics slightly, putting the phrase "A-number-one" into the list of things the singer wants to be. Ebb didn't care for the change, but he did like the fact that Sinatra made the song a hit. See www.npr.org/programs/morning/features/patc/newyorknewyork/.

3. Alger, *Ragged Dick*, pp. 110, 115, 245.

4. E. B. White, *Here is New York* (1949; New York: Little Book Room, 2000), pp. 34–36. Further references appear in the text.

5. Kenneth T. Jackson and David S. Dunbar, eds., *Empire City: New York through the Centuries* (New York: Columbia University Press, 2002), p. 26.

6. Philip Lopate, Introduction to *Writing New York* (New York: Library of America, 1998), p. xviii.

7. Thomas Bender, "New York as a Center of Difference," in his *The Unfinished City: New York and the Metropolitan Idea* (New York: New Press, 2002), pp. 185–86.

8. Kwame Anthony Appiah, "The Case for Contamination," *New York Times Magazine* (January 1, 2006): 52.

9. Kwame Anthony Appiah, *Cosmopolitanism: Ethics in a World of Strangers* (New York: Norton, 2006), p. xxi.

10. See Russell Shorto, *The Island at the Center of the World: The Epic Story of Dutch Manhattan and the Forgotten Colony that Shaped America* (New York: Doubleday, 2004).

11. See The New Netherland Project online (www.nnp.org).

12. Adam Gopnik, "Gothamitis," *The New Yorker* (January 8, 2007).

I

ROBERT LAWSON-PEEBLES

From British outpost to
American metropolis

In 1828, James Kirke Paulding summarized the changes that New York had undergone since September 1664, when the Dutch had surrendered to the forces of James Stuart, Duke of York. Paulding's account is still disquietingly relevant today:

> New York, though a very honest and well-intentioned city as times go, (with the exception of Wall Street, which labours under a sort of a shadow of suspicion,) has changed its name almost as often as some graceless rogues, though doubtless not for the same reasons. The Indian name was Manhadoes; the Dutch called it New Orange and New Amsterdam; the English New York, which name all the world knows it still retains. In 1673, it was a small village, and the richest man in it was Frederick Philipse, or *Flypse*, who was rated at 80,000 guilders. Now it is the greatest city in the new world; the third, if not the second, in commerce of all the world, old and new; and there are men in it, who were yesterday worth millions of guilders – in paper money: what they may be worth to-morrow, we cant [*sic*] say, as that will depend on a speculation. In 1660, the salaries of ministers and public officers were paid in beaver skins: now they are paid in bank notes. The beaver skins were always worth the money, which is more than can be said of the bank notes. New York contains one university and two medical colleges … twenty-two banks – good, bad and indifferent; forty-three insurance companies – solvent and insolvent; and one public library: from whence it may be reasonably inferred, that money is plenty as dirt – insurance bonds still more so – and that both are held in greater estimation than learning. There are also one hundred churches, and almost as many lottery offices, which accounts for the people of New York being so much better than their neighbours … there is an academy of arts, an athenæum, and several other institutions for the discouragement of literature, the arts and sciences … New York supports six theatres, of various kinds: from whence it may be inferred, the people are almost as fond of theatres as churches. There *was* an Italian opera last year. But … the birds are flown to other climes, and left the sweet singers of the nations, as it were, howling in the wilderness.

The final clause here takes an image from Deuteronomy 32:10 in the King James Version. In 1662, Michael Wigglesworth used the same image to argue that Malden, Massachusetts was set in a "region of darkness," devoid of religion. In 1828, Paulding wittily reapplied the metaphor to music to confirm that New York was a cultural wasteland dominated by fashion and finance. The wild beasts that stalked the streets of Manhattan were not Wigglesworth's "hellish fiends and brutish men," but belles and bankers. The institutions created to support the arts subscribed instead to the latest fashionable magazines from Britain. The result, Paulding suggested, was the decline of religion and the demise of literature and learning, and the ironic emergence of "the noble science of gastronomy" in Manhattan, superior even to Paris.[1]

To an extent, Paulding discusses New York in *The New Mirror for Travellers* as an illustration of the British assessment of the United States. For more than fifty years after the Revolution, Anglo-American relationships were characterized by a cultural and economic cold war that flared up briefly into the hot war of 1812. Sydney Smith, a founder of the *Edinburgh Review*, sounded an infamous keynote in 1820 when he asked: "In the four quarters of the globe, who reads an American book? or goes to an American play? or looks at an American picture or statue?"[2] Nine years later, the *Edinburgh Review* returned to the theme when it reviewed two books published within a few months of *The New Mirror for Travellers*, both by retired naval officers. One was *Notions of the Americans*, published in 1828, by James Fenimore Cooper, formerly of the United States Navy. The other was *Travels in North America* published in 1829 by Basil Hall, who had recently retired from the Royal Navy. In summary, the *Edinburgh Review* asserted that the United States had accomplished little for human happiness, and wondered if "the appetite for gain may be as devouring and as cannibal-like as that for blood."[3] The reviewer, who did not mention Paulding, nevertheless confirms Paulding's analysis by using degustatory imagery.

Gastronomy indeed provides an entrée to the literature of New York as the city changed from a British outpost to the American metropolis. The first English account, by Daniel Denton in 1670, talked of Manhattan as an Isle of the Blest, but one prepared for living heroes with a cornucopia, overflowing with goodies. Denton turned the word "blessed" into an incantation in honor of this "terrestrial *Canaan* ... where the Land floweth with milk and honey." The inhabitants are "blessed in their Bisket, and in their Store." They are "blest" by the extravagant produce of their fields and their animals – and by their own extravagantly procreating bodies.[4] Inevitably, a population explosion followed. When the English assumed power, New York was a small town of some 1,500 citizens, occupying the southern tip of

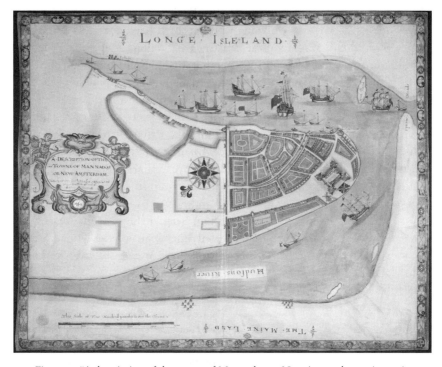

Figure 1: "A description of the towne of Mannados or New Amsterdam as it was in September 1661." This map is probably a copy of one drawn by surveyor Jacques Cortelyou in 1660, with English ships added to emphasize the victory over the Dutch. One Dutch name for the most prominent street was "De Heere Straet" (Gentlemen's Street); the English renamed it Broadway. The Battery (or fort) is now Battery Park, while the town wall gave its name to Wall Street. This plan is also known as "The Duke's Plan" because it was presented to the Duke of York, later James II. The map became part of the royal map collection, and then, with the books of George III, formed the basis of the British Library.

the island, enclosed by a town wall (now Wall Street, see *Figure 1*). By 1830 the population exceeded 200,000, and building had spread northwards past Washington Square.

The consequence of this population explosion was hedonism, the principle of pleasure, a fantasy of excess. The epic that is New York was founded in conquest, and then transformed into the capacious corporeality that would be celebrated by Whitman.[5] This chapter therefore limits itself to literature as it relates to the physical presence of the city, or, to use the title of the 1913 Francis Picabia watercolor, *New York as Seen from Across the Body*. Work that omits that physical presence has been omitted here.

Paulding in *The New Mirror for Travellers* had suggested that the enlargement of the city had led merely to the twin forces of speculation and conspicuous consumption. His analysis was right; his ironic dismissal of gastronomy wrong. Gourmandizing lies alongside fornication at the incontinent heart of epic. Paulding had not yet understood because his language, using the inhibiting structures of irony, had tended toward politeness. Cooper and Hall came closer to understanding the truth that, unlike politeness, which presses toward the resolution of comedy, excess demands epic grandeur. Together, Cooper and Hall suggest that the languages of politeness and excess provide the matrix for the literature of New York.

Cooper certainly agreed with Paulding about Manhattan cooking. He devoted several pages of *Notions of the Americans* to listing "the rare bounties of Nature" that were available for the "gratification" of New Yorkers. The city was "an unrivalled mart" because of its fertile environment, excellent inland and maritime connections, and access to the produce of differing cultures and climates. Unlike Paulding, Cooper did not indulge in irony about the city's culinary status, saying only that "the empire of gastronomy will sooner or later be transferred to this spot." He was diffident about the transfer of the empire of literature. American Literature would remain a tributary of English Literature:

> The Authors previously to the revolution are common Property, and it is quite idle to say that the American has not just as good a right to claim Milton, and Shakspeare, and all the old masters of the language, for his countrymen, as an Englishman. The Americans having continued to cultivate, and to cultivate extensively, an acquaintance with the writers of the mother Country since the separation, it is evident they must have kept pace with the trifling changes of the day. The only peculiarity that can, or ought to be, expected in their Literature, is that which is connected with the promulgation of their distinctive political opinions.

That was the problem. 1828 was also the year of the victory of Jacksonian democracy, a triumph of the commonplace that de Tocqueville would shortly turn into the tyranny of the majority. Cooper used the term "baldness" to characterize ordinary American life. This was a creative choice of noun, meaning simplicity and plainness, but as a follicular metaphor also suggesting absence. Several pages earlier, Cooper had warmed to the theme of "poverty of materials" by creating a negative catalogue: "no follies ... for the satirist; no manners, for the dramatist."[6] Fifty-one years later Henry James would produce a parody that closed by grumbling about a United States that had "no Epsom nor Ascot!" Both James and Cooper were indebted to Joseph Green Cogswell, who, writing anonymously for *Blackwood's*, began his own negative catalog by asserting that "there is nothing to awaken fancy in that land of dull realities."[7]

Cogswell tried to supply the lack of "fancy" by editing the *New York Review* from 1839 to 1842, and assisting John Jacob Astor in the foundation of the library that in 1895 became part of the New York Public Library. In 1828 the only major non-academic library was the New York Society Library, its name suggesting its clientele and reading matter.[8] Cooper was more ambitious than Cogswell. First, he noted that American writing was indeed emerging, and he instanced the New York Knickerbocker group, named in honor of "Diedrich Knickerbocker," the fictional narrator of Washington Irving's burlesque *History of New York from the Beginning of the World to the End of the Dutch Dynasty* (1809). The group included William Cullen Bryant, Lydia M. Child, Joseph Rodman Drake, Fitz-Greene Halleck, Charles Fenno Hoffman, Giulian Verplanck, and Nathaniel Parker Willis, many of them excoriated by Edgar Allan Poe, to terminal effect. Poe thought slightly better of *The Knickerbocker Magazine*. "It seems to have in it some important elements of success," he wrote, but "is deficient in that absolutely indispensable element, *individuality*."[9] The magazine lasted from 1833 to 1865, and also included material by New Englanders such as Hawthorne, Longfellow, Parkman, and Whittier. The amused, condescending style of the Knickerbocker group, if not the magazine, is well illustrated by Paulding's description of New York. Second, Cooper made a vital contribution to the literary life of New York, shortly after he moved there in October 1822, by founding the Bread and Cheese Club. It met initially at 300 Broadway, on the premises of an African American cook, who likely provided dinners much more exotic than bread and cheese, for the club became the meeting place for the city's notables, including politicians, merchants, lawyers, military and medical men, newspapermen and publishers. A number of painters (such as Asher Durand and Samuel Morse) took part, as did the Knickerbocker group. Cooper was quietly proud of his club, for he was aware of the role that such clubs played in literary life.[10] The Bread and Cheese Club was a direct descendant of the coffee house, which had played an important role in the changes to the structure of Anglo-American literary practice since Shakespeare and Milton.

Those changes were far from being "trifling," and they are demonstrated by the second book reviewed in 1829 by the *Edinburgh Review*, Captain Basil Hall's *Travels in North America*. The *Edinburgh Review* noted that Hall's experiences in the United States had led to "the destruction of his hopes" for the country, and Frances Trollope reported that the *Travels* caused there "a sort of moral earthquake," which would only be exceeded by the tremors caused by her own *Domestic Manners of the Americans*, published in 1832.[11] These comments are not supported by Hall's account of his arrival, which reveal a very happy man. For, at 8.30 a.m. on May 16, 1827, Basil Hall enjoyed the best breakfast of his life, at the well-named American Hotel:

A thousand years would not wipe out the recollection of our first breakfast at New York ... We had asked merely for some fresh shad, a fish reported to be excellent, as indeed it proved. But a great steaming, juicy beefsteak, also made its appearance, flanked by a dish of mutton cutlets. The Shad is a native of the American waters, I believe exclusively, and if so, it is almost worthy of a voyage across the Atlantic to make its acquaintance. To these viands were added a splendid arrangement of snow-white rolls, regiments of hot toast, with oceans of tea and coffee ... The luxury of silver forks and spoons, Indian china teacups, a damask table-cloth, in rooms free from any close, tarry, pitchy, remainder-biscuit smell, space to turn about in, soft seats to loll upon, and a firm ground on which to stand, with the addition of the aforesaid magnificent meal, formed altogether, whether from contrast or from intrinsic excellence, as lively a picture of Mahomet's sensual paradise as could be imagined.

Like Cooper, Basil Hall was no ordinary seaman. He had traveled extensively in Europe and further abroad, sailed round the Cape of Good Hope to the East Indies and to China, and round Cape Horn to Northern Mexico. He had made excellent use of his experiences, undertaking scientific experiments and publishing the journals of his travels. He had already, at the age of twenty-seven, been elected a Fellow of the Royal Society. But the opening hyperbole, followed by a delay of two pages, suggests that the "glorious breakfast" presented a challenge even to Hall's sophisticated analytical powers.[12] He responded by shaping his description into two related if rough-hewn parts. Hall begins with the language of excess, then tries and fails to contain it with the language of politeness.

Starting with *The Spectator*, the London magazine of Joseph Addison and Richard Steele, and developing with the circles around Samuel Richardson and Samuel Johnson, the relationship between writer and audience diversified markedly during the eighteenth century. In short, the social environment of writers moved from the court and the church into the street. The result was a much wider audience, a closer relationship between publication and mercantilism, and related changes in censorship laws. The language of politeness replaced centralized authority. This language was employed to instruct an expanding and increasingly sophisticated transnational readership by means, for instance, of essays, conduct books, and novels.[13] The eminent lawyer Sir William Blackstone understood the importance of these changes. In his *Commentaries on the Laws of England* (1765–69), Blackstone asserted that both "arbitrary governments" (for instance, that of Russia and, by implication, England before 1688) and "wild and uncultivated nations" (such as Africans and Native Americans) needed only a "paucity of laws." In contrast, the English common law was complex because it served "a polite and commercial people." Blackstone briefly compared mercantile and marital behavior in his three model societies and concluded: "the causes therefore of the multiplicity of the English laws are, the extent of the country which they govern; the commerce and refinement of it's [*sic*] inhabitants; but, above all, the liberty and property of the subject."[14] Blackstone's indebtedness to John Locke is clear; and by means of a set of key words he develops Locke's political theories in a dynamic and expansive context of politics, property, wealth, trade, consumption, the practices of writing, publishing, and reading, and codes of social behavior and personal deportment, all moderated by the English common law. Politeness (as its Latin root suggests) acted as form of police, providing a standard against which this complex material and social environment was tested. Although politeness had its origin in the formal behavior of aristocratic courts, Blackstone indicated that during the eighteenth century it had spread far beyond behavioral standards of the nobility to encompass the everyday life of a much broader social network of the upwardly mobile and their aspiring servants.[15]

The inclusion of the case of John Peter Zenger in collections of state trials for high treason highlights the changes that Blackstone described. Zenger was a journalist and printer who was arrested and jailed when in 1734 his New York *Weekly Journal* criticized William Cosby, the Governor of New York. Zenger's lawyer, Andrew Hamilton, argued at the trial for seditious libel that Zenger was exercising his liberty to express his opinion, and that "every Freeman that lives under a *British* Government on the Main of *America*" had the legal right "of exposing and opposing arbitrary Power (in these parts of the World, at least) by speaking and writing Truth." Hamilton's libertarian language rather than the issue of truth had its effect, and the jurors found Zenger not guilty. Zenger began his subsequent account of the trial by remarking that he published his paper because "I might make it worth my while."[16] In 1829, James Fenimore Cooper repeated that important connection of the profit motive with liberty. In a draft for Letter II of *Notions of the Americans*, Cooper wrote that "commerce is universally acknowledged to be both the parent and offspring of liberty." In Letter II itself, Cooper compared the "civil and religious liberty" of Britain with that of the United States. "Possessing those inestimable blessings in a still greater degree," the United States would, he hoped, achieve "commercial ascendancy." Cooper repeated that vision in 1851. In his introduction to the book he intended to call *The Towns of Manhattan* (for, unlike Paulding, he much preferred that name), Cooper reasserted that New York was "the mart of America" and prophesied that, if all went well, "a century will unquestionably place the United States of America prominently at the head of civilized nations."[17]

A civilized nation is characterized by a civilized dining room. Basil Hall's description of the dining room at the American Hotel therefore does more than simply reflect his pleasure on landing after twenty-eight days in ship's quarters. His brief but detailed account of the environment emphasizes its comfort and refinement – and his own comforting, refined ability to describe it. Hall's description of the dining room falls into the same category as John Lambert's account of a walk, twenty-one years earlier, down Broadway:

> New York is the first city in the United States for wealth, commerce, and population; as it also is the finest and most agreeable for its situation and buildings ... Broadway is lined with large commodious shops of every description, well stocked with European and India goods, and exhibiting as splendid and varied a show in their windows as can be met with in London. There are several extensive book stores, print-shops, music-shops, jewellers, and silversmiths; hatters, linen-drapers, milliners, pastry-cooks, coach-makers, hotels, and coffee-houses. The street is well paved, and the foot-paths are chiefly bricked. In Robinson-street the pavement before one of the houses, and the steps of the door, are composed entirely of *marble* [emphasis in original].

Little is known about Lambert, save that he was an Englishman who traveled through Canada and the United States from 1806 to 1808, painting watercolors that were reproduced as lithographs in the first of his two books. His eye for detail is evident in his appreciative description of a busy urban environment. Lambert's dense portrayal of the close relation between trade and politeness is capped by an emphasis on the hard stone used for buildings and sculptures. Marble symbolizes refinement because of its allusion to classical antiquity and its susceptibility to high polish. For these reasons Lambert believed that New York was "an exact epitome" of London.[18] He was not alone. Travelers, both in Britain and the United States, thought that London set the standard against which other towns were to be judged. Indeed, after his second residence in the United States, the radical journalist William Cobbett, writing of an 1818 stay, vigorously extended Blackstone's libertarian language to suggest that New York approached the perfection of politeness. The British visitor to New York, he wrote, "will miss by day only the nobility and the beggars, and by night only the street-walkers and pickpockets." Poverty and aristocracy walked hand in hand. For Cobbett, criminality was the natural result of an established church and a corrupt political system. That Cobbett had several brushes with the law, including two years in Newgate jail, simply proved his point that Blackstone's collocations of commerce and refinement, liberty and property, would not result in a unified, polite system until Britain had completed the libertarian revolution rooted in the English common law and now, in his view, realized by the United States.[19]

Basil Hall's breakfast, however, shows that New York could offer its own challenges to politeness. Hall's description of his food is in a different register from his description of the dining room. Although the language of politeness made room for sensuality, it was held in check by refinement. But refinement is unable to restrain the language of excess. "A great steaming, juicy beefsteak" are the words of a hungry sailor, home from the sea, rather than those of a second son of a baronet and Fellow of the Royal Society. After this lubricious outburst, the profusion of the food challenges Hall's repertoire of images, and pushes him beyond pleasure, further into a hedonism confirmed by the quotation from John Donne's "Elegy XIX: To his Mistress Going to Bed." For Donne, "Mahomet's paradise" was merely a way-stage in disrobing en route to sexual afflux, celebrated by the cry "O my America, my new found land." Hall reassigns Donne's reference to the Koran from the sexual to the gustatory organ and – naval discipline reasserting itself – does not overindulge it. Although Hall knows that the culinary is less carnal than concupiscence, he realizes that he has still exceeded the bounds of politeness. Protesting that he is no "gourmand, or epicure," Hall declares that he has "made upon this occasion a most enormous breakfast," and is too embarrassed to ask for more. So, with reluctance, he "rose at last with the hungry edge taken off, [if] not entirely blunted."[20]

Hall is able therefore to keep at bay his animal appetite, but his training in politeness doesn't equip him to resist another sensory excess, pyromania. New York ministers to this pleasure, too. After two false alarms in his hotel, he learns of a fire on Broadway. By running quickly he is just able to keep abreast of the fire engine and, "pleased with his good fortune," witnesses the "gallant" failure of the firemen to put out the blaze. Six months later, Hall permitted his young wife to share his passion, and she wrote excitedly back home:

> At length I have seen a fire, and a most magnificent one it was ... I ran for my bonnet and cloak, and off we set in pursuit of the fire, which altho' no great distance proved to be much further than we imagined from the bright light that spread around. When we got sight of it I was astonished by the magnificence, indeed I am told by those who are accustomed to see fires in this inflammable city that I was in very great luck in the spectacle I witnessed. There were four houses destroyed.

The behavior of the Halls is most impolite. The conduct book that for over a century was widely read in Britain and America, Lord Chesterfield's *Advice to His Son*, asserts that only "little minds are in a hurry ... they run, they hare, they puzzle, confound, and perplex themselves." But, in New York, Hall seems to have ignored Chesterfield when it suited him. He hares after the firemen. He is able, with some difficulty, to desist from over-eating – perhaps

to avoid Chesterfield's prescription of senna-tea in the morning and rhu-
barb at night – but as a loyal sailor he turns a Nelsonic eye to "lolling" in
the American Hotel. At the safe distance of Baltimore, Hall opens a copy
of *The American Chesterfield*, and uses it to remind American youth that
lolling, together with spitting and chewing tobacco, is bad form. If lolling is bad form for men, running for ladies is unspeakable. The conduct
books for ladies considered running such an alarming activity that they only
referred to it as a metaphor. Hence the Marchioness de Lambert's advice
to her daughter: "If you have a very warm and active imagination, and a
curiosity which nothing can stop, it is much better to employ these disposi-
tions in the sciences, than to run the hazard of their being turned to serve
your passions."[21] As her letters were private, Margaret Hall did not initially
repent her unwarranted exuberance in New York. During their subsequent
tour, as far north as Canada and south as the Gulf of Mexico, the Halls
found nothing to equal the excesses of New York. In comparison, Boston
was notable for Unitarianism; Philadelphia for its great prison and charities;
Washington for its decorous but long-winded politicians; and New Orleans
not only for the size of the Mississippi, but also for its gumbo, which the
Halls took some time to appreciate. Yet when she passed through New York
on the way back to Britain, Margaret Hall reflected that her experiences had
a dreamlike quality. The dream had not been "disagreeable," but she was
"not sorry that the dream was over."[22] New York had provoked emotions in
the Halls that they would prefer to renounce.

The conduct books provided theoretical advice. The increasing numbers
of novels written by women and using women as protagonists aimed to give
practical lessons to their female readership. The extent to which New York
is presented as an environment for testing politeness can be traced through
three novels, two by Charlotte Lennox and one by Susannah Rowson.
Charlotte Lennox was born, around 1730, in Gibraltar, where her father
was an army officer. The family lived in Albany, New York, from 1738 until
1742, when her father died. She subsequently moved to London, where she
became part of Samuel Johnson's circle. Her childhood memories of New
York are sketchy, and her two novels that handle a transatlantic plot present
the city in less detail than London. The first novel, *Harriot Stuart* (1750),
is set during the recent War of Jenkins' Ear (1739–42), an Anglo-Spanish
conflict. Harriot's first sight of the city indicates its role: "That city making a
delightful appearance from the water, I stood some moments contemplating
it with great pleasure." This is a rare moment of tranquillity, for New York
is a boundary between two wild areas, the hinterland of forests surrounding
Albany and the similarly dangerous Atlantic. The threats to Harriot's virtue,
however, come from unexpected quarters. Crossing the Atlantic, Harriot is

captured by Spanish privateers. But she receives "Spanish politeness" at the hands of her captors that has its counterpart in the woods of New York. Mohawks abduct her, but "this nation frequently celebrated for its politeness" is merely acting under the command of the villainous Captain Belmein, who masquerades as a native. The British, supposedly defending civilized values, are to the contrary often shown as "perfidious and designing." The men are violent; the women opportunistic: both are characterized by excessive movement. For instance, a Mrs. Villars runs until she is "quite out of breath." The first-person narrative handles Harriot's many vicissitudes by presenting a close-up account of her emotions until, in the final sentence of the novel, she achieves again the "serenity" that marked her first view of New York.[23]

Lennox repeated her transatlantic theme in *Euphemia* (1790). In the forty years since *Harriot Stuart* the growing conflicts in North America had prompted a great increase in publications. While preparing *Euphemia*, Lennox had refreshed her memory of New York through reading. She may have read Thomas Anburey's account, published in 1789. Anburey had been a lieutenant in General John Burgoyne's expeditionary force, and had been captured at the Battle of Saratoga. After being exchanged in 1781 he returned home via New York, but avoided describing the damage done to the city (from two serious fires and the years of British occupation) by plagiarizing, from a 1770 English translation, the Swedish scientist Per Kalm's 1750 account of the city. Whether borrowing from Anburey or from Kalm, Lennox's description of New York talks of the "flourishing trade" and "extremely fruitful" soil that would later be praised by James Fenimore Cooper. A less specific colonial time frame counterpoints the more exact description of New York. This allows Lennox to minimize shipboard incidents, so that the focus is now a comparison between London and Albany, with almost two volumes devoted to each. The eponymous heroine is married to an officer posted to America. Consequently, the debate is less about the threats to female virtue and more about questions of social relations. The epistolary form assists in replacing emotionality with fastidiousness. Euphemia's account of New York with its "succession of visits, balls, and entertainments" is used to highlight the affected social pretensions and superficial politeness of the British, and their condescension to the "uncouth" and "rudely familiar" Dutch whom they shortly meet in Albany.[24]

A year later, Susanna Rowson published *Charlotte Temple*. Rowson was the daughter of William Haswell, a Royal Navy lieutenant. They lived near Boston from 1766 to 1778, when they were returned to Britain in a prisoner exchange. The experience of revolutionary America undoubtedly affected the moral landscape of her best-known novel. Charlotte Temple's childhood home, somewhere in southern England, is presented as a place of peace and plenty. Hell is everywhere else. Britain and the United States differ only in the nature of their moral turpitude. In a flashback, the narrative describes a British aristocracy founded in primogeniture and arranged marriages, and plagued by snobbery, profligacy, and penury. New York is a lower circle of Hell, portrayed only in terms of space and economics. If the environment is lightly sketched in, the time is precise. A reference to St. Eustatia, the Leeward Island fought over by the British, Dutch, and French in 1781, indicates that the setting is during the British occupation of New York. The peripatetic nature of British military families strips from Charlotte the moral supports that should otherwise have been available. Left alone, Charlotte is at the mercy of economics, which turns up in the shape of "her barbarous landlady," who has come for the rent. In response to Charlotte's request for charity, she breaks out, in Rowson's rendering of vernacular:

> charity indeed: why, Mistress, charity begins at home, and I have seven children at home, *honest, lawful* children, and it is my duty to keep them; and do you think I will give away my property to a nasty, impudent hussey, to maintain her and her bastard; an I was saying to my husband the other day what will this world come to; honest women are nothing now-a-days, while the harlotings are set up for fine ladies, and look upon us no more nor the dirt they walk upon: but let me tell you, my fine spoken Ma'am, I must have my money; so seeing as how you can't pay it, why you must troop, and leave all your fine gimcracks and fal der ralls behind you. I don't ask for no more nor my right, and nobody shall dare for to go for to hinder me of it. [Rowson's emphases]

Constructed as just two sentences, this torrent of words, many of them redundant, reveals the impoliteness at the heart of the new economic order created by social mobility. Charity may begin at home, but home for Charlotte is thousands of miles away, and now unreachable. "Doomed to linger out a wretched existence in a strange land," she wanders off, into the snow and intense cold that is New York in winter. The novel's emotional appeal made it the biggest bestseller until *Uncle Tom's Cabin*. The novel reappeared in many different forms, one of them asserting that Charlotte was "the fastest girl in New York." Like another death, that of Willy Loman in Arthur Miller's *Death of a Salesman*, Charlotte's demise rubbed raw the emotions of American audiences because it exposed the outcome of the American Dream.[25]

The landlady's excessive, vernacular language is a foretaste of the future direction of American literature as it began to emerge from under the influence of its English progenitor. Cooper was right that the "peculiarity" of American literature would result from the "distinctive political opinions" of the United States and, even before *Notions of the Americans*, he had provided a more worthy counterpart to the landlady in the figure of Natty Bumppo.[26] James Kirke Paulding, too, would create a vernacular figure to answer the pretensions of the English. The origin of this figure may be seen in the character of the Yankee Jonathan in Royall Tyler's play *The Contrast*, first performed in New York in 1787. Jonathan's blundering courtship may have lost him his love Jenny, but his popularity with the audience was confirmed by his preference for such creole habits as "a little peaceable bundling," singing "Yankee Doodle," and exclamations such as: "Burning rivers! cooling flames! red-hot roses! pig-nuts! hasty-pudding and ambrosia!"[27] Paulding would develop the figure of Jonathan in *The Diverting History of John Bull and Brother Jonathan* (1812), a roman à clef about the events leading up to the second war between Britain and its former colony; and in *John Bull in America* (1825), a burlesque, as Paulding's son put it, "of the rabble of English travellers in this country."[28]

The environment for Brother Jonathan may be found in *Salmagundi*, a series of essays written by Paulding with William and Washington Irving, and collected into a book in 1808. When John Lambert introduced *Salmagundi* to London in 1811, he suggested that "it will act like a stimulating curry of India" because the essays "partake more of the broad humour of Rabelais and Swift than the refined morality of Addison and Johnson."[29] Lambert might have added, had he been aware of them, the "Silence Dogood" essays of Benjamin Franklin in *The New England Courant*. The seventeenth essay of *Salmagundi*, written by Washington Irving, provided a further name for New York. Irving told the story of "the thrice renowned and delectable city of GOTHAM" that was invaded by the Hoppingtots who, "impelled by a superfluity of appetite," did "make themselves masters" of the city and its abundance of "all manner of fish and flesh, and eatables and drinkables," compelling the earlier inhabitants to become, like themselves, "flagrant, outrageous, and abandoned dancers."[30]

The original Gotham is a village in Nottinghamshire, close to Sherwood Forest. Perhaps inspired by the outlaw tradition of Robin Hood, cheaply produced compilations of ballads and bad jokes with variations on the ironic title of *The Merry Tales of the Wise Men of Gotham* were popular for almost three centuries. Paulding would borrow that title in 1826 to tell the story of three such "wise" men to satirize utopianism and would repeat the exercise four years later to attack contemporary fashions and political chicanery. Gotham has, of course, since become the home town of Batman and Robin, successors to the outlaw of Sherwood Forest.[31] Homegrown character and home town are at last united in *The Lion of the West*. Paulding's play survives only in a British adaptation of 1833. It concerns the meeting between a Kentucky colonel named Nimrod Wildfire, who is "half horse, half alligator, a touch of the airth-quake, with a sprinkling of the steamboat," and one Mrs. Wollope, who recites extracts from her *Domestic Manners of the Americans*. Wildfire is a nephew to a New York merchant named Freeman, and probably also related to Natty Bumppo and Davy Crockett. Wildfire is an outrageous dancer and knows no peer in his command of Kentucky vocabulary. At one point he is in danger of being "*te-to-taciously ex-flunctified.*" But not by Mrs. Wollope, who is sent packing to England at the play's close. He also resolves a quarrel between Freeman and Percival, a British merchant. In the face of Wildfire's eloquence, they propose to "quench the petty fires of dissension." Wildfire offers to divide his land in "Kaintuck ... free gratis and for nothing," where "the ground's so rich there that if you plant a crowbar over night it will sprout tenpenny nails afore mornin'." Wildfire himself hopes to return to New York.[32] The audience joins him in that hope for, well before Damon Runyon, such linguistic invention finds its natural environment in Gotham. The play thus ends with a reconciliation between Britain and the United States, and between city and country. As we know from Leonard Bernstein's *On the Town*, it could only happen in New York.

Three hundred and fourteen years after Daniel Denton, in *New York Days, New York Nights* (1984), Stephen Brook showed that New York requires from its onlookers a fantasy of excess, with its joys, confusions, and occasional griefs. It must be described in superlatives, for "it is an idea, an assertion." Paradigm, in other words, is inseparable from place, archetype from architecture. New York awaits "your deepest pleasure" and requires from visitor and resident alike "your fullest participation," sexual and otherwise. Unlike Denton, however, Brook understands that superlatives can be bad as well as good. New York is both Hell and Heaven, "its exhilaration is also a kind of terror."[33] In 2001 the terror was realized to its fullest extent, and received an appropriate response from British spectators. Many Britons remember where they were when the attacks on the World Trade Center were first shown on their television screens; many then signed Books of Condolence. (I signed a Book in Boston, Lincolnshire.) Two days after the attacks, the band of the Coldstream Guards played the "Star-Spangled Banner" at the changing of the guard at Buckingham Palace in front of an unusually large and emotional crowd of between three and five thousand people.[34] The "Star-Spangled Banner" was an apt if possibly unwitting choice. The newspaper reporters seemed unaware that the lyrics were written at one of the worst moments in Anglo-American relations, when in 1814 the Royal Navy bombarded Fort McHenry in Baltimore. But historical accuracy has no part to play in the construction of the epic city.

NOTES

* This essay is dedicated to the memory of Emory Elliott.

1. An Amateur [J. K. Paulding], *The New Mirror for Travellers* (New York: G. & C. Carvill, 1828), pp. 10–11. Michael Wigglesworth, "God's Controversy with New-England," in *The Poems of Michael Wigglesworth*, ed. Ronald A. Bosco (Lanham, MD: University Press of America, 1989), p. 90.

2. Sydney Smith, "Review of Adam Seybert, *Statistical Annals of the United States of America*," *Edinburgh Review* 33 (January 1820): 79. On the cultural cold war, see Benjamin Lease, *Anglo-American Encounters: England and the Rise of American Literature* (Cambridge: Cambridge University Press, 1981).

3. [William Empson], "Review of James Fenimore Cooper, *Notions of the Americans* and Basil Hall, *Travels in North America in the Years 1827 & 1828*," *Edinburgh Review* 49 (June 1829): 473, 490.

4. Daniel Denton, *A Brief Description of New-York* (London: John Hancock, 1670), pp. 19–20.

5. See Peter Conrad, *The Art of the City: Views and Versions of New York* (New York: Oxford University Press, 1984), esp. pp. 3–23, 54–56, 323.

6. James Fenimore Cooper, *Notions of the Americans* (1828; Albany: State University of New York Press, 1991), pp. 116, 123–27, 342, 348, 352.

7. Henry James, *Hawthorne* (1879; London: Macmillan, 1967), p. 55; [Joseph Green Cogswell], "On the State of Learning in the United States of America," *Blackwood's Edinburgh Magazine* 4 (March 1819): 641–49.

8. Edwin G. Burrows and Mike Wallace, *Gotham: A History of New York City to 1898* (New York: Oxford University Press, 1999), p. 378.

9. See especially Edgar Allan Poe, "Joseph Rodman Drake – Fitz-Greene Halleck" (1836) and "The Literati of New York City" (1846), in *Essays and Reviews* (New York: Library of America, 1984), pp. 505–39, 1118–222.

10. Wayne Franklin, *James Fenimore Cooper: The Early Years* (New Haven, CT: Yale University Press, 2007), pp. 367–69.

11. [William Empson], "Review of James Fenimore Cooper, *Notions of the Americans* and Basil Hall, *Travels in North America*," 477; Frances Trollope, *Domestic Manners of the Americans*, ed. Richard Mullen (Oxford: Oxford University Press, 1984), p. 297.

12. Basil Hall, *Travels in North America in the Years 1827 & 1828*, 3 vols. (Edinburgh: Cadell & Co., 1829), I, pp. 5–8.

13. John Brewer, *The Pleasures of the Imagination: English Culture in the Eighteenth Century* (London: HarperCollins, 1997); Ann Bermingham and John Brewer, eds., *The Consumption of Culture 1600–1800: Image, Object, Text* (London: Routledge, 1995); Michael Warner, *The Letters of the Republic: Publication and the Public Sphere in Eighteenth-Century America* (Cambridge, MA: Harvard University Press, 1990).

14. Sir William Blackstone, *Commentaries on the Laws of England*, 4 vols. (London: T. Cadell and W. Davies, 1800), iii, pp. 325–27.

15. See Paul Langford, "The Uses of Eighteenth-Century Politeness," *Transactions of the Royal Historical Society*, 6th ser., 12 (2002): 311–31; Robert Darnton, "The Unity of Europe: Culture and Politeness," *George Washington's False Teeth* (New York: W. W. Norton, 2003), pp. 76–88; Lawrence E. Klein, "Politeness and

the Interpretation of the British Eighteenth Century," *The Historical Journal* 45 (2002): 869–98.

16. John Peter Zenger, *A Brief Narrative of the Case and Trial of John Peter Zenger* ([London], n. p., [1738?]), pp. 1, 29; *A Complete Collection of State-Trials and Proceedings for High-Treason*, 4th edn., 11 vols. (London: printed by T. Wright, 1776–81), ix, cols. 275–316.

17. Cooper, *Notions*, pp. 806, 22, 25; Cooper, *New York ... Being an introduction to the unpublished manuscript ... entitled The Towns of Manhattan* (1930; Folcroft, PA: Folcroft Library Editions, 1973), pp. 17, 37.

18. John Lambert, *Travels through Canada and the United States of North America in the Years 1806, 1807, & 1808*, 3rd edn. (London: Baldwin, Cradock & Joy, 1816), pp. 49, 55.

19. William Cobbett, *A Year's Residence in the United States of America*, ed. J. E. Morpurgo (Fontwell, Sussex [Eng.]: Centaur Press, 1964), p. 231; R. H. Sweet, "Topographies of Politeness," *Transactions of the Royal Historical Society* 12 (2002): 355–74.

20. Hall, *Travels in North America*, i, p. 8; John Donne, *The Complete English Poems*, ed. A. J. Smith (Harmondsworth: Penguin, 1971), p. 124.

21. Philip Dormer Stanhope, *Lord Chesterfield's Advice to His Son*, 3rd edn. (London: Richardson & Urquhart, 1777), pp. 34, 44; Philip Dormer Stanhope, *Letters Written ... to His Son*, 8th edn., 4 vols. (London: J. Dodsley, 1777), IV, p. 8; *The Young Lady's Pocket Library, or Parental Monitor* (Dublin: John Archer, 1790), p. 157.

22. Margaret Hunter Hall, *The Aristocratic Journey. Being the Outspoken Letters of Mrs. Basil Hall, Written during a Fourteen Months' Sojourn in America, 1827–1828*, ed. Una Pope Hennessy (New York: G. P. Putnam's Sons, 1931), pp. 24, 122, 298; Hall, *Travels in North America*, i, p. 19; ii, pp. iii, 343, 405; iii, p. 6.

23. Charlotte Lennox, *The Life of Harriot Stuart, Written by Herself*, ed. Susan Kubica Howard (London: Associated University Presses, 1995), pp. 68, 81, 104, 108, 138, 282.

24. Charlotte Lennox, *Euphemia*, 4 vols. in 2, introd. Peter Garside (London: Routledge/Thoemmes Press, 1992), ii, pp. 220, 224; iii, p. 33. See also Philippe Séjourné, *The Mystery of Charlotte Lennox: First Novelist of Colonial America* (Aix-en-Provence: Publications des Annales de la Faculté des Lettres, 1967), pp. 58–59, 71; and Eve Tavor Bannet, "The Theater of Politeness in Charlotte Lennox's British-American Novels," *Novel: A Forum on Fiction* 33:1 (Autumn 1999): 73–92.

25. Susanna Rowson, *Charlotte Temple*, ed. Ann Douglas (Harmondsworth: Penguin, 1991), pp. 77, 113, 116. R. W. G. Vail, "Susanna Haswell Rowson, the Author of *Charlotte Temple*: A Bibliographical Study," *Proceedings of the American Antiquarian Society*, n.s. 42 (1932): 62–64, 91–125. Cathy N. Davidson, "Introduction" to *Charlotte Temple* (New York: Oxford University Press, 1986), p. xxxi.

26. Cooper, *Notions*, p. 342.

27. Royall Tyler, *The Contrast* (1790), in *Early American Drama*, ed. Jeffrey H. Richards (New York: Penguin, 1997), pp. 37–38.

28. James Kirke Paulding, *The Bulls and the Jonathans: Comprising John Bull and Brother Jonathan and John Bull in America*, ed. William I. Paulding (New York: Charles Scribner and Company, 1867), p. 149.

29. *Salmagundi; or, the Whim-Whams and Opinions of Launcelot Langstaff*, introd. John Lambert (London: J. M. Richardson, 1811), pp. ix, xxxvii.

30. Washington Irving, *"Letters of Jonathan Oldstyle, Gent," and "Salmagundi,"* ed. Bruce I. Granger and Martha Hartzog (Boston: Twayne, 1977), pp. 272–77.

31. [J. K. Paulding], *The Merry Tales of the Wise Men of Gotham* (New York: G. & C. & H. Carvill, 1826); [J. K. Paulding], *Chronicles of the City of Gotham, from the Papers of a Councilman* (New York: G. & C. & H. Carvill, 1830); Edwin G. Burrows and Mike Wallace, *Gotham: A History of New York City to 1898* (New York: Oxford University Press, 1999), pp. xii–xiii.

32. James Kirke Paulding, *"The Lion of the West" and "The Bucktails,"* ed. Frank Grado (Lanham, MD: Rowman and Littlefield, 1994), pp. 99, 102, 117, 134–35.

33. Stephen Brook, *New York Days, New York Nights* (London: Hamish Hamilton, 1984), pp. 16, 284.

34. *The Guardian* (September 14, 2001); *The Telegraph* (September 14, 2001).

2

ELIZABETH L. BRADLEY

Dutch New York from Irving to Wharton

"DISTRESSING,"

Left his lodgings some time since, and has not since been heard of, a small elderly gentleman, dressed in an old black coat and cocked hat, by the name of KNICKERBOCKER. As there are some reasons for believing he is not entirely in his right mind, and as great anxiety is entertained about him, any information concerning him left either at the Columbian Hotel, Mulberry street, or at the office of this paper will be thankfully received.

This notice, published in the October 26, 1809 issue of the New York paper the *Evening Post*, was followed by subsequent announcements from the land-lord of the Columbian Hotel, who threatened to sell a "*very curious kind of a written book*" that had been found in the aforementioned Knickerbocker's rooms, as payment for rent the missing man owed him.[1] The ads were a hoax, the landlord fictional, but the book was quite real. It was made available for sale in New York City on December 6, 1809, with the title

A History of New-York, from the Beginning of the World to the End of the Dutch Dynasty; Containing, among Many Surprising and Curious Matters, the Unutterable Ponderings of Walter the Doubter, the Disastrous Projects of William the Testy, and the Chivalric Achievements of Peter the Headstrong – The Three Dutch Governors of New Amsterdam: Being the Only Authentic History of the Times that Ever Hath Been or Ever Will Be Published.

The narrator of this daunting tome was given as "Diedrich Knickerbocker," he of the cocked hat and unpaid bills (see *Figure 2*). The real author is much more familiar to posterity: it was a 26-year-old Washington Irving.

The *History of New York* was a near-instant success and jump-started the literary career of its young author, who would later be hailed as the first American humorist to achieve international renown. The *History*, however, was an unlikely favorite: it was a meandering, hyperbolic account of the discovery, colonization, cultivation, and ultimate surrender of the New Amsterdam settlement, as told by a New Yorker of Dutch descent.

Figure 2: Drawing of Diedrich Knickerbocker by Felix O. C. Darley for the 1849 edition of *A History of New York*. This representation of Knickerbocker, picturing him as slight of frame and quizzical of expression, wearing his battered hat and shabby cloak, received Irving's official stamp of approval.

Whether or not such a partisan account should qualify as "history" was doubtful: Irving's satirical, semi-fictional book more nearly resembled Jonathan Swift's *Gulliver's Travels* (1726) than William Bradford's *Of Plymouth Plantation* (1620–47). Why, then, was the *History* such a success? The book succeeded in large part because it gave New York City a founding mythology, a lasting narrative of exceptionalism that would, in time, completely eclipse Boston's Puritan "city on a hill." The New Yorker's sense of his own difference from the rest of the new United States, Irving's invented Dutch narrator insists, has its roots not in the English colony for which the city was named, but in the far more idiosyncratic, cosmopolitan, and charming traditions of New Amsterdam. And it is there, according to Knickerbocker, that readers should look for the solid foundation on which to anchor their own infinitely mutable and expanding city.

From a 21st-century vantage point, the act of celebrating New York as a place without peer is familiar, even banal: the city has been "sung" by everyone from Walt Whitman to Junot Diaz. But contemplating New York's particularity, not to mention its origins, was a relatively new impulse for Irving's readership. Before the *History*, few writers (either American or European) had taken the time to try to define New York, possibly because after the Revolutionary War all human exertion in New York was directed toward the rebuilding of the city itself. Visitors marveled at the ceaseless activity of post-war Manhattan, and at how New Yorkers seemed to derive their energy and excitement from "the perpetual motion of the busy."[2] New roads were barely in place in one city ward before additional housing and commercial developments, creeping ever northward over the island's farms, pastures, and filled-in marshlands, necessitated more of the same. At the same time, the city was not without visible traces of its Dutch past, including the crooked downtown lanes from which the new roads branched in an ever-increasing proliferation. In fact, those crooked streets were arguably the most complete source of information about the vanished Dutch settlement, for they were often named for the colonists who had first lived there. When the city rechristened many of its colonial roads to rid them of their Hanoverian associations (George Street became Spruce Street, King Street was dubbed Pine Street, and Little Queen Street was changed to Cedar Street), the Dutch ones were largely exempted, and these "grandfathered" byways of New Amsterdam came to serve as a kind of roadside concordance to actual city fathers, offering clues for contemporary New Yorkers to the people and events that had shaped the Dutch colony.[3] Irving's book was the first to put a figurative halt to that expansion, and the first to invite readers to embark on an archeological dig into New York's past – specifically, its Dutch founding and development. The result of this exploration and education is a city with stories, mysteries, and depth; a city, finally, with historical memory.

But the search for Dutch New York did not, in fact, begin with Irving. Instead, his book was inspired by the example of the New-York Historical Society, an organization of prominent New Yorkers founded in 1804 with the stated mission of collecting and preserving "whatever may relate to the natural, civic, or ecclesiastical History of the United States in general, and of this State in particular."[4] Unfortunately, as the Society quickly discovered, between the seven years of British wartime occupation and a series of large-scale fires that had ravaged the southern end of Manhattan, most of the archival holdings and city records from the New Amsterdam settlement had been destroyed. Nor, embarrassingly, could anyone be found who could understand the few state documents that remained in Albany – the Dutch-speaking local who had been commissioned to translate them into English in 1805 had made off with his fee in advance, and the first significant (but by no means thorough or error-free) translation was only completed in 1822. These losses were a torment to the Historical Society, which chided New Yorkers for their apparent lack of concern, and insisted that "without the aid of original records and authentic documents, history will be nothing more than a well-combined series of ingenious conjectures and amusing fables."[5] In other words, not even a regimented and growing street grid could secure a city built on historical quicksand.

This gap in New York's story was not only due to the devastations of war, however. Prior to Irving's fanciful appropriations in the *History*, few accounts of the New Amsterdam settlement had ever been made available to non-Dutch New Yorkers. While the governors of the English colony of New York had seen the value of naming high-ranking Dutch residents to their economic councils in order to maintain ties with Holland, the Dutch communities in Kings and Queens counties (known today as the boroughs of Brooklyn and Queens, respectively) and along the Hudson River were notoriously clannish, maintaining Dutch as their primary language, in some cases well into the nineteenth century.[6] These descendants of the original colonists showed little interest in promulgating Dutch literature or presenting Dutch-American histories to an English-speaking world. While their reticence was Irving's opportunity, the satirist did not create his New Amsterdam from nothing: as Elisabeth Paling Funk has pointed out, Irving's Dutch-descended friend and fellow New Yorker Henry Brevoort loaned him works from his private collection of rare Dutch books and manuscripts to further his research and lend historical gravitas to his "Knickerbocker" narrative voice.[7]

The Society also tried to augment its library of primary documents, but in lieu of Brevoort's Old World texts, the group solicited new research from their membership. The most famous of these efforts to capture the "state of the city" was Dr. Samuel Latham Mitchill's *The Picture of New York: Or, The Traveller's Guide Through the Commercial Metropolis of the United States, By a Gentleman Residing in this City* (1807). This catalog of New York's landscape, history, and contemporary civic institutions was one of the first urban guides to be written by a New York resident. The book, as befits its author, a founder of the College of Physicians and Surgeons and a peerless naturalist, is scrupulous in its detail, regardless of whether Mitchill is describing the constellation of islands in New York harbor or providing the municipal requirements for "Cargo-Pork" ("[it] shall not contain in one barrel more than four shoulders without the legs, nor more than 2 heads with the ears and snouts cut off and brains and bloody grizzle taken out").[8] However, Mitchill's comprehensive survey of New York bears few marks of Dutch civilization. He belittles the old Dutch place names in the city, dismisses the sale of "Hudson's River" to the Dutch as a minor transaction, and dispatches the surrender of the Dutch colony to the English in a single paragraph. Not one aspect of the New Amsterdam settlement, its government, or its society is explored in the *Picture of New York*, and the author devotes more space to a description of the "strata" of New York "granite" than he does to the entire Dutch rule. It was Mitchill's dismissal of New Netherlands, more than anything else, that laid the groundwork for Irving's satirical *History*: in later years, Irving admitted that his book had been intended to "burlesque the pedantic lore displayed in certain American works," such as Mitchill's "small handbook." Irving had also hastened to add that he had intended Knickerbocker's *History* as nothing more than a "temporary *jeu d'esprit*," not a statement of outright protest, but his charming competing account of New York, arriving so closely on the heels of Mitchill's book, could not help but be interpreted by its readers as a direct reproach to those who would deny the city its eccentric past, or allow its Dutch customs to become quietly extinct.[9]

The *History* is intended, Knickerbocker notes in his introduction, to pay "just tribute" to the "many great and wonderful transactions" of the Dutch colony, including their various attempts at statecraft and self-fashioning – basically, all those events for which the Historical Society could find no documentation. Knickerbocker's account of these events interleaves verifiable historical fact (drawn from footnoted sources, such as the journal of Robert Juet, first mate on Henry Hudson's *De Halve Maen*) with outrageous falsehood, such as when Knickerbocker suggests that Manhattan's Native Americans were not completely decimated by the settlers, but in some cases just scared away by the "tremendous and uncouth sound of the low dutch language." Irving also takes care that Knickerbocker offers periodic assurance that his outlandish tales have verifiable, pedigreed sources, whether they were "gleaned ... among the family chests and lumber garrets of our respectable dutch citizens," or taken from an "elaborate manuscript ... found in the archives of the Stuyvesant family," or by consulting "sundry family traditions, handed down from Knickerbocker's great great Grandfather," purportedly a "cabin boy" to Henry Hudson.[10] In this way, the narrator's assertions of privileged information (although he never mentions Henry Brevoort) mock the efforts of the Historical Society, by offering the same assemblage of "unverifiable facts" about New York that the Society had most feared and predicted. Throughout the *History*, the suggestion is made that an element of self-invention, of fable, is essential to the story of New York. "For after all, gentle reader," Knickerbocker notes with a wink, "cities *of themselves* ... are nothing without an historian" (379).

And, in fact, Knickerbocker's colonial history offers persuasive explanations for the archaic customs, structures, and names that haunted the contemporary city. These include crediting the New Amsterdam cows with devising the aforementioned twisting streets of lower Manhattan; the New Year's Day celebrations of New York's elites; the veneration of St. Nicholas; and the creation of the humble doughnut. For this last innovation, Irving seems to have taken his cue from the American poet Joel Barlow, whose 1793 ode to "Hasty Pudding" glorified the New England origins of corn-meal mush. In like fashion, Irving hailed the doughnut as New York's signature dessert, and insists that this "delicious kind of cake" was a feature of his ancestor's tea-tables, "called dough nuts, or oly koeks –at present, scarce known in this city, excepting in genuine dutch families" (480). Not only did the doughnut belong to New York but, as the invention of "genuine dutch families," it was *older* than New York, and thus part of the legacy of the New Amsterdam settlement, to be revered as a holy and delicious relic of the city's primordial past.[11] Like Barlow's ode to porridge, Irving's hymn to pastry drew early attention to the concept of regional identities, and suggested another, still-important way for New York to set itself apart from its American rivals: through the heritage of local cuisine.[12] This conjunction would have delighted (but not surprised) Irving's New York readership, who had already adopted street-eating (everything from oysters to "hot corn") and devised the first variation on urban takeout – as early as the 1760s, Samuel Fraunces was delivering meals to the captains and passengers aboard the ships that docked in the harbor, just a few blocks from his famous tavern.

As self-appointed curator of the vanishing culture of Dutch New York, Knickerbocker also eulogizes the colony's founding families. In the narrator's estimation, the true glory of the colony lies in the "regular, well organized, antediluvian dutch families" by whom it was first settled and protected, and whom he calls "the only local nobility [in New York], and the real lords of the soil."[13] Irving takes pains to show just how earthy Knickerbocker's "lords of the soil" really were, and lampoons the aristocratic pretensions of his readership with his mock genealogies. The "Van Nests of Kinderhook," for example, are praised for being "valiant robbers of birds' nests, as their name denotes; to these, if report may be believed, we are indebted for the invention of slap jacks, or buck-wheat cakes" (630). At the same time, there is a perverse, meritocratic streak to his Dutch class hierarchy; in the

Knickerbockerian universe, it is genteel to be shabby. The "higher classes, or noblesse," the historian insists, were those who "kept their own cows, and drove their own wagons," and "neither drove in their curricles nor sported their tandems, for as yet those gaudy vehicles were not even dreamt of" by a population that tended cabbage-gardens and were all "in full snore before nine o'clock" each night.[14] Despite the author's comic emphasis on the bourgeois, prosaic nature of the Dutch burghers and their colony, the "nobility" described in the *History* was soon appropriated by American readers who mistook Irving's mischievous heraldries for sober genealogical fact, and built their own aspirational fantasies on his satirical foundation.

Indeed, to Irving's delighted surprise, it took less than a year after publication for New Yorkers to adopt Knickerbocker's mythical Dutch forebears as their very own. Local writers soon began to imitate Irving's comically florid rhetorical style and borrow his nostalgic New Netherlands backdrop for stories of their own, while social groups sprang up to claim the New Amsterdam customs that Knickerbocker described with such loving precision. And New Yorkers began to call themselves – or to be called – "Knickerbockers." Buoyed by the success of his "*jeu d'esprit*," Irving added to (and would continue to rework) his Dutch repertoire in several of the collections of literary "sketches" that he published in the years after the *History*. Among these were a number of stories ostensibly narrated (or "found") by Diedrich Knickerbocker, including, most famously, the two stories that are now widely considered to be Irving's most lasting contributions to American literature: "Rip Van Winkle" and "The Legend of Sleepy Hollow." Along with "Dolph Heyliger," "Wolfert Webber: Or, Golden Dreams," "The Storm-Ship," and "The Money-Diggers," these further adventures of Dutch New Yorkers reiterated the homespun traditions and easy hospitality of that dwindling population, both in the Hudson River Valley and in the colonial and post-colonial city, and championed their fierce adherence to ancestral mores in the face of cultural and geographical upheaval. These refinements to the "Knickerbocker" vision of New York proved irresistible to Irving's readers, who reconstructed the city's past to suit their various agendas, with the help of his nostalgic tropes.

While commercial enterprises were the first to recognize the market potential in Diedrich Knickerbocker, Irving's appealing cast of Dutch "patriarchs" was soon seized by nativists, patriots, pulp fiction writers, and society novelists, and "Knickerbocker" quickly entered the literary lexicon as shorthand for an authentic New Yorker.[15] Some of the earliest fiction writers to invoke the Dutch legacy after Irving included his childhood friend and early collaborator (on the 1807 magazine *Salmagundi*) James Kirke Paulding, a writer of Dutch descent who contributed a sentimental novel, *The Dutchman's Fireside*

(1831), and a book of stories, *The Book of St. Nicholas* (1837), to what was quickly becoming a New Amsterdam genre, as well as *The Knickerbocker* magazine, founded in 1833 by Charles Fenno Hoffman (and later edited by Lewis Gaylord Clark), which claimed Knickerbocker as its muse at the outset, and ultimately hired Irving as a celebrity correspondent. Even before he joined the staff of *The Knickerbocker*, however, the magazine had turned Irving's Hudson River Valley sketches into a cottage industry, and churned out such hackneyed variations on his signature themes as "The Legend of Whooping Hollow," "A Dutchman 'Done,'" and "Reminiscences in the Little Church at Lake George." The magazine's trademark (and, for a time, highly lucrative) adherence to the blandest and most "refined" aspects of Irving's oeuvre would result in some of its more prominent contributors being grouped together, post facto, as the "Knickerbocker School" of literature. The nickname is something of a misnomer, for the most celebrated writers in the group, which included the poets William Cullen Bryant and Fitz-Greene Halleck and the essayist Nathaniel Parker Willis, are best known today, if at all, not for their *Knickerbocker* contributions, but for their independent work on non-Dutch themes, such as Bryant's poem "Thanatopsis" (1817).

And yet, as mediocre as *The Knickerbocker* may have proved to be, it is a useful early measure of the extent to which Irving's tales had become, and would continue to be, a source of valuable social and civic identification in the antebellum city. A cottage industry of New York histories emerged at this time to expand and correct the work of early chroniclers such as Mitchill and Irving, and to hold a mirror to a city that was growing increasingly self-conscious. The most enduring among these were David Valentine's *Manuals of the Corporation of the City of New York*, which began serial publication in 1841, and Edmund O'Callaghan's two-volume *History of New Netherland: Or, New York Under the Dutch*, published from 1846 to 1848.[16] Valentine's *Manuals* promised to "trace the progress of the city of New York ... from a wilderness condition" to the present day by offering salvaged founding documents, maps, and lithographs in each edition. O'Callaghan's *History* was made possible by the crusading work of John Romeyn Brodhead, an American historian who discovered papers relating to the Dutch settlement of the city while serving as an attaché to the American legation at The Hague and who was subsequently commissioned by the Governor of New York to translate them (from 1841 to 1844). But new scholarly efforts such as these did not satisfy the popular fascination with New York's Dutch heritage, which quickly spread to pulp literature and could even be found in the earliest New York *noir*, such as the "gaslight" stories of George G. Foster, whose *New York in Slices, by an Experienced Carver* (1849) and *New York by Gas-Light*

(1850) made a distinction between amoral American "merchant princes" and the New Yorkers of "old aristocratic Knickerbocker blood," whose style and behavior his books openly approve.[17] "New York is undoubtedly the greatest place for dancing in all Anglo-Saxondom," Foster declares in *New York by Gas-Light*, because "nowhere else ... has the light-toed goddess so many and such enthusiastic worshippers as in this staid old Dutch settlement of Gotham. There seems to be something in the intermixture of Puritan and Knickerbocker blood which gives peculiar activity to the heels and elasticity to the toes."[18] The reverential repetition of "Knickerbocker blood" starkly contrasts with the unalloyed disgust with which Foster describes some of the residents of the Five Points slums: "the descendants of Israel ... as celebrated for fecundity as cats or Irish women."[19] The immigrant ghettoes and the "staid old Dutch settlement of Gotham" hardly seem to be the same city.

Foster's bigoted language reveals how effortlessly Irving's Dutch historian could be employed in the service of an ever-growing American preoccupation with ethnicity and race. Terms such as "blood" were by no means unique to Foster, or to the gaslight genre: despite its vaunted cosmopolitanism, nineteenth-century New York would prove to be a critical hub for nativist sentiment in the decades leading up to the Civil War. Against this backdrop, it is hardly a surprise that the first American novel to capitalize on Irving's Knickerbocker worldview was itself an exercise in snobbery. Charles Astor Bristed's *The Upper Ten Thousand* (1852) was advertised to the reading public as a primer on "old New York," and a window, not unlike the one Edith Wharton would offer half a century later, on the customs and pretensions of the city's elite at play (see *Figure 8*, p. 95). The pedagogical twist to the novel is, without a doubt, its most interesting feature; Bristed borrows shamelessly from Irving and Paulding, as well as from James Fenimore Cooper's Dutch-inflected *Littlepage Manuscripts* trilogy (1845–46) to assemble his portrait of a family of patrician, Patroon-descended New Yorkers in Manhattan, at their country seat, Devilshoof (a blatant take-off of Cooper's Littlepage homestead, which is called "Satanstoe"), and in Saratoga Springs. *The Upper Ten Thousand* offers vocabulary tutorials, such as when Bristed's American protagonist helpfully exclaims to his English guest, "Oh, you don't know what *stoop* means! It is a Dutch word we Gothamites have retained. Well, then, come out on the front piazza"; or instructs readers that "Kaatskill" is "the genuine Dutch orthography" for "Catskill."[20] The book was the first to describe a Dutch-descended character as a "genuine Knickerbocker," turning Irving's imaginary historian into a bona fide New York archetype. Bristed drives the point home by reconstructing the *History*'s faux family trees in order to identify *parvenu* New Yorkers who were not, "in point of birth, ... related to the Van Hornes, the Masters, the Vanderlyns, or any of the old Dutch settlers[.]"[21]

A pulp romance published the same year demonstrates just how widespread New York's romance with the Dutch had become. John D. Vose's *Fresh Leaves from the Diary of a Broadway Dandy* details the adventures of a wealthy young man raised "above Bleecker," who ultimately renounces the "Hudson-street belle, the St. Mark's Place princess, the Waverly Place beauty ... [and] the Broadway heiress" in favor of his true love, a penniless girl "from the best old stock of blood in the state – the real, pure Knickerbocker of the old school – those days of Rip Van Winkle."[22] Naturally, as in Irving's own Hudson Valley tales, the lovely, seemingly destitute wife turns out to possess not only "the best blood of New York ... that genuine, whole-souled Knickerbocker, Rip Van Winkle and Livingston stock," but also "property deeded in [her] name, which includes a block of stores in Pearl-street, and a mansion in Ninth-street, on the west side of Broadway" (122–23). Like *The Upper Ten Thousand*, *Fresh Leaves* attaches real estate to pedigreed ancestry, the better to maintain the fantasy that the primordial "best blood" of Manhattan might, in fact, triumph over the city's emerging hierarchy: one of rampant development and ahistorical speculation.

The Gilded Age only reinforced the literary appropriation of Irving's Dutch clans and their picturesque Hudson Valley folkways. In conjunction with the antimodern movement that encouraged Americans to form genealogical societies (which included, not incidentally, the St. Nicholas Society, the Holland Society, and the Society of Holland Dames) and research the family crests of their Anglo-Saxon ancestors, the symbols of New Amsterdam became totems of class and race prejudice, and "Knickerbocker New York" became a synonym for "old money New York." This direction is exemplified by *The Last of the Knickerbockers* (1901), a "comic romance" that followed the fortunes of Alida Van Wandeleer, a Dutch-descended New York native whose "social talent," "perfect breeding," and affection for New York ensure that hansom cab drivers and titled nobility alike instantly identify her as "a real, live Knickerbocker." The author of this novel was himself a "real, live Knickerbocker": Herman Knickerbocker Vielé was a lineal descendant of the Knickerbocker family of Schagticoke, New York, from whom Irving had (he later confessed) borrowed his historian's now-famous surname. With this advantage, Vielé is in a position to undermine the authority of his more famous, fictional "cousin," but the author chooses instead to authenticate his heroine's Dutch pedigree by using Irving's book as Irving himself so often did: as a kind of circular proof. When asked whether she has ever read Irving's *History of New York*, his heroine replies: "Oh, yes ... I am descended from nearly everybody mentioned in it!" (18, 121). Unlike some of her real-life, Dutch-descended counterparts (such as the writer Giulian Verplanck, who protested Irving's satirical treatment of his ancestors), the fictional Alida is proud to be associated with her city's semi-apocryphal founding text.

Vielé's portrait of New Yorkers with a "burgher's birthright" is unquestionably a love letter to the "old stock," and a primer in historical consciousness for the "new people, whose names mean absolutely nothing, and [who are] frightfully overdressed" (48, 5). To this end, his characters are frankly ambassadorial about New York, calling Croton water their "vin du pays" and educating strangers to the subtle delights of the city, encouraging them to look beyond its advertised "theaters and department stores and noise" (98, 123). And, like Irving's narrator, the Van Wandeleers and their ilk remind the reader time and again that New York's Dutch inheritance is, in fact, history. "But I am not like you, I have no traditions to fall back on," a Peoria-born "dollar princess" says to Alida, more in wistfulness than in envy. "You are born knowing things we have to learn" (159–60). Ultimately, Vielé's heroine finds another "last" Knickerbocker to marry, one who has grown conveniently rich by prospecting in the mythical mining town of "Oro City, somewhere in the Rocky Mountains," but who still values the singular New York identity, as she does (29).[23] With this intercession, the author ends his valentine to the city, having rescued his Holland Dame from the genteel poverty that would undo one of the most famous heroines of another New York novelist, Edith Wharton.

"For the first time, the veil has been lifted from New York society," the dust jacket of the first edition of *The House of Mirth* announced, promising that Edith Wharton's 1905 novel would truly be an insider's account of the "Upper Ten Thousand."[24] Although Wharton apparently insisted that Scribner remove the statement from future editions of the book, it was by no means the last time that such a claim would be made about her work. From a commercial perspective, Wharton's Dutch pedigree and "Four Hundred" status gave her work instant authenticity. "On both sides," Wharton acknowledged in her memoir *A Backward Glance*, "our colonial ancestry goes back for nearly three hundred years, and on both sides the colonists in question seem to have been identified since early days with New York."[25] And yet unlike her own predecessors, Wharton's Manhattan "tribes" consistently deny that their own tribal identifications even exist: "Don't tell me," Mrs. Archer would say to her children, "all this modern newspaper rubbish about a New York aristocracy. If there is one, neither the Mingotts nor the Mansons belong to it; no, nor the Newlands or the Chiverses either. Our grandfathers and great-grandfathers were just respectable English or Dutch merchants, who came to the colonies to make their fortune, and stayed here because they did so well."[26]

These protestations from *The Age of Innocence* are echoed by Wharton's own assertion that (despite Scribner's advertisement) her family's antecedents were "purely middle class ... merchants, bankers, and lawyers."[27] However, while Wharton's novels adhere to the letter of these inclusive, republican principles, they universally depart from them in spirit, and while they decline the role of instruction manual, still painstakingly enumerate the inherited attributes that comprise a particular kind of New York aristocracy, closely resembling the one all her literary and tabloid peers were calling "Knickerbocker."

The gently born descendants of the "purely middle class" Dutch and English merchants whose lives are portrayed in novels such as *The House of Mirth*, *The Custom of the Country*, and *The Age of Innocence*, as well as in the novellas that make up the collection *Old New York*, derive their authority over their respective New Yorks from an innate grasp of the fine-grained linguistic and aesthetic cues that governed high society after the Civil War – what one Wharton character describes, with airy assurance, as "certain *nuances*" (1043). The crucial importance of these "nuances" is most keenly felt in *The House of Mirth*, where wealthy climbers ask for the native New Yorker Lily Bart's help in fine-tuning their "flamboyant copy" of high society, and later, in *The Custom of the Country*, where the inability of nouveaux riches to get the details of haute bourgeois "aspect and manner" right is handled with a Jamesian allusiveness by the narrator. In every case, the society depicted in Wharton's novels is governed with a "Dutch deliberateness" by mandarins who adhere to old traditions and even older kinship ties, whether they be the "viceregal" van der Luydens of *The Age of Innocence* overseeing their vast cousinship from the Patroon's house at "Skuytercliff"; the Trenors arranging tactical maneuvers in *The House of Mirth* from the terraces of Bellomont, their Hudson Valley seat; or the ethereal Ralph Marvell and his sister, Clare Van Degen, clinging to the values and Vermeer-like decorations of their ancestors in *The Custom of the Country*.[28]

Unlike her literary predecessors, Wharton does not always trumpet the New Amsterdam foundations of the insular world she depicts, but they are no less apparent for being so rarely spoken aloud. Perhaps the most telling evidence of her debt to the Knickerbocker landscape may be found in the repeated mentions – in both her fictions and her memoir – of Knickerbocker's creator himself. "We were brought up on the best books – Scott, and Washington Irving, and old whats-his-name who wrote the *Spectator*, and Gibbon and so forth," a character in *The Spark* insists, "cheap journalism – that's what most modern books are."[29] Whether or not Wharton agrees with this assessment, her own urban stories betray their debt to Irving's first attempt to capture the traces of Dutch New York.

In fact, the history that Irving bestowed on his protean, self-preoccupied hometown remained New York's preferred founding myth for the twentieth century and beyond. "Father Knickerbocker" became the mascot of New York City during the consolidation of the five boroughs in 1898, and this caricature of a seventeenth-century Dutch burgher (loosely interpreted) was used to promote not only the city (Knickerbocker was a ribbon-cutting ambassador to both World's Fairs) but also many of the city's commercial ventures, from Knickerbocker Beer and the Knickerbocker Hotel to a subsidized housing project called "Knickerbocker Village" and the New York Knickerbockers, a founding team of the NBA. Other Dutch tropes from Irving's *History* were not ignored: Franklin Delano Roosevelt's Works Progress Administration added decorative seals with windmills to its new municipal structures such as the East River Drive, and the Metropolitan Museum of Art acquired the "New York Alcove," consisting of furniture, paneling, and a fireplace wall from a Dutch colonial home in Ulster County. But literature about or by Dutch New Yorkers largely evaporated with the Gilded Age, and the new immigrant populations brought their own myths, and created their own literatures in their adoptive city. By the beginning of the twenty-first century, the Dutch presence in New York writing was a ghostly trace, and the historian's once-merry warning had largely come true: the memory of the colony he championed had dwindled almost to the "nothing" he predicted (379).

NOTES

1. Andrew Burstein, *The Original Knickerbocker: The Life of Washington Irving* (New York: Basic Books, 2007), p. 72. Burstein, Irving's most recent biographer, notes that some New Yorkers were taken in by the hoax advertisements and suggested posting a reward for Knickerbocker's safe recovery. Burstein adds that Irving's identity was kept secret by his publishers, Inskeep and Bradford, until the actual day of publication.
2. Theodore Dwight, quoted in Ric Burns and James Sanders, *New York: An Illustrated History* (New York: Alfred A. Knopf, 1999), p. 51.
3. The patriotic name changes took place gradually: Little George Street, Thames Street, and Duke Street may still be found on the 1807 Kirkham Map of New York City.
4. John Pintard, "To the Public, New-York Historical Society," *New-York Herald* (February 12, 1805).
5. *Collections of the New-York Historical Society for the Year 1809* (New York: I. Riley, 1811), p. 7.

6. Russell Shorto, *The Island at the Center of the World* (New York: Doubleday, 2004), p. 303; Edwin G. Burrows, "Kings County," in *The Other New York: The American Revolution beyond New York City, 1763–1787*, ed. Joseph S. Tiedemann and Eugene R. Fingerhut (Albany, NY: SUNY Press, 2005), p. 22; Thomas Wermuth, *Rip Van Winkle's Neighbors: The Transformation of Rural Society in the Hudson River Valley, 1720–1850* (Albany, NY: SUNY Press, 2001), p. 43. Shorto notes that "as late as the 1750s, English officials in [the Albany area] needed to find Dutch speakers to help them treat with Indians because Dutch was still the only European language the tribes spoke" (*Island*, p. 311).

7. Funk argues for the influence of one work in particular: an aphoristic moral guide or "emblem book" by the Dutch author Jacob Cats, entitled *Spiegel van den Ouden en Niewen Tyt* (1632), which was brought by Dutch settlers to New Amsterdam and continued to be imported by their descendants. Elisabeth Paling Funk, "Kindred Spirits: Jacob Cats and Washington Irving," in *From "De Halve Maen" to KLM: 400 Years of Dutch-American Exchange*, ed. M. Brigit Lacy, Charles Gehring, and J. Oosterhoof (Munster, Germany: Nodus, 2008), pp. 339–52.

8. Samuel L. Mitchill, *The Picture of New York: Or, The Traveller's Guide Through the Commercial Metropolis of the United States, By a Gentleman Residing in This City* (New York: I. Riley, 1807), p. 96.

9. Washington Irving, "The Author's Apology," in *A History of New York* (1848), ed. Edwin T. Bowden (Albany, NY: Twayne, 1964), p. 350.

10. Irving, *A History of New York* (1809), in *Washington Irving: Tales, History and Sketches*, ed. James W. Tuttleton (New York: Library of America, 1983), pp. 436, 378, 427. Further references appear in the text.

11. For a careful analysis of Dutch culinary traditions in New Amsterdam, see Peter Rose's delightful guide, *The Sensible Cook: Dutch Foodways in the Old and the New World* (Syracuse, NY: Syracuse University Press, 1989). Rose gives several recipes for "Krullen," "Oly-Koecks," and "Oly-Bollen," as well as one for "Suppaen," or cornmeal mush, which supports Irving's claim on Barlow's poetic dish.

12. The first American cookbook was Amelia Simmons's *American Cookery*, published in 1796, which included specifically "American" recipes such as "Indian Slapjack." Irving might have registered the competitive market created by the subsequent publication of *New England Cookery* in 1808, or, as John T. Edge's *Doughnuts: An American Passion* (New York: G. P. Putnam, 2006) suggests, Irving may have known about a piece of New Amsterdam "folklore," in which "a lady named Joralemon … a 'genuine *vrouw*' … opened Manhattan's first donut shop in 1796, selling *olykoeks* and coffee in the financial district between Broadway and Maiden Lane" (pp. 14, 16). Regardless of whether or not Mrs. Joralemon is apocryphal, Edge concurs that while the "donut [*sic*] is not endemic to America," the Dutch claim to have popularized the doughnut, as demonstrated in Irving's Knickerbocker works, and supported by Peter Rose, is highly credible. Indeed, Fannie Farmer's *Boston Cook Book* (Boston, MA: Jaynes, 1896) gives Irving credit for christening "oliekocken … doughnuts."

13. It is interesting to note that the 1848 edition of Irving's *History* expands on these ideas, replacing "local nobility" with "legitimate nobility," and championing the "well authenticated claims of our genuine Dutch families … that have been somewhat elbowed aside in latter days by foreign intruders" (p. 302).

14. Irving, *History* (1809), pp. 480, 485.
15. As Irving noted in the "Author's Apology" he appended to the 1848 edition of the *History*, "Knickerbocker" almost immediately became the namesake for local bakeries, ice distributors, spice merchants, baseball teams, omnibuses, and steamship companies, to name just a few that sprang up during the author's lifetime.
16. Burrows and Wallace suggest that this study of the Dutch colony, which included interviews with "old Dutch families in Flatbush and Gravesend," the very communities singled out by Samuel Mitchill, "came as a revelation to those who had incautiously assumed Irving's satirical 'history' was the real thing." Edwin G. Burrows and Mike Wallace, *Gotham: A History of New York City to 1898* (New York: Oxford University Press, 1999), p. 696.
17. George G. Foster, *New York in Slices* (New York: W. F. Burgess, 1849), p. 61.
18. George G. Foster, *"New York by Gas-Light" and Other Urban Sketches*, ed. Stuart Blumin (Berkeley: University of California Press, 1990), p. 163.
19. Foster, *New York by Gas-Light*, p. 127.
20. Charles Astor Bristed, *The Upper Ten Thousand: Sketches of American Society* (New York: Stringer and Townsend, 1852), pp. 47, 58–59.
21. *Ibid.*, p. 147. Interestingly, the author himself had only recently allied his own famous name (he was an Astor cousin) to one of the oldest of the "old Dutch" families of New York; he had married a daughter of Henry Brevoort, Jr., a patrician son of New Amsterdam, and Irving himself had attended the wedding.
22. John Vose, *Fresh Leaves from the Diary of a Broadway Dandy* (New York: Bunnell and Price, 1852), pp. 117–18. Further references appear in the text.
23. It may be speculated that "Oro City" inspired Wharton's fictional "Apex City," birthplace of the socially ambitious Undine Spragg, heroine of *The Custom of the Country*, published in 1913.
24. See Amy Kaplan, *The Social Construction of American Realism* (Chicago, IL: University of Chicago Press, 1988), pp. 84–85.
25. Edith Wharton, *A Backward Glance* (1933; New York: Scribner, 1964), p. 9.
26. Edith Wharton, *The Age of Innocence* (1920; New York: Library of America, 1985), p. 1054.
27. Wharton, *A Backward Glance*, pp. 10–11.
28. Edith Wharton, *Old New York* (1924; New York: Scribner, 1951), p. 164; Wharton, *Age of Innocence*, p. 1058.
29. Wharton, *Old New York*, p. 206.

3

BRYAN WATERMAN

The city on stage

Something which concerns themselves

The French traveler and critic Alexis de Tocqueville likely had in mind
New York City theaters like the Bowery and the Park when he wrote, in
Democracy in America (1835), that

> [a]t the theater alone, the higher ranks mix with the middle and lower classes;
> there alone do the former consent to listen to the opinion of the latter, or at
> least to allow them to give an opinion at all. At the theater men of cultivation
> and of literary attainments have always had more difficulty than elsewhere in
> making their taste prevail over that of the people and in preventing themselves
> from being carried away by the latter. The pit has frequently made laws for
> the boxes.[1]

Tocqueville's description indicates the ways in which the early theater in
New York (as in larger cities such as London or Paris) both accommodated
all classes and segregated them in carefully demarcated architectural spaces,
the "pit" on the floor and the private "boxes" – belonging to wealthy sub-
scribers – above and to the sides. He doesn't mention the third space common to early New York theaters, the "gallery," made up of balcony seating
that reached up to nosebleed heights, including a "third tier" that often
housed prostitutes and their customers. The "gallery gods," young working-
class patrons, were commonly understood to rule theaters by threatening to
shower food or even furniture on performers or viewers in other portions
of the house. The combined audiences in the pit, boxes, and gallery were
generally thought to represent "the entire public," though these audiences,
well into the nineteenth century, were overwhelmingly white and male.[2]
Though Tocqueville held that even in aristocratic nations the stage was the
most democratic branch of literature, the features outlined above were, he
believed, most true of post-revolutionary societies, which cultivated very specific tastes in drama: "Democratic communities hold erudition very cheap,"
he wrote, "and care but little for what occurred at Rome and Athens; they

42

want to hear something which concerns themselves, and the delineation of the present age is what they demand."[3]

Such demands conflicted, at times, with the desires of stage managers. The founding of the Bowery Theater in 1826 was understood by Mayor Hone and others of the patrician class both as a chance to siphon off the more unruly portions of the Park Theater's audience – the Park had been New York's principal theater since 1798 – and as a way to provide uplift and control for unruly Bowery denizens. The new theater, Hone said at the laying of the cornerstone, would "improve the taste, correct the morals, and soften the manners of the people."[4] In addition, he hoped the new theater would bring to the neighborhood gentry families moving uptown. A looming neo-classical temple of culture designed by Ithiel Town (whose new Custom House on Wall Street – known today as "Federal Hall" – would begin construction in 1833), the Bowery Theater was built on the site of the bustling Bull's Head Tavern, a hangout of butchers and cattle peddlers.[5]

The mixing of classes and cultures in the early nineteenth-century theater may have reflected a democratic culture, but such mingling was anything but irenic. Tensions among audiences, actors, and managers, and even among partisans of rival playhouses (as in the notorious Astor Place riots of 1849) persisted through the century, in spite of efforts to establish different venues to cater to different class, ethnic, and racial groups. One thing these diverse audiences shared, however, was the characteristic Tocqueville had identified with theatergoers in democratic societies: a desire above all to see "something which concerns themselves." From Royall Tyler's *The Contrast* (1787) to Clyde Fitch's *The City* (1909), New York audiences of various stripes flocked to see representations of themselves on stage. Plays as diverse as William Henry Smith's temperance melodrama *The Drunkard* (1844), Anna Cora Mowatt's genteel comedy *Fashion* (1845), Benjamin Baker's working-class farce *A Glance at New York* (1848), and sensation plays such as Dion Boucicault's *The Poor of New York* (1866) and Augustin Daly's *Under the Gaslight* (1867) all took the contemporary city as their settings. In doing so, they made the comparison of city to stage one of the theater's enduring concerns and used a variety of theatrical settings as laboratories for working out anxieties about the nature of social interactions in urban society.

"Pretty much like other families": *The Contrast*

Royall Tyler's *The Contrast* (1787) is best known to theater historians as the first play by an American writer to be professionally staged. Written by a young New Englander in town on government business, this comedy of manners sets up several contrasts: between the new nation and the mother country, between country and city, between Boston and New York. Critics commonly treat the play as a brief for the classical republican ideology of the revolutionary generation: an attack on British "luxury" as effeminizing and a plea for young Americans to cultivate homespun virtues, fashion, and entertainment. In making such arguments, the play would seem divided against itself, since the theater itself was taken by some old-guard republicans to be one of the chief European vices that needed to be stamped out. During the Revolution, the Continental Congress outlawed all "shews, plays, and other expensive diversions."[6] New York's major theater troupe, the American Company, most of whom were natives of Great Britain, left for the British West Indies, where they stayed for eight years, waiting out the war. The British, who eventually came to occupy New York City for the duration of the Revolution, continued to sponsor amateur theatricals (with British soldiers staging plays of their own). When the American Company returned following the evacuation of the British, the New York City council denounced them for performing "while so great a part of this city still lies in ruins, and many of the citizens continue to be pressed with the distresses brought on them in consequence of the late war."[7] Tyler, whose native Boston would not legalize the theater until 1794, was treading a thin line in writing for the stage.

Perhaps it's not surprising, then, that *The Contrast* is so preoccupied with theater conventions themselves. The play mines the idea of *theatrum mundi* – "all the world's a stage," in Shakespeare's formulation – to its fullest comic potential in a series of metatheatrical moments, or situations in which the play comments on the conventions of the theater itself. The most exemplary of these moments involves Jonathan, a country bumpkin from Massachusetts in town as an attendant to the Revolutionary War officer Colonel Manly. Jonathan explores the city in company with two local servants, Jessamy and Jenny, while Manly finds himself caught up in a seduction plot involving his sister, Charlotte. While the romance plots and subplots unfold among the upper-class characters, the unsophisticated Jonathan accidentally finds himself in New York's John Street Theater, a precursor to the Park. He mistakes the playhouse, though, for a church – unwitting commentary on similarities between stage and pulpit – and when the curtain goes up, he assumes he's somehow peeping on the family living next door. When Jessamy and Jenny ask him later for details about what he saw, his confusion is apparent: "Why, I vow they were pretty much like other families," he says of the people he saw on stage. "[T]here was a poor, good-natured, curse of a husband, and a sad rantipole of a wife."[8] He goes on to offer details that would make it clear to Jonathan's audiences, on stage and off, that he was describing a performance of Richard Brinsley Sheridan's extraordinarily popular play *The School for Scandal* (1777), along with John O'Keefe's *The Poor Soldier* (1783), both British imports. The actor playing Jonathan even winds up commenting on what would have been his prior performance in the latter. Though readers today need footnotes to make sense of some of these intertextual references, Tyler's initial audience would not have needed any, which is precisely the point and the source of Tyler's humor. The inside joke does depend, however, on the audience's *refusal* to suspend its disbelief, or to differentiate between the theater and real life – on its ability, that is, to see the actor and his character on stage at the same time. The line between stage and "real life" has been stretched precariously thin.

Jonathan's experience at the theater helps us see yet another "contrast" the play stages: between a sophisticated theater audience (represented on stage by Dimple, Jessamy, and Jenny) and a bumbling rube, Jonathan, the intellectual and cultural victim of the theater's ignorant opponents. What does it mean, then, that the play aligns its own knowing audience – the people who understand all the self-referential joking – with derided characters like Dimple and Jessamy, who turn their backs on the performers to watch elite women in the boxes "play the fine woman to perfection" (45)? To the extent that Jonathan represents audience members he is a rather poor and unsophisticated one here and elsewhere. Jonathan continually misreads the city, assuming that Jessamy is a member of congress, that a theater and a brothel are both churches, that the theater's stage is a neighbor's house, and that a prostitute is a deacon's daughter.

But Jonathan does get something fundamentally *right* about the theater's relationship to life: that the theater is *like* life in some ways. If his peep into the "neighbor's household" convinces him that Sheridan's characters are essentially like any other family, the observation implies that most members of society are caught up in various kinds of performance themselves. *The Contrast*'s opening scene makes much the same point, in Charlotte Manly's account of a walk on the Battery, at the bottom of Broadway, before an audience of admiring soldiers and beaux. Broadway, which ran close to the sites of both the John Street and the Park theaters, from very early on was a place for fashionable promenades, becoming a contested territory in the nineteenth century as multiple social groups wanted to display their taste.[9] Tyler, poking fun at such pretension, makes visible something that would remain a part of New York's characterization as a city all the way to the present: the popular conflation of the city with the theater itself.

Tyler's play shows how manners or politeness help institutionalize divisions based on class, sex, and race. For Tyler, social theatricality poses a problem, to be sure, but most particularly when members of the servant class seek to climb above their stations. We are to understand it as dangerous, for instance, when Jessamy recites Lord Chesterfield's advice (from his oft-reprinted if controversial *Letters to His Son*) on how to behave in polite society. Even Jonathan, whose rural simplicity is sometimes understood as native worth, is marked as an outsider to metropolitan manners and, in the process, kept in a lower-class position. Two virtues, as it were, for the price of one. At the same time, Manly's ability to perform his role as a natural aristocrat and to appear artless and sincere while doing so offers just one example of the cultural work such a play could perform in the name of patriotism. *The Contrast*'s conclusion – the promise of a wedding between New England and New York landed gentry, and between "virtuous patriotism and economic and political power" – leaves those who can't comprehend theatrical and social cues out in the cold.[10]

Broadway v. Bowery manners: *Fashion* and *A Glance at New York*

Tyler's satire on John Street audiences – that they ignore the stage to watch the performances of ladies in the boxes – is echoed a little over a decade later by Washington Irving's comedic theater-critic persona, Jonathan Oldstyle, who held that the audience itself "furnish[ed] no inconsiderable part of the entertainment" at the Park Theater.[11] This preoccupation with audience-watching was confirmed two decades later in John Searle's watercolor of the Park in the early 1820s (see *Figure 3*). The painting shows a more respectable crowd in the pit than Oldstyle's letter represents, but the fascination with the audience remains. (In fact, this painting – two-thirds of which is devoted to the audience – is filled with portraits of real people. Some members of the painting's contemporary audience would have recognized themselves or friends or prominent society members in the crowd, including Searle himself, who faces the viewer directly from the center of the bottom row of spectators.[12])

By the 1830s, separate venues had begun to accommodate widely varying audience expectations. The "fashionable" public, finally rid of Bowery audiences, made the Park more exclusive, with an eye toward the reforms Irving's Jonathan Oldstyle had endorsed: more attentive audiences, better music and décor, and a refined acting style. The new Bowery Theater and others like it attracted a working-class audience interested not in refinement but in what Walt Whitman called "the heavy tragedy business."[13] Its audiences cheered for cut-and-paste Shakespeare: the most famous pieces of heroic oratory followed by elaborate swordplay and battle scenes. Bowery audiences also thrilled to "apocalyptic" melodrama, in which a common-man hero battles

Figure 3: John Searle, *Interior of the Park Theater*, watercolor, 1822. Searle's picture dwells as much or more on the audience than on the performers on stage; several of the faces in the pit (including Searle himself, at the bottom of the frame, facing the painting's viewer) would have been immediately recognizable to insiders among Searle's contemporaries.

against oppression, a type played to perfection by the blood-and-thunder actor Edwin Forrest.[14]

The air of refinement that was coming to prevail at the Park was adopted by others who wanted to appeal to middle-class women and families. Beginning in 1850, P. T. Barnum used temperance plays such as William H. Smith's *The Drunkard* – in which a young Boston father winds up in a Five Points gutter almost the moment he arrives in New York – to attract evangelical Christian audiences, who previously had shunned theaters, to the 3,000-seat "lecture room" at his American museum. (*The Drunkard* remained on stage in New York for a quarter-century.[15]) Revivalists like Charles Grandison Finney built new megachurches such as the Broadway Tabernacle, constructed on the scale and model of large theaters, and in their sermons provided some of the hottest shows in town. In such settings, audiences repelled by the behavior at the Bowery might confirm their own performances with, as Whitman put it, "a dash of superiority."[16]

Two popular plays from the mid-1840s exemplify the growing divisions between genteel and working-class audiences, even as they demonstrate the ongoing fascination among audiences of various classes with seeing representations of oneself on stage. *Fashion* (1845), written by the self-avowedly respectable actress Anna Cora Mowatt, premiered in the waning days of the Park Theater and looks backward to eighteenth-century comedies of manners such as *The Contrast* and *The School for Scandal* even as it takes up some of the trappings of melodrama (the dominant stage form by mid-century). Benjamin Baker's *A Glance at New York* (1848), a working-class comedy written by a working-class playwright and produced for working-class audiences, premiered at the Olympic Theater, a cousin to the Bowery. Both plays serve as particularly sensitive registers of shifting codes of class and gender behavior – and of the anxieties these shifts produced, especially for the upper classes.

Fashion opens with a conversation between two servants, important figures of class anxiety for Mowatt as they were for Tyler, though the character types are slightly more complicated a half-century later. These servants work not for the landed gentry but for the nouveau riche, who turn out to be even more dangerous, in the play's judgment, than servants with class aspirations or low-bred foreigners who pretend to be aristocrats. The opening line, commentary from a black servant named Zeke on the new livery he has received from his mistress, Mrs. Tiffany, sums up the play's tensions in a nutshell. "Dere's a coat to take de eyes ob all Broadway! Ah! Missy," he says to the French maid, "it am de fixins dat make de natural born gemman. A libery for ever! Dere's a pair of insuppressibles to 'stonish de colored population."[17] Zeke fantasizes here, first, about being the focus of "all Broadway," the still-fashionable promenade that ran just outside the theater's doors. His desire to parade his new fashions mimics the pretensions of higher classes, even as he unwittingly spoofs their paradoxical belief that natural aristocracy is evident in what one wears. Furthermore, Zeke conflates "livery" with "liberty," a word that takes on multiple meanings in such a racially loaded scene. It soon becomes clear that Mrs. Tiffany – a former milliner who has married up – uses Zeke as a prop to signify her own class status. She renames him Adolph, because it sounds more aristocratic and, she thinks, more French. The renaming ceremony seems intended to invoke slavery: "I'm rather sorry that he is black," Mrs. Tiffany complains of Zeke, "but to obtain a white American for a domestic is almost impossible; and they call this a free country!" (315).

Throughout the play, Mrs. Tiffany aims to gather in her parlor New York's fashionable society. Though she has no real interest in literature, she invites a poet named T. Tennyson Twinkle – a send-up of Edgar Allen Poe – to read in her parlor because it is "all the rage to patronize poets!" (317). A dull young man, Augustus Fogg, from "one of our oldest families," competes in a lackluster way with Twinkle for the attention of Seraphina, Mrs. Tiffany's daughter, and her level-headed companion, Gertrude. The circle is rounded out by a mustachioed French nobleman, Count Jolimaitre, who turns out to be a common cook running a con on these gullible New Yorkers who aspire to Old World aristocracy. The antidote to the fashionable nonsense of Mrs. Tiffany's drawing room arrives with a visitor from upstate, Adam Trueblood, who, like Colonel Manly in *The Contrast*, aims to teach these misguided New Yorkers some lessons about American simplicity and virtue. Trueblood, in the end, turns out to be Gertrude's grandfather, who sent her away when she was a child to prevent her from being corrupted by his money; her mother had been the victim of a gold-digging seducer. Gertrude will of course inherit Trueblood's fortune now that her true identity is revealed and her virtue proven.

Along with what by 1845 must have seemed like an old-fashioned encomium to republican virtue, *Fashion* shares with Tyler's *The Contrast* a number of other things: a half-hearted preference for the country over the city, a simultaneous discomfort with and accommodation of social theatricality, and an elitism rooted in a notion of natural aristocracy. *Fashion* unveils the latter in Trueman's closing speech, using terms that would have been unthinkable immediately following the American Revolution. "[W]e *have* kings, princes, and nobles in abundance" in America, he tells the French pretenders, but they are "of *Nature's* stamp, if not of *Fashion's*" (366). With this moral in place, a comical epilogue both praises *Fashion* for becoming fashionable and asks the audience not to reject fashion outright but to learn to "prize [it] at its just value" (367). Those Trueblood represents, the moneyed, moralizing elite, turn out to be those best equipped to appraise. Thus *Fashion* allowed middle-class audiences to congratulate themselves that they were not Mrs. Tiffany and in doing so let themselves off the hook from the play's old-guard republican critique of fashion.[18]

Like *Fashion*, Benjamin Baker's *A Glance at New York* focuses on gender and class performance, though the emphasis here is on male working-class

F.S.CHANFRAU IN THE CHARACTER OF "MOSE"

Figure 4: F. S. Chanfrau as Mose in *A Glance at New York*, 1848. Mose, the quintessential "Bowery B'hoy," says he would "spile" (spoil) if he didn't "muss" (fight) regularly, but he is equally inclined to save babies from burning buildings. The legendary Mose became a mythical patron saint to Bowery denizens for the duration of the nineteenth century.

culture. The appearance of Frank Chanfrau as Mose (see *Figure 4*), the original Bowery B'hoy, constituted an almost literal instance of placing the contemporary city on stage. Chanfrau was raised on the Bowery and, like his famous character, had been a volunteer fireman. As Mose, who was generally supposed to be based on a real Bowery butcher named Moses Humphreys, Chanfrau voiced working-class complaints.[19] Striding onto the stage, chawing a cigar, he complains bitterly about his fire company: "I've made up my mind not to run wid der machine anymore."[20]

That line, on opening night, reportedly brought down the house. The play solidified Bowery B'hoy getup – top hats, great coats, hair worn in "soap-locks" – as a fashion craze, appropriated and amended signs of genteel masculinity. In *Glance*, though, the working classes are not troublesome aspirants to high society. Mose wouldn't follow in Mrs. Tiffany's steps if you paid him. *Glance* also replaces the social-climbing servants from *The Contrast* and *Fashion* with wise-cracking, street-smart youngsters: the comedic team of Mike and Jake. Like Jessamy and Jenny in *The Contrast*, they fleece a naive visitor from the country, but Mike and Jake's antics are celebrated by Baker and his audience whereas Jessamy was clearly the object of Tyler's scorn.

Glance highlights the theatrical nature of working-class masculinity in a cross-dressing episode early in the play, when Mose, serving as an impromptu tour guide of his Bowery neighborhood, takes some upper-class interlopers to a Ladies' Bowling Saloon. Rather than threatening his masculinity, the comedy actually serves to reinforce Mose's heteronormative manhood. Mose may be able to dress in women's clothing to pull a prank, but as his girl, Lize, points out emphatically, "Dere's no mistake but he's one of de b'hoys" (194). In its final scene, with characters of all classes amicably sharing a meal at the Vauxhall Gardens (a once-tony leisure spot being gradually taken over by the working class), *Glance* again emphasizes the physicality central to the performance of white working-class masculinity: Lize gloats about the way Mose, who typifies Bowery butchers, cuts meat. He eats and drinks like a man, too: "Bring me a plate of pork and beans," Mose tells a waiter. "Say, a large piece of pork, and don't stop to count de beans" (195). Spending money lavishly reinforces Mose's masculine performance; Lize gets all the doughnuts she can off him.[21]

In spite of the rosy cross-class friendships at the end of *Glance*, the class tensions in these plays – and the competing codes of masculine behavior among audiences – would culminate in one of the most famous episodes in New York theater history: the Astor Place riots of 1849, only a year after *Glance* premiered and four after *Fashion*, when working-class audience members of one theater – many of them butchers and fans of Edwin Forrest – stormed the new opera house and threatened to drive out of town a British actor starring in a rival performance of *Macbeth*. Newspaper accounts picked up on the class politics and framed the event as stemming from working-class resentment against "aristocratizing the pit."[22] The riots helped to speed up the city's complete social segregation of public space by class. After Astor Place, Tocqueville's description of upper-class audiences being forced to submit to the law of the pit no longer had any real application as far as theater itself was concerned.[23]

Naturalizing class difference: *The Poor of New York* and *Under the Gaslight*

In the 1860s and 70s, middle-class audiences developed tastes for extravagant stage spectacles that in some ways resembled the apocalyptic melodramas favored by working-class audiences decades earlier. Blockbusters like Dion Boucicault's *The Poor of New York* (1866) and Augustin Daly's *Under the Gaslight* (1867), both of which could otherwise have passed for run-of-the-mill sentimental melodrama, organized themselves around a key moment that aimed for extraordinary realism: a tenement fire in the former, and a thundering train passing across the stage in the latter. (Daly's play provided the prototypical train-tracks rescue, though in his version it's the heroine who saves a poverty-stricken *male* admirer from certain death on the rails.) Such scenes, touted for their verisimilitude, were the real draw of these plays, much as the delirium-tremens scene – often advertised as being played by a reformed drunk – was a central attraction of temperance plays earlier in the century. Certainly the desire for realism speaks to the long-standing impulse to consume representations of oneself and one's society. But unlike earlier instances of the city on stage, "sensation plays," as these dramas became known, represented stratified classes as permanent rather than permeable. Even the threat of class-climbing seems to have been neutered. The performance of polite manners was no longer an indication of one's quality: anyone could learn to speak properly or earn money. Rather, verifiable bloodlines carried renewed significance. In addition to the magnificent spectacle these plays offered, they also reinforced a message that outside forces, larger than individual choice or virtue, might dramatically alter one's destiny.[24]

In sensation plays of the 1860s and 70s, characters divide into rich and poor, with some virtuous and vicious members in each group. The concern with the nouveau riche is not as much in evidence here as it was in *Fashion*; nor are servants universally scheming to rise above their stations. Rather, the poor (often marked as immigrants) tend toward virtue; their poverty is sentimentalized but not particularly seen as a problem to be solved through economic or social reform. These are business-class plays, designed to appeal to middle-class viewers by showing them a version of themselves that conflates a tenuous economic reality with a fantasy of permanent – and permanently deserved – wealth. Audiences for these plays, more predominantly female than ever before, know they are above the virtuous poor, who clearly deserve condescension and sympathy; but viewers also know their more fitting fate would lie with the rich, providing for a "unity of the business class, often by an alliance between respectable families of moderate means and the old-moneyed elite."[25]

Sensation plays contained no direct assault on money or fashion. Rather, the most virtuous are uniformly shown to be deserving of wealth, even if economic misfortune has stripped them of it. The real crime in these plays lies in social cruelty, not inequality. When Laura, the heroine of *Gaslight*, is temporarily thought to be low-born, the ladies of New York's old-money families are "insulted by the girl's presence" and conspire to exile her.[26] Her fiancé, though he compares society to a pack of wolves, finds himself unable to defend her in the moment of her exposure. Still, he accurately diagnoses the problem: "Laura has mocked [society] with a pretense, and society, which is made up of pretenses, will bitterly resent the mockery" (260). In the world of sensation plays, there is no attempt to undo or resist society's theatricality; it has long since been taken for granted. One is either born for the role or not. Resolution comes for Laura and her lover only because her aristocratic lineage – which she deserves because she is virtuous – is eventually proven. (Her virtue alone would not have earned her the happy conclusion.) A similar end comes to the hero of *The Poor of New York*, who has meanwhile complained that the "most miserable of the poor of New York" are not the permanently impoverished but rather those who have lost fortunes in the recent economic downturn; these true unfortunates are bound by politeness to "drag from their pockets their last quarter to cast it with studied carelessness to the beggar, whose mattress at home is lined with gold."[27]

The advent of sensation plays solidified a new identity for theater audiences as consumers rather than governors of the stage; the audience's role is reduced, in accounts of such plays, with attention focused on the spectacle of the sensation scene and the duration of the play's run. "In their precision," one scholar writes, sensation plays' "sets were spectacles of nineteenth-century commodity culture, their builders using and replicating the familiar objects that filled Victorian streets and homes as well as the grander manufactured items (like trains) that propelled Victorian industry."[28] Audiences paid for the opportunity to assent to the thrilling illusion of danger – replicas of natural or industrial disasters that could be experienced as "impervious to the controls of culture or class"; at the same time, they assented to the impervious nature of class itself. The replica of Delmonico's lavish interior in *Gaslight*, that is, might be as overwhelming as the train scene. Either you survive a disaster or you don't; either you're born to survive a society that functions like a pack of Siberian wolves, or you naturally belong somewhere else. And as *Gaslight* shows, when class problems make their way even to country estates on Long Island, the country is not inherently more virtuous than the city.

If Clyde Fitch's 1909 play *The City* is any indication, by the early twentieth century the blame for vice had fully shifted from the metropolis itself to the individuals who inhabited it, and the question of social theatricality had become more a matter of natural selection – the knowledge of what's appropriate to wear appears to be inborn, not learned – rather than a contest between sincerity and artificiality. The central family in Fitch's play moves to the city from "Middleburg," a typical American small town, where they enjoyed social prominence. The children are anxious for more excitement and opportunity ("Who wants to smell new-mown hay if he can breathe in gasoline on Fifth Avenue instead! Think of the theatres! the crowds!") and the mother wants bigger social circles ("I'm tired of being the leading woman in a society where there's no one to lead!").[29] When the father, the only one in the family reluctant to leave Middleburg, suddenly dies, the family relocates immediately. In the city George, the eldest son, skyrockets to political prominence, but his bid for governor is jeopardized by a family secret: George's confidential secretary (a heroin fiend who had long blackmailed George's father) is, unknown to all but George himself, a bastard half-brother. When the secretary elopes with George's younger sister, only to discover later that they are actually siblings, he panics and kills his new bride. (This shocking catastrophe is just one of the moments, wrote a reviewer for the *Times*, in which "the artificial pass[es] for the real so perfectly as to create as complete a sense of illusion as the theatre often holds."[30]) In a society in which scandal has become "public property" (495), there's no hope of keeping this skeleton in the closet, especially since the secretary has been privy to two generations of the family's crooked business schemes. George's mother is more than willing to blame their bad fortune on the city itself: "Why didn't we stay home?" she asks her children after the youngest daughter's death. "I amounted to something there. I had as much sense as my neighbors. I could hold my own! Here, I've been made to understand I was such a nonentity – that I've grown actually to be the fool they believe me!" (533); her unfitness for the city is evident in her lack of fashion sense: "I haven't the remotest idea what's the thing to wear. In Middleburg I'd have known – but here I'm always wrong!"

Instead of either endorsing Mrs. Rand's critique or indicting society's fashionable demands, a chastened George begs his mother and the audience not to blame the city: "It's not her fault! It's our own! What the City does is to bring out what's strongest in us. If at heart we're good, the good in us will win! If the bad is strongest, God help us!" In *The City*, New York has become a stage on which one proves oneself, in a way a country village will never allow you. If you can make it here, in other words, you can make it anywhere. A "big, and busy, and selfish, and self-centered" city is, for this reason, a virtue: "she comes to her gates" and welcomes the man coming from the country village, George explains, "and she stands him in the middle of her market place ... and there she strips him naked of all his disguises – and all his hypocrisies, – and she paints his ambition on her fences, and lights up her skyscrapers with it! – what *he wants* to be and *what he thinks he is*! – and then she says to him, Make good if you can, or to Hell with you! And what is in him comes out to clothe his nakedness, and to the City he can't lie!" The emphasis here on advertising, clothing, ambition, and the market suggests that one function of the "City on Stage" trajectory over the course of the century was to naturalize what was still deeply problematic when Tyler wrote *The Contrast*: in Fitch's play, there's no distance at all and little tension between the stage and street. The "middle of her market place," in George's long-winded defense of the city, is an imaginary intersection of residential, business, fashion, and theater districts: "where Wall Street and Herald Square and Fifth Avenue and the Bowery, and Harlem, and Forty-Second Street all meet." By the early twentieth century performance and artifice – even fashion – were taken to be the deepest expression of who a person really is. This is not to say that anyone with the right clothes can make it; celebrity can come even to the undeserving. Personality may be something you can purchase on the consumer market, but only those whose value is inborn will have the innate taste to purchase the right one, and in Fitch's *The City* the constant scrutiny built into the urban environment brings to the surface whatever an impostor might be inclined to hide. The biggest lesson to be learned from the century-long pattern of New Yorkers putting themselves on stage is the relationship that evolves between the institution of the theater and what would become a culture of consumption, leading audiences (who have gone, over the course of the century, from governing the stage to being passive consumers of it) to believe that the kinds of performance involved in high-fashion promenades – the problematic starting point of Tyler's play – are precisely what will confirm one's personality rather than covering over or hiding one's authentic self.[31]

NOTES

1. Qtd. in Robert C. Allen, *Horrible Prettiness: Burlesque and American Culture* (Chapel Hill: University of North Carolina Press, 1991), p. 44.
2. On the early nineteenth-century theater's accommodation of the "entire public," see Lawrence Levine, *Highbrow/Lowbrow: The Emergence of Cultural Hierarchy in America* (New York: Oxford University Press, 1988), pp. 56–60. On the theater public's routine exclusion of women before the middle of the nineteenth century, see Allen, *Horrible Prettiness*, pp. 51–55.
3. Alexis de Tocqueville, *Democracy in America* (1835; Cambridge: Seaver and Francis, 1863), p. 97.

4. Qtd. in Allen, *Horrible Prettiness*, p. 51.

5. Edwin Burrows and Mike Wallace, *Gotham: A History of New York City to 1898* (New York: Oxford University Press, 1999), p. 475.

6. Qtd. in Bruce McConachie, "American Theater in Context, from the Beginnings to 1870," in *The Cambridge History of the American Theatre*, vol. 1: *Beginnings to 1870*, ed. Don B. Wilmeth and C. W. E. Bigsby (New York: Cambridge University Press, 1998), p. 128.

7. William Dunlap, *History of the American Theatre* (London: Richard Bentley, 1833), i, p. 111.

8. Royall Tyler, *The Contrast*, in *Early American Drama*, ed. Jeffrey H. Richards (New York: Penguin, 1997), p. 34. Further references appear in the text.

9. On controversies over black families promenading on Broadway see Marvin McAllister, *White People Do Not Know How to Behave at Entertainments Designed for Ladies and Gentlemen of Color* (Chapel Hill: University of North Carolina Press, 2003), p. 22. For very specific prescriptions for women's fashion on Broadway see George Ellington, *The Women of New York, or The Underworld of the Great City* (New York: New York Book Co., 1869), pp. 34–36.

10. John Evelev, "*The Contrast*: The Problem of Theatricality and Social Crisis in Postrevolutionary America," *Early American Literature* 31 (1996): 74–97, quote on 91.

11. Washington Irving, "*Letters of Jonathan Oldstyle, Gent.*" and "*Salmagundi: Or, The Whim-whams and Opinions of Launcelot Langstaff, Esq. & Others*," ed. Bruce I. Granger and Martha Hartzog (Boston, MA: Twayne, 1977), p. 12. Newspaper accounts of the Park Theater's opening and architecture also emphasized audiences as forming "no uninteresting part of the *spectacle*." See "Communication. New Theater," *Commercial Advertiser* (January 31, 1798), qtd. in Bryan Waterman, *Republic of Intellect: The Friendly Club of New York City and the Making of American Literature* (Baltimore, MD: Johns Hopkins University Press, 2007), p. 167.

12. See Heather Nathans, *The Early American Theatre from the Revolution to Thomas Jefferson: Into the Hands of the People* (New York: Cambridge University Press, 2003), p. 169; John Kasson, *Rudeness and Civility: Manners in Nineteenth-Century Urban America* (New York: Macmillan, 1991), p. 226.

13. Walt Whitman, "The Old Bowery," in *Complete Prose Works* (Philadelphia, PA: David McKay, 1892), p. 424.

14. See Bruce A. McConachie, *Melodramatic Formations: American Theatre and Society, 1820–1870* (Iowa City: University of Iowa Press, 1992), chs. 4–5.

15. For the popularity of Smith's and other temperance melodramas, see John W. Frick, *Theatre, Culture and Temperance Reform in Nineteenth-Century America* (New York: Cambridge University Press, 2003).

16. Qtd. in Levine, *Highbrow/Lowbrow*, p. 57. On Finney, preachers as actors, and the Broadway Tabernacle as a theater space, see R. Laurence Moore, *Selling God: American Religion in the Marketplace of Culture* (New York: Oxford University Press, 1994), pp. 50–51; and Jeanne Halgren Kilde, *When Church Became Theatre: The Transformation of Evangelical Architecture and Worship in Nineteenth-Century America* (New York: Oxford University Press, 2002), pp. 42–44.

17. Anna Cora Mowatt, *Fashion*, in *Early American Drama*, ed. Richards, p. 313. Further references appear in the text.
18. For this reading of the play, see especially Karen Haltunnen, *Confidence Men and Painted Women: A Study of Middle-Class Culture in America, 1830–1870* (New Haven, CT: Yale University Press, 1982), ch. 6.
19. The most detailed history of *Glance*'s reception and Mose's elevation to an American folk hero remains Richard M. Dorson, "Mose the Far-Famed and World Renowned," *American Literature* 15:3 (Nov. 1943): 288–300.
20. Benjamin Baker, *A Glance at New York*, in *On Stage, America! A Selection of Distinctly American Plays*, ed. Walter J. Meserve (Brooklin, ME: Feedback Theatrebooks & Prospero Press, 1996), p. 171. Further references appear in the text.
21. For more on the relationship between working-class literary consumption and Mose's physical appetite see David M. Stewart, "Consuming George Thompson," *American Literature* 80:2 (June 2008): 233–63.
22. Qtd. in Levine, *Highbrow/Lowbrow*, p. 306.
23. Nigel Cliff, *The Shakespeare Riots: Revenge, Drama, and Death in Nineteenth-Century America* (New York: Random House, 2007).
24. McConachie, *Melodramatic Formations*, ch. 7.
25. *Ibid.*, p. 216; on the rising number of women in sensation plays' audiences, see Richard Butsch, *The Making of American Audiences: From Stage to Television, 1750–1990* (Cambridge: Cambridge University Press, 2000), pp. 77–78.
26. Augustin Daly, *Under the Gaslight*, in *On Stage, America!*, ed. Meserve, p. 260. Further references appear in the text.
27. Dion Boucicault, *The Poor of New York*, in *Staging the Nation: Plays from the American Theater 1787–1909*, ed. Don B. Wilmeth (Boston, MA: Bedford Books, 1998), pp. 260–61.
28. Lynn M. Voskuil, "Feeling Public: Sensation Theater, Commodity Culture, and the Victorian Public Sphere," *Victorian Studies* 44:2 (2002): 245–74, quote on 258.
29. Clyde Fitch, *The City*, in *On Stage, America!*, ed. Meserve, pp. 482, 485. Further references appear in the text.
30. "Climax of 'The City' Has Terrific Power," *New York Times* (December 22, 1909).
31. On the growing importance of "personality" at the turn of the century see Warren Susman, "'Personality' and the Making of Twentieth-Century Culture," in *Culture as History: The Transformation of American Society in the Twentieth Century* (New York: Pantheon, 1984), pp. 271–85.

4

THOMAS AUGST

Melville, at sea in the city

Call me Ishmael. Some years ago – never mind how long ago precisely – having little or no money in my purse, and nothing particular to interest me on shore, I thought I would sail about a little and see the watery part of the world. It is a way I have of driving off the spleen, and regulating the circulation. Whenever I find myself growing grim about the mouth; whenever it is a damp, drizzly November in my soul; whenever I find myself involuntarily pausing before coffin warehouses, and bringing up the rear of every funeral I meet; and especially whenever my hypos get such an upper hand of me, that it requires a strong moral principle to prevent me from deliberately stepping into the street, and methodically knocking people's hats off – then, I account it high time to get to sea as soon as I can.

Melville, *Moby-Dick* (1851)[1]

Like a stranger suddenly sidling up as you walk down Broadway, or perhaps some young eccentric sitting alone at a bar determined to bend your ear a little, Herman Melville's novel of 1851, *Moby-Dick*, introduces itself to readers in an abrupt but engaging manner. Through a narrator named Ishmael, Melville gives voice to a modern consciousness as original as any in American literature. It is a voice as startling and unselfconscious as the manner in which people sometimes talk to themselves as they walk crowded streets of modern cities, or wander crowded thoughts of modern life.

Though Melville will devote most of his novel's great length to a whaling enterprise and shipboard life, the first chapter of *Moby-Dick* remains anchored in a brief tour of lower Manhattan (see *Figure 5*). Before returning to sea to be cured of his melancholy – "the drizzly November in my soul" – Ishmael insists we see where he is coming from: "Circumambulate the city of a dreamy Sabbath afternoon. Go from Corlears Hook to Coenties Slip, and from thence, by Whitehall, Northward." Taking us from the Battery to the seaport, along a part of what is now FDR Drive, past the financial district toward the west-side piers, Ishmael points out peculiar sights: "What do you see? – Posted like silent sentinels all around the town, stand thousands upon thousands of mortal men fixed in ocean reveries. Some leaning against

Figure 5: "Bird's-eye view of New York City with Battery Park in the Foreground," 1851. The Battery is the southernmost point of the island, and Corlears Hook juts out to the east near the edge of the frame. Ishmael imagines walking southward from the Hook to Coenties Slip just above the Battery, then cutting across on Whitehall, which runs diagonally to the northwest.

the piles: some seated upon the pier-heads; some looking over the bulwarks of ships from China; some high aloft in the rigging, as if striving to get a still better seaward peep. But these are all landsmen; of week days pent up in lath and plaster – tied to counters, nailed to benches, clinched to desks" (18–19). We never learn where Ishmael was born and raised, but as his walk downtown makes clear, he is familiar not only with the geography of Manhattan but with the anomie of modern life it seems to harbor. He walks anonymous streets, amongst the seaward-gazing masses that he points out along the way: "Look at the crowds of water-gazers there": "But look! here come more crowds, pacing straight for the water" (18–19). Ishmael speaks with a peculiar attitude, at once rude and sophisticated, sarcastic and sincere – with the boisterous savvy of someone who long ago learned never to become "pent up in lath and plaster," spiritually and physically immobilized by the routines and cares of work. Wherever he came from, and wherever he will go, Ishmael is a New Yorker.

Like Ishmael, Herman Melville embarked from Manhattan on his first ocean voyage, at the age of twenty, having himself become one of the city's transients. Melville was born at 6 Pearl Street, near the waterfront of New York City, the descendant of prominent, aristocratic families. An importer of French dry goods and a lousy businessman, his father had borrowed for years against his wife's legacy as he moved his family to fancier digs uptown – Cortlandt Street, Bleecker Street, and then to Broadway, furnishing his family with servants and the trappings of gentility. In October of 1830, an eleven-year-old Herman Melville fled the city with his father, who was three months behind with the rent and worried creditors would have him arrested. Following the family's furniture, which had gone on up the Hudson to Albany with Melville's mother and older brother the previous day, father and son boarded a steamboat at the pier at 82 Cortlandt Street. Called, sadly enough, *Swiftsure*, the boat was kept at the dock overnight by bad weather, and father and son huddled together for hours as they were rocked by the storm. It was, as Hershel Parker notes, "the last night Herman ever spent in the city of his birth with his father, and the trip upriver would be the last time he was ever alone anywhere with his father," before Allan Melvill died a few years later, a broken-down and exhausted man.[2]

New York City appears as a setting in only a small fraction of Melville's major works: in the first chapter of *Moby-Dick*, in the last third of his 1852 novel *Pierre*, and in "Bartleby, the Scrivener." Melville would return many times to New York, and live permanently there for the last two decades of his life until his death in 1891, but his work remains haunted by this primal scene of dispossession. In his autobiographical novel *Redburn*, the narrator avows, "I must not think of those delightful days, before my father became a bankrupt ... and we removed from the city; for when I think of those days, something rises up in my throat and almost strangles me."[3] At the outset of *Pierre*, Melville declares: "in our cities, families rise and burst like bubbles in a vat. For indeed the democratic element operates as subtle acid among us."[4] In the tale "Jimmy Rose," "Sudden and terrible reverses in business" reduce a once-wealthy merchant to a man "as poor as any rat; poor in the last dregs of poverty; a pauper beyond alms-house pauperism, a promenading pauper in a thread bare, careful coat; a pauper with wealth of polished words; a courteous, smiling, shivering gentleman."[5] As these works suggest, the sudden loss of Melville's seemingly comfortable childhood would complicate his ideas of class, giving him, as one critic notes, "the capacity to identify with the suffering of the dispossessed," while continuing to owe allegiance to the aristocratic lineage of his parents' respective families – indeed to cultivated, genteel tastes which, until his father's flight from creditors, the boy might have mistaken for his birthright.[6] In Melville's New York, it is the fate of economic cycles in the United States to dissolve the social ties in which individuals normally understand and locate their identities.

In one of the most famous short stories of American literature, Melville engages in both direct and oblique ways the psychological and social consequences of modern capitalism. In particular, "Bartleby, the Scrivener" is, as

Melville's original subtitle declares, a "story of Wall Street," exploring the meaning and value of work in a neighborhood that by the mid nineteenth century already symbolized New York City's central role as the engine of American business and finance. Narrated by a lawyer who "does a snug business among rich men's bonds and mortgages and title-deeds,"[7] the story offers a case study in the management of an office devoted to copying documents, and perhaps a reflection as well on the status of clerical work.[8] Though much of the story will describe the consequences of hiring the odd, inscrutable clerk named Bartleby, the narrator begins by describing in detail how the labor of his two other clerks is impaired by their respective defects of temperament and character. One, nicknamed Turkey, is about sixty years old, "the blandest and most reverential man in the morning." He worked effectively, but with lunch (and a drink or two) acquired an "inflamed, flurried, flighty recklessness," impairing his penmanship and distracting the office with all manner of "unpleasant racket" and "indecorous" activity. The other clerk, nicknamed Nippers, is "a whiskered, sallow, and, upon the whole, rather piratical-looking young man of about five and twenty," who is "the victim of two evil powers – ambition and indigestion" (638) and whose "irritability and consequent nervousness ... were mainly observable in the morning, while in the afternoon he was comparatively mild" (640).

With these two clerks, "Bartleby, the Scrivener" inaugurates a genre of writing about the alienation of modern officework that would flourish in American literature and culture into the twentieth century and beyond. In its dramatic mode, this literature depicted the anomie that bank clerk and poet T. S. Eliot would ascribe to his urban anti-hero, J. Alfred Prufrock, measuring out his life in coffee spoons; popular sociology and fiction of the 1950s would ascribe to corporate life images of the lonely crowd, other-directed personalities, men in grey flannel suits, or the "Mad Men" of advertising depicted in a recent television show. In its comic mode, this genre would include 1990s movies such as *Clerks*, and another recent television show "The Office," depicting slackers and oddballs inhabiting dead-end clerical positions in cubicles and convenience stores. Before taking up the tragic case of Bartleby, Melville's story puts the travails of office life to comic effect with Nippers and Turkey. The success of the office depends, as the lawyer notes, upon keeping the personal tics and habits of his employees in check, so that "I never had to do with their eccentricities at one time. Their fits relieved each other like guards. When Nippers' was on, Turkey's was off; and vice versa. This was a good natural arrangement under the circumstances" (640–41). With each clerk, personality – expressing the ambition of youth and the frustration of age – predictably intrudes on the "bland" and "mild" anonymity requisite to efficient service work. Taken together, Nippers and Turkey give their boss one good day's work; but they also offer a composite portrait of the damage exacted by even the respectable, if menial, white-collar career. The discipline of the workplace deforms the character of clerks, ensuring that one's labor will always be valued apart from "eccentricities" that distinguish individuals, and thwarting hope for advancement. The unnatural conditions to which we become fixed by work – "tied to counters, nailed to benches, clinched to desks," as Ishmael points out in "Loomings" – can never be compatible with the development of one's character.

Whether young or old, the clerks in "Bartleby" belie the American faith in social mobility and self-making already being mythologized, by the middle of the nineteenth century, in relation to business success, as well as the protean possibilities of self-reliance promised by Emerson and Thoreau in the same period. The title character epitomizes this inertness of human personality in the workplace. First described as "pallidly neat, pitiably respectable, incurably forlorn" (642), Bartleby becomes increasingly restricted in his words, answering each request from his boss and coworkers with the same phrase: "I would prefer not to." His physical movements become increasingly restricted as well, as Bartleby confines himself to his cubicle: "He was always there, – first in the morning, continually through the day, and the last at night," the lawyer declares, and with "his great stillness, his unalterableness of demeanor under all circumstances" (649). Over the course of the story, Bartleby apparently becomes homeless by taking up residence in the office – violating the separation of work and home, private and public, by which middle-class citizens sought to organize and manage character. In refusing finally to work, Bartleby ceases to be a member of the office community, and comes to seem less a person than an object. Though the lawyer asks him to go and offers a generous severance package, he "remained as ever, a fixture in my chamber" (657). At last Bartleby refuses to work at all, and the narrator tells us that "Bartleby did nothing but stand at his window in his dead-wall reverie" (656). When the narrator relocates his office to different premises, he leaves Bartleby "like the last column of some ruined temple, ... standing mute and solitary in the middle of the otherwise deserted room" (658).

Throughout the mid nineteenth century, fiction and journalism that focused on the mysteries of the city affirmed the ability of middle-class readers and social reformers to know the poor and abject of New York as a class, usually as melodramatic types safely confined to the stage of neighborhoods like the Five Points, rendered in what the narrator of *Pierre* sarcastically describes as the spectacle of the *pauvretesque*. By contrast, Melville insists that we see urban identity as both unstable and elusive. Bartleby and Jimmy Rose *become* individuals with downward mobility, as they slip through the web of shared assumptions and symbolic values that defined the collective identity of an emerging middle class: the separation of public and private, for example, or the genteel rituals of hospitality at which Jimmy Rose continues to appear in his ragged coat for "poor alms of tea and toast." So, too, these figures increasingly frustrate the self-consciously literary efforts of their narrators to explain them to their readers.[9] With its account of a spectator confronting a complex social environment, "Bartleby, the Scrivener" exemplifies narrative strategies that Melville would employ elsewhere in his fiction, in more exotic and far-flung settings ranging from the city of London in *Redburn* to the South Pacific in *Typee*.[10]

At a moment when middle-class individualism was being defined by new institutions and practices of literary culture, Melville's story finally exposes the failure of literary imagination to breach the economic and social barriers that rationalize the lives of urban dwellers.[11] Confronted with so unmoved and unmoving an employee, Bartleby's employer declares that "For the first time in my life a feeling of overpowering stinging melancholy seized me." The lawyer indulges in subjective reveries about "the bond of a common humanity" – "fraternal melancholy" and "sad fancyings" that serve finally to excuse him of responsibility for Bartleby:

> My first emotions had been those of pure melancholy and sincerest pity; but just in proportion as the forlornness of Bartleby grew and grew to my imagination, did that same melancholy merge into fear, that pity into repulsion. So true it is, and so terrible too, that up to a certain point the thought or sight of misery enlists our best affections; but in certain special cases, beyond that point it does not ... To a sensitive being, pity is not seldom pain. And when at last it is perceived that such pity cannot lead to effectual succor, common sense bids the soul be rid of it. What I saw that morning persuaded me that the scrivener was the victim of innate and incurable disorder. I might give alms to his body; but his body did not pain him; it was his soul that suffered, and his soul I could not reach.
>
> (653)

In the breakdown of his office's efficient "natural arrangement," the lawyer confronts the limits of his own subjectivity. The employee who is most physically present to the lawyer, Bartleby is at last unknowable – and finally undeserving of his personal benevolence.

In bending personality to the discipline of enterprise, Melville's New York proves corrosive not only of families, but of moral order itself, challenging the literary strategies and social values by which Americans sought to insulate themselves from the violent dislocations of modernity. The narrator's attempt to satisfy "curiosity as to who Bartleby was, and what manner of life he led," was futile, as he admits after visiting the half-dead Bartleby, incarcerated for vagrancy at New York's infamous prison, the Tombs. The story's last line leaves us with an impotent shrug of sentiment: "Ah Bartleby! Ah humanity!" (672).[12] As with homeless men or hustlers who take up favored spots on Manhattan streets to panhandle or sleep, Bartleby's eccentricity finally becomes another sort of urban anonymity. In moving readers beyond the narrative reach of sympathy, Melville exposes our desire to identify with the coworkers and strangers in our midst as an illusory conceit of class privilege.[13] After all, as one anthropologist has recently observed in a study of cannibalism, "sympathy exists only when survival looks promising."[14]

During the middle third of his life, when he struggled to pursue a career as a professional writer, New York City was Melville's professional home. At every point of its success and failure, Melville's literary career as a writer was decisively shaped by the city's publishing industry and cultural ferment. By the 1840s, scheduled steamboat service on the Hudson River made travel to Manhattan newly convenient from upstate towns such as Lansingburgh, to where Melville returned after a two-year trip to the South Pacific. Melville composed parts of his first novel, *Typee*, during several months of visits to the city with his brothers Allan and Gansevoort in late 1844 or 1845. He moved back to Manhattan in 1847 with his new wife Lizzie Shaw, where he occupied a town house on Fourth Avenue with Allan and his wife. Although he would live there only until 1850, when he moved to Pittsfield, Massachusetts, during his time in Manhattan Melville wrote *Mardi* (1847), *White-Jacket* (1848), and *Redburn* (1849), and also drafted the first chapters of *Moby-Dick*. "I have swam through libraries," Ishmael declares in his chapter on "Cetology," and in trying to explain retrospectively the mystery of the white whale, the narrator of *Moby-Dick* embodies the precocious intellectual and artistic aspirations that Melville came to nurture during this brief residence.

Melville himself swam through libraries – specifically, the large collection of his friend the literary editor Evert Duyckinck at Clinton Street, as well as that of the New York Society Library on Broadway, which he joined in 1848. Besides vastly expanding the intellectual reach of his writing, these years in Manhattan left their mark on "the nerve and sinew of his prose," as Andrew Delbanco observes: "Melville does not exactly write *about* the city, but the patter of images has the city's pulse and moves towards the rambling anthological prose of *Moby-Dick*." Not unlike strolling along a city street, "there is always the feeling of quickened pulse, of some unpredictable excitement, in aftermath or anticipation."[15]

At the outset of *Moby-Dick*, Ishmael's words embody an entirely new style of intellectual ambition. He speaks with unusual erudition, already suggesting the encyclopedic range of learning that will unfurl throughout the novel. American gentlemen of the eighteenth century might have used such erudition to identify themselves with an international republic of letters, to advance the mission of Western enlightenment to far-flung and provincial colonies. For Ishmael, however, learning is not an achievement, to be impersonally valued for its own intrinsic worth. Rather, it is street-wise: flaunted with boisterous self-consciousness, variously tossed off with the aggressive masculinity of the strut, a dare, a brag, a joke. Explaining the attraction of going to sea, Ishmael refers to classical philosophy and mythology, to Danish Royalty, to the Book of Genesis and the New Testament, but he also rejects "all honorable respectable toils," and insists on carrying learning into the most menial labor for pay. "No, when I go to sea, I go as a simple sailor, right before the mast, plumb down into the forecastle, aloft there to the royal mast-head," he declares, stripping the quest for knowledge of its physical exemption from manual labor as well as its social exclusion of the mass of men (20). Ishmael's adventure will entail not only climbing the rigging of philosophical speculation but also embracing humanity, amidst the roughest crowd of working men in the forecastle, representing every part of the globe.

Explaining the motives that drive New Yorkers to the water and justifying his own transition "from a schoolmaster to a sailor," Ishmael introduces us to a democratic cosmopolitanism, a taste for knowledge formed less by books than by the peripatetic, subjective experience endemic to wandering the streets, the protean capacity of individuals like Ishmael to inhabit multiple social worlds. This wisdom emerges from the youthful confidence with which a creative soul can sacrifice, if only temporarily, the security of personal identity to consciousness of universal community. "Who aint a slave? Tell me that," our guide demands, as though we might excuse the social, economic, and political inequalities of life – most apparent on the streets of Manhattan, in 1850 or today – with the finally ambivalent perspective of some existential pluralism: "that everybody is one way or other served in much the same way – either in a physical or metaphysical point of view, that is; and so the universal thump is passed round, and all hands should rub each other's should-blades, and be content" (21). At a historical moment when Karl Marx was recommending a new class consciousness as a solution to the alienation of capitalist labor, Ishmael seems to cure the melancholy of modern "weekdays pent up in lath and plaster" with a romance of universal fraternity. For the physical reserve and psychological solitude of middle-class individualism to which Bartleby gives such perverse and tragic expression, Ishmael prescribes a contentment of massaging one another's shoulders, of a collective belonging that throughout the novel will be continually evoked in images of the bodies of "common sailors" engaged in communal toil. As David Reynolds has suggested, Ishmael's references to fraternal labor and Andrew Jackson evoke the image of the Manhattan "b'hoy" that became a popular stereotype of young, native-born New York men.[16]

With its youthful energy and democratic polemic, Ishmael's voice echoes a new cultural and artistic nationalism that emerged in New York City in the 1840s. The new dominance that the city came to have in publishing before the Civil War was facilitated by the emergence of "Young America," a coterie of intellectuals and critics broadly seeking to articulate a nationalist creed of cultural independence. As Ted Widmer has suggested, Young America was not only a political movement, specifically identified with the Democratic Party and the expansionist doctrine that Louis O'Sullivan termed "Manifest Destiny" in 1845, but a cultural insurgency directed against a literary establishment dominated by Whig critics and intellectuals, centered in New England, and overly devoted to anglophile traditions. With O'Sullivan, leaders of Young America such as the novelist Cornelius Mathews and the editor and critic Evert Duyckinck announced the arrival of a new generation who would, at long last, realize the intellectual and artistic promise of political independence. In an address given at New York University in 1845, Mathews declared that his was the "first generation reared, from infancy to manhood – along the whole line of our lives, minute by minute, year by year – in the doctrine and under the discipline of Republican Truth." To give voice to this new generation, the Young America movement sought to move the nation's literary capital from Boston to New York, while at the same time proclaiming the revolutionary power of literature to promote an "original" national consciousness: "Here, in New York, is the seat and stronghold of this young power; but all over the land, day by day, new men are emerging into activity."[17]

Young America played a key role not only in promoting literary taste for newly self-conscious American writing, but in publishing important young writers and expanding the market for their work. In place of staid bastions of "old fogeyism" such as the *Knickerbocker Magazine* and the *North American Review*, Young America founded periodicals such as O'Sullivan's *Democratic Review*, where Hawthorne published important stories throughout the 1840s, and Duyckinck's *Literary World*, which published Melville's famous 1850 review "Hawthorne and His Mosses." Mathews and Duyckinck would wage an unsuccessful battle for international copyright, to give American authors economic protection against the pirating of their words, and to stem the inexpensive reprinting of British fiction that dominated the American periodical and book market. Answering the appeal of

Young America to make quality literature more affordable to a "popular" caste of American readers, the New York publisher Wiley and Putnam aggressively challenged Harper Brothers' dominance of the literature market by establishing a new series, the Library of American Books. "Not only did it introduce many of the country's most exciting young authors," as Widmer observes, but "it was the first series to even consider the radical notion Americans might be interested in reading a set of books by their own writers."[18] The series would issue a collection of Hawthorne's stories, *Mosses from an Old Manse*, as well as work by Margaret Fuller, William Gilmore Simms, and Robert Greenleaf Whittier. In 1846 it would issue two of Edgar Allen Poe's publications, *The Raven and Other Poems* and *Tales*. Also in 1846, the series would launch Herman Melville's career by publishing his first book, *Typee*, to both critical and popular acclaim.

No other antebellum writer so directly explored the cultural conflicts attending the emergence of a distinctively American literature as Herman Melville. Published in 1851, *Moby-Dick* was the realization of Young America's dream of a great American novel. As Widmer notes, Melville's nationalism was "inflamed by Young American teachings of the 1840s," and "*Moby-Dick* never could have been written without them."[19] The novel took up the idea that "American novels would have democracy at their core," but it did so by channeling the rebellious energy of Young America into what Duyckinck's influential review in the *Literary World* called a "piratical running down of creeds and opinions."[20] As a result of the novel's formal experimentation and cosmopolitan skepticism, critical reception of *Moby-Dick* disappointed the high expectations that Melville had come to have for the novel. But then, as he had recognized in his review "Hawthorne and His Mosses," in the midst of discovering his own artistic ambitions for his whale book, "it is the least part of genius that commands admiration": the moral and spiritual value of great literature would disclose itself only to individuals courageous, sensitive, and intelligent enough to see what others could not, to probe depths of meaning that, "like a scared white doe in the woodlands," could only elude the received opinions and complacent tastes of popular opinion.[21] Ironically, it would take successive generations of young upstarts – the New York Intellectuals of the 1910s and 1920s, as well as the New York School of poets and painters of the 1940s and 1950s, staging their own generational revolts, to install Melville in the modernist canon of American literature.

Melville returned to New York City in January of 1852, at the moment when he was completing his manuscript for his next novel, *Pierre*. By then it was already apparent that *Moby-Dick* would not meet with the great success he felt it deserved. At a meeting, Melville's one-time ally in the New York publishing world conveyed to him in person Duyckinck's objections to his latest manuscript. While staying with his brother Allan, Melville would add new, ill-fitting sections to his completed manuscript. Hershel Parker has surmised that Melville wrote some 150 new pages during this visit to the city, additions which "wrecked the next best crafted thing he had yet written."[22] Without warning, only a chapter after Pierre's elopement from the Berkshires to New York with his half-sister Isabel, the novel's narrator tells us that he will disregard prevailing conventions of narrative exposition. Suddenly, he informs the reader of Pierre's early career as an author, satirizing the literary standards and hypocrisy of the publishing industry. As the narrator declares at the outset of this seemingly capricious detour: "I write precisely as I please" (286). Indeed, as if giving overt expression to Melville's literary unconscious, Pierre's newfound life as a writer represents the disorderly irruption of New York City itself into the narrative design and thematic concerns of the novel, exposing the frustrated ambitions and artistic compromises that had attended Melville's early success and incipient decline.

If Young America had successfully moved the capital of American literature to New York, Melville chose now to satirize the local processes and provincial tastes through which literary tastes are manufactured for a reading public. In a chapter entitled "Young America in Literature," Pierre's juvenile writing is met by "applauses of the always intelligent, and extremely discriminating public"; editors "confessed their complete inability to restrain their unqualified admiration for the highly judicious smoothness and genteelness of the sentiments and fancies expressed" (287). Specious praise about the writer's "taste" makes literature an adjunct to the fashion trade, and Wonder & Wen, two former tailors now in the publishing business, offer to dress "your pantaloons – productions, we mean – ... in the library form" (289). Thus did literary reputation itself become a generic platform for advertising in the urban marketplace: "It was plain that they esteemed one's title page but another unwindowed wall, infinitely more available than most walls, since here was at least one spot in the city where no rival billstickers dared to encroach" (291). As Melville shrewdly observes in this chapter, the seemingly impersonal processes of mass-marketing literature are bound up with local sorts of reputation – becoming the infatuation of the respectable, album-bearing ladies of parlor society, for example, juggling obsequious requests for appearances by lecture societies and for autographs and portraits by magazines. Melville cast his Duyckinck in the part of an editor of "Captain Kidd Monthly," harassing Pierre for a Daguerreotype which, instead of immortalizing a genius, as with portraits of old, "now only *dayalized* a dunce" (297). Even the Harper Brothers, with whom Allan Melville negotiated a humiliating contract for *Pierre* during Herman's stay, would come in for a spanking.[23]

Although motivated by personal resentment and bridge-burning rather than narrative coherence, the new material that Melville added to his manuscript for *Pierre* nevertheless gives us his most direct reflections about his own career as an author, as well as his most sophisticated portrait of New York City as a site of artistic creation. Through the example of Pierre, Melville exposes the intimate, if not claustrophobic, social matrix in which he had first achieved short-lived literary fame with *Typee*:

> It was when thus haunted by publishers, engravers, editors, critics, autograph-collectors, portrait fanciers, biographers, and petitioning and remonstrating literary friends of all sorts; it was then, that there stole into the youthful soul of Pierre melancholy forebodings of the utter unsatisfactoriness of all human fame; since the most ardent profferings of the most martyrizing demonstrations in his behalf, – these he was sorrowfully obliged to turn away.
>
> (299)

Here, at the metropolitan center of emerging systems and institutions of mass culture, one discovers a peculiarly modern sort of artistic will-to-power, motivated by "melancholy forebodings of the utter unsatisfactoriness of all human fame," expressed as a renunciation of literary ambition. Where the possibility of fame and success were most intimately available and viscerally near, the true artist was *obliged* to turn away, as though taking an ethical stand. In a furious few weeks of writing, then, Melville would deliberately welcome the professional fate that had already been handed to him.

If Melville owed New York City for whatever success he achieved as an author, he also owed it for the peculiarly modern sense of autonomy – less economic or political than spiritual and psychological – that is variously dramatized throughout his work. Pierre's turn away from the Vanity Fair of the New York publishing world, for instance, entails an embrace of a bohemian subculture that would become a distinctive feature of the modern metropolis. Pierre takes lodging in the old Church of the Apostles. "Built when that part of the city was devoted to private residences, and not to warehouses and offices as now," the "tide of change and progress" had turned the church into mere real estate: "It must be divided into stores; cut into offices; and given for a roost to the gregarious lawyers" (309–10). Like Grace Church, at Broadway and Rector Street, which had been sold in 1845 and turned into stores and a museum of Chinese curiosities, Pierre's new housing is, as Hershel Parker notes, a "fit emblem of the fate of Christianity in commercial society where the better people were retreating farther and farther uptown."[24] But it represents not only the loss of a traditional model of organic community – a village blending spaces of home and work in the orbit of a church – but also a purposeful bifurcation of urban culture that would characterize the city's warehouse and business districts. These areas are populated by accountants and lawyers by day, but at night given over, like the Church of the Apostles, to "scores of those miscellaneous, bread-and-cheese adventures, and ambiguously professional nondescripts in very genteel but shabby black, and unaccountable foreign-looking fellows in blue spectacles" (311).

In making neighborhoods inhospitable to family life, the triumph of commerce at the street level paradoxically affords, by way of cheap attics and single-room occupancies, a breeding ground for a hipster lifestyle. As the narrator observes, residents at the converted church "are mostly artists of various sorts; painters, or sculptors, or indigent students, or teachers of languages, of poets, or fugitive French politicians, or German philosophers" (311). Like Pierre, the residents of the Apostles have chosen to live in such a place not out of desperation, but for the sake of artistic, intellectual, or political idealism:

> Often groping in vain in their pockets, they can not but give in to the Descartian vortices; while the abundance of leisure in their attics (physical and figurative), unites with the leisure in their stomachs, to fit them in an eminent degree for that undivided attention indispensable to the proper digesting of the sublimated Categories of Kant; especially Kant (can't) is the one great palpable fact of their pervadingly impalpable lives. These are the glorious paupers, from whom I learn the profoundest mysteries of things.
>
> (311)

Like often-privileged college graduates who in the later nineteenth and twentieth centuries would suddenly renounce their formerly dutiful over-achievement to explore themselves or write the great American novel, they are experimenting with a romantic individuality entirely divorced from utilitarian ends of production or consumption. Presumably some of these "adventurers" will soon quit urban slumming, as though it were an internship or rite of passage one undergoes on the way to adult maturity or career building. Others, however, will commit to it as an *ethos* – a particularly modern art of living, creatively committed to views that, "however heterodox at times, are still very fine and spiritual on the whole." Embracing the spiritual vocation of the artist at the cost of professional success, Pierre also embraces an existential isolation unique to urban bohemia: "one in a city of hundreds of thousands of human beings, Pierre was solitary as at the Pole" (392–93). This image of isolation would surface again a few years later, when Melville's narrator describes Bartleby: "He seemed alone, absolutely alone in the universe. A bit of wreck in the mid Atlantic" (657).

At this point in *Pierre*, Melville offers an acute portrait of a psychology of alienation that, like Ishmael's melancholy "November in my soul," becomes most seductive within the crowded anonymity of New York. While living in the city a few years earlier as a newlywed, Melville would take regular walks on Broadway in the late afternoon with his wife Lizzie, and then long walks by himself in the early evening. Again in New York in January of 1852, at the moment when his career suddenly foundered, Melville found himself writing furiously about Pierre's writerly estrangement from the urban environment:

> In the earlier progress of his book, he had found some relief in making his regular evening walk through the greatest thoroughfare of the city; that so, the utter isolation of his soul, might feel itself the more intensely from the incessant jogglings of his body against the bodies of the hurrying thousands. Then he began to be sensible of more fancying stormy nights, than pleasant ones; for then, the great thoroughfares were less thronged, and the innumerable shop-awnings flapped and beat like schooners' broad sails in a gale, and the shutters banged like lashed bulwarks; and the slates fell hurtling like displaced ship's blocks from aloft. Stemming such tempests through the deserted streets, Pierre felt a dark, triumphant joy; that while others had crawled in fear to their kennels, he alone defied the storm-admiral, whose most vindictive peltings of hail-stones, – striking his iron-framed fiery furnace of a body, – melted into soft dew, and so, harmlessly trickled from off him.
>
> (395)

If he starts out feeling the "utter isolation of his soul" more intensely by being buffeted "against the bodies of the hurrying thousands," Pierre soon finds himself braving this isolation, as if in heroic defiance of creation: to walk the city is, finally, to put one's very soul to sea, courting the most violent of storms. "By-and-by," as the narrator continues, "of such howling, pelting nights," Pierre seeks out "the more secluded taprooms," where he eyes "the varied faces of the social castaways, who here had their haunts from the bitterest midnights. But at last he began to feel a distaste for even these; and now nothing but the utter night-desolation of the obscurest warehousing lanes would content him, or be at all sufferable to him" (395). Because it feeds on withdrawals from the social world, this desire for solitude risks psychic dissociation of the soul from the body, transforming the author from "castaway" to derelict. One night Pierre seems to pass out, and when "he came to himself he found that he was lying crosswise in the gutter, dabbled with mud and slime." From its reckless self-absorption, the voyage of the soul to urban isolation finally wrecks one's body on the shoals of reality.

Like *Moby-Dick* and "Bartleby, the Scrivener," then, *Pierre* discovers a solitude that, for all the throngs on Broadway, the crowds of office workers, and huddled immigrant masses, best defines life in Melville's New York. Here, individuals find intellectual and spiritual freedom, but they also dwell in emotional poverty and abject loneliness. Men like Pierre seek to penetrate elusive truths that most men miss, "and by advancing, leave the rest behind; cutting themselves forever adrift from their sympathy" (196). Melville would continue to seek these elusive truths in his writing, but so too he would cut himself adrift. Following the publication of *The Confidence-Man* in 1857, he essentially gave up on the quest for professional success that had begun a little over a decade earlier, publishing poetry and occasional pieces but finally embracing writing as a private vocation, done in the solitude of his study after long workdays; he labored for years revising his last masterpiece *Billy Budd*, but made no attempt to publish it while he was alive. A few years after Melville and his family returned to live in New York, on East 26th Street, in 1863, he took a job as one of dozens of customs inspectors employed by the US Customs Service. For almost two decades, Melville made his way to the piers six days a week, for $4 a day, and vanished into anonymity. As he walked the island city of Manhattan, he perhaps became what Ishmael calls an *Isolato*: "not acknowledging the common continent of men," but, like the islanders who make up the crew of the *Pequod*, "living on a separate continent of his own" (107).

If Manhattan is the beginning of Ishmael's adventure, it is also the end – indeed, a port for departures and routines, a home for the finally rootless quality of mind and spirit that has no home. The most remarkable thing about the melancholy of which Ishmael speaks at the outset of *Moby-Dick* is its evident routine – "whenever" it arrives, his mood is as familiar in its contours as the light and weather of November days. Evidently, Ishmael has learned to inhabit the alienation of city life, to convert the solitude of its physical and spiritual isolation into an occasion for metaphysical adventure, for "ocean reveries" that will cast Melville's readers on a sea of words. While "Loomings" begins with Ishmael walking crowded streets in Manhattan, it ends with the image of a vast interior space: "the great flood-gates of the wonder-world," swinging open to my "inmost soul." If, as Ishmael declares, it was an "idea of the whale" that finally took him offshore, the scale and scope of Ishmael's metaphysical pursuit allows us to see "that the absolute is there all around us, formidable and familiar," as Jean-Paul Sartre observed in 1941.[25] The amplitude and multiplicity of Ishmael's intellectual, spiritual, and social quests are finally reflections of an existential solitude: an epic introspection born of living amongst the most diverse, diverting, and finally lonely of crowds. At the end of *Moby-Dick*, after all, it is Ishmael who alone survives to the tell the tale, whose voice floats up from the wreck of the *Pequod*, speaking to both the loneliness and the liberty of the crowd, to the imagination in isolation that Melville and his characters owed to urban modernity. For Melville's readers, Ishmael continues to walk the streets of Manhattan, in the wake of experience but forever open to our ocean reveries.

NOTES

1. Herman Melville, *Moby-Dick* (1851), ed. Hershel Parker (New York: W. W. Norton, 2002), p. 18. Further references appear in the text.

2. Hershel Parker, *Herman Melville: A Biography*, vol. 1: *1819–1851* (Baltimore, MD: Johns Hopkins University Press, 1996), p. 2: "Herman Melville became peculiarly sensitive to the overlayings of past and present in places where significant experiences of his life had occurred, so his father and other members of his family haunted the river and lower Manhattan whenever he walked there, even many decades later." As if to escape Allan's sorry legacy, Melville's mother changed her family's name following her husband's death by adding the letter e to Melvill.

3. Melville, *Redburn: His First Voyage* (1849), in *Redburn, White-Jacket, Moby Dick* (New York: Library of America, 1983), p. 44.

4. Melville, *Pierre, or The Ambiguities* (1852), in *Pierre, Israel Potter, The Piazza Tales, The Confidence-Man, Billy Budd, Uncollected Prose* (New York: Library of America), p. 13. Further references appear in the text.

5. Melville, "Jimmy Rose," in *Pierre, Israel Potter, The Piazza Tales, The Confidence-Man, Billy Budd, Uncollected Prose*, pp. 1283, 1286.

6. Robert Milder, "Herman Melville 1819–1891: A Brief Biography," in *A Historical Guide to Herman Melville*, ed. Giles Gunn (New York: Oxford University Press, 2005), p. 20.

7. Melville, "Bartleby, the Scrivener," in *Pierre, Israel Potter, The Piazza Tales, The Confidence-Man, Uncollected Prose*, p. 635. Further references appear in the text.

8. In the mid nineteenth century, "clerk" constituted the third largest occupation for urban men. The value of a clerk's main skill – his handwriting – was poised between its earlier status as an achievement of professional character and its late-nineteenth-century association with manual, secretarial work. See Thomas Augst, *The Clerk's Tale: Young Men and Moral Life in 19th Century America* (Chicago, IL: University of Chicago Press, 2003).

9. As the narrator of "Jimmy Rose" observes: "Without rudely breaking him right down to it, fate slowly bent him more and more to the lowest deep ... no man could with impunity be allowed this life unless regarded as one who, free from vice, was by fortune brought so low that the plummet of pity alone could reach him" (p. 1287).

10. "At different times in his career," Wyn Kelley observes, Melville "adopted for his characters both patterns of mastery of and surrender to urban form." Often "grafting local urban form onto exotic landscape, Melville challenges the genteel urban culture from which the spectator comes." Kelley argues that Melville's narrators develop four discrete perspectives, those of the "spectator of large capital city, provincial entering labyrinth, sojourner in a wasteland, pilgrim in the

cosmopolis or city of god." His work thus drew on long-standing literary traditions by which authors created "fictional space in constricted urban terrain." Wyn Kelley, *Melville's City: Literary and Urban Form in Nineteenth-Century New York* (Cambridge: Cambridge University Press, 1996), pp. 59, 62.

11. On the relation of Melville's story to literary practices of middle-class character, see Augst, *The Clerk's Tale*, ch. 5.

12. "Jimmy Rose" features refrains of a similar sentimental lament: "Poor, poor Jimmy – God guard us all – poor Jimmy Rose!" Such sentimental rhetoric was typical of fiction published in *Harper's Magazine*, where "Jimmy Rose" appeared. In "Bartleby, the Scrivener," which appeared in the more intellectual *Putnam's Monthly*, Melville arguably parallels one story about the magazine's concern with Wall Street's exploitation of workers with another story about the periodical market's demands on writers for sentimental style. See Sheila Post, "Melville and the Marketplace," in *A Historical Guide to Herman Melville*, ed. Gunn, p. 126.

13. Barbara Foley situates Melville's story in specific autobiographical relation to the historical context of the Astor Place riots, arguing that the story's critical engagement with the ideological struggle and class polarization of the late 1840s emerges within "a controlled ironic framework within which the reader is invited to judge the inadequacies and hypocrisies of the tale's narrator." Foley, "From Wall Street to Astor Place: Historicizing Melville's Bartleby," *American Literature* 72:1 (March 2000): 109.

14. Carole Travis-Henikoff, *Dinner with a Cannibal: The Complete History of Mankind's Oldest Taboo* (Santa Monica, CA: Santa Monica Press, 2008), p. 99.

15. Andrew Delbanco, *Melville: His World and Work* (New York: Knopf, 2005), pp. 117, 119.

16. See David Reynolds, *Beneath the American Renaissance: The Subversive Imagination in the Age of Emerson and Whitman* (Cambridge, MA: Harvard University Press, 1989), pp. 463–65.

17. Cited in Ted Widmer, *Young America: The Flowering of Democracy in New York City* (New York: Oxford University Press, 1999), p. 103.

18. *Ibid.*, p. 104.

19. *Ibid.*, p. 120.

20. Cited in Hershel Parker, *Herman Melville: A Biography*, vol. II: *1851–1891* (Baltimore, MD: Johns Hopkins University Press, 2005), p. 24.

21. Melville, "Hawthorne and His Mosses," in *Pierre, Israel Potter, The Piazza Tales, The Confidence-Man, Billy Budd, Uncollected Prose*, p. 1160. Although it claims to discover Hawthorne as a home-grown literary genius, Melville's review is more accurately read as a record of the ideas about literary value that he developed in 1850, while writing *Moby-Dick*. On the one hand, Melville's review demanded that readers stop looking abroad for their standards of literary value, proclaiming that "Shakespeares are this day being born on the banks of the Ohio" (p. 1161). On the other hand, Melville disdained precisely the "popularizing noise and show of broad farce" that had made Shakespeare and his works so well loved by all classes.

22. Parker, *Herman Melville*, II, p. 85.

23. *Ibid.*, II, p. 77. The Harper brothers offered Melville 20 cents on the dollar after costs for *Pierre*, whereas his previous works had earned him 50 cents on the dollar.

24. *Ibid.*, II, p. 67.

25. "No one more than Hegel and Melville has sensed that the absolute is there all around us, formidable and familiar, that we can see it, white and polished like a sheep bone, if we only cast aside the multicolored veils with which we've covered it. We haunt the absolute; but no one, to my knowledge, no one except Melville, has attempted this extraordinary undertaking of retaining the indefinable taste of a pure quality – the purest quality, whiteness – and seeking in that taste itself the absolute which goes beyond it. If this is one of the directions in which contemporary literature is trying in a groping way to go, then Melville is the most 'modern' writer." Jean-Paul Sartre, "Herman Melville's *Moby-Dick*," in *Twentieth Century Interpretations of "Moby-Dick,"* ed. Michael T. Gilmore (Englewood Cliffs, NJ: Prentice-Hall, 1977), p. 95.

5

LYTLE SHAW

Whitman's urbanism

Remember … [*Leaves of Grass*] arose out of my life in Brooklyn and New York … absorbing a million people … with an intimacy, an eagerness, an abandon, probably never equaled.

Walt Whitman[1]

> Walt Whitman, a kosmos, of Manhattan the son,
> Turbulent, fleshy, sensual, eating, drinking and breeding,
> No sentimentalist, no stander above men and women or apart from them.

Walt Whitman, "Song of Myself"[2]

As Whitman himself suggests, the pleasure he took in New York City was something more than a happy backdrop for his *real* work as a poet. It was, rather, fundamental to his attempt to imagine – and to enact – a democratic poetics that would find its basic resources in the unacknowledged though universal fact of humans having bodies, and its site, as it were, in the dense interactions of such bodies made possible in the most populous cities, New York above all. It is in this sense that, despite his strong attachment to the category of the nation as a whole and his repeated thematization of regional vignettes, Whitman is also, centrally, an urbanist – and one grounded in the specific urban locale of Manhattan. For it is in the daily life available in cities like Manhattan that, according to Whitman, one can best "absorb" and be absorbed by the largest number of other people – that one can try on, learn from, identify with other subjectivities, other concretely embodied modes and styles of life. This is perhaps why Whitman uses the word "inspiriting" to describe his experience of "the hurrying and vast amplitude of those never ending human currents" on Broadway.[3]

And yet the use of the term intimacy to describe the process of "absorbing a million people" suggests the enduring strangeness of Whitman's version of urbanism, one that positions absorption precariously between the physical and the conceptual – between literal contact with bodies or actual exchange

Figure 6: Walt Whitman. Steel engraving by Samuel Hollyer from a lost daguerreotype by Gabriel Harrison. Used as frontispiece to the first edition of *Leaves of Grass* (1855). His clothing and posture are meant to suggest that he is "one of the roughs."

of glances and more mediated mental contact with ideas and idioms. This goal of contact governs not only present-tense encounters in Whitman but, paradoxically, much of the poet's anticipated, and imaginatively staged, reception by later readers, including perhaps the most famous articulation of this in "Crossing Brooklyn Ferry," where Whitman claims that "distance avails not, / I am with you, you men and women of a generation, or ever / so many generations hence" (*PW*, 133). The sense in which the speaker is "with us" shifts throughout the poem from the analogical – "I too walk'd the streets of Manhattan island ... I too had receiv'd identity by my body, / That I was I knew was of my body" (*PW*, 135) – to the literal, the claim – signaled by the lines, "Closer yet I approach you" – that the poem offers not simply a trans-historically accessible image of the embodied poet immersed in the daily life of New York City, but actual visual access, first with him "as good as looking / at you now" and then with the readerly you looking back, in an "actual" intersubjective exchange of glances: "What is more subtle than this which ties me to the woman or / man that looks in my face? / Which fuses me into you now, and pours my meaning into you?" (*PW*, 137; see *Figure 6*).

As much as such passages suggest an impossible metaphysics of immediacy, Whitman does at moments hint at how mediation (especially linguistic mediation) was not just grudgingly admitted but understood as a generative force for his poetics. In his essay "Slang in America," for instance, Whitman presented the English language in terms very similar to those he used for New York City: as "a sort of universal absorber, combiner, and conqueror" (*PW*, 557). While English may engulf other languages, what slang conquers – from the very beginning – is "bald literalism," this by exploring the "lawless germinal element" of language (*PW*, 557). In fact, Whitman suggests, "many of the oldest and solidest words we use, were originally generated from the daring and license of slang" (*PW*, 558). One example points to an alternate sense for his claim in "Crossing Brooklyn Ferry" to "pour my meaning into you": "If you influenc'd a man, you but flow'd into him" (*PW*, 558). Physicalizing language – so that its seemingly traceless aspects might have a kind of material, measurable basis – Whitman then goes on to detail a range of his own "influences." These, it's worth underlining, are not merely the bodies he saw and touched, but the idioms they uttered, like the slang heard on the "city horse cars" in New York, whose driver is called the "'snatcher' (i.e. because his characteristic duty is constantly to pull or snatch the bell-strap, to stop or go on)" (*PW*, 560). Whitman returns to and amplifies this same scene in "Specimen Days," offering it especially to doubting scholars: "(I suppose the critics will laugh heartily, but the influence of those Broadway omnibus jaunts and drivers and declamations and escapades undoubtedly enter'd into the gestation of 'Leaves of Grass')" (*PW*, 478).

Certainly Whitman's own writing has now "enter'd into the gestation" of a great number of later New York poets, who tend to be less embarrassed about appreciating the declamations of bus drivers, subway conductors, or cabbies. An account of Whitman's ongoing influence on poetry in New York City might reasonably include Langston Hughes's poetry, especially from the 1920s, Hart Crane's *The Bridge* (1930), Federico García Lorca's *Poet in New York* (1930), George Oppen's *Of Being Numerous* (1968), as well as most of Frank O'Hara's work from the 1950s and 1960s and much of the writing of Lower East Side poets of the 1960s and 1970s, directly in the early works of Ed Sanders and Anne Waldman, less directly but no less importantly in the poetry of Ted Berrigan and Bernadette Mayer.[4] Certainly all of these poets looked back to Whitman's rich engagement with the city as they articulated their own urbanist poetics – as they thought through the individual subject's (and more, the individual *body*'s) relation to a larger social totality, provided in condensed form by the city. It is a measure of Whitman's broad influence that his imprint can be found in such radically different stylistic stances: Crane's ornate ambiguities; Oppen's austere abstractions; O'Hara's exuberant demotic bursts; García Lorca's anxious and heated rants. But rather than trace the breadth of Whitman's influence on poetry in New York, I want here instead to focus on just one case study (that of Allen Ginsberg) in order to suggest how Ginsberg drew out the utopian, unfamiliar, and even contestatory elements of Whitman in order to turn him into a countercultural ally from the 1950s onward.

Rather than see Ginsberg, however, as simply clouding the blue Whitmanian skies over Manhattan, it is more accurate to understand him as focusing in on, and exploring, tensions already latent in Whitman's celebration of urbanism – his situating of the city at the center of his democratic, corporeal poetics (see *Figure 7*). Before accounting for these tensions, let me elaborate on the special position of the city in Whitman's seemingly all-inclusive poetics. Like several other passages in the poem, section 15 of "Song of Myself" presents a kind of macro-panorama of American trades, genre scenes embracing a broad array of regions, classes, social identities – from duck-shooters and deacons to spinning girls, whale-boat mates, and paving men, from "quadroons" and "half-breeds" to "squaws" and "newly-come immigrants"; this within the West, the Yankee East, the Great Lakes, the Southwest, with its "walls of Adobie," and the Missouri plains (*PW*, 17–19). Passages like this propose that, with Whitman's help, we might zoom across space to bring these disparate people and activities into a neat paratactic list – and that as we do so we experience American democratic possibility not just thematically through this array of variable vicarious occupations, subject positions, and regions but in a sense formally too through their conjoined equivalence. And yet part of the reason why the poet was so insistent upon identifying himself as "Walt Whitman, a Kosmos, of Manhattan the son," was, as I suggested, that the city seemed to offer a micro-Kosmos for its sons.

At times Whitman's interest in urban condensation could take on a quite literal cast. Whitman's biographer Justin Kaplan, for instance, notices such a

Figure 7: Allen Ginsberg, New York City, Fall 1953: "Myself seen by William Burroughs, my new-bought Kodak Retina from Bowery hock-shop in his hand, our apartment roof Lower East Side between Avenues B & C, Tompkins Park trees under new antennae, Kerouac, Corso and Alan Ansen visited, The Subterraneans records much of the scene, Burroughs & I worked editing manuscripts he'd sent me as letters from Mexico & South America, the neighborhood heavily Polish & Ukrainian, some artists, junkies & medical students, rent only 1/4 of my $120 monthly wage as newspaper copyboy. Fall 1953."

logic at work in the poet's fascination with a model of New York City made by E. Porter Belden and presented in the Minerva Room on Broadway in 1846:

> The work of one hundred and fifty artists and artisans, surmounted by a gorgeous canopy adorned with nearly one hundred paintings of business establishments and places of note, Belden's creation occupied 480 square feet of floor space. "It is a perfect facsimile of New York," [Whitman] declared, "representing every street, lane, building, shed, park, fence, tree, and every other object in the city." Over 200,000 houses, stores, and public buildings were depicted in carved wooden miniature along with five thousand boats and ships in the harbor. Belden's model replicated New York [Whitman] said, "almost as accurately as if the latter had been by some Immense Mechanical Power compressed into narrower limits!"[5]

This model's relation to New York was, as Kaplan points out, like New York's relation to the country as a whole.[6] Frequently the Whitmanian subject "models" larger forces at work – gleeful about its representativity, its typicality, its embodiment of larger totalities: "This is the city and I am one of the citizens, / Whatever interests the rest interests me, politics, wars, markets, / newspapers, schools, / The mayor and councils, banks, tariffs, steamships, factories, stocks, / stores, real estate and personal estate" (*PW*, 54). At other moments, however, the Whitmanian subject must challenge doxa in order to propose other values as crucial to both urban and national existence. Consider first this gushing passage from "Democratic Vistas" about returning to New York and Brooklyn in 1870:

> The splendor, picturesqueness, and oceanic amplitude and rush of the great cities, the unsurpass'd situation, rivers and bay, sparkling sea-tides, costly and lofty new buildings, facades of marble and iron, of original grandeur and elegance of design, with the masses of gay color, the preponderance of white and blue, the flags flying, the endless ships, the tumultuous streets, Broadway, the heavy, low, musical roar, hardly ever intermitted, even at night; the jobbers' houses, the rich shops, the wharves, the great Central Park, and the Brooklyn Park of hills (as I wander among them this beautiful fall weather, musing, watching, absorbing) – the assemblages of the citizens in their groups, conversations, trades, evening amusements, or along the by-quarters – these, I say, and the like of these, completely satisfy my sense of power, fullness, motion, &c., and give me, through such senses and appetites, and through my esthetic conscience, a continued exaltation and absolute fulfillment.
>
> (*PW*, 405)

After locating in cities a man-made sublimity on a par with natural varieties offered by storms, mountains, forests, and seas, Whitman changes his tone on a dime: "But sternly discarding, shutting our eyes to the glow and grandeur of the general superficial effect, coming down to what is of the only real importance, Personalities, and examining minutely, we question, we ask, Are there, indeed, men here worth the name?" (*PW*, 405). Whitman's answer, of course, is no: what this slovenly, unremarkable population needs in order to live up to its stupendous physical context is … literature, the binding power by which "the new blood, new frame of democracy shall be vivified and held together," a literature that might, as in "Song of Myself," "give more compaction … fusing contributions, races, far locations" (*PW*, 401).

Interested both in Whitman's perceived problems and his proposed solutions, Allen Ginsberg touches on a rare moment of the former in part two of "Song of Myself": "then [Whitman] looks out at the drawing rooms of Brooklyn and lower Manhattan and the rich of his day, and the sophisticated culture of his day, and he sees that it's pretty shallow:

> Houses and rooms are full of perfumes, the shelves are crowded
>   with perfumes
> I breathe the fragrance myself and know it and like it,

The distillation would intoxicate me also, but I shall not let it.
The atmosphere is not a perfume, it has no taste of the distillation,
  it is odorless." [7]

Before we dive into Ginsberg's larger reading, let me elaborate its context by playing out some of the dynamics in the passage he quotes. While the spatial distillation offered by the Belden Manhattan model exercises Whitman's synecdochic fascination and seems to stand as an emblem of his democratic poetics, somehow this olfactory distillation ushers in the opposite experience: the need to cleanse the senses, to establish their proper and absolute dimensions by distinguishing the particular and temporary allurements of perfumes from the universal and endless truth of the atmosphere.[8] Sometimes, though, these distillations seem to escape their chambers and waft out onto the sidewalk, in the form of dandies, or even white-collar workers. Encountering these apparitions presents problems for the well-intentioned Whitmanian subject:

> The little plentiful manikins skipping around in collars and tail'd coats,
> I am aware who they are, (they are positively not worms or fleas,)
> I acknowledge the duplicates of myself, the weakest and shallowest is
>   deathless with me,
> What I do and say waits for them,
> Every thought that flounders in me the same flounders in them.
>
> *(PW,* 54–55)

If the claimed result is still a process of duplication, this must now occur across a gap of negative presuppositions, of anxious glances and floundered thoughts, such, perhaps, as the thought (or dream) of superiority with which the passage appears to begin. Elsewhere the great equalizer, the force that would trump any temporary and distancing desire for distinction with the immediacy of touch, sensuous corporeal existence here struggles to perform its democratic function.

Too weak here, at other moments touch threatens to overstep its democratic position on the sensorium as but one among five equal senses.[9] This problem appears most centrally in section 28 of "Song of Myself":[10]

> Is this then a touch? quivering me to a new identity,
> Flames and ether making a rush for my veins,
> Treacherous tip of me reaching and crowding to help them,
> My flesh and blood playing out lightning to strike what is hardly different
>   from myself,
> On all sides prurient provokers stiffening my limbs,
> Straining the udder of my heart for its withheld drip,
> Behaving licentiously toward me, taking no denial,

Depriving me of my best as for a purpose,
Unbuttoning my clothes, holding me by the bare waist,
Deluding my confusion with the calm of sunlight and pasture-fields,
Immodestly sliding the fellow-sense away,
They bribed to swap off with touch and go and graze at the edges of me[.]

(*PW*, 33)

Unlike the former panoramas of industries and trades, where bodies are alternatively productive and/or attractive, now as one body comes into full contact with another, its desires threaten to take over, becoming semi-autonomous from consciousness, touch tyrannically dominating the other senses in a way that's neither rational nor democratic.[11] Much as, in singing the praises of progress and democracy, Whitman needs to make us aware that he also considers evil, now in singing the praises of the present-to-itself body he also needs to consider how complete corporeal being might actually *abstract* one from the world, rather than connecting one to it more intimately.

This moment presents a limit condition for the sensing body in "Song of Myself" – a condition in which excess contact produces the desire for privacy. We might pair this with a similar moment involving speech, language, and sound more generally in which the urban environment becomes a kind of infinite sonic archive of repression. In section 8 the beloved omnibus drivers replace their generative declarations with "interrogating thumb[s]." Now "The blab of the pave, tires of carts, sluff of boot-soles, talk of the / promenaders" and "the clank of the shod horses on the granite floor" frame a less inviting sonic landscape focused by "impassive stones that receive and return so many echoes" (*PW*, 11).

> What groans of over-fed or half-starv'd who fall sunstruck or in fits,
> What exclamations of women taken suddenly who hurry home and give
>   birth to babes,
> What living and buried speech is always vibrating here, what howls
>   restrain'd by decorum,
> Arrests of criminals, slights, adulterous offers made, acceptances, rejections
>   with convex lips,
> I mind them or the show or resonance of them – I come and I depart.

(*PW*, 11)

It is characteristic of Whitman that he claims autonomy from this affective environment; he can come and depart, can mind these howls merely for their "show or resonance." Subsequent New York poets, however, have often presented themselves as fundamentally subject to the social implications of these urban distress signals. Ginsberg, for instance, tunes directly into this frequency, dedicating not just his most famous poem, "Howl" (1956), but the entirety of his career to examining both how such noise is "restrained by decorum" and what might be done not merely to allow public howling, but to obviate it. Such differences, though, were not perceived as a limitation in Whitman, whom Ginsberg was careful to position as one of his central "spiritual teachers," a "prophet of American democracy," and one who had "completely possessed his own body."[12] In a 1969 interview Ginsberg expands on this:

> As Whitman observed, if the natural love of man for man is suppressed, men won't be good citizens and democracy will be enfeebled. What Whitman prophesied was an adhesive element between comrades – the "sane, healthy love of man for man." But because of suppression of feelings in America, the overemphasis on competition and rivalry – a tough guy, *macho*, hard, sadistic police-state mentality – American men are afraid of relationships with each other.
>
> (SM, 242)

One of the many reasons to howl in 1956, then, was because macho, tough guy, sadistic police-state decorum (even in the New York City Frank O'Hara called "Sodom-on-Hudson") still restrained this "natural love of man for man."[13] Though Whitman's "sane and healthy" antidote might seem to be the exclusive domain of gay men, it was interestingly not understood this way by Ginsberg: "men will love men, women love women, men love women, women love men," so that in the Whitmanian model "spontaneous tenderness" between any combination becomes "the basis of democracy" (SM, 286). But whether or not, from our current perspective, homosexual desire is essentialized, the very fact that it is included within a foundational celebration of desire would, of course, have been disturbing to most of Whitman's contemporaries. Fascinated by this, Ginsberg sees Whitman's proposal reaching its most extreme form in "Calamus": "Okay, so he's proposing that the dear love of comrades and the unabashed affection between citizens be acknowledged as it stands rather than mocked. And then, of course, not to get people upset, so:

> I hear it [was] charged against me that I sought to destroy institutions;
> But really I am neither for nor against institutions,
> (What indeed have I in common with them? or what with the
>   destruction of them?)
> Only I will establish in the Mannahatta and in every city of these States
>   inland and seaboard,
> And in the fields and woods, and above every keel little or large that
>   dents the water,
> Without edifices or rules or trustees or any argument,
> The institution of the dear love of comrades."
>
> (WW, 306)

"Howl," too, sought to ground the institution of the dear love of comrades in a reconfigured Manhattan, in Whitman's "City of Orgies," where comrades might found a "community rather than … a nation 'among the fabled damned of nations'" (SM, 242).[14]

Such love of comrades may still be suppressed in the world of "Howl." But the book at least shows it as possible and present – as, in fact, organizing a micro-society or coterie of initiates, the "best minds of my generation," who bond over their revulsion to Cold-War America but do not yet constitute a widespread counterculture.[15] Or at least they bond when they are not "destroyed by madness," "dragging themselves through the negro streets at dawn / looking for an angry fix," baring "their brains to Heaven under the El" (H, 9), "busted in their pubic beards returning through / Laredo with a belt of marijuana for New York" (H, 10), or crashing "through their minds in jail" (H, 18).

These variously psychic, pharmacological, or legal interludes – in which one Who is separated from another by the ultimate Grinch, Moloch – are central to the micro-social politics of the poem. Certainly they are instances in which "decorum" has swooped down and stifled howlers, necessitating further howls. But they are also moments that emphasize a latent atomism in a not-yet-articulated group of comrades whose primary logic of collectivity is their negative need to scream. This dynamic is emphasized by the fact that many avenues of symbolic protest seem to lead, in the poem, only to self-destruction: howling subjects are reduced to burning "cigarette holes in their arms protesting / the narcotic tobacco haze of Capitalism" (H, 13), or throwing "their watches off the roof to cast their ballot / for Eternity outside of Time" (H, 16). The futility of these modes of protest seems to be associated with the limits imposed by an "Absolute Reality" whose "drunken taxicabs" might run one down (H, 16). Even the more effective or classic protests are interwoven with psychic episodes that are not within the control of the speaker – with "groans" and "exclamations" that one cannot mind from a distance for their "show or resonance":

> who distributed Supercommunist pamphlets in Union
> Square weeping and undressing while the sirens
> of Los Alamos wailed them down, and wailed
> down Wall, and the Staten Island ferry also
> wailed,
> who broke down crying in white gymnasiums naked
> and trembling before the machinery of other
> skeletons,
> who bit detectives in the neck and shrieked with delight
> in policecars for committing no crime but their

own wild cooking pederasty and intoxication,
who howled on their knees in the subway and were
dragged off the roof waving genitals and manuscripts[.]

$$(H, 13)^{16}$$

For Ginsberg, these repressive elements of contemporary life, these howl-
inducing infrastructures, coalesce into a single term, noted above: Moloch,
the "sphinx of cement and aluminum [that] bashed open / their skulls and
ate up their brains and imagination" (H, 21). Moloch is at once what causes
one to howl and what decorously represses the sound:

Moloch whose eyes are a thousand blind windows!
Moloch whose skyscrapers stand in the long
street like endless Jehovahs! Moloch whose factories dream and croak in the fog! Moloch whose
smokestacks and antennae crown the cities!
Moloch whose love is endless oil and stone! Moloch
whose soul is electricity and banks! Moloch
whose poverty is the specter of genius! Moloch
whose fate is a cloud of sexless hydrogen!
Moloch whose name is the Mind!

$$(H, 21-22)$$

By the end of this passage Moloch's location, however, has moved crucially
from a secure exteriority, associated with the urban features of skyscrapers, factories, and smokestacks, to interior mental constructions.[17] Certainly
Whitman's "influence" involved tools for combating mental Molochs; but
what is more surprising, perhaps, is that Ginsberg was careful to associate
Whitman, too, with the kinds of more public, exterior modes of protest that
he developed over the course of the 1960s.

In a 1964 interview, for instance, in which he discusses his first demonstration (in San Francisco, against a visit by Madame Nhu, the wife of
Vietnam's chief of secret police), Ginsberg says: "It took a lot of nature in
[Whitman] to expose that tenderness openly for the first time in America but
that's the unconscious basis of our democracy and that's why I'm here today
on the picket line trying to be tender to Madame Nhu and Mao Tse-Tung.
Or better, asking them to be tender" (SM, 13).

As Ginsberg reads him, Whitman has become not just a countercultural
ally, but a theorist who *makes possible* a new and still unassimilated social
attitude – on the picket line, in the "negro streets," in the bedroom, and
even in the "neon fruit supermarket," where Ginsberg can dream of his
enumerations. It is telling, for instance, that in perhaps Ginsberg's most
famous calling out to Whitman – the poem "A Supermarket in California"

(1955) – the grey-bearded nineteenth-century bard becomes a character out of Genet or Godard, checking out the grocery boy, sampling foods, "and never passing the cashier." In the enormous supermarket of American trades, objects, and people that is Whitman's poems, the subject of desire is not alienated, not a "childless, lonely old grubber, poking among the meats in the refrigerator" (*H*, 29). Nor is he an object of surveillance, "followed in my imagination by the store detective" (*H*, 29). No one monitors the Whitmanian subject who zooms through space in his cross-country panoramas.

But this new situation is, arguably, less an ironic commentary than an attempt at translation across time: to take Whitman seriously, to make good on his claims, to restage his project in the present is to occupy a marginalized position in the United States of the 1950s, be it in a supermarket in California or in the streets of New York City in "Howl." This is in part because Whitman's constantly advertised "availability" depends, in fact, as he himself says in "Democratic Vistas," "on the assumption that the process of reading is not half-asleep, but, in the highest sense, an exercise, a gymnast's struggle [in which the reader is called upon to] construct indeed the poem, argument, history, metaphysical essay" (*PW*, 460). Awake and generous in his reading, Ginsberg sees Whitman's social theory, and his urbanism in particular, not just as a bodily poetics insufficiently attentive to howls restrained by decorum. Instead, Ginsberg focuses on the contestatory aspects of Whitman's poetics in order to position him, not as a poetic innovator excusable for his embarrassing models of progress and nationalism, but rather as a thinker whose radical propositions about a more fully democratic world of adhesive tenderness and infinite possible absorptions have still not been fully contemplated, let alone realized.

NOTES

1. Quoted in Justin Kaplan, *Walt Whitman: A Life* (New York: Simon and Schuster, 1980), p. 113. Other useful biographies are Gay Wilson Allen, *The Solitary Singer: A Critical Biography of Walt Whitman* (New York: New York University Press, 1967); David S. Reynolds, *Walt Whitman: A Cultural Biography* (New York: Knopf, 1995); and Jerome Loving, *Walt Whitman: The Song of Himself* (Berkeley: University of California Press, 1999). I am also indebted to Michael Moon's *Disseminating Whitman: Revision and Corporeality in "Leaves of Grass"* (Cambridge, MA: Harvard University Press, 1991) for its excellent account of the status of the body in Whitman in relation to the multiple editions of *Leaves of Grass*.
2. "Song of Myself," in *The Portable Walt Whitman*, ed. Michael Warner (New York: Penguin, 2004), p. 27. Further references appear in the text as *PW*.
3. From a section of "Specimen Days" entitled "Broadway Sights" (*PW*, 476).

4. Though written in 1930, García Lorca's book was first published posthumously in 1940 and first translated into English in 1988. Whitman could also be read in slightly less direct but no less significant ways in the works of a poet like Jackson Mac Low.

5. Kaplan, *Walt Whitman*, p. 113.

6. Kaplan continues: "Uncompressed by mechanical power, bustling and self-contradictory, New York, as Whitman knew it then, was itself a 'model,' of the nation reduced, of personality and mental life enlarged" (*ibid.*).

7. Allen Ginsberg, "On Walt Whitman, Composed on the Tongue," in *Deliberate Prose: Selected Essays, 1952–1995*, ed. Bill Morgan (New York: HarperCollins, 2000), p. 291. Further references appear in the text as WW.

8. Certainly an anxiety about domesticity was one of the engines that drove Beat writers like Ginsberg and Jack Kerouac on the road. But in identifying with a passage like this Ginsberg is also interested in repositioning the body in culture more broadly – and in ways whose gender politics are not quite so predetermined.

9. Like Whitman, Ginsberg would at key moments explore the limits of his own strongly advocated politics of touch – in moments we might read in relation to the "crisis" section in "Song of Myself." In 1967, for instance, Emmett Grogan of the Diggers was making a speech on the evils of private property and the necessity of replacing cash with barter. In the Haight Ashbury audience sat countercultural hero Allen Ginsberg – planner, with the Diggers, of the "Be-In" in Golden Gate Park and spiritual ally in general. And yet Ginsberg interrupted Grogan on this day, apparently to test the status of privacy in Grogan's proposed model of the social: "'What does a guy like me do who's making some bread and decides he wants to buy a little piece of land? ... *Just* for myself[.]'" Jane Kramer, *Allen Ginsberg in American* (New York: Vintage, 1970), p. 103.

10. In section 38, the other famous crisis section, the opposite logic seems to be at work: the panoramas threaten to remove one from bodily existence.

11. By framing this as a matter of the politics of the sensorium, of touch "Immodestly sliding the fellow-sense away," I do not mean to suggest that it is not, also, an obviously erotic scene that depicts a homosexual encounter in which the speaker's "flesh and blood ... strike what is hardly / different from myself." Nor should we ignore the more specific historical politics of figuration: that extreme, transformative states (eros for Whitman, death for Dickinson) are frequently figured by reference to Native American violence – Whitman's "red marauder," Dickinson's "Thunderbolt / That scalps your naked soul." For the latter reference, see Dickinson's "He fumbles at your soul," in *The Complete Poems of Emily Dickinson*, ed. Thomas H. Johnson (Boston: Little Brown, 1960), p. 148.

12. The first phrase comes from an interview collected in *Spontaneous Mind: Selected Interviews, 1958–1996*, ed. David Carter (New York: Perennial, 2001), p. 242. Further references to this collection of interviews appear in the text as SM. The next two phrases are from WW, pp. 285, 291.

13. "Commercial Variations," in *The Collected Poems of Frank O'Hara*, ed. Donald M. Allen (New York: Knopf, 1972), p. 85. For an account of this poem and of Ginsberg's relation to O'Hara, see my *Frank O'Hara: The Poetics of Coterie* (Iowa City: University of Iowa Press, 2006), pp. 115–50.

14. Ginsberg notes that Whitman called New York "City of Orgies." Ginsberg continues about Whitman, "he projected physical affection even to the sexual or his phrase is 'physical affection and all that is latently implied' between citizen and citizen as part of the adhesiveness which would make us function together as a community rather than as a nation 'among the fabled damned of nations,' which was his phrase in the essay 'Democratic Vistas.'" (*SM*, 242). The actual phrase from "Democratic Vistas" runs slightly differently: Whitman suggests that the "solely materialistic bearings upon current life in the United States" could put "our modern civilization ... on the road to a destiny, a status, equivalent, in its real world, to that of the fabled damned" (*PW*, 460).

15. Allen Ginsberg, *Howl and Other Poems* (San Francisco, CA: City Lights, 1956). Further references appear in the text as *H*.

16. Might one see the unforgettable "waving" of "genitals and manuscripts" as an updating of the more decorous, though purportedly immediate, transmission of literary culture in both "Crossing Brooklyn Ferry" and "Song of Myself"?

17. William Blake, another of Ginsberg's heroes, would call these "mind-forged manacles."

6

CALEB CRAIN

The early literature of New York's moneyed class

Because a June thunderstorm had washed out the railroad tracks ahead, the pleasure party would not be able to reach Saratoga that evening. Fortunately, a stone's throw from the stalled train was a hotel. It looked improbably grand, but the travelers – Harry Masters; his wife, Clara; and their friend Edward Ashburner – decided to stay there for the night. They were going to be roughing it. Despite the eight columns in the hotel's portico, the bedding turned out to have bugs, and the other guests were not the sort of people Harry and Clara Masters socialized with back in the city.

Ashburner, who was from England, was still learning the customs of the American leisure class. During dinner he observed a new one. All the guests ate at a common table, and in order to shut out the diners not of "our set," Harry and Clara spoke French. They spoke it rather freely, in fact – so freely that a man across the table began to stare. Ashburner was afraid that the staring man spoke French too and didn't like what he was hearing. But then the man ate some pound cake and cheese, together, and Ashburner knew they were safe.

"Oh, that's nothing," said Harry, when told of Ashburner's fear and how it had been dispelled. "Did you never, when you were on the lakes, see them eat ham and molasses?"[1]

So went the class war in mid-nineteenth-century New York. If you live in dread that the syrup will trickle over and contaminate the bacon, now you know why.

Harry, Clara, and Edward are fictional characters created by a writer named Charles Astor Bristed in 1850. Two years earlier, Bristed had inherited a Manhattan house, ninety city lots, and a country seat from his grandfather, John Jacob Astor, at his death the richest man in America. In other words, Bristed didn't write for money. He wrote because he wanted to record for posterity (or at any rate for the English, who doubted) that in New York there existed "a set of exquisites – daintily-arrayed men, who spend half their income on their persons, and shrink from the touch of a woolen glove." The word *metrosexual* had not yet been invented, but Bristed did have a name for the men and women he was describing. He called them the "upper ten thousand" – a phrase coined in 1844 by another chronicler of New York high society, Nathaniel Parker Willis. Bristed qualified the term, because he found it a bit too inclusive. Actually, he explained, "the people so designated are hardly as many hundreds."[2]

He was being snooty. But it was an important part of the myth of early America that its rich were puny in numbers and insignificant in the broader scheme of things. "In America there are but few wealthy persons," the French nobleman and amateur sociologist Alexis de Tocqueville wrote in 1835, adding that "In America most of the rich men were formerly poor." Even Herman Melville, who took few of America's myths about itself for granted, wrote in his 1852 novel *Pierre* that "In our cities families rise and burst like bubbles in a vat."[3]

For more than a century historians agreed. But in the late 1960s, when flattering generalizations about American equality came in for vigorous disrespect, a historian named Edward Pessen decided to sift through New York City's tax assessment records to find out if wealth had in fact been as evenly distributed and as unstable as Tocqueville thought. He discovered, among other things, that New York City had had approximately 113 millionaires in 1845.[4] And he rediscovered Bristed's world, in which wealthy New Yorkers were dyeing their mustaches and elaborating rules about cocktails while Henry James was still in short pants.

In his 1973 book *Riches, Class, and Power before the Civil War*, Pessen titled his chapters with Tocqueville-discomfiting questions: "Were There Truly Rich Americans in the 'Era of the Common Man'?", "Were Rich Americans ... Self-Made Men?", "Did Fortunes Rise and Fall Mercurially During the 'Age of Fluidity'?", and "Equality of Opportunity?" Yes, no, no, and forget about it, he answered, dourly and statistically. Furthermore, compared to their contemporaries, the rich of 1845 were not just rich but oppressively, disproportionately rich. By Pessen's reckoning, the top 1% of New York families then owned half the city's wealth. (For comparison's sake, consider that in 2004 the top 1% of American households owned 34% of the nation's wealth.) Despite Tocqueville's belief that "wealth circulates with inconceivable rapidity" in America, when Pessen checked the backgrounds of wealthy New Yorkers of 1828 and 1845, he found that 95% had been born to "rich and/or eminent" parents. In 1982, a scholar named Frederic Cople Jaher attempted to debunk Pessen, but his not altogether convincing analysis of the "vintage of fortune" in New York City in 1828 and 1856–57 only lowered the proportion of wealth that was inherited to 70%. In short, the way Charles Astor Bristed came into his money was the rule not the exception.[5]

*

New Yorkers of the day would not have been terrifically surprised to learn any of this; citizens were then fascinated by socioeconomic extremes and read about them avidly. The trend had begun in the 1830s, when a new breed of newspapers, known as the "penny press," sought to win a mass readership with lower prices and a lower moral tone. In search of cheap laughs, the *New York Sun*, the *New York Transcript*, and the *New York Herald* sent reporters to the police courts to collect funny things said by drunks, and in search of cheap thrills they published verbatim the transcripts of murder trials. In particularly sensational cases, such as that of Helen Jewett, a prostitute killed with a hatchet in 1836, the papers competed so fiercely to add detail that, almost incidentally, they invented investigative journalism – the practice of going out to find stories instead of waiting for them at one's desk.[6] Edgar A. Poe took an interest in the 1841 murder of Mary Rogers, an attractive twenty-year-old who sold cigars in downtown Manhattan. He transposed the case to Paris, renamed the victim "Marie Rogêt," and set his fictional creation C. Auguste Dupin, the first detective in literature, to solve the fictional case – which Poe carefully distinguished, in a metaphysical postscript, from the real one.[7]

In Britain and Europe, writers known today as flâneurs (French for "strollers") combed cities for urban vignettes – humorous, outrageous, or poignant – and in America, too, such essays appeared in relatively sophisticated magazines such as the *Knickerbocker* as early as the 1830s. Poe hated the *Knickerbocker* for its tame and genteel conservatism – of its editor he was to write that "an apple, in fact, or a pumpkin, has more angles" – and though he himself sometimes wrote as a New York flâneur, he questioned the premises of the genre in his 1840 story "The Man of the Crowd," in which the wish to find meaning in urban flotsam leads to a wild goose chase and the brink of a psychological abyss.[8]

The New York slice of life survived Poe's analysis, however, to be taken up by a very different literary genius, Charles Dickens, who visited the city in 1842. In *American Notes*, Dickens described fiddling and tambourine-playing at a mixed-race dance hall and squalor in a slum district known as Five Points. Taking a dim view of the young democracy, the novelist noted that swine ran free in the city. "He is in every respect a republican pig," Dickens wrote of a representative porker, "going wherever he pleases, and mingling with the best society, on an equal, if not superior footing." New Yorkers were appalled and mesmerized.[9]

Despite Dickens's pioneering example, however, down-and-out New York did not really come into its literary own until 1848. In February of that year, Benjamin A. Baker's play *A Glance at New York* introduced the character of Mose, a butcher and volunteer fireman who spoke in dialect, brawled readily, saved abandoned babies, and enjoyed minstrel songs (see *Figure 4* on p. 50). "The fire-boys may be a little rough outside, but they're all right here," Mose told the audience, touching his hand to his heart. New Yorkers loved him. Not only did *A Glance at New York* have a long run and more than a dozen sequels, but Mose leapt into American folk-lore.[10] That same winter, a journalist and former sailor named Edward Z. C. Judson, who called himself Ned Buntline, began to write and publish a novel titled *The Mysteries and Miseries of New York*. Mose appears in it, though his girlfriend, Lize, has a larger role, as a big-fisted thief with a soft heart. Buntline also borrows con men from Baker's play, the dance-hall and slum visited by Dickens, and the murdered cigar girl fictional-ized by Poe. Though at least one scholar has rightly called *Mysteries and Miseries* "a remarkably bad novel," it's a treasury of slang ("You look as if you'd just been dragged through a sick Frenchman," one character says to another, upon recognizing his hangover) and can still offer vulgar read-erly pleasures.[11] Its revelations of criminal life were plundered in turn by a third writer, George G. Foster, in the summer of 1848, for a series of *New York Tribune* vignettes collected as *New York in Slices, by an Experienced Carver* and soon followed up by a similar collection, *New York by Gas-Light, with Here and There a Streak of Sunshine*. Less cheery than Baker's play and less sentimental than Judson's novel, Foster's sketches offer jour-nalistic precision: the cries of waiters in cheap restaurants ("biledamand cabbage shillin, ricepudn sixpnce, eighteen-pence – at the barf you please – lobstaucensammingnumberfour – yes sir!"), what prostitutes really think of their profession ("I feel as if I ought to be pretty well satisfied with the way I have managed to get on in the world"), and the dark truth about couples who go to ice-cream parlors ("They are evidently man and wife – though not each other's!").[12]

The explosion of interest in New York's proletariat and lumpenproletar-iat was to touch writers of all kinds. When Walt Whitman self-published his book *Leaves of Grass* in 1855, the look that he affected in the frontis-piece – a work shirt with the collar open, a broad-brimmed hat, and a rakish sidways slouch – owed something to Mose (see *Figure 6*, p. 77). Whitman's reference to "foofoos" ("Washes and razors for foofoos ... for me freckles and a bristling beard") may puzzle readers today, but New Yorkers of his time would have known the word from *A Glance at New York*:

GEORGE. What's foo-foos?
MOSE. Why, foo-foos is outsiders, and outsiders is foo-foos.
GEORGE. I'm as wise now as ever.
MOSE. Well, as you're a greenhorn, I'll enlightin you. A foo-foo, or outsider, is
    a chap wot can't come de big figure.[13]

Herman Melville seems to have painted from Judson's and Foster's palette in the second half of his novel *Pierre*, when the hero takes two young women to an unnamed metropolis and they land on their first night in a police station full of prostitutes, drunks, and thieves. And though Melville shifted the setting from Broadway to a steamboat, he devoted an entire novel to one of the city's most colorful criminals, the Confidence Man, who first began asking citizens to trust him with their watches in 1847 and was given his name by the *New York Herald* as early as 1848.[14]

New York low life became a literary staple. Readers with a taste for it could turn to new, more subjective guides to the city like Joel H. Ross's *What I Saw in New-York* (1851) or William M. Bobo's *Glimpses of New-York City* (1852) and later to such compendia as Matthew Hale Smith's *Sunshine and Shadow in New York* (1868; see *Figure 9*) and James Dabney McCabe's *Lights and Shadows of New York Life* (1872). Urban crowding was satirized in Thomas Butler Gunn's *The Physiology of New York Boarding-Houses* (1857), and urban childhood was sentimentalized in Solon Robinson's *Hot Corn: Life Scenes in New York Illustrated* (1854) and Charles Loring Brace's *The Dangerous Classes of New York* (1872).[15] In the twentieth and twenty-first centuries, the genre has been studied by such scholars as Hans Bergmann, David Reynolds, Karen Halttunen, John F. Kasson, William Chapman Sharpe, Dell Upton, and Luc Sante, and thanks to Martin Scorsese's film *Gangs of New York* (2002), the image of the city projected in it has become widely known.[16]

But as it happens, the literature of New York's overclass in the decades before the Civil War was nearly as prolific as that of its underclass, though it is less well known. It was for the most part written by the rich themselves, and perhaps because of that, the touch of these writers was lighter. They were, however, just as prodigal with detail.

Bristed was an insider. At his death, one obituarist noted that he had "made himself a sort of champion of the cultivated minority of his countrymen." Another remarked that "It was pleasant to see him with his horses." He did not write about his world to share it with the poor and the middle classes. He wrote because he liked to show off.[17]

Like most people who write about their own class, Bristed gestured toward critique and reform. But in his case, the gestures were exceptionally mild. "Sometimes you will see *slices* of lemon put into a cobbler – nothing can be more destructive; avoid everything but the yellow peel," he cautioned those who aspired to mix his favorite drink, the sherry cobbler.[18]

It does not seem to have occurred to Bristed that readers who happened to lack a trust fund might find his tone off-putting. "There is something

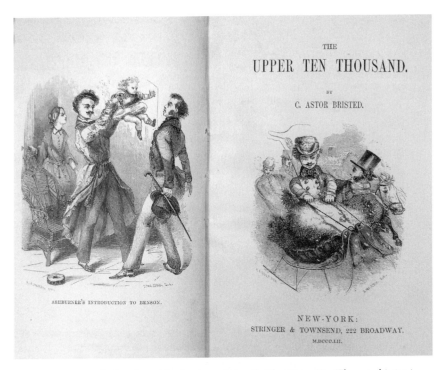

Figure 8: Frontispiece from Charles Astor Bristed's *The Upper Ten Thousand* (1852). Bristed, the heir to a New York real-estate fortune, drew his fictional self-portrait in the character of Harry Masters, who here shows off his son to an English visitor. "Isn't he a beauty?" Masters boasts. "Isn't he a whole team and one horse extra?" Bristed, for his part, seems even prouder of what Masters is wearing: an orange cashmere and rose silk dressing gown, tied with "a tasselled cord that looked like a very superior style of bell-pull."

peculiarly disagreeable in an American crowd," he complained, when Masters and Ashburner visited a racetrack, "from the fact that no class has any distinctive dress. The gentleman and the workingman, or the 'loafer,' wear clothes of the same kind, only in one case they are new and clean, in the other, old and dirty." It is *so* vexing of the poor to resist wearing something nicely distinctive, like sackcloth. Bristed's compassionless conservatism is strangely refreshing, if you are in the mood to indulge a fantasy identification with socioeconomic evil. And the sherry cobbler does sound nice. A sugared lemon peel, half a cup of pounded ice, and dark sherry. Shake in a tumbler and drink through a straw, *only* on a hot summer day. According to Bristed, three glasses an hour "will be enough."[19]

For a recognizably modern ambivalence toward the upper class, a reader must turn to the writer who invented the concept of the upper ten thousand, Nathaniel Parker Willis. The ambivalence may not at first be apparent,

Figure 9: Frontispiece from Matthew Hale Smith's *Sunshine and Shadow in New York* (1868). Smith's compendium treats such varied subjects as politics, religion, publishing, crime, and entertainment. Smith views New York as a city of extremes: its religious philanthropists are the world's finest, but at the same time a "worse population than can be found in New York does not inhabit the globe." Smith treats his readers to detailed discussions of high and low.

because Willis had a weakness for the trappings of wealth at their most fey. "Unmitigated new hat is truly frightful," he would advise a hypothetical college boy, while impersonating a decadent uncle. "Short hair on a young man looks to me madhousey. Ugh! Straight or curly, leave it long enough to make a bootlace for a lady! And see that it looks threadable by slight fingers." As for shoes: "Patent leather, of course, till death."[20]

But there was a serious mind beneath the camp and frippery. Or, as Willis put it, addressing himself in the voice of one of his friends, "Ah, mi-boy! that pious infancy of yours! It oozes through the after crust of your manhood in drops of poetry!" Willis was a child of New England, the eldest son of a strict Congregationalist deacon and his indulgent wife. The deacon had edited a religious newspaper in Boston, and he and his wife somehow endowed their offspring with all the genetic and cultural equipment necessary for ruthless ascent into New York literary celebrity.[21]

In capturing the attention of high society, the Willis siblings were formidable. Nathaniel founded and edited the *Home Journal*, ancestor to today's *Town and Country*. His brother Richard composed "It Came Upon a Midnight Clear" and became one of the city's most respected music critics. Sister Sara, under the name Fanny Fern, became the highest-paid newspaper columnist in America.[22] And brother Edward, after serving a prison sentence in Ohio for rape, served briefly as publicist and agent for Lola Montez, dancer and femme fatale. (The details are murky, but Edward was fired either because he embezzled or because he lapsed into family habits and wrote an unauthorized account of his employer for the *New York Herald*. After Montez recovered her temper, she hired him back. And then she fired him again.[23])

High society's respect, by contrast, often eluded the Willises. It didn't help that they quarreled with one another. After Nathaniel discouraged his sister's literary ambitions, she took revenge by caricaturing him in her autobiographical novel *Ruth Hall*. When the heroine is widowed, her brother frets that in her mourning she has given in too easily to a bad hair day. No one had any trouble recognizing Nathaniel. "Fashion is his God," another character says of him. "Sorrow in satin he can sympathize with, but sorrow in rags is too plebeian for his exquisite organization."[24]

This was accurate. Fashion was Nathaniel's god. But he wrote about it with more insight, nimbleness, and edge than any of his contemporaries. On a city without an opera: "Like a saloon without a mirror." On the depreciation of courtesy in New York: "Politeness has gradually grown to be a sign of a man in want of money." On a sudden vogue for a fabric still posh today: "'*She had on a real Cashmere*' would be sweeter, to a number of ladies, as a mention when absent, than 'she had a beautiful expression about her mouth,' or 'she had such loveable manners,' or 'she is always trying to make somebody happier.'"[25]

For all his talent, Willis never wrote a solid book. The need to earn a living fettered him to magazine ephemera, a fate he accepted with a pose of tragic resignation: "The hot needle through the eye of the goldfinch betters his singing, they say." After he abandoned sacred poetry in early youth,

Willis's ambition took a conventionally serious form only once, in a public lecture on fashion at the Broadway Tabernacle in 1844. In the lecture, Willis made explicit his peculiar, and peculiarly democratic, understanding of fashion, which he called an "inner republic."[26]

He began by defining fashion as "a position in society" that different cultures awarded to different traits. In France, it went to intellectual and artistic achievement; in England, to beauty and cocksureness. In both countries, according to Willis, the "first principle" of fashion was "rebellion against unnatural authority," because fashion forced the ruling class to acknowledge people of merit born outside it. The particular acknowledgment that he had in mind was sexual, although he didn't say so explicitly. Through fashion – that is, through a selection of spouses prompted by fashion – the English upper class ensured that their children would be attractive and bold, and the French, that theirs would be intelligent. Although the principle of fashion might be revolutionary, its effect was conservative, by a kind of sexual engrossment.

What did American fashion reward? "*Conspicuousness in expense,*" Willis wrote with dismay. (A few years later, he would identify New York as "*the point where money is spent most freely for pleasure.*") He hoped that this preference was temporary and that Americans could change it by force of will. But he feared that no one would bother to take the problem seriously. Like Willis himself, fashion seemed trifling to most people. He insisted it wasn't, because it determined which virtues the ruling class would welcome into their beds and thereby into the elite.[27]

Willis was an outsider. Nothing shows it so clearly as the frankness with which he analyzed how the insiders reproduced themselves. To observers who genuinely belonged to the elite, such a problem remained politely invisible. They found other issues much more urgent and alarming. It was, for example, a catastrophe that the standard New York brownstone was only 25 feet wide.

Because of it, New Yorkers could not throw parties in their home city as exquisite as those they threw in Paris, complained Régis de Trobriand, who knew whereof he spoke because he was a baron and was married to a daughter of the president of the Chemical Bank. Trobriand made his lament in the *Revue du nouveau-monde,* a biweekly journal that he edited and published in New York in 1849 and 1850. The French-language journal reprinted Lamartine's poetry and Sainte-Beuve's criticism, in the hope that Americans might come to know French culture directly rather than through "the deceitful veil of British lucubrations," as Trobriand put it. It also featured Trobriand's own commentary on New York high society.[28]

Given the miserable dimensions of a New York house, "one may guess what feeble resources are available to a host for assembling a dancing multitude inside it," Trobriand wrote. "He can only offer two or three rooms, with no passageway between them other than a narrow corridor, half of which is encroached upon by a staircase." Supper had to be served upstairs, and before a guest could make her formal entrée to a party, she had to climb as far as the third floor to deposit her coat. (Once she made the climb, however, she would discover a room where she could repair her toilette – a much-appreciated innovation that had not yet reached Paris, Trobriand admitted.) There was nowhere for the men to stand and talk, or sit and play cards. What was to be done? Fortunately, the baron was able to report that the revolution was *en marche*. Along Fifth Avenue a few altruistic New Yorkers had taken it upon themselves to build houses whose floorplans stretched across two, three, and in some cases four traditional lots.[29]

Not everyone recognized the tragedy of the "twenty-five-feet-front-and-take-off-your-things-in-the-third-story balls," as Willis called them. Bristed agreed that narrow buildings were "very inconvenient," but he saw a much graver threat to social order in the "foreign dances of luscious and familiar character" that were taking New York by storm – the polka, the redowa, and the schottisch. The polka, in particular, seemed to him as infectious and deleterious as a disease, and his dislike was widely shared. In fact the middle-aged rich men of 1850s New York hated the polka almost as consistently as they hated abolitionists. In his diary, the merchant George Templeton Strong denounced it as "a kind of insane Tartar jig performed to a disagreeable music of an uncivilized character." In the *Lorgnette*, another biweekly journal of New York high society, the satirist Donald G. Mitchell wrote that "I ... think it highly probable that the movement may have found its way into domestic arrangements, and the baby be lulled, the dumb waiter rise and fall, and the cook stove rotate – polka-wise."[30]

The polka was athletic. Sometimes a woman who danced it was obliged to borrow a gentleman's handkerchief to pat her neck dry. Sometimes the case was much worse. After "polking" with a Miss Friskin, who wore a green silk dress, Bristed's Harry Masters discovered that his white waistcoat, pants, and cravat "were all stained green, as if I had been playing with a gigantic butterfly." When Jonathan Slick, a Yankee hick invented by the novelist Ann S. Stephens, toured New York's high life, he saw a couple dance the polka and felt sure the woman had been ruined by the intimacy. "If the gal means to git married, her bread will be all dough again, arter this," Slick commented.[31]

Almost invariably, polka hatred was accompanied by a further regret, namely, that high society was not really fun for anyone but teenagers. Like the easily fatigued of every era, mature socialites protested that they went to parties to talk not to dance. Or rather, that's why they would go, if they did, but they didn't. According to Willis, a foreigner invited to a New York party was heard to exclaim, "Charming children! but where are the grown-up people?"[32]

In addressing this problem, there was not a surfeit of intellectual coherence. Some of the older men seem to have turned prickly because younger ones had sidelined them, and they vented their disgruntlement by deriding middle-aged women who tadpoled. In the *Lorgnette*, Mitchell sneered at women who, "grown a little anxious on the score of their own age, are very willing to commute the stock of years, by balancing the polka with a boy." Bristed concurred, and he argued, in a logic contorted by dudgeon, that since women acquired "world-knowledge" faster than men, equality of age between a man and a woman was in fact "virtual disproportion." Between a twenty-three-year-old woman and a twenty-three-year-old man, there was such an egregious disparity in emotional maturity that if they married, she would be tempted not only to despise him but also to "form a low of opinion of men, as men." Naturally this would lead to bankruptcy, early death, and season tickets to the opera.[33]

Bristed knew exactly what to do. Young men should be kept out of society until they acquired the mental wherewithal to dominate women. In the meantime the young women, Bristed generously conceded, could stay. Thus instead of parties where young men danced with middle-aged women, there would be parties where *middle-aged* men *talked* with *young* women. Now isn't that better? Before anyone spends too long wondering why Bristed thought so, it is worthwhile to consult George Templeton Strong's diary entry of April 13, 1852: "Much scandal afloat here touching our New York Society in Paris ... how Bristed keeps a grisette, and how Mrs. Bristed met the couple somewhere and the two ladies clapperclawed."[34]

As it happens, Willis also knew exactly what to do. According to him, middle-aged women weren't the problem. On the contrary, he exalted them. "The most delightful age of woman, in cultivated society, is ... when she is wise enough to be an adviser and counselor to a male friend, and yet attractive enough to awaken no less respect than admiration," he wrote. He was confident that the conversation of "married belles" would intellectualize the social gatherings now frittered away in carnal dancing, and so he urged them to rebel against the convention that retired women from society as soon as they were married – to resist "the re-podding of the once-shelled pea."[35]

When outraged husbands objected that Willis was encouraging immorality, he invited them to read an entomologist's description of the life cycle of the coccus:

> The males have wings, and, having no care for food, go and come as they please. The females have no wings, and live by suction of plants to which they fix themselves at an early period of their life and remain immovable till death. When impregnated, they spread their bodies over the eggs and so perish into a membrane, or egg, which the young ones break through and destroy, in coming into life.[36]

Did American wives have to share the fate of female scale insects?

According to family legend, when the Baron de Trobriand was nine years old, he and his classmate Baudelaire debated whether the sins they told in confessional were really kept secret. As a test, Trobriand volunteered to his confessor that he and some friends were planning to burn the school down. He was promptly expelled.[37] It would be pleasant to imagine that the incident decided Baudelaire's character, but at the time Baudelaire would have been four, which seems rather young for complicity, even in his case.

Whether the story is true or apocryphal, Trobriand grew up to be a person sophisticated about secrets and skeptical of pieties. (He also grew up to be brave: in the Civil War, he would command the Lafayette Guard, a militia of Franco-Americans, and would fight valiantly at Gettysburg.) In his column for the *Revue*, Trobriand agreed with Bristed, Mitchell, and Willis that New York society was overrun with the young. But his analysis went much further than theirs – so much further that he might qualify as the historical original of the amorous, mustache-twirling Frenchman of popular culture (cf., for example, Jacques, the bowling tutor who tried to estrange Marge Simpson from Homer).

In Europe, a party was a microcosm of the social world, Trobriand wrote. Every important kind of person could be found there, and a boy who attended in search of simple pleasures was soon challenged by complex ones, which inveigled him into a sentimental education. He met mature men he wished to emulate and mature women he wished to please. "La passion, c'est la vie," Trobriand proclaimed, and it was the romance of these new friendships that ripened boy into man.

Alas, "in America there is none of this," Trobriand continued, darkly. Parents sheltered their children from passion instead of prompting them to explore it. And they knew almost nothing about it themselves. Custom and a cycle of chores isolated mothers, and business-minded fathers thought socializing was ephemeral and silly.[38]

The result was the polka; society was insipid. A "*good* young man" might be satisfied by it, Trobriand supposed (here the reader must silently supply whatever the word for "ninny" is in French), but a passionate one would turn elsewhere. To a brothel, probably. If he could channel his thwarted passion into scholarship or politics, he might save his health and morals, but even then he would never develop the emotional richness that he would have in European society. In some unspecifiable, Jamesian way, he would remain stunted.

"Leave, cross the ocean; go spend a few years in Europe, and you will return from it men," Trobriand counseled the upper-class adolescent boys of America. But he wondered what would happen if they did. "Having become men, would they want to return?" he asked, anticipating by half a century the plot of *The Ambassadors*.[39]

In the meantime, on this side of the Atlantic, society would only improve if wives were allowed to indulge "the little passions that are, so to speak, the small change of the great ones." In Trobriand's opinion, it was "une injustice flagrante" that New Yorkers looked the other way when a girl flirted but refused to extend the same courtesy to a married woman. And while he was on the subject of passion, he had some advice for American husbands. Providing was not enough. What men gave their wives had to be "ennobled by that multitude of details in private life whose nuances are to the heart of women what tears of dew are to the calyx of flowers."[40]

Bristed of course objected: Trobriand's analysis was hopelessly French and largely immoral, and in marriage "if either party has a right to expect amusement of the other, it is the *man*."[41] So move to the provinces, Trobriand replied. There you will find all the stagnant domesticity and deference to male prerogative you desire. There the polka will not trouble you. Just bear in mind the verdict of the novelist Jules Sandeau: "There is nothing so odious as the race of small towns; it is the last degree of perversion and brutishness that a man living in society may come to."[42]

"I look in despairing bewilderment at my white gloves," the rich, young, bookish George Templeton Strong confided to his diary in 1846, after coming home from a tea party. "Confusion between the ego and the non-ego is embarrassing."[43]

The culture of wealth did not necessarily make those who lived in it happy or comfortable. Its best chroniclers, like Strong, are those who could see the existential chinks in the façade. While he was courting, Strong joked that he wished "there wasn't any such thing as money in the world, or that every one was comfortably supported by the state." He didn't really wish any such thing, but he worried that he wouldn't be able to afford the woman he fell in love with. He was a rising, successful lawyer, and his father was an established, successful lawyer, who would soon build him a large house on Gramercy Park. But the financial pressures on marriage were enormous. Rich young women went to rich young men, and the historian Sven Beckert has discovered that at least one credit agency reported on financially significant matches. When Bristed's fictional Englishman wondered aloud whether wealthy Americans married for money, his host told him, in a turn of phrase that evoked Mose the fireman, "They don't marry for anything else." For several years after his marriage, Strong's anxiety about money, if anything, increased. "Oh, for $100,000 – well invested!" he wrote in 1851. "A skillful operation resulting in an enormous profit with no risk has all the charm for me now of poetry or romance."[44]

The intersection of love and money made for "a sadness which can hardly be explained," according to George William Curtis, another keen inside observer of the mid-century elite. In his youth Curtis had seriously considered the socialism that Strong merely joked about. At Brook Farm, the Transcendentalist commune not far from Emerson's Concord, Curtis experienced "manure and dish-water" and debated utopian philosophy. Clothespins fell out of his pockets at the evening dances. He was said to have been so beautiful that boys and girls alike fell in love with him. He continued farming in Concord for a couple of years after he left the community, and in an accident he cut his hand. He carried the scar back to New York.[45]

It seems almost too perfect an emblem. No doubt there were many nights when the hand that Curtis had wounded in the service of idealism was worn inside a white glove like Strong's. *The Potiphar Papers*, Curtis's satire of high society, reads as if it had been written by that gloved hand and shared in its doubleness. In the fiction, each chapter of which is narrated by a different character, Curtis recorded the betrayals he saw among the wealthy, which were for the most part self-betrayals. Of the foppish, unemployed men too old to dance but not yet middle-aged, he wrote, "The seal of their shame is their own smile at their early dreams." Curtis wished to smile instead at the smilers. The humor doesn't quite come off. Despite his sarcasm, which is often cruel, his characters manage to be poignant. Mr. and Mrs. Potiphar feel bullied by the lifestyle that their social position obliges them to buy, but that is the least of their troubles. The worst is, neither of them has married for true love. They have compromised for the sake of money, and each turns now for comfort to a nostalgic fantasy of what might have been. Not even their disappointment is shared with each other – only with the reader. "I shall never be in love again," Mr. Potiphar soliloquizes, as he remembers the girl he didn't marry. Then he echoes the gospel of Mark, in a line that would have pleased Thoreau: "In getting my fortune I have lost my real life."[46]

NOTES

1. Charles Astor Bristed, *The Upper Ten Thousand* (New York: Stringer and Townsend, 1852), pp. 91–93.
2. Edward K. Spann, *The New Metropolis: New York City, 1840–1857* (New York: Columbia University Press, 1981), p. 208; Sven Beckert, *The Monied Metropolis: New York City and the Consolidation of the American Bourgeoisie, 1850–1896* (Cambridge: Cambridge University Press, 1993), p. 28; Bristed, *Upper Ten Thousand*, pp. 6, 271; Thomas N. Baker, *Sentiment & Celebrity: Nathaniel Parker Willis and the Trials of Literary Fame* (New York: Oxford University Press, 1999), p. 208 n. 40.
3. Alexis de Tocqueville, *Democracy in America*, trans. Henry Reeve, Francis Bowen, and Phillips Bradley (New York: Vintage, 1990), i, p. 52; Herman Melville, *Pierre; or, the Ambiguities* (Evanston and Chicago, IL: Northwestern University Press and the Newberry Library, 1971), p. 9.
4. Edward Pessen, *Riches, Class, and Power before the Civil War* (Lexington, MA: D. C. Heath, 1973), pp. vii–viii, 22.
5. *Ibid.*, pp. 35, 85; Edward N. Wolff, "Recent Trends in Household Wealth in the United States: Rising Debt and the Middle-Class Squeeze," Jerome Levy Economics Institute, Working Paper No. 502 (June 2007), www.levy.org/download.aspx?file=wp_502.pdf&pubid=929; Tocqueville, *Democracy in America*, 1, p. 51; Frederic Cople Jaher, *The Urban Establishment: Upper Strata in Boston, New York, Charleston, Chicago, and Los Angeles* (Urbana: University of Illinois Press, 1982), p. 202. Pessen and Jaher had to make many subjective judgments to compile their statistics. Because they made them slightly differently, comparing their results isn't straightforward. Pessen felt that he was able to determine the socioeconomic status of the parents of 90% of the individuals in his samples (those worth more than $100,000 in 1828 and more than $250,000 in 1845). Jaher only felt sure of parents' status in 64% of his 1828 sample (those worth more than $100,000) and 44% of his 1856–57 sample (worth more than $100,000). Jaher felt that in cases where he didn't know the parents' status, the parents were likely to have been poor. Pessen, by contrast, felt that the rags-to-riches ideology of the era would have tainted the evidence in the opposite direction, obscuring information about wealthy backgrounds. To come up with a statistic based on Jaher's data that is comparable to Pessen's 90% rate of inherited wealth, I added together the number of wealthy individuals in Jaher's 1828 and 1856–57 samples known to have come from wealthy backgrounds and divided it by all the wealthy individuals from those years whose backgrounds Jaher had been able to determine. (If I were to accept Jaher's premise that most of the wealthy whose backgrounds he could not determine were self-made men, I would have used as a denominator the total number of wealthy individuals in his samples for those years, and the resulting percentage would have been significantly lower than 70%.)
6. Hans Bergmann, *God in the Street: New York Writing from the Penny Press to Melville* (Philadelphia, PA: Temple University Press, 1995), pp. 19–40; Matthew Goodman, *The Sun and the Moon: The Remarkable True Account of Hoaxers, Showmen, Dueling Journalists, and Lunar Man-Bats in Nineteenth-Century New York* (New York: Basic Books, 2008), pp. 36–41; Andie Tucher, *Froth &*

Scum: *Truth, Beauty, Goodness, and the Ax Murder in America's First Mass Medium* (Chapel Hill: University of North Carolina Press, 1994), pp. 7–96; Patricia Cline Cohen, *The Murder of Helen Jewett: The Life and Death of a Prostitute in Nineteenth-Century New York* (New York: Knopf, 1998). For a survey of trial transcripts as a form of popular literature in Victorian America, see Caleb Crain, "In Search of Lost Crime: Bloated Bodies, Bigamous Love, and Other Literary Pleasures of the 19th-Century Trial Transcript," *Legal Affairs* 1:2 (July/August 2002): 28–33.

7. Amy Gilman Srebnick, *The Mysterious Death of Mary Rogers: Sex and Culture in Nineteenth-Century New York* (New York: Oxford University Press, 1995).

8. For accounts of New York flâneurs in the 1830s, see Bergmann, *God in the Street*, p. 63; Perry Miller, *The Raven and the Whale: The War of Words and Wits in the Era of Poe and Melville* (New York: Harcourt Brace, 1956), p. 162; and Edward L. Widmer, *Young America: The Flowering of Democracy in New York City* (New York: Oxford University Press, 1999), p. 96. Between them, Miller and Widmer offer a portrait of mid-nineteenth-century New York's literary infighting that will probably never be surpassed. (For a briefer account, see chapters 39–41 of Edwin G. Burrows and Mike Wallace, *Gotham: A History of New York City to 1898* [New York: Oxford University Press, 1999]). Edgar A. Poe, "Lewis Gaylord Clark," *The Literati of New York*, in *Essays and Reviews* (New York: Library of America, 1984), p. 1206. Edgar A. Poe, "The Man of the Crowd," in *Poetry and Tales* (New York: Library of America, 1984), pp. 388–96. For Poe as a flâneur, see Edgar A. Poe, "The Doings of Gotham," in *Writing New York: A Literary Anthology*, ed. Philip Lopate (New York: Library of America, 1998), pp. 91–106.

9. Charles Dickens, *American Notes*, in *Writing New York*, ed. Lopate, p. 58; Bergmann, *God in the Street*, pp. 115–24.

10. [Benjamin A. Baker], *A Glance at New York* (New York: Samuel French, n.d.), p. 20; Richard M. Dorson, "Mose the Far-Famed and World Renowned," *American Literature* 15:3 (Nov. 1943), pp. 288–300; Peter George Buckley, "To the Opera House: Culture and Society in New York City, 1820–1860" (unpublished Ph.D. thesis, State University of New York at Stony Brook, 1984), pp. 388–99; Constance Rourke, "The Comic Poet" (ch. 5), in *American Humor: A Study of National Character* (1931; rpt. Gainesville: Florida State University Press, 1986).

11. Buckley, "To the Opera House," pp. 431–68; Timothy J. Gilfoyle, *City of Eros: New York City, Prostitution, and the Commercialization of Sex, 1790–1920* (New York: Norton, 1992), pp. 144–48. The best edition of Judson's *Mysteries and Miseries* is Ned Buntline [Edward C. Judson], *Mysteries and Miseries of New York* (New York, 1848), which includes a glossary of "flash," or criminal slang, and a running commentary on opposition from real-life criminals that Judson believed his novel was exposing. The book is now rare, however, and for convenience I have drawn the quotation from a later, poorer edition that I happen to own, Ned Buntling [*sic*], *The Mysteries of New York* (London: Milner & Company, n.d.), p. 43.

12. George G. Foster, *New York by Gas-Light, and Other Urban Sketches*, ed. Stuart M. Blumin (1850; rpt. Berkeley: University of California Press, 1990), pp. 37, 214, 103, 134; Bergmann, *God in the Street*, pp. 58–59.

13. Bergmann, *God in the Street*, pp. 69–90; Walt Whitman, "Leaves of Grass" (1855), in *Complete Poetry and Collected Prose* (New York: Library of America, 1982), p. 48; Benjamin A. Baker, *A Glance at New York*, p. 16.

14. Melville, *Pierre; or, the Ambiguities*; Melville, *The Confidence-Man, His Masquerade* (1857; Evanston, IL: Northwestern University Press and Newberry Library, 1984); Bergmann, *God in the Street*, pp. 181–220; Michael S. Reynolds, "The Prototype for Melville's Confidence-Man," *PMLA* 86 (1971): 1009–13; Caleb Crain, "The Courtship of Henry Wikoff; or, a Spinster's Apprehensions," *American Literary History* 18:4 (2006): 679, 690 n. 6.

15. Joel H. Ross, *What I Saw in New-York; or, a Bird's Eye View of City Life* (Auburn, NY: Derby and Miller, 1851); [William M. Bobo], *Glimpses of New-York City, by a South Carolinian, (Who Had Nothing Else to Do)* (Charleston, SC: J. J. McCarter, 1852); Matthew Hale Smith, *Sunshine and Shadow in New York* (Hartford, CT: J. B. Burr, 1868); James D. McCabe, *Lights and Shadows of New York Life; or, the Sights and Sensations of the Great City* (Philadelphia, PA: National Publishing Company, 1872); Thomas Gunn, *The Physiology of New York Boarding-Houses* (1857; rpt. New Brunswick, NJ: Rutgers University Press, 2009); Solon Robinson, *Hot Corn: Life Scenes in New York Illustrated* (New York: Dewitt and Davenport, 1854); Charles Loring Brace, *The Dangerous Classes of New York, and Twenty Years' Work among Them* (New York: Wynkoop and Hallenbeck, 1872).

16. Bergmann, *God in the Street*; David Reynolds, *Beneath the American Renaissance: The Subversive Imagination in the Age of Emerson and Melville* (New York: Knopf, 1988); Karen Halttunen, *Confidence Men and Painted Women: A Study of Middle-Class Culture in America, 1830–1870* (New Haven, CT: Yale University Press, 1982); John F. Kasson, *Rudeness & Civility: Manners in Nineteenth-Century Urban America* (New York: Hill & Wang, 1990); William Chapman Sharpe, *New York Nocturne: The City After Dark in Literature, Painting, and Photography, 1850–1950* (Princeton, NJ: Princeton University Press, 2008); Dell Upton, *Another City: Urban Life and Urban Spaces in the New American Republic* (New Haven, CT: Yale University Press, 2008); Luc Sante, *Low Life: Lures and Snares of Old New York* (New York: Farrar, Straus & Giroux, 1991).

17. "The Late Charles Astor Bristed," *New York Times* (January 16, 1874): 4; M. E. W. S[herwood], "Charles Astor Bristed," *Galaxy* 17 (April 1874): 545–46.

18. Bristed, *Upper Ten Thousand*, p. 67.

19. *Ibid.*, pp. 227, 68.

20. Nathaniel Parker Willis, *Fun-Jottings; or, Laughs I Have Taken a Pen To* (New York: Scribner, 1853), p. 343; Nathaniel Parker Willis, *Dashes at Life with a Free Pencil* (New York: J. S. Redfield, 1845), p. 19.

21. Nathaniel Parker Willis, *The Rag-Bag: A Collection of Ephemera* (New York: Scribner, 1855), p. 315; Thomas N. Baker, *Sentiment & Celebrity*, pp. 17–18.

22. Fanny Fern [Sara Payson Willis], *"Ruth Hall" and Other Writings*, ed. Joyce W. Warren (New Brunswick, NJ: Rutgers University Press, 1986), p. xviii.

23. This is my interpretation of an ambiguous series of articles by and about Montez and Edward Willis that appeared in the *New York Herald* between December 25,

1851 and January 15, 1852. See also Thomas N. Baker, *Sentiment & Celebrity*, pp. 126, 212 n. 18.

24. Fern, *"Ruth Hall" and Other Writings*, pp. 58, 207.
25. Willis, *Rag-Bag*, p. 343; Nathaniel Parker Willis, *Hurry-Graphs; or, Sketches of Scenery, Celebrities and Society, Taken from Life* (New York: Scribner, 1851), pp. 298, 332.
26. Nathaniel Parker Willis, *Rural Letters and Other Records of Thought at Leisure* (Auburn, NY: Alden and Beardsley, 1856), p. viii; Thomas N. Baker, *Sentiment & Celebrity*, p. 98; Nathaniel Parker Willis, *Lecture on Fashion: Delivered before the New York Lyceum* (New York: Mirror Library, 1844), p. 12.
27. Willis, *Lecture on Fashion*, pp. 3, 9; Willis, *Rag-Bag*, p. 45.
28. M. E. W. Sherwood, "Gen. de Trobriand's Romantic Life," *New York Times* (August 14, 1897); Robert D. Bohanan, "Régis Dénis de Trobriand," *American National Biography Online*, February 2000, www.anb.org/articles/05/05–00182. html; Marie Caroline Post, *Life and Memoirs of Comte Régis de Trobriand, Major-General in the Army of the United States, by His Daughter* (New York: E. P. Dutton, 1910); Régis de Trobriand, "La Revue du nouveau-monde," *Revue du nouveau-monde* 1: 2 (my translation).
29. Régis de Trobriand, "Les Bals de New-York, premier article (Salons et soupers)," *Revue du nouveau-monde* 2: 8.
30. Willis, *Rag-Bag*, p. 42; Bristed, *Upper Ten Thousand*, p. 43; Charles Astor Bristed, "New York Society and the Writers Thereon," *The Literary World* 6 (March 23, 1850): 296; George Templeton Strong, *The Diary of George Templeton Strong*, ed. Allan Nevins & Milton Halsey Thomas (New York: Macmillan, 1952), i, p. 269; Donald G. Mitchell (pseudo. "John Timon"), *The Lorgnette: or, Studies of the Town, by an Opera Goer* (New York: Stringer & Townsend, 1850), ii, p. 18.
31. Mitchell, *Lorgnette*, i, p. 57; Bristed, *Upper Ten Thousand*, p. 219; Ann S. Stephens, *High Life in New York, by Jonathan Slick* (New York: Bunce & Brother, 1854), p. 65.
32. Willis, *Hurry-Graphs*, p. 270.
33. Mitchell, *Lorgnette*, i, pp. 30, 58; Bristed, "New York Society," pp. 296–97.
34. Strong, *Diary*, ii, p. 90.
35. Willis, *Hurry-Graphs*, p. 270; Willis, *Rag-Bag*, p. 62.
36. Willis, *Hurry-Graphs*, p. 272.
37. Post, *Life and Memoirs of Comte Régis de Trobriand*, p. 50.
38. Régis de Trobriand, "Les Bals de New-York. Deuxième article. Les Hommes," *Revue du nouveau-monde* 2: 66, 68.
39. Trobriand, "Les Bals de New-York," *Revue du nouveau-monde* 2: 70.
40. Régis de Trobriand, "Les Bals de New-York. Troisième article. Les Femmes," *Revue du nouveau-monde* 2: 137, 132.
41. Bristed, "New York Society," p. 414.
42. Régis de Trobriand, "La Société française à propos de la société de New-York," *Revue du nouveau-monde* 3: 125.
43. Strong, *Diary*, i, p. 273.
44. Strong, *Diary*, i, p. 264; Beckert, *Monied Metropolis*, p. 34; Bristed, *Upper Ten Thousand*, p. 119; Strong, *Diary*, ii, p. 67.

45. George William Curtis, *The Potiphar Papers* (New York: Harper & Brothers, 1856), p. 15; Henry W. Sams, *Autobiography of Brook Farm* (Englewood Cliffs, NJ: Prentice-Hall, 1958), pp. 134, 229, 241; John W. Chadwick, "Recollections of George William Curtis," *Harper's* 86 (February 1893): 469–70.

46. Curtis, *The Potiphar Papers*, pp. 16, 94.

7

MARTHA NADELL

Writing Brooklyn

The child is already born, and is now living, stout and healthy, who will see Brooklyn numbering one million inhabitants! Its situation for grandeur, beauty, and salubrity is unsurpassed probably on the whole surface of the globe; and its destiny is to be among the most famed and choice of the half dozen of the leading cities of the world. And all this, doubtless, before the close of the present century.

Walt Whitman, "Brooklyniana: No. 17" (1862)

Crowds of men and women attired in the usual costumes, how curious
   you are to me!
On the ferry-boats the hundred that cross, returning home, are more
   curious than you suppose,
And you that shall cross from shore to shore years hence are more to me,
   and more in my meditations, than you might suppose!

Walt Whitman, "Crossing Brooklyn Ferry" (1860)

In an 1862 article in the *Brooklyn Standard*, Walt Whitman imagined, less than four decades hence, Brooklyn's prominence among the cities of the world. At the time of his writing, Brooklyn was the United States' third largest city. Home to more than 260,000 people, Brooklyn rivaled New York, its neighbor across the East River, in size, industry, and population. Residents lived and worked on densely populated streets designed in 1839 as a grid; they rode the numerous ferries that daily crossed the East River. In an earlier article in the six-month series entitled "Brooklyniana," Whitman envisioned among future generations a widespread interest in the narratives of Brooklyn's diverse inhabitants, their stories of daily life, "personal chronicles and gossip," and most of all their "authentic reminiscences" and "memoirs" of urban life. Whitman was prescient.[1] Although it is no longer its own city – the consolidation into Greater New York City occurred in 1898 – Brooklyn's inhabitants and landscape are a recognizable and indeed iconic element of American arts and letters. Yet although Whitman foresaw the prevalence of Brooklyn memoirs, he did not anticipate the range and complexity of Brooklyn's literary history, one that both complements and complicates that of New York City as whole.

It is to another of Whitman's works that we must turn for the contours of Brooklyn writing of the twentieth and twenty-first centuries. In "Crossing Brooklyn Ferry," Whitman contemplates the daily commuters between Brooklyn and New York City, alternately finding kinship with and sensing distance from his fellow ferry-riders. He connects this urban phenomenon – the encounter with the nameless figures in a crowd – with the "flood-tide" and "ebb-tide" of the East River, the "tall masts of Manhatta" and the "beautiful hills of Brooklyn."[2] Indeed, in linking the cityscapes to their inhabitants and in distinguishing them from each other, he anticipates the emergence of the literal *topoi* of Brooklyn – its bridges and tunnels, its neighborhoods and streets, its buildings and parks – as its literary *topoi*. For twentieth- and twenty-first-century Brooklyn writers, the borough's material landscape becomes a figurative one. Through a number of genres – the coming-of-age novel, the crime tale, and the memoir – Brooklyn becomes a site for meditations on the language befitting modern urban life; on the contrast between an imagined New York cosmopolitanism and an ostensibly authentic ethnic, working-class, or religious provincialism; on the spatial and temporal construction of collective and individual identity; on the figuration of memory in the sights, smells, and sounds of the street; and on the physical and figurative cartography of social inclusion and exclusion.

The most familiar site in the literary history of Brooklyn is, of course, the Brooklyn Bridge (see *Figure 10*). Indeed, the bridge is one of the most iconic landmarks of New York and the United States as a whole. As the work of Alan Trachtenberg and Richard Haw reminds us, the Brooklyn Bridge has a cultural history all its own.[3] It not only appears throughout American arts and letters but also weaves through the print and visual culture of the United States and other countries. In the 1920s and 1930s, it was a favorite subject for modernist writers such as Hart Crane, Frederico García Lorca, John Dos Passos, and others. Phillip Lopate argues that it is the "mother of a local modernism," though many of these writers loosen the bridge from its Brooklyn moorings.[4] In *The Bridge* (1930), Hart Crane writes of the "harp and altar," affirming that its "curveship lend[s] a myth to God."[5] For him the bridge is more than the means of travel between Brooklyn and Manhattan; it is a technological and spiritual wonder that connects all of America, its past, and its future. Vladimir Mayakovsky juxtaposes the physical structure of the bridge – its "steel mile" and "rigorous calculation of bolts and steel" – against the generalized "shopkeeper," the "hungry," the "unemployed."[6] Charles Reznikoff's account of the bridge is brief – "In a cloud bones of steel" – and strips the structure of its anchor in urban space.[7] In "The Brooklyn

Figure 10: This photograph shows the pedestrian walkway on the Brooklyn Bridge, ca. 1898. What the poet Vladimir Mayakovsky would describe as the bridge's "rigorous calculation of bolts and steel" made it a favorite subject for modernist writers. The poet Hart Crane had rooms at 110 Columbia Heights in Brooklyn, the same rooms from which Washington Roebling supervised the bridge's construction as chief engineer. Crane begins the final section of *The Bridge* (1930) by invoking the technological wonder of the bridge: "Through the bound cable strands, the arching path / Upward, veering with light, the flight of strings, – / Taut miles of shuttling moonlight syncopate / The whispered rush, telepathy of wires."

Bridge Blues" (1956), Jack Kerouac roots the span in "Brooklyn in [Thomas] Wolfe's redbrick jungle," but after moving across the "bolts of the beams in the bridge steel," the poet reaches Spain rather than Manhattan. In Marianne Moore's "Granite and Steel" (1966), the bridge is a "climactic ornament, a double rainbow," created out of the "German tenacity" of its designer.

Other works deploy the bridge in a different way. Rather than concentrate on the beauty of its Gothic arches and the meshing of its diagonal suspenders and vertical stays, they firmly root it in its function as means of traversing the literal and metaphorical span that separates Brooklyn from Manhattan. Picture one of the final scenes in one of Brooklyn's iconic films, *Saturday Night Fever* (1977). As the camera hovers, a car carrying a mattress and Tony Manero's love interest speeds over the East River, moving literally from Brooklyn to Manhattan and figuratively from an ethnic, working-class community to a sophisticated life of art, or so the characters hope. This scene echoes those in numerous works, in which the bridge, because of its distinct structure and physical position in the East River, becomes a passage not only across space but also through time, social position, or aesthetic experience. In his *Sketches of Life* (1982), Louis Mumford walks the bridge and makes meaning out of its vistas on to Manhattan: "Here was my city, immense, overpowering, flooded with energy and light ... The world, at that moment, opened before me, challenging me, beckoning me, demanding something of me that it would take more than a lifetime to give, but raising all my energies by its own vivid promise to a higher pitch."[8] The walk across the bridge in Colson Whitehead's *The Colossus of New York* (2003), in contrast, ends in Manhattan with an absorption into the anonymity of the urban crowd.[9]

If the Brooklyn Bridge and other sites, such as Coney Island and Ebbets Field, the former home of baseball's Dodgers, are visually recognizable Brooklyn icons that stand in literature for a negotiation between literal place and social position, Brooklyn's neighborhoods, streets, and subways – all lines, of a sort, that spatially structure the borough – are equally important literary *topoi*. From Claude McKay's references to the African American residents around Myrtle Avenue in *Home to Harlem* (1928) to James Agee's 1939 tour of Flatbush, Midwood, Clinton Hill, and neighborhoods in *Brooklyn Is* (2005) to Jonathan Lethem's exploration of Gowanus cum Boerum Hill in the 1970s in *The Fortress of Solitude* (2003), the borough's cartography has become an essential element of its literary landscape.

The geography and architecture of the neighborhoods in which Eastern European, Jewish immigrants settled were the subject of a number of 1930s texts. Henry Roth's *Call It Sleep* (1935) is a modernist encounter with the street. The novel, set in Brownsville, or, as Roth writes in the immigrant vernacular, "Bronzeville," moves beyond the classic tale of immigrant arrival in New York into a family drama in multilingual experimental prose. It contrasts the language of the home (Yiddish rendered in an elevated English) and the broken English of the street. The Brooklyn street on which David lives and yet which he cannot identify in English – "Boddeh Street," "Body Street," "Pother," "Barhdee" – stands for the disruption and alienation of the new arrival.[10]

In his trilogy of Brooklyn novels, *Summer in Williamsburg* (1934), *Homage to Blenholt* (1936), and *Low Company* (1937), Daniel Fuchs considers the community's enmeshment in its physical environs. His characters rarely venture out of Williamsburg or Neptune (Brighton) Beach. While the novel is thus suggestive of a Brooklyn provincialism, the characters reveal themselves to be readers of the intricacies of social interaction in the topography of the area. In *Summer in Williamsburg*, the characters search for the reasons for a man's suicide:

If you would really discover the reason, you must pick Williamsburg to pieces until you have them all spread out on your table before you, a dictionary of Williamsburg. And then select. Pick and discard.[11]

Fuchs's "dictionary" suggests the complexity of the connections between the apartment buildings and streets and their denizens. Does the cityscape define its residents or is it the other way around? *Homage to Blenholt* approaches the interrelation of space and identity in a different way. The novel revolves around the residents of a Williamsburg apartment building, a comic cast of characters including the protagonist Max, a "schlemiel," his girlfriend Ruth, and an "amateur etymologist of distinction" named Mendel Munves. Within this discrete neighborhood, indeed living in a single apartment building, is a group of individuals, who are united in their common ethnicity, religion, and class status but are profoundly different in other ways. Fuchs's social architecture, emerging from the literal architecture of Williamsburg, suggests the complexity and the heterogeneity of the community.

Once the subway expanded into Brooklyn, it began to play a part in Brooklyn literature. Consider Thomas Wolfe's "Only the Dead Know Brooklyn" (1935), which closes with the famous lines, "It'd take a guy a lifetime to know Brooklyn t'roo an' t'roo. An' even den, yuh wouldn't know it all."[12] Described in the rough Brooklynese of its narrator, the subway is a liminal space akin to Whitman's ferry; neither public nor private, it enforces an intimacy of shared physical space and a consensual distance, as strangers crowd together during their commute. Staging an encounter between the Brooklyn-accented narrator and a map-bearing visitor, Wolfe's story begins as a disagreement about the correct subway route to "Bensonhoist" and becomes a subtle commentary in a Brooklyn vernacular on the instability of different kinds of cartography – the conventional map of paper and ink and the interior or native map of lived experience. In their exchange, the protagonist and his foil become exemplars of the insiders who populate Brooklyn's neighborhoods and the outsiders whom they resist.

Sol Yurick's novel *The Warriors* (1965), made famous by Walter Hill's 1979 film adaptation, uses the subway and the streets to suggest the limits of cosmopolitanism. The Coney Island Dominators are a gang whose turf is only a small, unmarked, yet palpable part of their Coney Island neighborhood – "No one had lined it, like on school maps, and there were no *visible* border guards."[13] After a violent ending to a city-wide gang summit, the Dominators travel the streets and subway back to Coney Island. Never having been outside of their immediate area, the adolescent boys experience the subway as an alienating, terrifying place. As the failure of cosmopolitanism reifies the metaphorical lines that separate communities, the subway serves to further split groups along arbitrary boundaries, which have come to be associated with race and ethnicity.

In her 2007 short story "Brooklyn Circle," Alice Mattison explores the map of the subway itself. She describes the manner in which the design of the subway system separates Brooklyn's neighborhoods and, hence, their residents: "The lines stretched from Manhattan like the tentacles of an octopus, but nothing connected them except in a very few places. To travel between some locations in Brooklyn, it was necessary – it is still necessary, Jerry pointed out – to travel into Manhattan and back." Mattison's story includes an imaginary episode in Brooklyn's history: the attempt by a multiracial descendant of immigrants – "Marcus Ogilvy's mother had been a German Jew, and on his father's side he even had one black grandparent" – to shift the subway's orientation from Manhattan to Brooklyn by connecting its neighborhoods, traditionally riven along ethnic, racial, and religious lines.[14] With the "Brooklyn Circle," a "mad scheme" of linking communities along an elevated train line, Mattison ponders the potential and failure of the subway to engender communities across difference.

If the Brooklyn Bridge, Coney Island, the neighborhood, and the subway are all icons of Brooklyn, so too is Betty Smith's *A Tree Grows in Brooklyn*. No other novel set in or about Brooklyn has been so inextricably linked to the borough. Published in 1943, the novel became an immediate bestseller, made into a movie in 1945 and subsequently into a play and a ballet. Even Bugs Bunny got in on the act, in "A Hare Grows in Manhattan" (1947).

Smith's novel is preoccupied with the resilience of the poor and the possibility of class mobility in early twentieth-century Brooklyn. Set in Williamsburg and concentrating on its protagonist Francie and her family, the novel is a narrative of ethnic assimilation and of what we can conceive of as the George Jefferson model of success: movin' on up, but in this case not to the East Side but to Queens or, eventually, to Michigan. Published in the middle of the Second World War, *A Tree Grows in Brooklyn* casts Brooklyn as both an old and a new country, and for some, a transitional place in between. It is an old country akin to Germany and Ireland, the birthplaces of a number of its characters; it is the locus of ethnic kinship, especially among first- and second-generation immigrants. And yet, it is an entry point to a new country in which education can begin to erase difference, where the third generation can consent to a new, broad American identity.

Consider this exchange in Francie's classroom, a key place for the process of assimilation:

> "I know you're American," said the easily exasperated teacher. "But what's your nationality?"
>
> "America!" insisted Francie even more proudly.

"Will you tell me what your parents are or do I have to send you to the principal?"

"My parents are American. They were born in Brooklyn."

All the children turned to look at a little girl whose parents had not come from the old country. And when Teacher said, "Brooklyn? Hm. I guess that makes you American all right," Francie was proud and happy. How wonderful was Brooklyn, she thought, when just being born there automatically made you an American![15]

Brooklyn entitles Francie to an identity as an American that earlier generations could not claim. And herein lies a central part of this novel's appeal, for this is a text about an alienated adolescent's coming of age into a generalized American identity.

Despite the text's embrace of narratives of the urban, immigrant poor, it nevertheless erases linguistic difference. *A Tree Grows in Brooklyn* almost exclusively employs standard English, except for the speech of the most marginal characters. Although we know that Francie has a Brooklyn accent, something she hopes to lose at the University of Michigan, none of her speech is rendered in the vernacular. Compare this to *Call It Sleep* or "Only the Dead Know Brooklyn," both of which render the Brooklyn accent so strongly that it is nearly impossible to read them silently. In its refusal to represent vernacular and multilingualism, *A Tree Grows in Brooklyn* trades the ethnic complexity of the borough for a more generic Brooklyn that can stand, however, for only some Americans: white ethnic ones.

Paule Marshall's 1959 novel *Brown Girl, Brownstones* tests the limits of *A Tree Grows in Brooklyn*'s understanding of Brooklyn's and America's ethnic and racial complexity. As in *A Tree Grows in Brooklyn*, we follow a coming-of-age narrative, this one of Selina, a young Barbadian girl. But *Brown Girl, Brownstones* departs from its precursor by attending to the diversity of Brooklyn's languages. Although the text is shot through with the Bajan vernacular, *Brown Girl, Brownstones* also speculates as to the narrative possibilities of a text written by and about non-white immigrants:

In the somnolent July afternoon the unbroken line of brownstone houses down the long Brooklyn street resembled an army massed at attention. They were all one uniform red-brown stone. All with high massive stone stoops and black iron-grille fences staving off the sun. All draped in ivy as though mourning ... Glancing down the interminable Brooklyn street you thought of those joined brownstones as one house reflected through a train of mirrors, with no walls between the houses but only vast rooms yawning endlessly one into each other. Yet, looking close, you saw that under the thick ivy each house had something distinctively its own. Some touch that was Gothic, Romanesque, baroque or Greek triumphed amid the Victorian clutter ... Behind those grim façades, in those high rooms, life soared and ebbed. Bodies crouched in the postures of love at night, children burst from the womb's thick shell, and death, when it was time, shuffled through the halls. First, there had been the Dutch-English and Scotch-Irish who had built the houses ... For a long time it had been only the whites, each generation unraveling in a quiet skein of years behind the green shades.[16]

This text employs the architecture of the Brooklyn street to suggest the complexity of writing about racial and national difference. Rather than attend to the uniformity of the houses, of narratives of ethnic assimilation, *Brown Girl, Brownstones* asks us to attend to differences amid common human experiences. Subtle variations of architecture among "Victorian clutter" are differences in language, in experience, departures from the formulae of *A Tree Grows in Brooklyn*. And there is tension in these differences, for Selina feels "odd speech clashed in the hushed rooms," as though she were "something vulgar in a holy place." Through its use of a similar plot with alternative formal and linguistic strategies, then, *Brown Girl, Brownstones* questions the assumptions about a racially homogeneous and authentic Brooklyn – and hence America – embedded in *A Tree Grows in Brooklyn*.

Later coming-of-age novels do not recapitulate the plot of *A Tree Grows in Brooklyn* as closely as Marshall's text. Edwige Danticat offers a transnational coming of age in her account of a young girl's movement between Haiti and Brooklyn in *Breath, Eyes, Memory* (1994).[17] Paul Auster reverses the trajectory in his coming-of-age-qua-coming-to-death novel *The Brooklyn Follies* (2005). At the end of his life, Auster's protagonist returns to Brooklyn, where he finds a community, a multi-ethnic one at that.[18] In 1951, Alfred Kazin published *A Walker in the City*. One of Brooklyn's many memoirs, albeit one of the few that isn't preoccupied with the Dodgers, Kazin's work follows his visit to Brownsville, "the margin of the city," ten years after he had left for "the city," meaning Manhattan. Concerned with memory itself, Kazin's text opens as he exits the subway and walks along the neighborhood streets, his senses bombarded by "the leak out of the men's room, then the pickles from the stand just below the subway's steps," by "the old women in their shapeless flowered housedresses and ritual wigs," "their soft dumpy bodies and the budging way they occupy the tenement stoops."[19]

Kazin maps Brooklyn and along with it ethnicity, race, and class:

We were the end of the line. We were the children of the immigrants who had camped at the city's back door, in New York's rawest, remotest, cheapest ghetto, enclosed on one side by the Canarsie flats and on the other by the hallowed middle-class districts that showed the way to New York: "New York" was what we put last on our address, but first in thinking of the others around us. *They* were New York, the Gentiles, America; we were Brownsville – *Brunzvil*, as the old folks said – the dust of the earth to all Jews with money, and notoriously a place that measured all success by our skill in getting away from it.

(12)

Echoing the model of success deployed in *A Tree Grows in Brooklyn*, the memoir casts Brooklyn as an ancestral place from which Kazin escapes. It is to Manhattan, "the city," that Kazin aspires:

> We were of the city, but somehow not in it. Whenever I went off on my favorite walk to Highland Park in the "American" district to the north, on the border of Queens, and climbed the hill to the old reservoir from which I could look straight across to the skyscrapers of Manhattan, I saw New York as a foreign city. There, brilliant and unreal, the city had its life, as Brownsville had ours.

(11)

With a literal vantage point from Brooklyn on to Manhattan, Kazin casts the two boroughs in opposition to one another. Brooklyn, or rather Brownsville, is the site of the domestic and the daily, while Manhattan, with its soaring vertical architecture, is modern and foreign.

If the coming-of-age novel and memoir are iconic Brooklyn literary forms, so too is the crime tale. Red Hook, an isolated area as well as a working port with a reputation as a hardscrabble, working-class, ethnic community, has come to be associated in Brooklyn literature with crime and justice. Arthur Miller, in his 1955 play *A View from the Bridge*, casts Red Hook as a site of conflict among generations of an immigrant group:

> But this is Red Hook, not Sicily. This is the slum that faces the bay on the seaward side of the Brooklyn Bridge. This is the gullet of New York swallowing the tonnage of the world. And now we are quite civilized, quite American.[20]

The play positions Eddie Carbone, whose desire for his niece clouds his judgment, against her suitor Rodolpho, who is an illegal immigrant, recently arrived with his brother Marco. Eddie becomes a "rat" and turns Rodolpho and Marco over to the authorities. Marco reacts violently, and the play concludes with Eddie's death. Eddie and Marco represent two competing systems of justice. Despite his complex motives, Eddie turns to the governmental and civic authority of the New World. Marco, instead, roots himself in retribution and vengeance, associated with an Old World system of justice.

This was not the first time that Red Hook had been associated with violence, ethnicity, and crime. H. P. Lovecraft's "The Horror at Red Hook" (1925) depicts the neighborhood as "a maze of hybrid squalor" and as a site of occult activities. It is home to a "population [that] is a hopeless tangle and enigma; Syrian, Spanish, Italian, and Negro elements impinging upon one another, and fragments of Scandinavian and American belts lying not far distant. It is a babel of sound and filth."²¹ The story recognizes and rejects the ethnic, racial, and linguistic differences in Red Hook.

In 1964, Hubert Selby depicted Red Hook as a lawless and hopeless frontier. *Last Exit to Brooklyn*, a graphic and disturbing account of violence and sexuality, comprises a series of interconnected stories revolving around a dismal bar in Red Hook. The characters range from a corrupt union official, taking advantage of a strike, to the infamous Tralala, a rough, unsympathetic, and promiscuous young woman who is gang-raped at the story's conclusion. Drugs, alcohol, sex, and seemingly little else preoccupy these characters. It is tempting to read Selby's novel as contemporary naturalism, akin to that of Frank Norris and Stephen Crane. Certainly the desperate conditions in which the characters live shape their desperate lives. Yet Selby's experimental prose denies that possibility; the novel avoids punctuation and employs stream of consciousness and an abbreviated vernacular. Refusing to be bound by syntax and grammar, set on the fringes of and isolated from the remainder of Brooklyn, the text suggests a place and a society that resists conventional rules of right and wrong.²²

Contemporary Brooklyn writers recapitulate many of the motifs of earlier Brooklyn writing. Perhaps the best known is Jonathan Lethem, who has published two Brooklyn novels, *Motherless Brooklyn* (1999) and *Fortress of Solitude*. *Motherless Brooklyn* is a coming-of-age novel, a crime novel (albeit a "soft-boiled" one, set in part in Red Hook), and a novel obsessed with neighborhoods, streets, language, and identity. It follows Lionel Essrog, an orphan with an extreme case of Tourette's Syndrome, as he comes into his own voice.

Lethem articulates a connection between the language of urban spaces – the linguistic codes of the neighborhood and the street – and the structure and codes of social relations. Ethnic insiders are the only individuals able to, indeed allowed to, navigate the world of the Brooklyn street: "Only Frank Minna was authorized to speculate on the secret systems that ran Court Street." He is anchored neither in place nor in language, although he possesses his own: "Like Court Street, I seethed behind the scenes with language and conspiracies, inversions of logic, sudden jerks and jabs of insult."²³ Akin to the outsider who does not respect the social and lingual rules of the street ("The homicide cop didn't know you weren't supposed to say those names aloud. Not anywhere, but especially not out on Smith Street"), Lionel has no access to the unspoken language and underground narratives that allow the ethnically similar residents of an area to understand each other (115). He wonders, for example, about how the mother of his mentor, his guide to Brooklyn's streets, sells her food to the community: "How her prices and schedule were conveyed I never understood – perhaps telepathically" (70).

In *The Fortress of Solitude*, coming of age and crime meet gentrification, a process that hinges on the association of place and social position. Near the setting of Truman Capote's posthumous *A House in the Heights* (2002) and Paula Fox's *Desperate Characters* (1970), employing the motif of the ailanthus tree of *A Tree Grows in Brooklyn*, and alluding to the sensory memory of *A Walker in the City*, the novel depicts Brooklyn in the 1970s through the childhood of Dylan Ebdus, the lone white child residing on Dean Street in a neighborhood in transition – racially, economically, even in name. It is known as Gowanus by its long-term non-white and working-class residents and as Boerum Hill by Isabel Vendle, a new resident with a plan to transform the neighborhood into a white, middle-class one. Like James Agee, who writes an almost obsessive cartography in *Brooklyn Is* (1939, pub. 1968), Dylan is obsessed with mapping not only his larger neighborhood but also his block of Dean Street, pavement by pavement ("an arrangement of zones in slate").[24] For Dylan, even a single sidewalk is fraught with race, and where one lives determines one's behavior and identity, from the street play of children to the yoking (mugging) of adolescence to the adult dramas of sexuality and addiction. Of all of Brooklyn's literature, *Fortress of Solitude* most clearly articulates the imbrication of urban location and urban identity. In it, as in other Brooklyn writing, the borough's social history, its architecture and infrastructure, and its population's codes and behaviors become its literary history and geography.

In *Brooklyn Is*, Agee contrasts Manhattan, where "the whole of living is drawn straining into verticals," with Brooklyn, where "this whole of living is ... relaxed upon horizontalities."[25] Agee's dichotomy may not hold – if it ever did – as the twenty-first century advances. Indeed, *The Fortress of Solitude* likely signals the end of an era, as the gentrification that Lethem's novel depicts spreads horizontally across much of Brooklyn. Real estate developers and politicians trade on nostalgia for the Dodgers and for an imagined authenticity of the working-class and ethnic communities of the mid-twentieth century in order to construct vertically. Erecting out-of-scale buildings that dwarf the horizontal cityscape, they attempt to transform gritty 4th Avenue into Brooklyn's Park Avenue. Selby's Red Hook is now the site of the Real World, MTV's take on adolescent *sturm und drang*. Brooklyn has become a place to go to rather than to get away from. Changes in the physical and social landscape of Brooklyn have begun to affect its presence in American popular culture and will indeed have an impact on its literature. While still home to writers, many of them well established, Brooklyn may become cast as "the city of yore," as neighborhoods that were once of little interest to writers of the come now preoccupy them. Narratives of immigration may emerge more in Queens, and the Bronx may begin to challenge Brooklyn's position as the setting for coming of age.

NOTES

1. Henry M. Christman, ed., *Walt Whitman's New York from Manhattan to Montauk* (New York: New Amsterdam, 1963), p. 3.
2. Walt Whitman, "Crossing Brooklyn Ferry," in *Broken Land: Poems of Brooklyn*, ed. Julia Spicher Kasdorf and Michael Tyrell (New York: New York University Press, 2007), p. 3.
3. Alan Trachtenberg, *The Brooklyn Bridge: Fact and Symbol* (Chicago, IL: University of Chicago Press, 1979); Richard Haw, *The Brooklyn Bridge: A Cultural History* (New Brunswick, NJ: Rutgers University Press, 2005).
4. Phillip Lopate, *Waterfront: A Walk around Manhattan* (New York: Anchor Books, 2005), p. 271.
5. Hart Crane, "Proem: To Brooklyn Bridge," in *Broken Land*, ed. Kasdorf and Tyrell, pp. 37–38.
6. Vladimir Vladimirovich Mayakovsky, "Brooklyn Bridge," in *Broken Land*, ed. Kasdorf and Tyrell, pp. 32–36.
7. Charles Reznikoff, "The Bridge," in *Broken Land*, ed. Kasdorf and Tyrell, p. 47.
8. Louis Mumford, "The Brooklyn Bridge," from *Sketches from Life*, in *Empire City: New York throughout the Centuries*, ed. Kenneth T. Jackson and David S. Dunbar (New York: Columbia University Press, 2002), p. 844.
9. Colson Whitehead, *The Colossus of New York* (New York: Anchor Books, 2003), p. 109.
10. Henry Roth, *Call It Sleep* (New York: Noonday Press, 1991), p. 101.
11. Daniel Fuchs, *The Brooklyn Novels* (New York: Black Sparrow Press, 2006), p. 11.
12. Thomas Wolfe, "Only the Dead Know Brooklyn," in *The Brooklyn Reader*, ed. Andrea Wyatt Sexton and Alice Leccese Powers (New York: Harmony Books, 1994), p. 281.
13. Sol Yurick, *The Warriors* (New York: Grove Press, 2003), p. 14.
14. Alice Mattison, "The Brooklyn Circle," *New Yorker* (November 12, 2007).
15. Betty Smith, *A Tree Grows in Brooklyn* (New York: Perennial Classics, 1998), p. 168.
16. Paule Marshall, *Brown Girl, Brownstones* (New York: Feminist Press, 1981), p. 3.
17. Edwige Danticat, *Breath, Eyes, Memory* (New York: Vintage, 1994).
18. Paul Auster, *The Brooklyn Follies* (London: Faber and Faber, 2005).
19. Alfred Kazin, *A Walker in the City* (New York: Harcourt, Brace, Jovanovich, 1979), pp. 5–6. Further references appear in the text.
20. Arthur Miller, *A View from the Bridge* (New York: Penguin, 1977), p. 4.
21. H. P. Lovecraft, "The Horror at Red Hook," in *Brooklyn Noir 2*, ed. Tim McLoughlin (Brooklyn, NY: Akashic Books, 2005), p. 21.
22. Hubert Selby, *Last Exit to Brooklyn* (New York: Grove Press, 1964).
23. Jonathan Lethem, *Motherless Brooklyn* (New York: Vintage, 1999), pp. 74, 57.
24. Jonathan Lethem, *The Fortress of Solitude* (New York: Vintage, 2003), p. 13.
25. James Agee, *Brooklyn Is: Southeast of the Island: Travel Notes* (New York: Fordham University Press, 2005), p. 4.

8

SARAH WILSON

New York and the novel of manners

At the conclusion of Edith Wharton's *The Age of Innocence* (1920), the gentlemen of the Welland-Mingott clan gather in Newland Archer's library, and their talk turns to the social disintegration implied in the rise of that "foreign upstart," Julius Beaufort. Lawrence Lefferts, the perennial (and hypocritical) defender of "society," thunders: "If things go on at this pace ... we shall see our children fighting for invitations to swindlers' houses, and marrying Beaufort's bastards."[1] Only a chapter (and twenty-six years) later, Lefferts's quintessential articulation of Old New York embattlement is driven home by the revelation that Newland Archer's eldest son plans to do just that. For *The Age of Innocence*, "Beaufort's bastards" come to stand for illegitimacy legitimized by the passage of time: more specifically, they speak to a struggle over manners staged through generational change. Like many New York novels of the turn of the twentieth century, Wharton's novel frames the rapid social change of the era in generational terms: cultural conflict comes off as family squabble. As the discussion of Beaufort's bastards suggests, generational change stages intimate clashes between what is and is not culturally acceptable, all while troubling existing divisions between what is "family" and what is "foreign," what is private and what is public. "Manners," in this sense, become the battleground through which turn-of-the-century New York writers bring cultural difference home; in particular, New York novels of manners reckon with such cultural difference by recognizing it as an inescapable force of historical change.[2]

In this sense the New York novel of manners both resembles and differentiates itself from traditional novels of manners. Like the traditional novel of manners (best exemplified by the novels of Austen), these texts are concerned with the social conventions by which communities and classes can be mapped. The fiction of Wharton and Henry James remains relatively true to this tradition, while beginning to gesture at the forms of difference that press at the boundaries of class and culture in New York. However, a significant proportion of turn-of-the-century New York novels expand the populations understood to be "mappable" by novels of manners: novels by William Dean Howells, Abraham Cahan, and Paul Laurence Dunbar bring into the tradition classes and cultures, races and ethnicities (and even literary genres, such as naturalism) not usually associated with manners literature as traditionally conceived. These novels share their preoccupation with manners with a polyglot host of other turn-of-the-century New York texts, reflecting the allure of manners – their diversity, even their exoticism – for chroniclers of a cosmopolitan society. From Brander Matthews's *Vignettes of Manhattan* (1894), Henry James's *The American Scene* (1907), Theodore Dreiser's *The Color of a Great City* (1923), and Konrad Bercovici's *Around the World in New York* (1924), which offer travelogue-like representations of the variety and wonder of Manhattan; to fictionalized autobiographies like Hutchins Hapgood's *Autobiography of a Thief* (1903), Dorothy Richardson's *The Long Day: The Story of a New York Working Girl* (1905), and William Riordon and George Washington Plunkitt's *A Series of Very Plain Talks on Very Practical Politics* (1905), which introduced readers to the manners of subcultures like career criminals, working girls, and Tammany politicians; to graphic texts like R. F. Outcault's "Yellow Kid" comic strip, which led readers of Joseph Pulitzer's *New York World* and William Randolph Hearst's *New York Journal* through rollicking tours of New York slums and beyond, turn-of-the-century New York texts emphasized the close proximity of cultural difference by anatomizing the diversity of manners in the city.

These turn-of-the-century New York texts represented *manners* as, in Lionel Trilling's famous words on the subject, "a culture's hum and buzz of implication ... the whole evanescent context in which its explicit statements are made." Trilling noted that "in any complex culture there is not a single system of manners but a conflicting variety of manners, and ... one of the jobs of a culture is the adjustment of this conflict."[3] New York *novels* of manners are distinguished, within this expanded category of manners writing, by the intensity of their skepticism about the possibility of "adjustment" of the conflict of manners. They communicate this skepticism through representations of families in conflict over generations. In the more traditional novels of manners, by Wharton and James, varieties of manners over generations reveal community to be a constructed and contentious thing: family conflict in particular adumbrates the dramatic effects of new cultural influences in the city. From William Dean Howells's *A Hazard of New Fortunes* (1890) through a series of less-traditional novels of manners, New York's diversity fundamentally alters the contours of intimate experience, to the point that the shock of intergenerational conflict resounds even in the fractured individual selves of the new century. In other words, New York novels of manners represent important early traces of the imaginative transformations – of selfhood, family, and ideas of difference and belonging – that would extend through the United States over the twentieth century.

In turn-of-the-century New York manners writing, manners do not represent a homogeneous cultural arena, but a site of always-surprising dynamism; they reflect the constant introduction of novelty through the intersections of varied populations.[4] Indeed, in New York novels of manners, intergenerational conflicts serve to introduce the idea of cultural change (primarily racial and ethnic, but also political) as a force marking intimate arenas of self-definition – something quite distinct from the forces that traditionally concern manners literature (gender and class identity). In the process, these texts inscribe the special conflicts and questions of a cosmopolitan city into the tradition of manners.

Novels of Old New York

Henry James's *Washington Square* (1881) offers a glimpse of the "old" New York that he found missing in the chaos of the turn-of-the-century city (he chronicled his late-life return in *The American Scene* [1907]). In the 1840s New York of *Washington Square*, the family is already a battleground over manners: Catherine Sloper's tasteless dresses and social timidity distress her father, a "man of the world" who might wish for a more unusual and vivacious daughter.[5] Instead, Catherine's "deepest desire" is "to please" her father (10). This anti-rebellion finds the daughter adamantly locating her happiness in the limited sphere of parental approval, and the parent dreaming of a broader sphere for his child's activities. Yet when Catherine clashes with her father over a marriage proposal from the fortune-hunter Morris Townsend, she does so in more predictable terms, surprising her father with her reluctance to cede to his judgment and her resolve to "stick" with the ill-favored connection (99). For Catherine there will be no ultimate act of defiance of parental authority, however. Her suitor abandons her when her father promises to disinherit her. She never marries, spending the rest of her days in the house on Washington Square, a dull and eager-to-please girl irrevocably marked by her experience of being a pawn in a game of intergenerational transfer.

Catherine emerges from this experience more attuned to the social dynamics of a later moment: as an older woman, "she mingled freely in the usual gaieties of the town, and she became at last an inevitable figure at all respectable entertainments. She was greatly liked, and as time went on she grew to be a sort of kindly maiden-aunt to the younger portion of society" (173). She straddles generations, combining her favored position among the youth with a conservatism that brands her, by forty, an "old-fashioned person, and an authority on customs that had passed away" (173). The social inheritance that Catherine thus claims is a constructed thing: her authority on the past is only recently gained and does not itself extend into the past.[6] For the youth who view her so sympathetically, she represents an Old New York ostensibly certain and solid, but in fact founded in uncertainty and conflict.

Lily Bart of Edith Wharton's *The House of Mirth* (1905) similarly reveals the insecure basis of Old New York: the young woman, the product of a lavishly spending respectable family hit by financial ruin, wavers ambivalently each time she is given the opportunity to marry for money and fulfill her mother's desire to secure her position. Indeed, as Lily's serial faltering and her limited cash flow inexorably diminish her marriage prospects, she finds herself considering the proposal of a man who is the social equivalent of "Beaufort's bastards": Simon Rosedale, a wealthy Jewish financier. If Lily's ambivalence and social struggles give her new insight into the arbitrary nature of the codes by which her friends live, Rosedale offers her an even more estranged perspective on those manners. The final bargain he proposes – that, in exchange for his backing, she should blackmail Bertha Dorset and thus reacquire her lost social status – strikes Lily as exhibiting a kind of disturbing genius: it transforms messy social conflict into "a private understanding, of which no third person need have the remotest hint. Put by Rosedale in terms of business-like give-and-take, this understanding took on the harmless air of a mutual accommodation, like a transfer of property or a revision of boundary lines. It certainly simplified life to view it as a perpetual adjustment, a play of party politics, in which every concession had its recognized equivalent."[7]

Lily recoils from this: *The House of Mirth* imagines no generation beyond anti-Semitism, in which Rosedale, like Beaufort's bastards, might cease to occasion social repugnance. However, Rosedale is in ascendancy when he opens this vision of manners to Lily, and his perspective productively troubles traditional boundaries between private and public, business and social life, even ethics and pragmatics. Lily will ultimately devote herself to the more rarefied vision represented by Laurence Selden, but the novel is unequivocal about Selden's increasing irrelevance in Rosedale's New York.[8] Lily's rather maudlin deathbed delusion (that she is cradling a child) only reinforces the failure of intergenerational struggle to transform the vision of manners fully in this novel. Where the conflict of manners does not spill into subsequent generations (indeed, when one attempts to encapsulate it in a single being, a single moment), Wharton finds only a stillborn version of cultural change.

This is not the case in *The Age of Innocence*, which though it concludes with Newland Archer refusing to reignite the passion of his youth – in a visit to Paris after his wife's death, he stays outside Ellen Olenska's apartment, explaining that he is "old-fashioned" (1302) – also includes Archer's wonder at a new generation "too busy – busy with reforms and 'movements,' with fads and fetishes and frivolities – to bother much with their neighbours. And of what account was anybody's past, in the huge kaleidoscope where all the social atoms spun around on the same plane?" (1295–96). If Newland Archer's rebellion against the manners of his age was untimely quashed, he lives to see his son self-consciously marry his own Ellen. And yet the overturn of the old regime of New York manners is also gradual enough, in this text, for each generation to express a certain fidelity to the preceding one. Newland stays true to the manners of his parents, despite being sorely tempted; his son Dallas, in turn, is true to a vision of Newland oriented toward Ellen Olenska, but adds to that a broader tribute to the manners of the earlier generation. Hearing that his father stayed with his mother without her directly asking him to abandon Ellen, Dallas observes, "You never did ask each other anything, did you? And you never told each other anything. You just sat and watched each other, and guessed at what was going on underneath ... Well, I back your generation for knowing more about each other's private thoughts than we ever have time to find out about our own" (1298). The "rush" with which Dallas breaks off this contemplative interlude further testifies that these kinds of manners, despite their communicative efficiency for another generation, have been relegated to the status of quaint and unthreatening artifacts for the new, brashly liberated generation.

Archer sees difference, if not conflict, between his own early struggles with right conduct and his son's "tumultuous enthusiasm and cock-sure criticism" (1300). Such difference is not entirely emancipatory: the new generation seems to have lost both intimate insight and cultural reading skills as it has moved beyond the constraints and prohibitions of old-fashioned manners: "the new generation ... had swept away all the old landmarks, and with them the sign-posts and the danger-signal" (1300). Without the sign-posts and the danger-signal – understanding manners descriptively rather than prescriptively, that is – Dallas's generation of post-Theodore Roosevelt Americans risks losing the sense of estrangement that offered Archer what little critical perspective he gained on his culture. Wharton's novel closes on the possibility that this new generation, in "the huge kaleidoscope where all the social atoms spun around on the same plane," accepts a vision of manners as homogeneous and in keeping with their self-assurance and lack of questioning as was the case in the generation preceding Newland. Ironically, intergenerational difference conceived in these terms produces an unnerving cultural continuity, an unabashed parochialism rather than the promised cosmopolitanism.

Novels of the "huge kaleidoscope"

Despite being published thirty years before *The Age of Innocence*, William Dean Howells's *A Hazard of New Fortunes* speaks directly to the anxieties that conclude Wharton's novel. Howells's novel includes only oblique looks at Old New York, but it insists upon cultural turbulence as a central characteristic of life in the wider city. New York stages an "experiment" that daunts Howells's protagonist Basil March, a genteel Boston man of letters, just as it "terrifies" his wife, who explains that she "can't find myself in it."[9] From March's disquisitions on the kinds of social existence produced by the design of New York flats and tenements, to his wife's admission that peering into strange homes from the elevated train produces "a domestic intensity mixed with a perfect repose that was the last effect of good society with all its security and exclusiveness" (76), to observations of the fleeting, "touch-and-go quality" (296) of social interactions and identity as experienced in New York, *A Hazard of New Fortunes* casts New York as a fecund and terrifying nexus of manners, one whose rush – unlike Dallas Archer's – never seems to favor cultural homogeneity.[10] Even the literary periodical that draws March to New York appeals to late-century forms of transnational commercial and aesthetic circulation.[11] If the complacent March children do seem to bear out the cultural threat hinted at by the self-confident Dallas Archer, the subplot that pits the earnest reformer Conrad Dryfoos against his wealthy father promises that the city will always draw new intergenerational conflicts to the fore.

The domestic, commercial, and political threads of Howells's novel intersect most tellingly in a late scene in which this Conrad Dryfoos, inspired in equal parts by love for a young woman reformer and by rejection of his father's venal politics, is killed in the fray associated with a streetcar strike. Conrad voluntarily steps forward to defend the German socialist Lindau (thus repeating Lindau's earlier cross-cultural voluntarism in the American Civil War). The labor-conflict mêlée of *A Hazard of New Fortunes* produces just such unlikely associations, mixing different ethnicities, classes, generations, and political visions: it costs the young man his life, but also has transformative effects on other players in the novel. (In this sense Howells anticipates later labor novels, such as Theresa Malkiel's *The Diary of a Shirtwaist Striker*, of 1910, and Arthur Bullard's *Comrade Yetta*, of 1913, in which physical proximity to labor conflict produces feelings of kinship between women of different classes and ethnicities.) In Howells's novel, as in Wharton's representation of Lily Bart, intergenerational conflict is cut short; however, Howells's novel is more successful than Wharton's at asserting alternative cultural kinships, or ways in which

Conrad's beliefs and actions might be transferred along non-traditional lines of affiliation.

Howells's Basil March is on hand to witness the labor fracas in which Conrad is killed, just as he is there later to witness Lindau's death from his injuries; he merges witnessing with an active engagement with both men's ideas of reform, modeling for the reader Howells's idea of intellectual kinship born of proximity. Yet these gestures of affiliation rest heavily on coincidence – on March's contemplative temperament, and on the chance intersections that position him as witness. Indeed, intersections like the scene of strike violence (as well as less shocking thematic and narrative coincidences) are more than a matter of plotting convenience in A Hazard of New Fortunes: Howells's novel is scripted by a faith that New York generally enacts a kind of enlightening social connection through proximity and intersection. A radical version of the same faith drives Lindau to live in a tenement; he explains that "you must zee it all the dtime – zee it, hear it, smell it, dtaste it – or you forget it. That is what I gome here for. I was begoming a ploated aristograt. I thought I was nodt like these beople down here, when I gome down once to look aroundt: I thought I must be somethings else, and zo I zaid I better take myself in time, and I gome here among my brothers – the beccars and the thiefs!" (190). Howells's novel suggests that New York constantly puts one among brothers like the beggars and the thieves; the mixed social contacts and juxtapositions of New York redefine "realistic" forms of kinship just as Lindau's tenement redefines the boundaries of class and family.[12] When Conrad Dryfoos, and indeed March, step forward to claim Lindau, they are also meant to be stepping into new, New York-mediated versions of affiliation (and even filiation).[13]

Howells's novel collapses social difference, urban distance, and patterns of domestic association to demonstrate New York's radical troubling of traditional boundaries. If the novel is ultimately wry (with March himself) about a literary gentleman's capacity to translate stirred sensibility into transformative political change, it also models a kind of intellectual engagement with manners and social relations that tempers its final disengagement from radical social change. One of Howells's realist protégés, Stephen Crane, however, used New York's collapses of social, physical, and even generational distance to very different effects. Just as A Hazard of New Fortunes reveals that, even after extensive wanderings in New York, the Marches' "point of view was singularly unchanged" (305), Crane's Maggie, A Girl of the Streets (1893) represents a low-life New York that, despite its vivid contrasts and violent collisions, remains uncannily unchanging.[14] Generational conflict, Crane's novel suggests, does not necessarily lead to the kinds of social transformation that even Wharton's novels flirt with. Instead,

Crane's novel paints a scene of social stasis, in which the home is a base for ever-repeating patterns: parental drunkenness, brotherly self-centeredness, neighborly censure and indifference. Even Maggie's impressions of the wider world seem cast from templates: her suitor Pete strikes her as a timeless masculine ideal, even as he goes on to ruin her; the melodramas he takes her to see seem to speak changeless truths, despite their remoteness from her own experience. Crane's narrator frames these assumptions of timelessness in the language of mock heroism, underlining both their pathos and their ridiculousness. Above all, the narrator's ironic remove from the manners and attitudes he describes reinforces the novel's naturalistic emphasis on the unchangeable nature of experience. The narrative progresses inexorably toward a ruin that was anticipated at its beginning: indeed, when Maggie's drunken mother asks of her son, "An' wid all deh bringin' up she had, how could she? ... Wid all deh talkin' wid her I did an' deh t'ings I tol' her to remember?", the complaint is notable not because it misrepresents the past (though it does), but because it reveals Maggie's mother's canny awareness that the past can be anything she says it is – as long as she turns to the language of manners to claim it was always and consistently so (thus the repeated locutions *all* the bringing up, *all* the talking).[15] The ironic contrast between the mother's claim and Maggie's actual history is fleeting, even despite the enabling skepticism of Crane's narrator; the familiar narrative of the fallen daughter re-describes generational conflict as a timeless truth subject to general consensus.

Crane's universe stands apart from the more optimistic employments of intergenerational clash to describe cultural change in New York novels of manners. In Crane's New York one generation is little different from another; among the Irish immigrants of *Maggie*, transformational rebellion against one's antecedents is neither formulated nor enacted. Crane's dark vision of cultural stasis contrasts starkly with the aspirational renditions of intergenerational conflict and change that played out in so many immigrant narratives of the turn of the century. For example, the title character of Abraham Cahan's *Yekl: A Tale of the New York Ghetto* (1896) self-consciously crafts a New-World self by adopting the manners he sees around him. Indeed, Yekl ("Jake" in America) is so anxious to drop the habits that might mark him as a "greenhorn" that he transposes the intergenerational conflict in manners into his domestic relationship with his more-recently arrived wife, Gitl. Jake is made young again by the "hum and buzz" of the New York scene; nostalgic and ambivalent as he may be about the loss of the timeless, changeless scenes that he associates with his roots, he can no longer accept the habits of dress and deportment that his more traditional wife preserves.[16] Yet after their divorce it seems that it is she who will best balance the manners of Old

World and New. Jake's headlong assimilation may produce the more perfect alignment of character and scene (his heart imitates each "violent lurch" by the cable car that he rides away from the scene of his divorce), but he senses the future promised by such assimilation to be "dark and impenetrable."[17]

Cahan's later novel of assimilation, *The Rise of David Levinsky* (1917), elaborates on this dark and impenetrable future. Orphaned and unmarried, Levinsky succeeds in the business world but finds no purchase on the kinds of intergenerational connection that family promises. His adoption of the American "gestures, manners, and mannerisms" that he, like Yekl, associates with communication, connections, and success, meets with little external resistance; indeed, his only problem seems to be that *he* feels lacking, especially in the "special slang sense" that he associates with native-born Americans.[18] But Levinsky does see an intergenerational drama play out in his acquaintance – he muses of his lover, Dora, that she observed her Americanized daughter "with a feeling akin to despair … It was as though she was pursuing the little girl, with outstretched arms, vainly trying to overtake her" (288). Despite his own aptitude for picking up a manner or a design (his eye and ear stand him in good stead in matters of business and of cultural assimilation), he identifies with Dora's despair and with the sense of inner deficiency that he sees as characteristic of her relation to her child. Though assimilation promises alternative cultural kinships akin to those implied in Howells's *A Hazard of New Fortunes*, in Cahan's later novel these alternative kinships cannot substitute for the traditional family-based belonging that assimilation erodes.

Levinsky sees a perfect synchrony of inner feeling and external manner as being reserved for the American-born children of the ghetto: they "are American not only in their language, tastes, and ambitions, but in outward appearance as well. Their bearing, gestures, the play of their features, and something in the very expression of their Semitic faces proclaim the land of their birth" (355). For himself and for immigrants like him, he imagines a quite different, quasi-intergenerational dynamic, but one figured as playing out within the individual self. He concludes his narration by describing a fragmentation of self that eloquently speaks to the problem of the unconnected individual as represented by Wharton's Lily Bart: "I cannot escape from my old self. My past and my present do not comport well. David, the poor lad swinging over a Talmud volume at the Preacher's Synagogue, seems to have more in common with my inner identity than David Levinsky, the well-known cloak-manufacturer" (530). "Inner identity," whatever it may be, is caught up in a familiar struggle between youth and age. Indeed, the uncomfortable incompatibility of Levinsky's boy and man figures (and the awkwardness of manners never fully naturalized) constitutes the fullest articulation of Jewish-American assimilation in Cahan's novel. Unlike *The House of Mirth*, however, Cahan's novel suggests just how fully the tropes of intergenerational conflict have infiltrated and transformed accounts of the individual self faced by the cultural variety of New York.

On the other hand, Paul Laurence Dunbar's *The Sport of the Gods* (1902) finds no stubborn "inner identity" by which young African American migrants might resist the corrupting effects of New York: it takes the city "barely five years to accomplish an entire metamorphosis" of the characters of Joe and Kitty Hamilton, new arrivals from the South.[19] Despite their hapless mother's attempts to keep them true to an older moral code, Joe ends up a drunk and a murderer, while Kitty abandons the down-home melodies she once sang for a life on the stage. While their parents put up a greater struggle against the temptations of the city, these migrant youths gravitate toward the entertainment-saturated life of theaters and nightclubs (and they are not alone: they join Maggie of Crane's *Maggie*, Carminella of Edward Townsend's *A Daughter of the Slums* [1895], Carrie of Theodore Dreiser's *Sister Carrie* [1900], the anonymous narrator of James Weldon Johnson's *The Autobiography of an Ex-Colored Man* [1912], and Levinsky of Cahan's *The Rise of David Levinsky*). Dunbar's novel is an extreme case: the novels of manners of the turn of the century do not always connect theatricality and musical performance with corruption. However, the widespread attraction to theatricality in New York novels of manners does put significant pressure on ideas of fixed "identity." Through the mediation of the many scenes of performance in New York novels of manners, selfhood itself begins to seem a kind of performance (a performance most effective when informed by a nuanced sense of manners).[20]

The narrator of James Weldon Johnson's *The Autobiography of an Ex-Colored Man* moves most fluidly between the sets of manners he observes in New York (from Tenderloin nightclubs to upper-class bohemian homes) as a chameleon-like mixed-race orphan. He remains a performer when he permanently adopts a white racial identity, but this new identity, closely associated with his fathering of two children and re-inscription into traditional models of familial belonging, is less mobile. Ironically, Johnson's narrator bequeaths a performed identity (one based on his light skin as well as his pitch-perfect sense of white New York manners) to a next generation unaware of the theatricality of their cultural inheritance. Theatricality thus becomes the means by which a sustained intergenerational conflict (as in Dunbar's novel) is effectively submerged in a more individualized struggle (as in both Johnson's and Cahan's novels). In this new form of individualized intergenerational conflict, "manners" come to represent the changeability of culture, rather than the overweening influence of the past. In fact, as opposed to Wharton's novels, which cast manners themselves as the battlefield, these later "kaleidoscope" novels begin to align manners with one side of the battle (changeability), while associating the family with biological heredity, inheritance, and continuity.

The novels of manners of the turn of the century set the stage for a central intellectual conflict of the 1920s – one most famously played out in F. Scott Fitzgerald's *The Great Gatsby* (1925), but also prominent in Anzia Yezierska's novels such as *Bread Givers* (1925) – between the power of origins (a class identity, a racial identity, or the like) and the power of self-fashioning (cultural change or shifting manners) in determining an individual's identity. Yet turn-of-the-century New York novels also offer a nuanced investigation into the nature and value of manners in their own right. In them, manners represent the primary measure of difference in an era of cultural turbulence; by emphasizing the play of cultural difference over time rather than over space (representing difference as "change" rather than difference as a form of identity), they subtly work to erode barriers between classes, races, and ethnicities. By focusing on intergenerational change, New York novels of manners frame both the shocks and the opportunities of a cosmopolitan society as intimate, domestic concerns, as opposed to purely external, public experiences. They not only thematize, but also enact, New York's revelation that "Beaufort's bastards" have been uncannily legitimized as one's own children and inheritors – that in this city and in the new century, cultural change comes home, to one's familiars and one's now-unfamiliar self.

NOTES

Thanks to Darren Gobert and Mark Stabile for their helpful readings and comments.

1. Edith Wharton, *The Age of Innocence* (1920), in *Novels* (New York: Library of America, 1985), p. 1284. Further references appear in the text.
2. It is not surprising, then, that Wharton and William Dean Howells, two premier practitioners of the novel of manners, both cast their novels as "historical." For closer discussion of these claims, see Susan Goodman, *Civil Wars: American Novelists and Manners, 1880–1940* (Baltimore, MD: Johns Hopkins University Press, 2003), esp. chs. 1 and 3. By "historical" these writers did not mean that they wrote historical romances; rather, they aspired to a literary form that, as Howells put it, documented *both* the inner complications and the "outer entirety" of experience. William Dean Howells, "Novel-Writing and Novel-Reading," in *Selected Literary Criticism*, ed. Ronald Gottesman, 3 vols. (Bloomington: Indiana University Press, 1993), III, p. 231.
3. Trilling continues: "It is that part of a culture which is made up of half-uttered or unuttered or unutterable expressions of value. They are hinted at by small actions, sometimes by the arts of dress or decoration, sometimes by tone, gesture, emphasis, or rhythm, sometimes by the words that are used with a special frequency or a special meaning. They are the things that for good or bad

draw the people of a culture together and that separate them from the people of another culture. They make the part of a culture which is not art, or religion, or morals, or politics, and yet it relates to all these highly formulated departments of culture. It is modified by them: it modifies them: it is generated by them: it generates them. In this part of culture assumption rules, which is often so much stronger than reason." Lionel Trilling, "Manners, Morals, and the Novel," in *The Liberal Imagination: Essays on Literature and Society* (New York: Macmillan, 1948), pp. 206–7.

4. In all of this New York writing, the change and conflict that characterizes representations of "manners" nudges the meaning of the term along the same path taken by the idea of "culture" in this period: that is, "manners" shift from a matter of prescription, in the style of Matthew Arnold (what is best to do), to a matter of description, in the style of Franz Boas (what is in fact done). But as even the change limned by "Beaufort's bastards" indicates, *novels* of manners become more insidiously prescriptive even as they become more descriptive in their approach to manners. (*The Age of Innocence*, for example, closes by seriously questioning the new generation's manners.) For the intersection of manners and anthropological writing (including that of Franz Boas), see Nancy Bentley, *The Ethnography of Manners: Hawthorne, James, Wharton* (Cambridge: Cambridge University Press, 1995).

5. Henry James, *Washington Square* (1881; New York: Library of America, 1990), p. 3. Further references appear in the text.

6. Though she is disinherited, Catherine retains the townhouse on Washington Square, a not-insignificant possession in a novel of this name. It is Washington Square that prompts James's narrator to break the narrative frame, musing that the neighborhood has "the look of having had some kind of a social history. It was here, as you might have been informed on good authority, that you had come into a world which appeared to offer a variety of sources of interest; it was here that your grandmother lived ... it was here that you took your first walks abroad" (p. 15). This "you," clearly autobiographical in its resonance for James, also opens up to the reader, suggesting the capaciousness and yet intimacy of the "social history" that becomes Catherine's alternate inheritance.

7. Edith Wharton, *The House of Mirth* (1905), in *Novels* (New York: Library of America, 1985), p. 271.

8. The social ascendancy of the *parvenu* (if not his Jewishness) is revisited in Wharton's *The Custom of the Country* (1913), in which Ralph Marvell plays the doomed scion of Old New York; Marvell's son Paul ends up utterly alienated from his Old New York roots, finally living with his social-climbing, multiply divorced mother, Undine, and her wealthy businessman of a husband, Elmer Moffatt.

9. William Dean Howells, *A Hazard of New Fortunes* (New York: Modern Library, 2002), pp. 22, 28. Further references appear in the text.

10. See, however, Amy Kaplan on the ways in which the Marches' observation of the city inscribes boundaries meant to assuage their middle-class anxieties about the porosity of such boundaries: *The Social Construction of American Realism* (Chicago, IL: University of Chicago Press, 1988), pp. 48–53.

11. See Brad Evans, *Before Cultures: The Ethnographic Imagination in American Literature, 1865–1920* (Chicago, IL: University of Chicago Press, 2005),

pp. 113–39. Evans argues, however, that the novel's interest in disorder remains confined to the aesthetic realm (with the disorderly social circulation represented by Lindau ultimately remaining unfathomable to March).

12. On the slumming tradition that Howells draws on here, see Chapter 6, as well as Robert Dowling, *Slumming in New York: From the Waterfront to Mythic Harlem* (Urbana: University of Illinois Press, 2007); Carrie Tirado Bramen, "The Urban Picturesque and the Spectacle of Americanization," *American Quarterly* 52 (2000): 444–77.

13. In Lindau's case, these new social and proto-familial configurations are linked with a disrespect for all manners, traditionally conceived (he lives in topsy-turvy squalor, and commits the ultimate act of bad taste by disparaging his host, Dryfoos, at a dinner given by the oil tycoon). The mad whirl of domestic couplings that unfold around Howells's political plot, however, provide a counterpoint to the relentless masculinism and anti-mannerliness of the Lindau-reconceived family unit.

14. See Keith Gandal on Crane's radical deviation from a previous tradition of emphasizing "moral transformation" in slum fiction: *The Virtues of the Vicious: Jacob Riis, Stephen Crane, and the Spectacle of the Slum* (New York: Oxford University Press, 1997), pp. 39–57.

15. Stephen Crane, *"Maggie, a Girl of the Streets," and Other New York Writings* (New York: Modern Library, 2001), p. 46. On the literary use of dialect (here, Maggie's mother's, but also used in Cahan's *Yekl*, below), particularly whether it acts as a force of homogenization or of destabilization, see Gavin Jones, *Strange Talk: The Politics of Dialect Literature in Gilded Age America* (Berkeley: University of California Press, 1999).

16. Abraham Cahan, *"Yekl" and "The Imported Bridegroom" and Other Stories of Yiddish New York* (New York: Dover, 1970), p. 31.

17. *Ibid.*, p. 89.

18. Abraham Cahan, *The Rise of David Levinsky* (New York: Penguin, 1993), pp. 129, 291. Further references appear in the text.

19. Paul Laurence Dunbar, *"The Sport of the Gods" and Other Essential Writings* (New York: Modern Library, 2005), p. 407. See Martha Banta on the larger African American debate over good manners and rebellion: *Barbaric Intercourse: Caricature and the Culture of Conduct, 1841–1936* (Chicago, IL: University of Chicago Press, 2003), pp. 268–93.

20. On the connections of theatricality and the society of spectacle and surveillance associated with the burgeoning consumer culture of the turn of the century (indeed, on the apparent possibility of resistance as in fact the mark of the operation of power through literature), see Mark Seltzer, *Henry James and the Art of Power* (Ithaca, NY: Cornell University Press, 1984).

9

ERIC HOMBERGER

Immigrants, politics, and the popular cultures of tolerance

When a Jewish boy marries a Catholic girl we can expect laughs aplenty, and maybe some tears along the way: and so it proved in *Abie's Irish Rose*, a wildly successful play by Anne Nichols, which had a triumphant five-year run on Broadway from 1922. By 1927 there had been over 2,000 performances on Broadway and more than 11,000 performances world-wide, including a notable five-year run in the West End of London. At no time was it regarded as anything other than popular schlock. Nichols's characters speak with stage Irish and Yiddish accents richly larded with New Yorkese: *vell* (well), *goil* (girl), *dose* (those), *pizziness* (business), *tink* (think), *nize* (nice), *mudder* (mother), *strit* (street), *hoits* (hurts), *spik* (speak), *pliz* (please), *vant* (want), *don'd* (don't), *peefle* (piffle). Solomon Levy, Abie's father, summons a "texes keb" (taxi cab), and so on. The dilemmas of ethnic difference are settled with comic deftness when Rose cooks kosher food for her Abie, and makes a ham for her friends.

Abie's Irish Rose is a commercial product of American popular culture. It is also a prism in which powerful cultural forces – ethnic relations, the impact of mass immigration, and the cross-generational complexities of assimilation – are refracted, exaggerated, and also unexpectedly clarified. Popular culture is perhaps more comfortable than "high" culture with the interplay of cultural production and the immigrant experience. (It took several generations of ethnic jokes, we might say, to make *Call It Sleep* possible.) I take the broad ethnic comedy of Nichols's play to constitute a fable of tolerance. In the face of great cultural pressures for assimilation, her play offered Jewish audiences, and not just Jews, a way to manage that pressure. It opened a little window for tolerance.

"Artistically one of the worst and financially the greatest achievement of the U. S. Theatre," noted *Time Magazine* (November 3, 1924), "Abie has put Miss Nichols upon uneasy street. It has rendered her prosperous in dollar bills and penniless in artistic admiration."[1] Robert Benchley sourly quipped that "people laugh at this every night which explains why democracy can never be a success."[2] The play's commercial success, sustained by road companies playing across the nation, made it something of a cultural phenomenon, one richly saturated in ethnic stereotypes and Broadway clichés.

Over the course of the half-century after its initial staging, *Abie's Irish Rose* metastasized into a formidable franchise, long before the concept of "franchise" was invented. The New York press loved the story of *Abie's Irish Rose*. Its unknown (and female) author and her Broadway triumph attracted press reviews, profiles of the author, and cartoons in the *New Yorker*. Victor Fleming directed a silent movie adaptation for Paramount which was released as a talkie in 1928. Nichols got a shared credit for the screenplay with Herman J. Mankowitz. Published initially as a play in 1924, it was novelized by Nichols in 1927 and reissued with a new dust jacket in a "photoplay" edition by Grosset & Dunlap in the same year. *Abie's Irish Rose* spawned a cascade of popular-culture products. There were numerous stage covers, knock-offs, and movie adaptations, such as *Kosher Kitty Kelly* (1925), *Abie's Imported Bride* (1925), and *The Cohens and the Kellys* (1926). The original play, with its readily marketable Catholic-Jewish romance plot, was made into movies at least six times. The most successful, or the most readily exploitable, was *The Cohens and the Kellys*, which began life as an obscure play, *Just Next Door*, which was bought by Carl Laemmle and Universal Studios and transformed into a 1929 movie starring Charlie Murray and George Sidney, and a series of follow-up films.

Universal was sued by Anne Nichols, whose lawyer, Moses Malevinsky, submitted a bill of particulars running to 657 pages, demonstrating the similarities between Nichols's play and the Universal movie. The judges, who included Learned Hand, were not persuaded. In a decision which has been described as the leading US case in copyright law in the 1930s, the court ruled that general themes or plots could not be copyrighted: "A comedy based upon conflicts between Irish and Jews, into which the marriage of their children enters, is no more susceptible of copyright than the outline of Romeo and Juliet."[3] Universal went on to release *The Cohens and Kellys in Trouble* in 1933.

Abie's Irish Rose was made into a weekly radio soap opera which ran for seven months in 1944, and was revived twice on Broadway by Nichols, with diminishing success, in 1937 and 1954. In 1946 *Abie's Irish Rose* was remade as a movie by United Artists/Bing Crosby, featuring Joanne Dru and an upbeat title song performed by Mel Tormé, in which Rose thinks positively about the world: "What ever happens she'll find a little good in ev'rything." Nichols received a joint writing credit for the screenplay.

An unpublished play by Philip Roth, *A Nice Jewish Boy*, performed at the American Place Theater in 1964, was a comic rewrite of *Abie's Irish Rose*.

Dustin Hoffman played the lead. The warm liberal conclusion of Stanley Kramer's 1967 movie, *Guess Who's Coming to Dinner* – nominated for ten Oscars – affirmed its roots in *Abie's Irish Rose*. The Supreme Court in *Living* v. *Virginia* had just struck down as unconstitutional laws which banned interracial marriage. And here were Spencer Tracy and Katharine Hepburn playing crusty but lovable parents whose daughter has just married a black man, played by the eloquent, handsome Sidney Poitier. The issue of interracial marriage was an explosive one and Kramer's film upset a lot of people. It also gave a tag, a little shared joke, which over the following decades accompanied the question of racial integration.

As late as 1972, *Abie's Irish Rose* provided the plot for *Bridget Loves Bernie*, a 24-part television comedy series directed by Ozzie Nelson, in which the upper-class Irish-American Bridget (played by Meredith Baxter) marries Bernie Steinberg (David Birney), a Jewish taxi driver from Brooklyn. The kids love each other, but there are problems with their parents, who are uncomfortable about the differences in class and religion separating the two families. The audience's response was quite positive, and it became the fifth-ranked show for CBS that year. But *Bridget Loves Bernie* was unexpectedly cancelled at the end of the first season. The story went around New York that the studio executives were fed up with the barrage of anti-Semitic hate mail which greeted their cute little comedy. It was also attacked by indignant rabbis for encouraging intermarriage. The level of hostility towards *Bridget Loves Bernie* surprised everyone. That wasn't supposed to be the American way. Warner Brothers' short-lived 1998 sitcom *You're the One* gave us much the same plot, Manhattan setting, and plentiful ethnic stereotypes.

The success of *Abie's Irish Rose* was not solely due to effective exploitation, though it made Anne Nichols a very wealthy woman; it is also a striking instance of the interplay of cultural production and the immigrant experience in New York City. At every stage in the history of *Abie's Irish Rose*, as author, director, and producer, Nichols was a serious professional in the management of her interests. She exploited the commercial possibilities of the play, and assertively defended her rights. The source of this cascade of light entertainment, Anne Nichols, was born in 1891 and raised in a strict Baptist family in rural Georgia. She was not an "ethnic" and not a New Yorker, at least not until she began to write and produce plays in the early 1920s. We are used to the notion that "ethnic literature" is written by, and reflects the experience, of "ethnics." Nichols reminds us that a somewhat wider understanding of the uses of ethnicity is called for.

Running away from Georgia at the age of sixteen, she turned up in Philadelphia where she found work as a singer and pursued a career as an actor and writer. She married and then divorced Henry Duffy, an Irish

Catholic actor and producer. Settling in New York after the war ended, she wrote vaudeville sketches and had two plays produced on Broadway. She later claimed to have written *Abie's Irish Rose* in a mere three hours, and persuaded the Broadway producer Oliver Morosco to stage it in Los Angeles and San Francisco. But they fell out when Nichols proposed to bring the play to New York. Perhaps Morosco doubted that the play was right for the sophisticated Broadway audience. Nichols promptly sued Morosco for breach of contract, and set out to direct and produce the play herself. *Abie's Irish Rose* opened at the Fulton Theatre on West 46th Street on May 22, 1922. After mixed reviews, the play limped along to half-empty houses for several months. Desperate to give the play a proper chance, Nichols needed to borrow money. No one would touch a new play by an little-known playwright, and so she approached Arnold Rothstein, the city's leading gambler and loan-shark. She offered Rothstein a half interest in the show for $25,000. Not being particularly interested in the theater (his wife Carolyn claimed that he had seldom if ever attended a play), Rothstein preferred collateral, and Nichols signed over to him the mortgage on her house. At the end of the run, Rothstein had made $3,000 profit. Nichols was a millionaire.[4] It is hard to imagine that the backing of Rothstein hurt the play's popular appeal.

Fathers and sons

Nichols's Abie is not an immigrant but lives utterly within the complexities of immigrant life and the travails of assimilation in New York City. Her characters speak English (the son more comfortably than the father), and move with growing confidence in the urban milieu. Abie's father Solomon, who has a department store in the Bronx, is an orthodox Jew, a traditionalist proud of being old-fashioned. It is unthinkable for Solomon that his thoroughly Americanized son Abie would not marry a "nice Jewish girl." But Abie's rapid assimilation carried with it a threat. The more "American" he became, the deeper his implicit rejection of his father's life and values – and his Judaism.

Nichols identified a paradox at the heart of assimilation: that the search for liberation and self-fulfillment carried with it the prospect of weakening Jewish identity and perhaps its dissolution altogether. This paradox exists in *Abie's Irish Rose* at the level of ethnic jokes, and the customary mechanisms of light entertainment, but the deeper meaning persists. The figure of David Levinsky in Abraham Cahan's 1917 novel embodies the paradox. He has made a fortune as a cloak-manufacturer in the shark-pool of American commerce. But at the end of the novel Levinsky knows he has betrayed his deepest instincts, and that his wealth has been paid for by personal isolation and emotional emptiness. His is not a classic American rags-to-riches success story, but a study in ambivalence which connects Levinsky's ghetto striving to Howells's Silas Lapham, Dreiser's Carrie Meeber, and Fitzgerald's James Gatz, among other casualties in the American struggle for success.[5]

The literary model for Solomon Levy was perhaps Asriel Stroon in Cahan's *The Imported Bridegroom* (1898), driven by fear that his Americanized daughter Flora will be lost to the Jewish faith if something is not done to prevent her seduction by the secular, free-thinking ways of American youth. Stroon is homesick for the old piety, and brings a learned yeshiva scholar from his native village in the Old World to New York, hoping that he will marry Flora. Cahan, the most ironic of immigrant writers, saw clearly that the memory of the Old World was a constant reproach to Jewish immigrants making their way in the New World, and one which they jettisoned at some emotional cost. The nostalgic memory of *shtetl* piety, Sabbath observance, and deep immersion in the study of Torah was not shared by their children, for whom it became an annoying reproach. *Shtetl*-nostalgia is not exclusively a post-Holocaust phenomenon, as readers of Cahan's novels know. But the nostalgic portrayal of the *shtetl* in *Fiddler on the Roof* (1971) and *Yentl* (1983) are products of American culture and its dynamics, irrevocably distanced from the *shtetl* as it once was.

Nichols gave Solomon Levy a *shtetl* backstory in *Abie's Irish Rose*: born in Russia to a life of hardship and persecution, Levy was orphaned in a Cossack pogrom, and illegally smuggled out of Russia. He sailed for America, married, and was soon a widower when his wife died after giving birth to their son Abie. Judaism is the central pillar of Solomon Levy's identity. But that is not the case with Abie, who sees his father as someone who needs to lighten up, who must be weaned away from his entrenched prejudices, and ancestral dislike of Christians. There is much about the reality of immigrant life in New York that makes no appearance in Nichols's story, not least its instability, the incessant changes in residence that tenement life and employment demanded, and the profound sense of dislocation that immigrants felt. "People who had labored in the same workshop or neighborhood in the Old World," wrote Michael R. Weisser, "now faced the prospect of changing employers and work locations several times each year. The frenzy of immigrant life in New York, its rapid and unforeseen change, was the antithesis of the *shtetl* experience, and all the traditional definitions and habits were suddenly without meaning."[6] Popular culture can do many things with the immigrant experience, but broad ethnic comedy captures little of the vertiginous, existential dislocation experienced by immigrants. No wonder those who were like Solomon Levy clung ever more desperately to the old values.

Families were universally perceived as the custodians of ethnic and religious tradition, but it was in the primal conflicts between fathers and sons that the Jewish struggle toward modernity was at its most intense. The generational gap between parents, born and shaped by the experience of the *shtetl*, and the streetwise, ambitious, American-raised children, with a "peculiar air of self-confidence" unknown to their ghetto-born parents, was a staple of early twentieth-century Jewish culture.[7] Arnold Rothstein, the son of an owner of a dry-goods store who was raised in a townhouse on the Upper East Side, suggests the same pattern of experience. While still a teenager Rothstein fled from the iron constraints of bourgeois Jewish respectability and sought out the saloons, jazz clubs, and gambling dens of the Lower East Side. When he brought a girlfriend home to meet his father, he explained that she was not, actually, Jewish, and would not convert. "Well, I hope you'll be happy," Abraham Rothstein said. After his son's wedding he covered the mirrors in his townhouse and said Kaddish, the traditional prayer for the dead.[8] No less than Solomon Levy in *Abie's Irish Rose*, Rothstein's father was mourning for a dead son.

American Jewish literature from Anzia Yezierska to Michael Gold reads like a series of battle reports between fathers and sons (and daughters). Gold's *Jews Without Money* (1930), set in the tenement world of the Lower East Side, drew a contrast between the author's hard-won lessons on the streets of New York, and the defeated, fearful lives of his parents, for whom virtually every aspect of American life, with its political corruption, prostitutes, and gangsters, was "treyf," an affront. Despite these fears, the protagonist of *Jews Without Money* played with the children of his Irish neighbors.[9] The Americanized children of Hannah Breineh in Anzia Yezierska's story "The Fat of the Land" are embarrassed by their mother's foreign accent and crude manners. Reversing the plot in "Children of Loneliness" (in the volume of that title), a modern daughter, Rachel Ravinsky, tries to teach her parents good table manners. Rejecting her mother's latkes (potato pancakes), she rejects her mother's world.[10] It is the assimilated children in *Hungry Hearts, Children of Loneliness, Abie's Irish Rose*, and *Jews Without Money* who become the teachers of their parents, reality-instructors in new ways of American life. The children hope to transcend the old tribalisms and entrenched prejudices, and win a place in American life. Their *allrightnik* optimism sets the scene for yet further opportunities for disillusionment and irony.

There was a narrative need for a vantage point outside the claustrophobic family and the embattled urban ghetto. Nichols began the novelized *Abie's Irish Rose* with Abie's military service during the First World War. Although the American experience of war was brief (from April 1917 until November

1918), for ethnic communities in New York and elsewhere its consequences were vast. The war virtually stopped the conveyor belt of immigration to America, which was further restricted by the Johnson-Reed act of 1924. The number of new immigrants was cut to no more than 2 percent of the total foreign-born population of that nationality present in the United States in 1890. The "national origins" quota system remained in force until the 1960s. Nowhere was the impact of Johnson-Reed felt more strongly than in New York, which had traditionally been the most "foreign" of American cities. In 1910 over 40 percent of the city's population was foreign-born. The New York of *Abie's Irish Rose* was gradually becoming a more "American" city.

Service in the American Expeditionary Force in Europe, and the shared experience of combat, acted as a powerful solvent to the old divisions and hostilities in the streets of New York. Religious divisions were among the first things to be challenged by service overseas. Chaplain Samuels in the novelized *Abie's Irish Rose* recounts the story of finding a badly wounded soldier, Patsy Dunn, who asks the rabbi to "say the right word" for him. It was a request which could not be refused.

> "I'm glad to hear you say that, Father. And I do think the boy died comforted."
> "Of course he did! A lad doesn't think of creeds at such a moment. He's got other things to think about – "
> "Yes."
> " – More important things. When death is just around the corner …"
> "Men forget their prejudices."
> "They do. And I hold it's the will of God. For, after all, 'tis the same God above us."[11]

In *Abie's Irish Rose*, war taught the benefits of "a little tolerance toward other people."[12] On the home front, rampant anti-foreign and antiradical propaganda entrenched the old political, racial, and religious prejudices. With its love-conquers-all plot, and comic resolution of religious tensions, Nichols's play, a fable of tolerance, was a tremendous success in a wintry time for liberal values.

Americanism, Americanization, and tolerance

Americans firmly believed that there was a prophetic American identity, and a distinctive American way of life. Waving the flag was the American way. Resistance to assimilation, assertions of apartness, were greeted with indignation. Hyphenated Americans (as they were called) came under strong pressure to learn English, and enter fully and without reservation into American life. In a lecture in 1893, Theodore Roosevelt, then a member of the United States Civil Service Commission, stated before an audience in Boston that "we have a right to demand that every man, native born or foreign born, shall in American life act merely as an American ... we don't wish any hyphenated Americans; we do not wish you to act as Irish-Americans, or British-Americans, or native Americans, but as Americans pure and simple."[13] (Saying this in 1890s Boston carried additional layers of local meaning.) Against the darkening background of national debate after 1914 about neutrality and intervention, demands for "100% Americanism" intensified. The tell-tale hyphen was a political red flag. Citizenship classes were made compulsory in public schools, and the school day began with the Pledge of Allegiance to the flag. It is important to stress that the project of "Americanizing" the immigrant won widespread, indeed even messianic support, not least in the ghetto itself.

The heated polemics about the need to Americanize the immigrant were closely paralleled by debates within each immigrant community about Americanization, and what it might mean. And what it might cost. The Orthodox, a conservative minority in the American Jewish community, feared that becoming a "good American" entailed dangers. They resisted the incessant clamor to adapt to American ways, and were more likely to read the Orthodox (i.e., conservative) Yiddish paper *Tageblatt*, with its hatred for "reform sects in religion and the socialistic tendencies in politics and economics," than the socialistic polemics of Cahan's *Forverts*.[14]

The metaphor of the "Melting Pot" was given wide publicity by the success of Israel Zangwill's play of that name, first produced in Washington, DC, in 1908. He envisaged a new American identity being forged out of the process of "melting" the different national groups. The most enthusiastic proponents of the "Melting Pot" advocated a merger of the immigrant communities with the dominant Anglo-Saxon culture of America. The precise mechanism envisaged does not bear much scrutiny: that kind of mingling, to say nothing of racial "amalgamation," had few advocates in America in 1908. In fact, the idea of the "Melting Pot" failed to win support from any immigrant community. In the early twentieth century, intermarriage for Jews hovered around 2 or 3 percent. The long tradition of diaspora inculcated the belief that Jews must remain a people apart to survive. They were the least assimilated of all immigrant communities. For observant Jews, the prospect of the "Melting Pot" was a nightmarish threat to Jewish identity. They feared that the Americanized young would marry outside the religion. Lurking behind their fears was the seductive figure Lilith, the night-demon and seductress, who was the embodiment of Orthodox fears of the sexual and cultural danger of the *shiksa*. For a minority, then, Americanization was seen as a one-way ticket to group suicide.

Theodore Roosevelt remained a strong supporter of the ideal of the "fusing of all foreign nationalities into an American nationality."[15] Flatly rejecting "sectarian intolerance" and the extremes of prejudice, the ultimate absorption of American diversity into the reigning Anglo-Saxon model would not have surprised or disappointed him. Zangwill, who dedicated his play to Roosevelt, inserted a caveat in the 1914 text of the play: "The process of American amalgamation is not assimilation or simple surrender to the dominant type, as is popularly supposed, but an all-round give-and-take by which the final type may be enriched or impoverished."[16] In his hands, the "Melting Pot" or Americanization sought more cautiously to be a response to inter-ethnic resentments. The majority of American Jews were strongly attracted to the liberal ideal of tolerance and, as Zangwill suggested, to its "all-round give-and-take." Tolerance could temper the harshest implications of Americanization, and that is the context in which *Abie's Irish Rose* triumphed in New York.

The outward signs of Americanization were to be seen everywhere on the city streets. Jews wore three-piece suits and derbies. Traditional long black coats and broad-brimmed hats looked wildly out of place. Tradition and ritual, the outward signs of Jewishness, meant little in the "Land of Hurry-Up."[17] A visceral hunger for economic opportunities shattered traditional communal loyalties. Baseball, the Fourth of July, hotdogs – the whole panoply of secular pleasures of American life – irresistibly drew Abie and his generation toward a new kind of social identity as Jews and Americans. Assimilation promised an escape from poverty, and acceptance in the larger community. While turning their back against tyrannical ideas of compulsory assimilation, the *idea* of assimilation represented opportunities which most immigrants welcomed – providing of course that there was a way to control the process, to pick and choose, at least to the point where some sense of personal identity survived. Despite the anxieties of the pious, the process of Americanization uneasily continued.

The path toward "100% Americanism" was more contentious, and more overtly political. Throughout the decade which preceded *Abie's Irish Rose*, there were important Jewish communal leaders in New York who flatly disagreed about what Americanism involved. Rabbi Joseph Silverman of Temple Emanu-El, the oldest Reform synagogue in the United States, promulgated a "Ten Commandments of True Americanism" in 1915.[18] Rejecting all jingoism, Silverman's "True Americanism" strongly supported preparedness and internationalism. In an address on "Americanism and Hyphenism," Dr. Stephen S. Wise of the Free Synagogue in New York, a freewheeling advocate of reform Judaism and ethical earnestness, denounced militarism and claimed that military preparedness was "fundamentally wrong."[19]

Despite the sentiment expressed in Emma Lazarus's celebrated poem "The New Colossus" ("Give me your tired, your poor, / Your huddled masses yearning to breathe free, / The wretched refuse of your teeming shore. / Send these, the homeless, tempest-tost to me, / I lift my lamp beside the golden door"), this was no golden age of sympathy for foreigners, huddled or otherwise. A generation had passed since the Jewish banker Jesse Seligman was humiliatingly turned away at the Grand Union Hotel at Saratoga, being told by the manager that "Mr. Seligman, I am required to inform you that no Israelites shall be permitted in future to stop at this hotel."[20] Judge Henry Hilton, administering the estate of the recently deceased merchant A. T. Stewart, later explained that he was opposed to what he described as the "Seligman Jew." Protest meetings were held, letters written by William Cullen Bryant, sermons preached against the exclusion by Henry Ward Beecher, but to no avail. What so shattered Jewish morale in New York was the unexpected extent of support for the exclusion. The memory of that event long shaped Jewish insecurities in New York.

In the 1920s the enemies of tolerance, led by the Ku Klux Klan, were organized and aggressive. The American Legion had a threatening Committee on Americanism. Discrimination was near universal: suburban golf clubs and major manufacturers and financial institutions regularly excluded blacks, women, and Jews. Quotas governed Jewish admission to the nation's most distinguished Ivy League universities.[21] Where tolerance existed, it was limited in scope. But so far as New York Jews were concerned, liberal tolerance – religious liberty, separation of church and state, and social and political equality – was the only game in town.

The most important liberal engagement with Americanization occurred in New York, and preceded *Abie's Irish Rose* by barely a half-dozen years. A Harvard-trained philosopher, Horace Kallen, first coined the phrase "cultural pluralism" in 1915.[22] Kallen believed that the culture of the immigrants was intrinsically of value in the formation of American society. He also feared the potentially tyrannical pressure for conformity, arguing that patriotism, chauvinism, and religious triumphalism endangered American values. Kallen's ideas met with the enthusiastic approval of American liberals like John Dewey, and it was Dewey's pupil, Randolph Bourne, who restated Kallen's argument in articles in *The Atlantic Monthly* and the *Menorah Journal* in 1916.[23] Bourne saw the repressive potential of Americanization, particularly at a moment when the United States was on the verge of entering the war in Europe. He proposed as an alternative to the blanket assimilation of immigrant groups the concept of dual citizenship or what he called cooperative Americanism. This echoes Zangwill's belief in the desirability of "an all-round give-and-take." The American culture envisaged by Kallen and Bourne would be composed of diverse groups within the state in more or less open and tolerant competition. They assumed, perhaps naively, that none of the separate ethnic groups would seek to assert hegemonic authority over the cultural aspirations of the others. The radical edge of Kallen's and especially Bourne's argument was diluted, perhaps in the hope of making it more widely acceptable. In its softest form it was assembled by the Roosevelt coalition in the 1930s and was harnessed to the war effort in the 1940s. It celebrated a mildly tolerant diversity and an Americanness which defined itself, not in terms of the traditional Anglo-dominant model, but of a mixture of people from all backgrounds united in support of a national purpose. Hollywood grasped the cinematic possibilities of the emerging model of Americanism. The new platoon stumbles off the bus, as the crusty drill-sergeant calls roll. Wearing funny hats and sweatshirts, they stand there, slouching, waiting for something to happen. There is a Gonzalez, a Greenbaum, and a Pellegrini; there are whites and blacks, Hispanics, and snobbish types from Harvard; farm boys and city delinquents. At the end of the movie, the platoon marches with pride; their uniforms reflect their new unity; officers salute; the flag crisply waves; the families are thrilled. They have become one out of many.

Abie's Irish Rose connects us to the enduring American engagement with the ideal of tolerance. It is, for all its evident limitations, a play which belongs to the seed-time of twentieth-century American liberalism.

NOTES

1. www.time.com/time/magazine/article/0,9171,736441,00.html.
2. www.actorsequity.org/aboutequity/timeline/timeline_1920.html.
3. *Nichols* v. *Universal Pictures Corporation et al.* No. 4. Circuit Court of Appeals, Second Circuit, 45 F.2d 119; 1930 U.S. App. Lexis 3587.
4. Leo Katcher, *The Big Bankroll: The Life and Times of Arnold Rothstein* (New York: Harper & Brothers, 1959), pp. 303–4; Nick Tosches, *King of the Jews: The Arnold Rothstein Story* (New York: Ecco, 2005), p. 293.
5. Abraham Cahan, *The Rise of David Levinsky: A Novel* (New York: Harper & Brothers, 1917); Jules Chametzky, *From the Ghetto: The Fiction of Abraham Cahan* (Amherst: University of Massachusetts Press, 1977), ch. 9.
6. Michael R. Weisser, *A Brotherhood of Memory: Jewish Landsmanshaftn in the New World* (Ithaca, NY: Cornell University Press, 1989), p. 76.
7. Thus Gitl in Abraham Cahan, *Yekl* (New York: Dover, 1970), p. 83.
8. Rich Cohen, *Tough Jews* (New York: Simon & Schuster, 1998), p. 47.
9. Michael Gold, *Jews Without Money* (New York: Horace Liveright, 1930), pp. 163–65.
10. Anzia Yezierska, *Hungry Hearts* (Boston and New York: Houghton Mifflin, 1920), pp. 178–223; Anzia Yezierska, *Children of Loneliness* (London: Cassell, 1923), pp. 29–56.

11. Anne Nichols, *Abie's Irish Rose* (New York: Harper & Brothers, 1927), p. 31.
12. *Ibid.*, p. 32.
13. "The True American Spirit," *New York Times* (November 19, 1893).
14. Hutchins Hapgood, *The Spirit of the Ghetto: Stories of the Jewish Quarter of New York, with drawings from life by Jacob Epstein* (New York: Funk & Wagnalls, 1902), p. 179.
15. Roosevelt to Israel Zangwill, November 27, 1912, Roosevelt Collection, Library of Congress, cited in Thomas G. Dyer, *Theodore Roosevelt and the Idea of Race* (Baton Rouge: Louisiana State University Press, 1992), p. 131.
16. Israel Zangwill, "Afterword," in *The Melting Pot: A Drama in Four Acts* (London: William Heinemann, 1914), p. 203.
17. Gold, *Jews Without Money*, p. 107.
18. "'True Americanism' in a New Decalogue," *New York Times* (December 20, 1915).
19. "Loyal, But Is For Peace," *New York Times* (December 20, 1915).
20. "A Sensation at Saratoga," *New York Times* (June 19, 1877).
21. Jerome Karabel, *The Chosen: The Hidden History of Admission and Exclusion at Harvard, Yale, and Princeton* (Boston, MA: Houghton Mifflin, 2005).
22. Horace M. Kallen, "Democracy versus the Melting Pot," *The Nation* 100 (February 18 and 25, 1915): 190–94, 217–20.
23. Randolph Bourne, "Trans-National America," *Atlantic Monthly* 118 (July 1916): 86–97; Randolph Bourne, "The Jew and Trans-National America," *Menorah Journal* 2 (December 1916): 277–84.

10

MELISSA BRADSHAW

Performing Greenwich Village bohemianism

And so the people are standing before Greenwich Village murmuring in pitying tones, "It is not permanent, the colors will fade. It is not based on good judgment. It is not of that sturdy and healthy material from which, thank providence, we of the real Manhattan have been fashioned." There are others who sigh, "It is beautiful in places!" while others add, "That is only an accident."

Djuna Barnes, "Greenwich Village as It Is"[1]

As one of Amy Lowell's young Harvard acolytes left Boston for a new life in Greenwich Village, the poet sent him off with this warning: "The only thing I beg of you is not to be fooled by Greenwich Village. There are no good people there. They are just failures who agreed to admire each other, since the world refuses to do it for them."[2] Lowell had good reason to distrust the denizens of Greenwich Village. Though they shared similar artistic tastes and a similar drive to reform American literature, their ends differed dramatically. Lowell's was a conservative, anti-unionist, capitalist, pro-war mindset. The bohemians of the Village, on the other hand, believed in free love, labor reform, socialism, and pacifism. And yet Lowell's snide admonition, however unwittingly, gets at one of the most compelling paradoxes of bohemian Greenwich Village: a belief in failure as the only real mark of success in an America that the activists, anarchists, feminists, artists, writers, and poets who made it their home saw as increasingly smug, acquisitive, and anti-intellectual. Where Lowell notoriously pitched her writing to the general public, working to make the avant-garde accessible and commercially lucrative, the Villagers reveled in rejection by this same audience. They believed art could enlighten minds, shatter social prohibitions, even ameliorate inequities among the classes, and when middle-class audiences responded to their work with confusion and derision, they felt confident they had hit their mark. In rejecting the bourgeois desires of mainstream America, with its hunger for social position and material success, they turned the Village into a place where art reigned supreme as the highest, most noble human achievement.

The writers and artists who made the Village an enclave of countercultural forces in the first decades of the twentieth century read like a who's who of American artistic, literary, and intellectual history: playwrights Susan Glaspell and Eugene O'Neill; journalists Floyd Dell, John Reed, Randolph Bourne, Neith Boyce, and Djuna Barnes; poets Edna St. Vincent Millay, William Carlos Williams, and Hart Crane; memoirists Van Wyck Brooks and Mary Heaton Vorse; suffragists and social reformers Crystal Eastman, Emma Goldman, Henrietta Rodman, Inez Mullholland, and Ida Rauh. Mabel Dodge's weekly salons brought together disparate groups of reformers and artists – birth control advocates and imagist poets; union organizers and disciples of Sigmund Freud; socialist revolutionaries and modern dancers – proving that what they fought for was not as important as the mind-numbing culture they fought against.[3] Journals and "little magazines" such as Max Eastman's *The Masses*, Margaret Anderson and Jane Heap's *The Little Review*, Alfred Kreymbourg's *Others*, and James Oppenheimer's *Seven Arts* gave modernist artists and writers a vehicle for their stylistic experiments and inextricably linked art and social reform. It is impossible, in fact, to overstate the connection between art and social revolution in the Village ethos. To be an artist in the first place required a rejection of bourgeois values, but the art itself, sexually frank and eschewing traditional forms and conventions, constituted as well an aggressive rebuke of genteel artistic and literary traditions.

Americans imported the idea of bohemia from European artists' enclaves, especially nineteenth-century Paris, as romanticized in George du Maurier's novel *Trilby* (1894) and Giacomo Puccini's opera *La Bohème* (1896). Meant to evoke the hedonism and anti-materialism of the Gypsies, purportedly from Bohemia, bohemianism is both a style and a fantasy. There is no such thing as an "authentic" bohemianism: it is always an affectation, a self-conscious performance of an antiestablishment sensibility, expressed through art, non-marital and homosexual liaisons, and a rejection of bourgeois comforts. Village bohemians, the majority of whom were college educated and from middle-class backgrounds, came from all over the United States to participate in a subculture that shared their ideological convictions. They congregated in cafes and restaurants like Polly Holladay's on Fourth Street. There Polly's sometime lover, anarchist philosopher and Village personality Hippolyte Havel cooked and promulgated revolution, while members of the women-only Heterodoxy club argued over free-speech principles, and members of the Liberal Club upstairs drank, debated, and flirted during their wild weekly dances. New Women, eschewing the culturally mandated roles of wife and mother to pursue careers as journalists, artists, editors, and social workers; young men fresh from their Ivy League degrees; along with Jewish intellectuals, Russian revolutionaries, and German immigrants mingled in these gathering places, staying up all night, immersed in what historian Christine Stansell describes as a culture of talking, "self-conscious, flashy, daring, ostentatiously honest and sexual."[4]

A 1935 Columbia University sociological survey of Greenwich Village divided its population into two mutually exclusive groups: "local people" and "Villagers." The locals were the Italian, Irish, and Jewish families who lived in the tenements, went to church, had large families, and adhered to the fairly mainstream American value of social betterment through hard work and the gradual accumulation of capital. While the locals generally aspired to the social status and material comforts of the middle class, the Villagers flocked to Greenwich Village precisely so they could repudiate the bourgeois mentality and repressive morality of "the Babbitt-ridden communities from which they had escaped."[5] They settled into the Village loudly, eager to live among "the people" in noble poverty, with all the tone-deafness and condescension of those who have the luxury to choose their living conditions. Their neighbors eyed them with suspicion and then proceeded to double their rents and raise food prices, happy to bilk the newcomers of money carelessly spent. As the Columbia study explains, the two groups lived in entirely different worlds, though they lived side by side, the gulf between them "wide and unbridged."[6] Locals worried about the pernicious effects of their neighbors' unsavory lifestyles, their looseness with money, and their socialist leanings, and complained that they had taken over their neighborhood; Villagers criticized the locals' large families, their lack of education, and their foreignness, and characterized them as noisy and unkempt.

For all their inability, or unwillingness, to integrate with the locals, Village artists found them good artistic fodder, drawing on the disparities between the two groups for dramatic effect in their art. Djuna Barnes wrote local-color sketches for New York daily newspapers, for example, which often romanticized the locals as earthier, more authentic figures than the Villagers. In "Paprika Johnson" (1915) she tells the story of a stenographer who becomes the "first cabaret artist." Paprika is a beauty, "as good to look upon as a yard of slick taffy, and twice as alluring," but for the men in Swingerhoger's Beer Garden, her allure is in her voice, as she sits on her fire escape Saturday evenings, singing and playing on her banjo eight floors above the revelers in the garden below.[7]

Convinced that she is the beer garden's real draw, Swingerhoger offers her a job as paid entertainment, but Paprika demurs, certain she'll find a husband and a life away from her fire escape. In the meantime, Paprika uses her lovely voice to help her unlovely best friend, Leah – "thin, pock-marked and colorless" – woo Gus, a blind man (36). Once Leah is married, Paprika is free to pursue her own interests and eagerly accepts the epistolary courtship of the boy who tends the donkeys at Stroud's. On the very night that they are to meet face to face, however, Gus's vision is restored, and Leah begs Paprika to sit at his bedside in order to soften the blow of realizing he has a homely wife. As Paprika sits at Gus's bedside, the boy from Stroud's arrives at her apartment, and seeing Leah, "laugh[s] suddenly, with a hard, disillusioned break," and leaves (46). Her dreams of leaving the city for marital happiness in Yonkers, or the Bronx, of trading popular songs for lullabies, crushed, Paprika accepts Swingerhoger's offer, and as the story ends is still, at thirty, sitting on her fire escape, strumming on her banjo, singing to the men below.

"Paprika Johnson" critiques bourgeois desires as they fester, unattainable and unworthy, in the urban working class. Paprika's desires are simple: she wants a husband; she wants to move from the eighth floor to the second-floor front apartment. Were it not for her loyalty to her bosom friend, she might have had them. But as Barnes's narrative makes clear, Paprika's loss might be for the best. The boy from Stroud's is no catch, a pampered only child "who had put his hands into his mother's hair and shaken it free of gold" (38). His hasty departure after he mistakes the homely Leah for Paprika suggests he is no spiritual match for the noble heroine.

Ironically, when Paprika Johnson's trustworthiness and compassion get in the way of her dreams, she accidentally achieves what Villagers like Barnes hunger for by becoming an artist. This dense character study offers an enigmatic moral: Paprika achieves the Village ideal – she escapes the bourgeois institutions of marriage and motherhood, and finds a venue and an adoring audience for her art – precisely because she did not want or try for it. Paprika's lonely banjo songs, free of symbolic import or political significance, exist only as art. Effortlessly countercultural, Barnes's heroine represents the authenticity of the proletariat.

By contrast, the Village couple Barnes depicts in her satire "The Terrorists" are charlatans. She sardonically introduces one of her protagonists, Pilaat, by explaining that although his long hair and artistic dress make him appear bohemian, he has been cursed with the health and vigor of one who has known a pampered life. His youthful love of the "people" has given way in middle age to disdain, a disregard that Barnes ascribes to having "been comforted and maimed in his conceptions and his fellow love by too many clean shirts in youth." He approaches the social revolution he has devoted his life to "as one cleans up a floor, not as one binds up a wound."[8] With this striking metaphor Barnes gets at the character's primary flaw: his incapacity for tenderness. One cleans a floor vigorously, and without thought, taking satisfaction from efficiently solving the problem of the dirty floor.

But binding wounds requires not only skill and efficiency, but also empathy, as the problem is inextricable from the human who bears the wound. His young wife, meanwhile, has worked to obliterate her tenderness, thinking this a critical component of performing a bohemian identity. In order "to annihilate any slovenly ease of mind in herself, ... she deliberately set about annihilating her own soul and her own delicate, sensitive, and keen insight." Adopting the clothing and postures of the intellectual, she has literally weighted herself, wearing heavy boots "that seemed to be drawing her down" and loose, paint-smeared shirts that hide her thin body.

The problem with this couple, Barnes suggests, is that their anger at capitalist greed and their concern for the sufferings of the "people" is an affectation. The nameless wife spends her days in cafes, pretending to read a book of poems written by her husband, so that when strangers ask her about it she can brag that it was written by "Pilaat Korb – you know, the Terrorist" (163). During impassioned conversations she "permit[s] herself the pleasure of pretending to feel human suffering very deeply." She imitates Pilaat's conversational style, leaning "far back in her chair as he did when he had finished a sentence," as she accuses others of "wander[ing] ... about the world like shadows" separated from their bodies (163–64). When Pilaat and his friends finally plot to overthrow the capitalist regime, Barnes captures the fury and indignation of the would-be revolutionaries: "Lips protruded, ears trembled, the very beards began to shake. Fists doubled up, eyes sparkled, and the tongue knew no forbidden thing" (170). Certain that "with the dawn [they] shall creep forth to make the world better for men," they search the room for makeshift weapons. Once they have experienced the rage of revolutionaries, however, they pass out drunk, their revolution confined to tearing apart furniture for weaponry.

Barnes's cynical character sketch paints Village socialism as more talk than action, a criticism common enough that she could assume readers of the daily newspaper would get her joke. Her terrorists are harmless because they are more interested in the pose of countercultural revolutionaries than in actually bringing about social change. But the Village was, in fact, home to a large number of devoted socialists, unionists, anarchists, and radicals, such as Mary Heaton Vorse, a labor reporter whose stories brought the realities of workers' lives into middle-class America's living rooms; John Reed, founding member of the Communist Party of the United States of America (CPUSA); and Big Bill Haywood, founding member and first leader of the Industrial Workers of the World. Members of the IWW, known as Wobblies, believed that workers should be united as one class, rather than split among craft-based unions, in order to fight exploitation by the employing class more effectively. Two major actions of the nineteen-teens found major support from Village radicals: the 1912 Lawrence textile strike in Lawrence, Massachusetts, and the 1913 Paterson Silk Workers' Strike in Paterson, New Jersey. Villagers not only participated in the Paterson strike, which was ultimately unsuccessful, but also, led by Jack Reed and Mabel Dodge, reenacted it in pageant form in Madison Square Garden in order to raise awareness and bring in funds. The Paterson Strike Pageant offered a bizarre aestheticization of the labor movement that assumed the theatricality of protest was transferrable, detached from its context as political action.

The struggles of the laboring class were a dominant theme of actual Village theatrical productions, as well. The Provincetown Players, one of the only theatrical troupes in the Village at the time, took its inspiration from the Irish National Theatre, which toured the United States in 1911 promoting the modern social realism of native Irish playwrights.[9] Developed to combat the superficiality and commercialism of Broadway, the Provincetown Players wanted to return theater to the quasi-religious function of ancient Greek theater by using minimalist sets and amateur acting to emphasize the communal importance of drama as social ritual. They believed their do-it-yourself, not-for-profit productions could have both social and aesthetic impact. Unlike the sometimes-rival Washington Square Players, who premiered works by George Bernard Shaw, Anton Chekov, and Henrik Ibsen, the Provincetown Players only produced works by American playwrights and most often by themselves, including Susan Glaspell, Edna St. Vincent Millay, and most significantly Eugene O'Neill.

O'Neill's career began with the Players, who produced all of his short plays, beginning with *Bound East for Cardiff* in 1916, up until his move to Broadway with *Beyond the Horizon* in 1920. He returned to the Players with *The Hairy Ape* (1922), a play about an alienated laborer coming to understand his oppression, which was deemed too controversial for Broadway because it stoked anxieties produced by the labor movement.[10] As the play opens, the protagonist, Yank, feels empowered in his position stoking the engines of an ocean liner, sure that his labor, though unglamorous and unseen, commands respect: "We run de whole woiks. All de rich guys dat tink dey're somep'n, dey ain't nothin'! Dey don't belong. But us guys, we're in de move, we're at de bottom, de whole ting is us!"[11] When a wealthy young woman who has wandered down to the stoke hold recoils at Yank's appearance, calling him a "filthy beast" and fainting in horror, his pride turns to fury. He becomes enraged at "them lazy, bloated swine what travels first cabin," who, in the words of his fellow worker, a socialist named Long, "dragged us down 'til we're on'y wage slaves in the bowels of a bloody ship, sweatin', burnin' up, eatin' coal dust! Hit's them's ter blame – the damned Capitalist clarss!"

(44). His class rage lands him in jail, where he learns about the Wobblies, then takes him to the offices of the IWW, where his violent plans to make the upper classes suffer by "blow[ing] tings up" alarm the unionists, who suspect he might be an infiltrator. After they throw him out, calling him "a brainless ape," he makes his way to the zoo, hoping to find camaraderie with the animals. He releases a gorilla from its cage so that together they can terrorize those who have tyrannized them, but the animal crushes Yank, leaving him to die alone and despondent, belonging nowhere.

O'Neill described the play as expressionistic, with the protagonist representing the alienation and dehumanization of modern man in industrial society. "Yank," he explained, "is really yourself, and myself. He is *every* human being ... His struggle to 'belong,' to find the thread that will make him a part of the fabric of Life – we are all struggling to do just that."[12] The New York City police, however, found the play far too realistic. They tried to have it closed on the grounds that it was "obscene, indecent, and impure."[13] Though they were ostensibly offended by the play's "naturalistic" language – O'Neill's protagonist uses phrases like "Yuh lousy, stinkin', yellow mut of a Catholic-moiderin' bastard!" (58) – its larger offense was its sympathetic portrayal of laborers and its clear articulation of the IWW's mission statement. For example, when Yank is sent to jail for blocking a wealthy man's entry onto a bus, he learns about the IWW and the Wobblies from the other prisoners. In a scene of extended exposition he learns that mainstream America fears the IWW's power to undermine capitalist hierarchies, and he has an epistemological shift: whereas he once saw himself with pride as existing at the bottom – literally, the energy from within the ship that drives it forward – he now sees himself as trapped and oppressed by the upper classes who alone benefit from his labors. While Yank, in his murderous rage, reflects popular conceptions of IWW members as irrational and dangerously seditious, O'Neill challenges this perception by characterizing the men in the IWW office as reasoned and thoughtful, clear about what they want to accomplish and determined to do so peacefully. Wary of the play as symptomatic of the social unrest emanating from the Village, the New York police asked the mayor to close down the play, fearing it would embolden laborers and cause riots.

O'Neill's less literal, more symbolic interpretation reflects a crucial aspect of the Village ethos, that capitalist industrial society represents not progress, but devolution, robbing all humans of their humanity – the upper classes their ability to feel human suffering, the lower classes their dignity.[14] And while Villagers were routinely accused of lacking patriotism, they saw their drive to allow people of all classes to live with self-respect and to profit from their labors as deeply patriotic, as central to the promises of America.

If the police worried that O'Neill's play too neatly disseminated the case against capitalism and propagated bohemian ideas about laborers' rights and the promise of social revolution, a more insidious, and ultimately successful, threat to the social order lay in the Villagers' championing of free love and their conviction that feminism could make both women's and men's lives better. Freed from the de facto roles of mother and helpmate that came with marriage, New Women could develop into individuals with drives and desires beyond these gendered roles. Men, similarly freed from the stultifying role of provider and head of household, found themselves at liberty to pursue careers as artists and intellectuals.[15] They gained as well the possibility of more authentic companionship – sexual as well as emotional – with their female lovers. Maxwell Bodenheim, in fact, argued that the common-law marriages popular in the Village were more meaningful, and lasted longer than traditional marriages, because they were based on true affection rather than legal stipulations and economic necessities. Marriages, he claimed, are easier to end than long-term love affairs, because divorce courts do the messy work of separating lives once entwined. "In the Village where couples marry or bundle together because of love and love alone, conscience is a great bulwark against marital failure."[16] Of course the New Woman was also free to eschew romantic entanglements altogether, and exult in her sexuality without commitments of any kind.

No one exemplified this spirit of daring New Womanhood, as sexually driven as any man and just as wary of entrapment, like the Village golden girl, Edna St. Vincent Millay (see *Figure 11*). Millay's time in the Village was relatively brief, from 1917 until 1922, when she left for two years in Europe, returning briefly in 1925. Giddy with desire, and ready to flee at the first sign of sentiment, she was already famous when she came to the Village, having shot to stardom in 1912 when her poem "Renascence" – a long, mystical, Whitmanesque meditation on nature and God – did not win one of the top three prizes in a poetry contest for an anthology called *The Lyric Year*. This loss was so debated and so denounced that the twenty-year-old became an overnight poetic cause célèbre, taken up by everyone from Harriet Monroe to Louis Untermeyer to the mortified and repentant first-place winner of the contest, Orrick Johns, who offered Millay his prize money. Fresh from Vassar, which the impoverished girl poet attended thanks to the support of a patron, Millay arrived in New York City just as her first book came out.[17]

Renascence and Other Poems (1917) solidified her reputation as an important poet, proving that the title poem had not been a fluke, but it was her second book – *A Few Figs from Thistles* (1920), epitomizing the spirit of the bohemian New Woman – that established her as the It-girl of Greenwich Village. The familiar lines of "First Fig" packaged the defiant *carpe diem*

Figure 11: Publicity photo of Edna St. Vincent Millay, taken by Arnold Genthe at the publisher Mitchell Kennerly's Mamaroneck, NY estate in 1914, a few years before Millay's arrival in Greenwich Village. This photo, which emphasizes her youth and femininity, was used to market Millay's first volume of poetry as the work of a female wunderkind.

exuberance of bohemian life into the bite-sized refrain mainstream America wanted and expected from Millay:

> My candle burns at both ends
> It will not last the night;
> But ah, my foes, and oh, my friends –
> It gives a lovely light![18]

Because she was famous before she came to New York, anything she did there resonated far beyond MacDougal Street, and because she rejected the modernist experimentation of Village poets like William Carlos Williams, instead writing poetry that was modern in sensibility but traditional in form, Millay offered up an accessible version of quasi-mythical bohemian profligacy. *A Few Figs from Thistles* served as a bridge between the reality of bohemian Greenwich Village and national fantasies of the Village.[19] "Recuerdo," for example, captures the naughty urbanity of staying up all night wasting time: "We were very tired, we were very merry – / We had gone back and forth all night on the ferry" (2). As much a metaphor for bohemian art for art's sake as it is a representation of Village life, the poem argues that doing something just for the fun of it is wonderful and worthwhile.

It was in this volume that Millay dropped the role of ingénue and created the poetic persona still most closely associated with her: that of a sexually sophisticated, unsentimental modern woman. In "Thursday" she tells a disconsolate lover that having loved him on Wednesday is no guarantee that she will love him on Thursday:

> And why you come complaining
> Is more than I can see.
> I loved you Wednesday, – yes – but what
> Is that to me?
>
> (4)

In "The Penitent" she brags: "[']I've been a wicked girl,' said I; / 'But if I can't be sorry, why, / I might as well be glad!'" (17). Sonnet III, "Oh, think not I am faithful to a vow!," casts the poet as sexual aggressor, "faithless … save to love's self alone," who warns her lover that she will stay only as long as she is satisfied: "Were you not lovely I would leave you now … And seek another as I sought you first" (31). Similarly, in Sonnet IV, "I shall forget you presently, my dear," she challenges her lover to enjoy her love while it lasts. "Make the most of this, your little day, / Your little month, your little half a year," for the vows dictated by social custom are "brittle" and short-lived, while nature's inconstancy – the sex drive that defies monogamy – alone is constant: "nature has contrived / To struggle on without a break thus far, – / Whether or not we find what we are seeking / Is idle, biologically speaking" (32).

What is most disruptive about these bold assertions of desire, however, is the way they articulate the bohemian philosophy of free love to a middle-brow audience. Sonnet III, for example, turns the idea of commitment upside down, arguing that vows are antithetical to love, as they create unions sustained by a sense of obligation more than affection. The speaker's refusal to be faithful to a mere vow emerges as the truest guarantor of love she can offer. She will be constant only so long as she finds her lover "hunger's rarest food, / and water ever to my wildest thirst." The impermanence of her love makes it more valuable. "I am most faithless," she warns, "when I am most true" (31).

Millay's 1917 arrival in the Village coincided with what the first generation of bohemians bemoaned as the end of a golden era, a time period described in retrospect as a "Little Renaissance," when Villagers played, plotted, created, and fought in self-imposed exile, far from the commercial concerns of mainstream culture. Nina Miller describes this moment as "the cusp of two ideological eras," with "Millay figur[ing] importantly for both: the older generation, who claimed her as the emblem of waning bohemian authenticity and the younger generation, who turned to bohemia as part of a national urge to do so."[20]

Of course, Millay's arrival in Greenwich Village also coincided with the United States' entry into the First World War. In his memoir, *Exile's Return*, Malcolm Cowley, himself a member of this younger generation, describes how the war changed the Village. Before the war Greenwich Village "contained two types of revolt, the individual and the social – or the aesthetic and the political, or the revolt against puritanism and the revolt against capitalism."[21] The war ushered in an era of nativism and jingoism; told that it was their patriotic duty, people were asked to sacrifice personal comforts. They learned to ration food, clothing, and metal, while industrial energies turned to producing clothing, food, and weaponry in support of the war effort. In this climate labor organizers who fought for workers' rights suddenly seemed unpatriotic; pacifists who had spent the last several years trying to keep the United States out of the war were seen as traitors; communists and socialists who had advocated a revolt against capitalist social and economic structures were now perceived as dangerous threats. The social radicals who had been such an important part of Greenwich Village either left the country, served jail time as conscientious objectors, or turned their energies inward. As Cowley sarcastically notes, right around the time the socialist magazine *The Masses* was shut down by the government for its determinedly anti-war stance and for linking capitalism with militarism, "talk about revolution gave way to talk about psychoanalysis" (67).

When Cowley's generation arrived in the Village, many of them coming straight from active duty, the Village's political vibrancy had been stamped out, with the remaining vestiges of cultural rebellion focused on sexual and artistic self-realization. These remaining rebellions, moreover, had solidified into a codifiable product. When post-war American industry needed to turn thrifty workers into avid consumers, it looked, Cowley explains, to the Village for inspiration. Bohemian principles once considered corrupt morphed into advertising slogans: "*self-expression* and *paganism* encouraged a demand for ... modern furniture, beach pajamas, cosmetics ... *Living for the moment* meant buying an automobile, radio, or house, using it now and paying for it tomorrow. *Female equality* was capable of doubling the consumption of products – cigarettes for example – that had formerly been used by men alone" (62). To the *Saturday Evening Post*'s repeated claims that the Village, its long-standing ideological nemesis, was dead, Cowley argues:

> If … the Village was really dying, it was dying of success. It was dying because it became so popular that too many people insisted on living there. It was dying because women smoked cigarettes on the streets of the Bronx, drank gin cocktails in Omaha and had perfectly swell parties in Seattle and Middletown – in other words, because American business and the whole of middle-class America had been going Greenwich Village.
>
> (65)

With their customs appropriated, commodified, and folded into middle-class American life, post-war Greenwich Village bohemians were in crisis. A new generation of artists and writers, one that had fought in the First World War, settled in the Village with no illusions as to the country's potential and no patience for the bohemian "funny clothes," social causes, and individualism they viewed as mere affectation.[22] Defining themselves decisively against the older generation, they eschewed "artiness" and self-important intellectualism and drank and danced and had sex with an abandon born of two years' fighting a war they did not expect to return from. Cowley, who saw his circle of friends as existing apart from the older generation, describes them as broken and demoralized. "The Village in 1919 was like a conquered country … 'They' had been rebels: they wanted to change the world, be leaders in the fight for justice and art, help to create a society in which individuals could express themselves … Now they were relics" (71–72). As Cowley's generation settled into the Village they too produced a stylized affect, one antithetical to that of their idealistic elders and premised on an ideal of austere masculinity, butch and brutal.

Even as Cowley disparages the previous generation, his tone belies a nostalgia for the Village as they knew it, a place where ideas and -isms – Marxism, Cubism, feminism, anarchism – intermingled and interacted. As he describes "Bill Haywood, the one-eyed man-mountain, the Cyclops of the IWW," mesmerizing a roomful of artists at Mabel Dodge's with stories of violent labor rebellion in the gold mines of Idaho, or Villagers getting "their heads broken in Union Square by the police before appearing at the Liberal Club to recite Swinburne in bloody bandages," his sardonicism gives way to tenderness. In writing his longing for a Village he just missed, he joins a long tradition of missing bohemia. To belong to bohemian Greenwich Village is to star in a meta-narrative about the experience of experiencing Greenwich Village. And for every generation, the Village they experience is just a little less edgy, a little less authentic than that of the preceding generation. Mourning this lost authenticity, then, is part of being a bohemian, as is understanding the elusiveness of authentic experience. Savoring this impermanence, taking comfort in this loss as a secret only those in the know are in on, while gullible tourists squeeze into cafes and wander winding Village streets looking for glimpses of artists or Marxists or free-love prophets, becomes itself a marker of the true Greenwich Village bohemian.

NOTES

1. Djuna Barnes, "Greenwich Village as It Is," in *New York*, ed. Alyce Barry (Los Angeles, CA: Sun and Moon Press, 1989), p. 224.
2. Amy Lowell to S. Foster Damon, April 25, 1918, bMS Lowell 19.1 (348). Amy Lowell Papers, Houghton Library, Harvard University.
3. Ross Wetzsteon offers a rousing description of Mabel Dodge's salon in *Republic of Dreams: Greenwich Village, the American Bohemia, 1910–1960* (New York: Simon & Schuster, 2002), pp. 15–47. According to Wetzsteon, Dodge's most important accomplishment was in understanding that "the repressive traditions against which the Village radicals were rebelling – political, economic, sexual, artistic – were inextricably linked, and that the most immediately necessary radical act was not to focus on specific reforms but to break down the barriers between the radicals themselves" (p. 25).
4. Christine Stansell, *American Moderns: Bohemian New York and the Creation of a New Century* (New York: Henry Holt and Company, 2000), p. 74.
5. Caroline F. Ware, *Greenwich Village, 1920–1930: A Comment on American Civilization in the Post-War Years* (Boston, MA: Houghton Mifflin, 1935), p. 244.
6. *Ibid.*, p. 244.
7. Djuna Barnes, "Paprika Johnson," in *"Smoke" and Other Early Stories* (Los Angeles, CA: Sun and Moon Press, 1982), p. 38. Further references appear in the text.
8. Djuna Barnes, "The Terrorists," in *"Smoke" and Other Early Stories* (Los Angeles, CA: Sun and Moon Press, 1982), p. 162. Further references appear in the text.
9. See Brenda Murphy, *The Provincetown Players and the Culture of Modernity* (New York: Cambridge University Press, 2005). Her first chapter, "The Founding: Myth and History," outlines the Little Theater movement in the United States and its indebtedness to the Irish Players, to the popular pageant movement in the United States, and to European avant-garde literary and artistic experimentation.
10. The play moved to Broadway after three weeks of performances at the Provincetown Players Playhouse.
11. Eugene O'Neill, *The Hairy Ape*, in *Nine Plays by Eugene O'Neill* (New York: Garden City Publishing Co., 1940), p. 48. Further references appear in the text.
12. Quoted in Murphy, *The Provincetown Players*, p. 206.
13. "Object to 'The Hairy Ape,'" *New York Times* (May 19, 1922).

14. See Lois Cuddy and Claire M. Roche's introduction to *Evolution and Eugenics in American Literature and Culture, 1880–1940: Essays on Ideological Conflict and Complicity* (Lewisburg, PA: Bucknell University Press, 2003) for a discussion of *The Hairy Ape* as showing "the consequences of the 'descent' of the human race for both the upper and under classes" (p. 44).

15. For a forceful statement of this ideal, see Emma Goldman, "The Tragedy of Women's Emancipation," in *"Anarchism" and Other Essays* (New York: Dover, 1969), pp. 213–25.

16. Maxwell Bodenheim, *My Life and Loves in Greenwich Village* (New York: Bridgehead Books, 1954), p. 56.

17. See biographical accounts of Millay's time in the Village in Nancy Milford, *Savage Beauty: The Life of Edna St. Vincent Millay* (New York: Random House, 2001); Anne Cheney, *Millay in Greenwich Village* (Birmingham, AL: University of Alabama Press, 1975); and Jean Gould, *The Poet and Her Book: A Biography of Edna St. Vincent Millay* (New York: Dodd Mead and Company, 1970).

18. Edna St. Vincent Millay, "First Fig," in *A Few Figs from Thistles* (1920; New York: Harper & Brothers, 1922), p. 1. Further references appear in the text.

19. See Nina Miller, *Making Love Modern: The Intimate Public Worlds of New York's Literary Women* (New York: Cambridge University Press, 1998). Miller argues that Millay "gave focus to the culture's diffuse ambivalence abut contemporary social change … provid[ing] symbolic access to modernity for her national audience" (p. 17).

20. *Ibid.*, p. 18.

21. Malcolm Cowley, *The Exile's Return: A Literary Odyssey of the 1920's* (New York: Viking Press, 1934), p. 66. Subsequent citations appear in the text.

22. Among the "Village ideas" that Cowley deemed irrelevant to his generation were progressive education, self-expression, "the crusade against puritanism" [*sic*], and female equality.

II

THULANI DAVIS

African American literary
movements

Harlem, the first neighborhood famed as a global black metropolis, has stood for a century as this country's largest and most iconic black community. When this once white neighborhood became a black one, however, it was the sixth home in New York for African Americans before law and custom began to allow them access to the entire city. I often joke that whenever Europe sailed off to discover the rest of the world there was always an African aboard. In the case of New York, this was doubly true. A black Portuguese navigator came up the Hudson in 1525, and in 1613 Jan Rodriguez, a free black sailor, was dropped off from a Dutch trader on Manhattan and stayed.[1]

The African influence on New York has its origins in the steady stream of people of African descent imported by the Dutch as slaves to build New Amsterdam. During the mid-1600s some held in bondage were freed and given land to provide a buffer zone against attacks from Native Americans at the northern end of New Amsterdam. When the British took over in 1664, thousands more captives were imported directly from West Africa into slavery in New York and a more repressive bondage than under the Dutch. The earliest African communities were near the present African Burial Ground and in the Five Points area. After the draft riots of 1863 a residential area known as "Little Africa" was in the West Village (until about 1890), and others developed in Brooklyn. From the 1880s until about 1910, most African Americans moved into the Tenderloin along Eighth and Ninth Avenues from 23rd Street to 42nd and San Juan Hill, between 58th and 65th Streets on the West Side.[2]

Early twentieth-century originators

The rise of the Tenderloin coincided with the post-Reconstruction waves of violence against African Americans, who were made aware by the political aims of the attacks that their rights of citizenship had vanished before they were fully acquired. The first epidemic of lynching and the legalization of Jim Crow segregation drove people out of the South. Among the migrants were New York's first jazz artists, including "Jelly Roll" Morton, Willie "the Lion" Smith, and James Reese Europe. Black theater countered minstrelsy, fed songs to early vaudeville and laid the groundwork for today's musicals. One group of showmen, many of them minstrel performers, formed a club designed to put their source of bread and butter out of business. "The Frogs," as they called themselves, included Europe, Bert Williams, George Walker, J. Rosamond Johnson, Bob Cole, Jesse Shipp, and others. They waged a long struggle at the turn of the twentieth century against minstrelsy's stereotypes.

The writers of the time were members of an educated, middle-class elite, some of whom were engaged in a drive for assimilation and, though their names are now obscure, they unfairly marked the period as a nadir in African American letters. Notable exceptions were a wildly diverse group ranging from the widely accepted dialect poet Paul Laurence Dunbar and the fiction writer Charles Chesnutt, to early feminist and educator Anna Julia Cooper and the progressive journalist Ida B. Wells.

Wells came to New York fleeing Memphis under threat for writing fierce editorials on lynching. Her paper was destroyed in her absence and she stayed and wrote for *The New York Age*. Her autobiography, *Crusade for Justice: The Autobiography of Ida B. Wells*, gives one of the few firsthand accounts of the political crises facing African Americans during the post-Reconstruction era. Elizabeth McHenry has pointed out that access to mainstream publication was so limited for African Americans at the time that even famous writers like Dunbar and Chesnutt were under-published, and literary scholars "have been content to steer clear of this period, maintaining our focus more profitably on the more easily recognizable authors, published works, and established publishing venues associated with the Harlem Renaissance."[3]

The two most influential books of the century's dawning were *Up From Slavery* (1901) by Booker T. Washington and *Souls of Black Folk* (1903) by W. E. B. Du Bois. Washington's hugely successful memoir made an artful use of the conventions of the slave narrative and was the last important work in that lineage. The book included a speech conciliatory toward southern white supremacist tradition that both made him famous and opened a bitter debate among African Americans.

The slave narrative tradition itself was relegated to the past by Du Bois's book, a collection of linked essays mixing historiography and memory that followed only Wells and Frederick Douglass in attacking the state's negligence toward African Americans after Emancipation. *Souls* stepped beyond its predecessors in innovation, style, and depth and in various ways influenced a wide array of writers. The impact of Du Bois's prodigious work as a scholar (especially the 1899 *The Philadelphia Negro* and the 1935 *Black Reconstruction*), journalist (particularly as editor of *The Crisis*), and activist (notably as a founder of the National Association for the Advancement of Colored People), cannot be overstated, yet *Souls* is perhaps his most-read and best-loved work for its portrait of the emergence from bondage.

Arguably the most important antecedent to the work of the Harlem Renaissance was *The Autobiography of an Ex-Colored Man* (1912), written by James Weldon Johnson, a poet from Jacksonville, Florida, who had come to New York in 1902 to write shows. He and his brother, the composer J. Rosamond Johnson, and the performer Bob Cole formed one of the most successful theater teams in New York. In this novel, which was initially published anonymously and taken to be a genuine autobiography of "passing," Johnson created a groundbreaking work endowed with an urbane central character whose complex internal life excavates some of the conflicts of racial identity fifty years out of slavery. The ex-colored man, the child of a white man and his black mistress in Georgia, grows up in New England, becomes a ragtime player in the Tenderloin, and is then taken abroad by a white patron. A later trip to Georgia to search out black folk music exposes him to a lynching, and sets his mind on passing. Some of the book's most detailed passages recall the novelty of New York's language, food, rhythms, and diversity. He later documented the growth of the city's black community and its migration to Harlem in *Black Manhattan* (1930).

Now that we are in an era likely to be named after the country's first African American president, the work of Wells, Du Bois, and Johnson has even greater significance because of their interest in the breadth of the African American journey out of legal bondage and their focus on our relationship to the American state. They were asking the most pertinent questions, and in time we shall have to examine whether they've been answered.

In December 1905 the *New York Herald* ran a story under the headline, "Negroes Move to Harlem," announcing that whites had been replaced by black tenants in flats on 134th between Seventh and Lenox Avenues. The article reported "the cause of the colored influx was inexplicable."[4] A murder had actually allowed a young African American realtor to begin placing black tenants – at higher rents – into buildings on that street. In 1908, the black expansion into Harlem began in earnest. Theater artists were also driven out of Broadway to Harlem from about 1909 until the end of the First World War.[5] Many small bars sprang up along 133rd ("The Jungle") and 134th, offering blues, booze, and dancing, and some catered to gay night life.[6] The area became home to Florence Mills, Bessie Smith, and Alain

Locke, as well as James Weldon Johnson and Fats Waller, to name a few. My uncle, the critic Arthur P. Davis, often told the story of seeing Du Bois and Garvey, who had little use for each other, passing one another on Seventh Avenue without acknowledgment, one in quasi-military gear and the other with fedora and cane.

By 1920, the African American population was larger than in any other American city. For artists during the 1920s, important anchors in the community included the 135th branch of the NY Public Library, the 135th Street YMCA, the Lafayette Theater, the Lincoln Theater, and the literary salon known as the Dark Tower on 136th. It was not until the 1930s that Harlem took on its present dimensions, with the exception of the business corridor of 125th Street, which was white-owned and hostile terrain for blacks.

According to many of the writers who were there, the Harlem community coalescing after the First World War was, in its size, diversity, and sophistication, a source of amazement to its new arrivals from the South and Midwest and from Africa and the Caribbean. Black Harlemites forged a cultural milieu that explored and exploited the arts and folklore of island, plantation, and southern town and delved into the African connection uniting their past. Not only was there a sense of discovery for black artists, but mass political organizing and protest movements became possible along with the transplanted parades of benevolent societies and churches.

What is blackness? Harlem Renaissance innovators

On July 28, 1917, not long after whites in East St. Louis, Illinois rioted, killing nearly 200 African Americans and burning their community in a labor dispute, between 8,000 and 10,000 residents of Harlem marched down Fifth Avenue in a silent vigil protesting mob violence, lynching, disenfranchisement, and all forms of discrimination. The march was the first mass protest in New York and symbolically announced the onset of the Harlem Renaissance, or the New Negro Movement as it was then known (see *Figure 12*).[7]

The job of organizing African Americans only became more urgent during the "Red Summer" of 1919, in which whites suffering the post-war economic troubles struck out with mob violence against blacks in cities from South Carolina to Washington, DC and across the Midwest, culminating in violence in Chicago. In several of these riots, blacks organized armed self-defense and fought back. "If We Must Die," a sonnet written that year by Jamaican-born Claude McKay, became the calling card of the era:

> If we must die, let it not be like hogs
> Hunted and penned in an inglorious spot,
> While round us bark the mad and hungry dogs,

Figure 12: Silent protest parade on Fifth Avenue, New York City, July 28, 1917, in response to the East St. Louis race riot. In the front row are James Weldon Johnson (far right); W. E. B. Du Bois (2nd from right); Rev. Hutchens Chew Bishop, rector of St. Philip's Episcopal Church, Harlem; and realtor John E. Nail.

> Making their mock at our accursèd lot ...
> Like men we'll face the murderous, cowardly pack,
> Pressed to the wall, dying, but fighting back![8]

This gendered representation of black resistance became widespread, abetted perhaps by the withdrawal of many women from civil rights protest into the reform movements of the Uplift era. Without the dominance of an Ida B. Wells, who encountered much hostility as a woman leader, "manhood" became a centerpiece of the language of the day. In this environment, Marcus Garvey amassed his troops. By the mid-1920s, Garvey, who had arrived from Jamaica to organize blacks in a movement for race pride and self-determination, shocked many by assembling rallies with crowds of 20,000, and delighted Harlem with parades of the uniformed members of the Universal Negro Improvement Association (UNIA) down Seventh Avenue. Harlem was shown the power of street theater, radio broadcasts, and sheer numbers.

One of the engines powering Harlem's intellectual ferment was a black-owned press. A broad range of publications concerned with the political and material conditions of African Americans were employers and outlets for writers. *The New York Age*, in print since the late 1880s, had made

Wells a household name, and in 1903 hired James Weldon Johnson. Du Bois founded the *Crisis* magazine in 1910, the most prominent, widely read, and long-lived of the magazines, and published many of the Renaissance writers, including novelist Jessie Fauset and conservative satirist George S. Schuyler, who were *Crisis* employees. Novelist and playwright Wallace Thurman worked for the radical *Messenger*, founded by Chandler Owen and A. Philip Randolph. The poet Countee Cullen wrote for *Opportunity Magazine*, and fiction writer Eric Walrond worked there and at Garvey's paper, *The Negro World*. McKay worked as a co-editor downtown at Max Eastman's *Liberator*, while novelists Dorothy West and Richard Wright ran *The Challenge*. Also in the late 1930s, novelist Ann Petry was an editor at the *Amsterdam News* and *The People's Voice*. This tradition of journalistic practice among Harlem writers continues today. These publications also became the primary outlets for the pioneer black critics.

The literary publications of the Harlem Renaissance began to appear in the mid-1920s. Their manifesto was *The New Negro* (1925), a collection edited by philosopher and critic Alain Locke and first published as a special issue of the journal *Survey Graphic*. Locke wrote:

> Of all the voluminous literature on the Negro, so much is mere external view and commentary that we may warrantably say that nine-tenths of it is *about* the Negro rather than of him, so that it is the Negro problem rather than the Negro that is known and mooted in the general mind. We turn therefore in the other direction to the elements of truest social portraiture, and discover in the artistic self-expression of the Negro to-day a new figure on the national canvas and a new force in the foreground of affairs.[9]

Locke cited the Great Migration as the "main change" and one of its consequences that "with renewed self-respect and self-dependence, the life of the Negro community is bound to enter a new dynamic phase." Locke announced, "The day of the 'aunties,' 'uncles' and 'mammies' is equally gone. Uncle Tom and Sambo have passed on" (4, 5). Locke's vision was integrationist and based on the assumption that if the races do not know each other through genuine self-expression "the race situation in America becomes desperate" (9). With this idea of engaging the "truest self portraiture," in 1922 James Weldon Johnson had published *The Book of American Negro Poetry*, the first collection of its kind, to be followed by two volumes of collected Negro spirituals. Decades later, writers of my generation would discover these still to be among the few sources of primary materials on African American literature and folklore.

One of the finest and most influential works to come from the Harlem Renaissance, *Cane* (1923), was written by a native of Washington, DC, Jean

Toomer, who spent little time in Harlem and did not write about Harlem, but illuminates Harlem by his somewhat contentious relationship to the leading figures of its movement. Toomer spent a few childhood years in Brooklyn and in 1917 took classes at NYU and City College, and it was the literary environment in the city that caused him to turn to writing.[10] After *Cane* was published Toomer broke with the race-consciousness of the Harlem writers and many of them in turn disparaged his abandonment of blackness in favor of a spiritual quest. But his break with the older literary traditions was widely admired and set a standard others would emulate. The luminous *Cane* is a collage of prose, poetry, and drama evoking the rural South with incantatory prose. That southern landscape was familiar to many who had made the journey north, but for Toomer it was a newly discovered path into racial identification. The book's portraits of black women – complex, lyrical, mysterious – were also utterly new to all American literature.

A kindred spirit was the Guyanese writer Eric Walrond, whose lush evocations of Panama and the Caribbean written in a loosely narrated and poetic style made his only work of short stories, *Tropic Death* (1926), unusual for the day. Walrond, like Toomer, wrote only this book before setting off on another quest. Unlike Toomer, he was an ardent race man and a Garvey follower until he became disillusioned with Garvey's mismanagement of UNIA projects.

Color (1925), the first volume of poems by Countee Cullen, is representative of one aspect of the Renaissance sensibility, turning a curious eye to the legacy of Africa. In his case, it is a mythical place, little known to a descendant of slaves born in the South, adopted by a Harlem minister, and educated at NYU and Harvard. "What is Africa to me," he asks in the opening line of "Heritage," responding variously:

> Africa? A book one thumbs
> Listlessly, til slumber comes.
> Unremembered are her bats
> Circling through the night, her cats
> Crouching in the river reeds
> …
> So I lie, who find no peace
> Night or day, no slight release
> From the unremittent beat
> Made by cruel padded feet
> Walking through by body's street.
> Up and down they go, and back,
> Treading out a jungle track.[11]

Outstripping Cullen in his broad impact was Langston Hughes, a poet from
Joplin, Missouri, whose itinerant life would take him to West Africa and for
whom that continent was not so much the question as the struggle of daily
life among the day laborers and bar patrons of Harlem. Hughes's modernist verse deploying the rhythms, humor, and rich play of urban black vernacular speech, influenced writers of the several generations to come in the
twentieth century. He celebrated blackness itself, not for its African origins
but for its adaptations in the here and now. In poems such as "Harlem Night
Club" in his first volume, *The Weary Blues* (1926), he toys with the jungle
tracks Cullen ponders so solemnly:

> "Sleek black boys in a cabaret.
> Jazz-band, jazz-band –
> Play, plAY, PLAY!
> Tomorrow ... who knows?
> Dance today!"
> White girls' eyes
> Call gay black boys.
> Black boys' lips
> Grin jungle joys.[12]

Hughes followed *Weary Blues* with *Fine Clothes to the Jew* (1927),
which some of the image-conscious black critics faulted for its unblinking
working-class focus. His novel, *Not Without Laughter* (1930), received some
criticism too for its exploration of the depredations of Harlem life among
the poor but as David Levering Lewis writes, "Since Toomer, no Harlem
writer had written as beautifully about the vices and virtues of ordinary
Afro-Americans and the truths governing their lives."[13] Hughes came out
with *The Ways of White Folks* in 1934 and *Montage of a Dream Deferred*
in 1951, and with his last books in the 1960s such as *The Panther and the
Lash* (1967) he became an elder statesman of the Black Arts Movement. He
was widely printed, his stories ran in black newspapers for decades, and he
became the country's most well-known African American writer. Hughes's
work also had a populist impact, inspiring widespread schools of urban
working-class vernacular poetry, laying the foundation for the sixties' voices
of Amiri Baraka, Sonia Sanchez, and others, and the later work of Pedro
Pietri, the Last Poets, Gil Scott-Heron, and Ntozake Shange.

Two novels became touchstones in a debate over the degree to which portrayals of the urban communities in formation should reflect the damag-
ing effects of poverty such as prostitution, gambling, and drug use. *Nigger
Heaven* (1926) by Carl Van Vechten, an important white patron and pro-
moter of Harlem Renaissance artists, was taken to task for contributing

to negative impressions of the race already created by stereotyping. *Home to Harlem* (1927), the first novel by Claude McKay, was better received but still enraged some of the Renaissance literati for its frank depiction of working-class Harlem. Du Bois surmised that McKay had "set out to cater to that prurient demand on the part of white folks."[14] It became the first commercially successful novel by an African American writer, which perhaps further fueled anxieties after its publication.

McKay's main character, Jake, a deserter from a First World War labor battalion in France and a footloose laborer, takes the reader on a journey through the working-class black metropolis. Jake's unanchored life is countered by that of his friend, Ray, an educated West Indian and aspiring writer much like McKay, whom he meets while working the railroads. The novel is an invaluable portrait of the conditions facing blacks after the First World War. Clearly set in 1919, one sees that long before the Depression apartments in Harlem might have five day workers sleeping in the living room, gambling saloons were busy every night, and blacks were often used as scab workers on the docks. Hazel Carby has written of Van Vechten and McKay that the latter "has a much deeper, richer, and more complex understanding of the cultural forms of the black urban landscape on which he draws than Van Vechten." Still, she critiques the use of female characters in both novels as problematic compared to the portraits of "masculinity in formation."[15]

The Harlem Renaissance had a number of important women writers who have been rescued from near-obscurity over the years. Gifted writer Nella Larsen wrote about characters who felt marginalized in both the black and white worlds. Larsen was the bi-racial child of a black father from the Virgin Islands and a Danish mother, and spent many of her formative years in a Danish-American community and several years in Denmark. Her novels *Quicksand* (1928) and *Passing* (1929) are centered on complex female characters given to destructive decisions and burdened with a fragility contrary to black female stereotypes of the day. In the psychological emphasis of her work, she anticipates the fiction of Toni Cade Bambara, Alice Walker, Gayl Jones, and others appearing in the 1970s.

Zora Neale Hurston looms much larger over the Renaissance today than she did in her lifetime. Many of her peers, including Wallace Thurman and Langston Hughes, wrote portraits of her that dismissed her talents in favor of mocking her penchant for enacting southern black folklore before whites. Hurston, trained under the anthropologist Franz Boas, did field work in Alabama, Florida, and Louisiana and produced not only folk studies (including audio tapes and film), but also fiction and plays. In recent years, scholars have acknowledged the full extent of her body of work and its contribution to knowledge of American folkways.

Hurston's second novel, *Their Eyes Were Watching God* (1937), now considered a classic, was not given its full due for years, perhaps because it was written in dialect, centered on a journey into unfettered womanhood that defied conventions of the day, or because it focused so tightly on black experience that the broader, oppressive presence of white supremacy in the South was peripheral to the story. *Their Eyes* shows more subtly the relationship of southern blacks to whites bossing the levees or other workplaces in rural areas. The novel's ultimate crisis takes place during a disastrous Florida hurricane that she uses in part as a brilliant metaphor explaining black/white relations at the time – half of the African Americans are doomed by their willingness to take the word of white employers that no harm will come of the storm and the other half are saved by heeding their knowledge of the natural environment and fleeing.

The word Renaissance as a label for this period should perhaps be seen not as the rebirth of a given community or its arts but as the birth of a collective African American sensibility outside of bondage – an expression of the singular people forged by bondage from many. This movement, which produced a great deal of work in literature, visual arts, theater, and even film, rises amidst the huge dislocation of the Great Migration during the years of the First World War and is in discourse with the dominant ideology of white supremacy, the Victorian ideal of womanhood, and blackface minstrelsy in all the performing arts. Its arrival comes in the context of cosmopolitan centers, access to education, and political organizing during the widespread adoption of Jim Crow practice even where it was not the law.

Blackness as the ghetto: rise of the Negro novelist

In the late 1930s several new novelists came to Harlem, some finding work with the Workers Progress Administration. The Harlem Riot of 1935 brought the beginnings of awareness of the problems uptown. In the work following the Depression years into the early 1960s, the dense, sprawling black metropolis became the Negro ghetto, no longer promising ground but a grinding mill of hardship. Richard Wright was born in Mississippi to a sharecropping family and then migrated in 1927 to Chicago, where he got involved in progressive movements and with the Negro Federal Theater of Chicago. He moved to New York in 1937 to become the Harlem correspondent of the *Daily Worker* and to finish his novel *Native Son* (1940). During the next few years he published his most masterful work: *Uncle Tom's Children* (1938), *Twelve Million Black Voices* (1941), and *Black Boy* (1945). While in New York, he wrote for *The New Republic, Partisan*

Review, *New Masses*, and other journals. In the mid-1940s he moved to Paris where he lived until his death in 1960.

Native Son was the most successful book by an African American author up to that time and put its author in a singular place among his peers, particularly given his years as a member of the Communist Party in the early forties and his criticism of Renaissance writers so beloved in black communities. The book told powerfully the story of Bigger Thomas, now an iconic character representing the transplanted southerners trapped in rat-infested tenements in the North without hope of employment beyond day labor and domestic service. Thomas is a young man who, after gaining a chauffeur's job, accidentally kills his employer's daughter in a panic at the possibility of being discovered as he helped the drunken young woman to her bed. He is fashioned as a creature of feelings, instincts, and reactions, unable to make an analysis of his own condition.

The generation of critics who came of age with the growth of militant nationalist groups in the 1960s dubbed Wright a "protest writer," a label that has over time diminished awareness of the acute analysis in his work as well as the visceral power of his prose. At the same time, these later critics were promoting male-centered political and artistic movements that muted discussion of the heavy-handed ideological passages in *Native Son* and the author's faulty treatment of female characters.

Ann Petry, who came to New York in the late 1930s from Connecticut, found the basis for her first and most successful novel in a newspaper story. *The Street* (1946), the tragic story of Lutie Johnson, a single mother in Harlem, is often paired with *Native Son* as a work of naturalist determinism. While *The Street* does focus narrowly on the accumulating damages of life among the urban poor, the significance of her revelations concerning the specific gendered oppressions and sexual exploitation of black women were long overlooked. The novel endured and in time became the first by an African American woman to sell a million copies.

Wright and Petry made mainstream America aware of the perils facing the millions struggling in the rubble of all the black meccas of the Great Migration. Wright especially was foundational for much of the work of the late 1960s and to many writers of the Black Arts Movement, but the naturalists also bred important resistance. Two major writers of twentieth-century American literature made the most brilliant pushes against the limitations of Wrightian ideology – Ralph Ellison and James Baldwin.

Ralph Ellison left three remarkable works: the 1952 novel *Invisible Man*, the essay collection *Shadow and Act* (1953), and *Going to the Territory* (1986), a collection of essays and stories. Born in Oklahoma City, Ellison became an avid student of 1920s jazz and aspired to be a musician. He went to Tuskegee Institute where he studied composition and encountered the work of T. S. Eliot, a major influence, but he abandoned his education for New York. Like many of the young Harlem writers to follow, he was mentored by two old hands of the Renaissance, Locke and Hughes, as well as by Wright, who published him in *The New Challenge*.

Ellison's *Invisible Man*, an audacious literary debut, rewrote the grand narrative of the African American man of the first half of the twentieth century inside the framework of a man's existential decision to step outside the course of his own expected narrative. His "invisible" protagonist journeys, much as Ellison did, from the West to the deep South for education, and deserts the anti-intellectual, plantation mentality of the southern black college for Harlem and the ferment there in the early 1930s. He spends some time engaged in progressive organizing before growing disgusted with his comrades and the failure of Marxism to address the persistence of racism. The novel weaves elements of Ellison's wide-ranging passions from jazz to European and American literature into episodes that continue to stand as vital metaphors for aspects of the African American experience. He also showed the potential for African American narrative to contain portraits of the larger culture as had Melville and Twain. The novel was declared a masterpiece and placed Ellison in the most celebrated ranks of contemporary literature, a position that proved crippling to his subsequent production in fiction.

Blackness as resistance: elders of 1960s literature

It is perhaps fitting that the first prominent Harlem writer actually born in Harlem was the eloquent and prophetic James Baldwin, who gave voice to the despair and anger of the powerless urban poor struggling in Harlem as its white landlords and employers abandoned the area and the middle class fled to the suburbs. Beginning in 1949, Baldwin caused a stir in the pages of *Partisan Review*, *Harper's*, and *Commentary*, among other publications, and hit his stride from 1955 to the early 1960s. In 1948 he wrote of Harlem: "All of Harlem is pervaded by a sense of congestion rather like the insistent, maddening, claustrophobic pounding in the skull that comes from trying to breathe in a very small room with all the windows shut."[16] Baldwin exposed the failure of American democracy, and the strange role of the African American as object in his own culture, echoing Locke in saying that so much had been written about the race that the race was more mythic than known.

Baldwin's poignant first novel, *Go Tell It On the Mountain* (1953), is largely autobiographical, retelling his experiences as a child whose stepfather brutally fought the young Baldwin's desire to write, pushing him instead to become a youthful preacher. Steeped as the writer was in the Christian gospel and the rhetoric and rhythms of the African American sermon, Baldwin's essay writing wielded a fierce authority and a familiar beauty. In addition to the novel, in the 1950s, he produced a collection of his prose, *Notes of a Native Son* (1955); a play, *Amen Corner* (1955); and the novel *Giovanni's Room* (1956), which dealt candidly with a homosexual relationship. In the 1960s, he published a second novel, *Another Country* (1962), a frank and tragic exploration of the intertwined lives of several black and white New Yorkers at mid-century; *Nobody Knows My Name* (1961), which covered his years living in Europe and his first immersion into the southern civil rights movement; and *The Fire Next Time* (1963), his most startling and prophetic work, coming as it did before the years of most widespread rioting in the United States. The essays of James Baldwin became the gold standard for those of us who would follow, and remain unmatched in African American non-fiction when it comes to incisive analysis, candor, and eloquence.

The Baldwin I knew – only slightly – was graying and gracious, but the impatient young Baldwin sick to death of blind bigotry made me want to write. That Baldwin never faded. I last saw him when I found myself seated next to him at an off-Broadway revival of the mordantly brilliant play, *The Black Picture Show*, written and directed by Bill Gunn. In reviving it Gunn had revealed the homosexual subtext obscured in its earlier marvelous Lincoln Center production. Baldwin's friend Gunn made a name for himself more as one of the first black directors doing Hollywood films (*The Landlord, Ganja & Hess, The Greatest*) than as a playwright, but his last play, *Forbidden City* (1989), which opened to outrageously ignorant and mean reviews literally as he died in a New York hospital, plumbs as deeply as Baldwin did the complex fruits of black self-loathing. Baldwin too received brutal reviews for his later work and he returned to Europe, where he remained until his death.

Baldwin the giant media presence eclipsed several other writers producing at the time. Chester Himes produced a series of novels beginning with *If He Hollers Let Him Go* (1945) and *Lonely Crusade* (1947), and later works including *Pinktoes* (1961) and *Cotton Comes to Harlem* (1965). Paule Marshall (1929–), a native of Brooklyn, published her landmark novel *Brown Girl, Brownstones* in 1959, the first of four novels. She has also produced a collection of novellas and continues to explore the connections between Africa, the Caribbean, and the US in her work. John A. Williams (1925–), who emerged with his third novel, *The Man Who Cried I Am* in 1967, one of the quintessential texts of 1960s, began publishing novels with *The Angry Ones* (1960), *Night Song* (1961), and *Sissie* (1963).

Funnyhouse of a Negro (1960), the first play by Adrienne Kennedy (1931–), opened in New York in 1962, astounding many with an unbridled and disturbing journey into the psychopathology that is part of slavery's legacy. The OBIE-winning play was termed experimental at the time. Its multi-layered use of four alternate personas – Patrice Lumumba, Jesus, Queen Victoria, and the Duchesss of Hapsburg – within the character of an African American woman could also be read as work in dialogue with Frantz Fanon and as a response to a mainstream culture completely unprepared to confront the racial, sexual, and political complexities facing African American women. Kennedy anticipated the explorations of women and madness in the fiction of Gayl Jones and Alice Walker. She is very significant for playwrights of my generation and those interested in moving beyond naturalism toward a theater of ideas.

As the era of the civil rights movement in the South came to the forefront of news across the country, other voices of northern urban militancy began to be heard along with Baldwin. Lorraine Hansberry, whose play *Raisin in the Sun*, set an African American landmark by opening on Broadway in 1959. *Raisin* concerns a black family trying to escape the Chicago ghetto for a home in a white suburb. Its rich portrayal of Walter Lee Younger was for many an iconic representation of black manhood, and Lena Younger held sway for decades as the voice of the older generation who had labored in menial work and survived the stifling tenements. For others, the play offered a portrayal of new generation of African Americans, particularly educated and ambitious black women like the character of Beneatha Younger, who searches for a path out of the specific oppressions of her gender. Hansberry moved to New York where her play, *The Sign in Sidney Brustein's Window*, opened in 1964, shortly before her death.

Also in 1964, Baldwin's *Blues for Mr. Charlie*, a tragedy airing the battles between generations in the southern civil rights movement, between northern and southern strategies of resistance, and echoing the martyrdom of activists like Medgar Evers, opened to hostile reviews, despite its many virtues.

That same year, *The Dutchman*, a play by LeRoi Jones (Amiri Baraka) (1934–), opened and shook the New York theater world with its brutally honest portrayal of the ancient, unspoken war simmering between the races by the mid-1960s. The OBIE-winning play also announced the arrival of one of the major African American writers of the 20th century, a poet from Newark, New Jersey, educated at Howard University. Baraka had joined the Beats in Greenwich Village in the 1950s, publishing *Preface to a Twenty Volume Suicide Note* (1961) and *The Dead Lecturer* (1964), and published an innovative and dynamic column on jazz in the *Village Voice* for several years. Hearing Malcolm X, bearing witness to Harlem riots, and taking a trip to Cuba radicalized him and he moved to Harlem and began building arts institutions. Amiri Baraka became a founder of the Black Arts Movement, a second explosion of African American arts which limited space constrains me from exploring here. His *Home: Social Essays* (1965), *Tales* (1967), *Black Music* (1968), and the anthology *Black Fire* (1968) are the foundational texts of that movement. The play *Slave Ship* (1969/70), more akin to the Living Theater process than to plays as text, was for those who saw it the shocking first depiction of Middle Passage in performance. Baraka continues to produce vital, challenging work.

The Autobiography of Malcolm X, written with Alex Haley and published after Malcolm's assassination in 1965, has given millions an understanding of the black rage of the 1960s. Tutored by Harlem Renaissance historian J. A. Rogers, Malcolm focused readers on their own conditioned thinking and the widespread impact of white supremacy in the American mind. The years following his death would bring a new generation of writers carrying forward the concerns of earlier authors over the conditions facing their race and creating an even greater diversity of language, styles, and forms in American literature.

The major movements among African American writers all have roots in New York, in part because it is a publishing center, and in part because the writers here have had fairly close connections to black writers elsewhere. The global community of writers of African descent in formation in the 1920s continues. While the first generations were marked by a diverse set of origins and roving lives, the de facto segregation of the city put them in close proximity with each other and confined them to a small number of outlets for publication. In the 1920s and the 1960s and 1970s arts movements resulted in the founding of numerous small publications and venues for readings, productions and workshops, many of which persist today. Tensions continue over the gatekeepers to publication and their penchant for the unusual, even unrepresentative black voice, and debate still percolates over the role of the artist with regard to resistance to oppression.

NOTES

1. Howard Dodson, Christopher Moore, and Roberta Yancy, *The Black New Yorkers: The Schomburg Illustrated Chronology* (New York: John Wiley & Sons, 2000).
2. Ira Berlin and Leslie M. Harris, eds., *Slavery in New York* (New York: New Press, 2005), pp. 6, 8, 43, 60–61, 78–82, 110.
3. Elizabeth McHenry, "Toward a History of Access: The Case of Mary Church Terrell," *American Literary History* 19 (2007): 383.

4. Dodson, Moore, and Yancy, eds., *The Black New Yorkers*, p. 27.

5. David Levering Lewis, *When Harlem Was in Vogue* (New York: Knopf, 1981), p. 25; James Weldon Johnson, *Black Manhattan* (1930; New York: DaCapo, 1991), p. 171.

6. George Chauncey, *Gay New York: Gender, Urban Culture, and the Making of the Gay Male World, 1890–1940* (New York: Basic Books, 1994), p. 252.

7. James Weldon Johnson, *Along This Way: The Autobiography of James Weldon Johnson* (1933; New York: Penguin, 1990), p. 320; Lewis, *When Harlem Was in Vogue*, p. 9.

8. James Weldon Johnson, ed., *The Book of American Negro Poetry* (1922; New York: Harcourt Brace Jovanovich, 1969), pp. 168–69.

9. Alain Locke, ed., *The New Negro* (1925; New York: Atheneum, 1975), p. xv. Further references appear in the text.

10. Lewis, *When Harlem Was in Vogue*, p. 63.

11. In *The New Negro*, ed. Locke, pp. 250–53.

12. In *The New Negro Renaissance: An Anthology*, ed. Michael W. Peplow and Arthur P. Davis (New York: Holt, Rinehart & Winston, 1975), p. 147.

13. Lewis, *When Harlem Was in Vogue*, p. 251.

14. Arthur P. Davis, *From the Dark Tower: Afro-American Writers 1900 to 1960* (Washington, DC: Howard University Press, 1974), p. 41.

15. Hazel V. Carby, "Policing the Black Woman's Body in an Urban Context," *Critical Inquiry* 18 (1992): 747–49.

16. James Baldwin, *Notes of a Native Son* (New York: Bantam, 1972), p. 47.

12

TRYSH TRAVIS

New York's cultures of print

Pluralities of print

Where to begin a discussion of "New York's cultures of print"? A logical starting point might be the national magazines founded in the city around the turn of the nineteenth century, large-format monthlies like *Munsey's* (1889–1921), *Collier's* (1888–1919), and *McClure's* (1893–1911). These popular publications drew on New York's cutting-edge publishing technology and marketing savvy, as well as on the city's wealth of journalistic talent, to help bring into being a national middle-class reading public. Their inheritors were the "smart" magazines of the 1920s and 30s – *Smart Set* (1900–30), *Vanity Fair* (1913–36), *The New Yorker* (1925–present), and *Esquire* (1933–present) – dedicated to bringing New York's culture and style to the hinterlands. Significantly, these publications began the segmentation of the national public by targeting a niche audience with high education and income levels for the advertisers of luxury goods.[1]

To get the full flavor of New York's cultures of print, however, we should juxtapose these frankly commercial endeavors with their more bohemian counterparts. Although they were scattered around the US and Europe, plenty of the "little magazines" that shaped the roaring twenties and radical thirties made their homes in New York, including *The Dial* (a revived and revised version of the Boston Transcendentalist publication of the same name, 1916–29), *The Seven Arts* (1916–17), *The Masses* (1911–17), and *The New Masses* (1926–48). They were succeeded by the Beat and progressive publications that hallmarked the mid-century "mimeograph revolution." Devoted to journalism, poetry, and other forms of word and print art, downtown publications like Gilbert Sorrentino's *Neon* (1956–60), Diane di Prima's *The Floating Bear* (1961–68), and Ed Sanders's *Fuck You/a Magazine of the Arts* (1962–65) helped to define a downtown print culture that saw itself as aesthetically, economically, and politically distinct from the publishing mainstream ensconced in midtown.[2] In addition to artsy journals, this print counterculture included newspapers like the *Village Voice* (1955–present) and the *East Village Other* (1965–72) and book publishers – internationally known houses like New Directions Publishing (fd. 1936) and Grove Press (fd. 1951) as well as smaller enterprises like Totem Press (fd. 1958) and Corinth Books (fd. 1959). It also extended to radical bookstores of all stripes, from literary enclaves like the Eighth Street Book Shop (fd. 1947), to overtly political enterprises like the Peace Eye Bookstore (fd. 1965) and early queer establishments like the Oscar Wilde Memorial Bookshop (fd. 1967).[3]

But even attention to this diversity does not capture the totality of New York's "cultures of print." The city has long nourished decidedly down-market forms of print culture alongside its more high-minded middlebrow and avant-garde undertakings. Thus a truly democratic survey would attend to the hugely successful pulp magazine and dime novel publishers like Street and Smith (1855–1949) and Beadle and Adams (1858–97), as well as to Bernarr Macfadden's sprawling "Physical Culture" empire of confessional and health publications (1899–1941). Their success spawned the comic book and genre fiction publishers that straddled the line between magazines and books – Experimenter Publishing Company (later Gernsback Publications, Inc., 1915–38), Thrilling Publications (1931–55), and Ace Books (1952–72), to name just a few – and specialized in graphic tales of the lurid and the tawdry.[4] Finally, any honest reckoning with the city's heterogeneous print cultures should acknowledge its many "bookleggers" – the publishers and peddlers of erotica and pornography. In the early twentieth century New York was America's porn capital, and its lowest of lowbrow publication circuits was as diverse and multi-faceted as its more staid coevals. Thus the anonymously produced smutty newsprint comics known as "Tijuana Bibles" circulated through channels quite different from, but just as well-established as, those that dealt in the aestheticized images known as "gallantia" produced by presses like Panurge (ca. 1929–35) and Falstaff (ca. 1934–38).[5]

Throughout the long twentieth century, this dizzying array of publishers, printers, retailers, and readers overlapped and intersected in New York, reflecting and giving voice to the city's unique pluralism. The various print trades – not merely publishing but also paper manufacturing, printing, binding, and the like – had long been significant contributors to New York's economy, and by 1900 their concentration in and around the city had created a self-sustaining synergy. The presence of so many print institutions created a marketplace of goods, labor, and ideas that drew literary talent in from across the nation and sent texts of all kinds back out in return. Critic and editor Malcolm Cowley spoke for many when he observed in 1934 that the ambitious litterateurs of his generation flocked to Manhattan because "living was cheap, because friends of ours had come already (and written letters full of enchantment), because it seemed that New York was the only city where a young writer could get published."[6] The city's complex web of print cultures invited competition and innovation, attracting talent and keeping the costs of entry for new enterprises relatively low.

At the center of that web sat a concern conspicuously absent from the cultures of print enumerated above: trade book publishing, which produces those volumes we think of when we think of the generic "book" – works of fiction, drama, and poetry, as well as all forms of non-fiction prose, from presidential biographies to the latest weight-loss manuals. Trade publishers' enterprise went unremarked in the earlier list of New York's print cultures because its size, longevity, and ubiquity have to a large extent naturalized its presence in the city, masking the fact that, like all those other cultures of print, it is the result of particular cultural and political-economic arrangements. But what seems a commonsense equation of New York City and book publishing has not always been so commonsensical, and this chapter examines the ways that trade publishers ("book men," as they liked to call themselves) constructed that equation between the late nineteenth and mid twentieth centuries. To do so, they deployed specific ideas about culture and democracy that both relied on and helped to create the image of New York as an "international capital of culture," a modern and modernist city emblematic of all that was best in the free world.[7]

The genteel tradition

In the eighteenth and early nineteenth centuries, trade publishing was concentrated in Boston, where the great houses of Ticknor and Fields (fd. 1832, became Houghton Mifflin in 1880) and Little, Brown (fd. 1837) published the authors whose names would become synonymous with the "American Renaissance": Nathaniel Hawthorne, Ralph Waldo Emerson, Henry David Thoreau, James Russell Lowell, and Harriet Beecher Stowe, among many others. By the end of the Civil War, however, "New York dominated the ... publishing scene in America," and its dominance only increased as the decades passed.[8] By 1920, the annual *Blue Book of Business* tallied the total number of US book publishers at 1,346; of those, 315 were in or around New York City, with 24 of the 29 major houses (those issuing more than 50 titles annually, according to trade journal *Publishers Weekly*) in Manhattan proper.[9]

Trade publishing grew enormously around the turn of the century as the number of Americans attending high school and college rose. With the increasing size of the middle class, the number of books – the material objects that both facilitated entrance into and reflected the status of that class – grew apace. While reliable figures are notoriously difficult to obtain, annual title production increased by orders of magnitude, jumping from 2,076 in 1880 to 10,187 in 1929.[10] Growth did not mean, however, that book men sought to "corporatize" their trade – to massify and rationalize production in search of profit and power like so many American industries during this period. Despite their concentration in New York, publishers retained a strong commitment to the genteel traditions associated with old New England culture, and resisted new business and management trends that might have put them in league with the robber barons of industry or the new cultural entrepreneurs of vaudeville, cinema, and radio.[11]

Part of their reluctance in this regard had to do with what they saw as the book's essential nature, its status as an object that resisted the schemes of modern cultural production. While individual *units*, or copies of books, could be produced en masse, the imaginative work that was the book's *essence* could not be industrialized. Furthermore, the trade was confident that long-standing traditions of book retailing were such that neither market research nor advertising would ever result in increased sales. The book's nature meant it could not be advertised or "puffed" because, unlike soap or crackers, each title was a new and unique artifact, a commodity form that defied the logic of branding, one of the most powerful engines driving the new consumer culture of the early twentieth century. As The Century Company's William Ellsworth explained, using the historical novel *Hugh Wynne* as his example: "The reader of *Hugh Wynne* doesn't go forth and buy another copy as soon as he has read the first; in fact, that is the last thing he does. He is through with *Hugh Wynne* forever, and he turns to another book, an entirely fresh one … for he is not impressed by the publisher's name [and therefore] doesn't say, as he lays down *Hugh Wynne*, 'Give me The Century Company's books or none.'"[12] Somewhat smugly, book men saw themselves and their houses not as manufacturers, but as stewards who maintained the channels through which unique cultural artifacts moved.

As a result, while trade publishing grew considerably during the first decades of the twentieth century, it retained a sense of itself as a gentleman's profession. Around it, culture industries serving the growing American middle class began increasingly to focus on the act of consumption – normalizing it, facilitating it, making it more pleasurable. But book publishing remained stubbornly centered on the process of production, as embodied in the relationship between editor and author. Out of that collaboration precipitated the iconic book – an enduring cultural object linked to the vision and labor of a select few individuals and, as a result, superior to the evanescent products of competing culture industries. Such books, book men believed, formed the foundation of a liberal democracy and provided enduring insight into the human condition. Thus while they believed themselves free of Victorian propriety, New York publishers nevertheless retained a strong commitment to the genteel; the book trade was at its best when its commercial dimensions were appropriately subordinated to its higher cultural calling.

The "golden age" of culture and democracy

For about the first half of the twentieth century, trade publishers successfully balanced the commercial and cultural aspects of their enterprise, simultaneously decrying the ongoing push to commodify aspects of their trade while using those commercial innovations to expand and deepen the book's claim to cultural centrality. Plenty of book men excoriated the jejune innovations engineered by their counterparts on Madison Avenue – book clubs, paperbacks, and cross-media promotions like turning novels into movies, or radio programs devoted to bookish topics – on the grounds that they cheapened and diluted traditional literary culture. Ultimately, however, most embraced these revenue-enhancing innovations, justifying their interest in cash flow on the grounds that it allowed for the production of larger lists and contributed to the overall growth of the world of books. This successful negotiation of the competing pulls of commerce and culture led many publishers to characterize the early to mid twentieth century as trade publishing's "golden age," an era when "print was still king, and literature was at the center of the nation's culture."[13]

Within these accounts of the golden age, opinions vary about precisely which fraction of the period was the most highly burnished. For some that honor goes to the interwar years. The continued growth of the middle class meant a broader reading public, one that both enjoyed unprecedented leisure time and felt new pressures to stay abreast of a rapidly changing culture. Both aspects of that middle-class life led to increased book-buying, and the expanding marketplace, in concert with improved technology for book manufacture and distribution, offset the rising prices of paper and labor. By the 1920s, million-sellers were not uncommon.[14]

This expansion of middle-class horizons also brought about the cultural formation historians call "the revolt from the village" – the turn against the constraints of an older literary style associated with Victorian New England that brought the likes of Malcolm Cowley and his friends to New York in search of new ways of thinking, writing, and living. As a result, old New York houses like Harper and Brothers (fd. 1813) and Charles Scribner's Sons (fd. 1846) swelled with new editorial and writing talent, and works by Midwestern and Southern authors like Ernest Hemingway, F. Scott

Fitzgerald, Thomas Wolfe, and Richard Wright emerged to reshape the image of "America" laid down by an earlier generation of writers.

At the same time, what historian Edward de Grazia has called a "new breed" of literary publishers appeared in the city, creating a more daring and cosmopolitan marketplace for literature. Unlike the founders of the old houses, many of this new breed – for example Alfred Knopf, Richard Simon and Max Schuster, and Alfred and Charles Boni and Horace Liveright, of the firms that bore their names, along with Harold Guinzberg of Viking, and Bennet Cerf and Donald Klopfer of Random House – were émigré or first-generation American Jews. Hailing from Western European bourgeois families, typically with deep roots in the intellectual and literary worlds of global capitals like Paris, Vienna, and Amsterdam, they had more in common with their WASP counterparts in New York publishing than with the Eastern European Jews who were simultaneously making a place for themselves in Hollywood.[15] Their good taste and sophistication allowed them to establish themselves quickly as culture brokers, and they capitalized on their familiarity with artistic currents flowing through Europe to challenge the lingering parochialism of US literary tradition. Sometimes in partnership and sometimes in tension with the "little magazines" described above, their houses not only published and marketed, but also actively helped to foment the modernist experimentations of the Jazz Age. As a result, New York became the center of a national literary scene that, for the first time, existed in sustained dialogue with its continental counterparts.[16]

In part because these new houses continued to nourish, to great effect, the roots of a recognizable literary culture, the trade overall was able to dismiss as insignificant the more commercial innovations going on in its midst. Schemes like Charles Boni and Harry Scherman's Little Leather Library – miniature reprints of classics, originally packaged inside of Whitman's candy boxes – and Scherman and Maxwell Sackheim's Book of the Month Club – a mail-order subscription service that sent a pre-selected title each month to would-be readers too busy to choose their own reading material – were perceived by plenty of book men as degradations of the iconic book and the hallowed act of reading. But, as evidenced by the awarding of the Nobel Prize in literature to novelist Sinclair Lewis in 1930, American literary culture had also never seemed so real and vital. When they remembered to take the long view, New York's book men could still see commerce serving culture.

If some commentators see the interwar period as the high tide of New York publishing, others, emphasizing the political rather than the cultural value of books, believe the post-war era deserves that encomium. Like every other industry, publishing used the Second World War to climb out of the trough of the Depression. Reading was promoted heavily – and successfully – after 1941 as a way to gain useful knowledge to advance the war effort at home and abroad. More important, it was depicted as an active and critical leisure pursuit that nourished democracy, directly contrasting the passive propagandistic media of film and radio that had fed fascism in Germany and Italy. In a meeting in New York's Town Hall in 1942, trade publishers rallied to form the Council on Books in Wartime (CBW), uniting around the slogan "books are weapons in the war of ideas!" That sensibility would carry them into the post-war era.

The book men's championing of democracy took several different forms. One early example was a changed industry attitude toward cheap paperback reprints. For decades, "fiction factories" like Street and Smith had been producing paperbound books for young and working-class audiences, but their flimsy construction and formulaic content had led generations of serious publishers to perceive such volumes as something less than real "books." During the war, however, this changed, as the CBW coordinated a massive paperback production and distribution campaign called the Armed Services Editions (ASEs). These cheap, half-sized books were printed on newsprint, using the many idle magazine presses in the New York region. Nearly 124,000,000 volumes, representing over 1,300 titles, were ultimately distributed to US servicemen around the globe. Early on, the CBW intended for the ASEs to introduce "culture" to enlisted men and junior officers, but by the end of the war, sympathy for battle-weary GIs looking for simple escape reading led the Council to concede that ambitious point and to publish more popular fare.[17] While some members groused that titles like *Tarzan of the Apes* and *The Case of the Half-Wakened Wife* pandered to the lowest common denominator of their audience, a growing majority insisted that simply putting books into readers' hands was important cultural work, the instigation of a reading habit that ideally would be fed with higher-quality fare in peacetime.

This move to promote reading, rather than specific book forms or content, became increasingly important during the post-war years, and paperbacks moved from the fringes to the center of respectable book culture. Cheap paperback genre fiction (often spun off from comic books or magazines by diversified publishers like Thrilling and Ace) flourished as never before, but so did new softcover reprints of classic and contemporary literature, philosophy, and history titles. Soberly packaged to demonstrate their legitimacy, titles from Kurt Enoch and Victor Weybright's New American Library series (fd. 1948) and Jason Epstein's Anchor Books (fd. 1952) became standard texts as college classrooms swelled to bursting with returning GIs. Rather than "cheapening" literary culture, paperbacks' presence in train stations, grocery stores, and five-and-dimes came to symbolize a new era of democratic book culture in the US.[18]

Anti-democratic elements outside the book men's traditional orbit also helped to consolidate the idea of reading – almost any kind of reading – as an emblem of democracy. Bids by the John Birch Society and other "concerned citizens" groups to ban specific titles, especially in the Midwest and the South, led publishers to mobilize to fight McCarthyism. Although the American Library Association (ALA), headquartered in Chicago, was an important site for book culture's resistance to illiberalism, New York's pluralist and combative reputation meant that the city emerged as the geographical and imaginative center of that resistance. In partnership with the ALA, the American Book Publishers Council (the trade organization that had replaced the Council on Books in Wartime in 1945) convened the Westchester Conference in the Manhattan suburbs in 1953. From it emerged "The Freedom to Read," a declaration of the book's central role in a free society and of the signatories' determination to defend their rights to publish and circulate all manner of printed materials, subject only to the approval of the marketplace.[19]

This commitment to print culture liberalism was enacted globally as well as domestically. Many book men had worked for the Office of Facts and Figures or its inheritor, the Office of War Information, during the war, which resulted in an unprecedented degree of cooperation between the US government and the private publishing industry. This collaboration paid concrete dividends: when the armistice came and the Department of State found itself helping to rebuild the civilian economies of much of Europe, including their publishing industries, key American publishers were on hand to offer assistance, as well as to strike deals for the publication and distribution of American titles abroad. But cozying up to the government also entailed costs.

As the US embarked on programs of cultural diplomacy in the developing world, its agents expected their publisher-partners to conform to their ideas of how best to go about "meeting the challenge of Communism on bookstands abroad."[20] Typically, this meant flooding foreign markets with free copies of poorly translated paeans to American democracy. The State Department's ham-fisted attempts at literary propaganda appalled publishers who believed that liberal democratic culture was its own best advertisement. To advance their own version of democracy, in 1952 a group of New York publishers founded the Franklin Book Programs, Inc., a non-profit consultancy that offered training and seed money to publishers, printers, and book retailers in countries deemed at risk of "going communist." Rejecting Washington's top-down diplomacy as inherently unworkable, Franklin

Books instead strove to cultivate the publishing infrastructures necessary to sustain free marketplaces of ideas within struggling democracies. By identifying and working with the book men – existing or nascent – in cities like Beirut, Lagos, and Jakarta, New York publishers believed they could recreate around the globe the kind of cosmopolitan liberalism that had come to be associated with their own city.

Good-bye to all that

These accounts of the golden age of New York publishing differ in emphasis, but they agree on two key points. First, what made the age "golden" was book publishers' ability to subordinate commercial imperatives to higher ideals, thereby maintaining the book's (and the book man's) elevated position in the increasingly crowded pantheon of American culture. Second, the golden age came to a close around 1960, when that ability exhausted itself and "the great old-line book people began to be replaced by bottom-line businessmen."[21] After that, the story goes, changes in technology, in the tax code, and in the entertainment market eliminated the slim margin of gentility that book men had so jealously guarded, and the trade was reduced to merely another culture industry. Beginning around 1970 – just as the financial fortunes of New York City itself began to decline – successive waves of mergers and acquisitions destroyed the autonomy of the old houses, and books became mere units on the balance sheets of international multimedia conglomerates, placeless and faceless entities driven by a crass quest for profit rather than any sense of cultural obligation.[22]

Like the stories of the golden age themselves, the truth value of this decline narrative remains open to debate. A careful reading of twentieth-century publishers' memoirs and trade journals, as well as of the popular press, reveals, perhaps unsurprisingly, that trade publishing in the golden age was just as marked by irrationality, cronyism, and the quest for commercial success as it was by the lofty pursuit of culture and democracy. Then as now, publishers carped that too many books were published each year (always by other houses, of course), that Americans were not serious readers, and that the overall quality of books and readers had never been lower. These shortcomings were blamed, just as they are today, on the disgraceful worship of money by an industry that, while it might never have been pure, had certainly once been a lot better.

Though we should certainly question whether the golden age of publishing existed in fact, there can be no debating that it existed – and still exists – as both an ideal and a norm against which subsequent print cultures are relentlessly judged. What is most notable about that ideal/norm is the special role that New York City plays within it. For geographical and demographic reasons that, over time, became economic assets – proximity to manufacturing and transportation options, for instance, as well as population density and connectedness to Europe – Manhattan during the nineteenth century had become the physical headquarters of the book publishing trade. In the twentieth century, as their cultural hegemony was challenged by new leisure entrepreneurs of various sorts, as well as by new forms and flows of knowledge and power, book men sought to capitalize on that location, to leverage New York's increasing visibility and power and its growing symbolic weight on behalf of their industry. While individual books or publishers may have been resistant to the logic of branding, the industry as a whole was not: New York became the brand for the books that were produced there.

Thus New York publishers welcomed experiment and sought new angles of literary vision from the rest of America as well as from abroad; in short, New York was not Boston. At the same time, it cared about quality, aesthetic rigor, and the life of the mind; New York was not Hollywood. In its steadfast commitment to pluralism and freedom, no matter how messy they might be, New York was not the backwater Midwest or an ideologically over-determined Washington. Through this series of negations, which were sometimes made tacitly, other times explicitly, publishers constructed New York as both the symbol and the workshop of liberal cosmopolitanism. The ultimate modernist space, it was uniquely positioned within its historical moment to serve the cultural needs of the world – needs that upper-middle-class white book men believed could best be met by the serious, well-considered, finely crafted trade books at the center of their city's print culture.

In the early decades of the twentieth century, then, trade publishers crafted an ideology of the book that rested upon and helped to promote an ideology of New York: the golden age was the product of a golden space and vice versa, each image working to render the hegemony of the other more attractive and more natural. The 1970s and after witnessed the return of what those ideologies had worked for decades to repress: race and gender tensions that a broad-minded pluralism could not dispel, a persistent imbalance of power between labor and capital, the most venal forms of social inequality, and the left- and right-wing anti-intellectualism that precipitated out of those frictions. As these energies welled up, they eroded not only the ideals of the glittering modernist city and its noble book culture, but also the institutions through which they had taken on cultural and material life. The golden-age-and-decline narrative is the product of that erosion: for the inhabitants of those institutions, book men chief among them, change could only be experienced as a tragic decline, a fall away from culture and democracy into hack commodification and anarchy.

To the denizens of New York's other cultures of print – journalists and genre publishers, devotees of the city's endlessly multiplying print undergrounds – the meaning of the post-1970s changes in the political economy of trade publishing was less precise. In the cracks and crevices opened up by the demise of an older ideology of print, new literary voices appeared, many of them insufficiently "respectable" to have been inscribed in the pages of older, more proper print forms. Postmodern and punk subcultures created both new spaces for publication and new modes of reading – slick enclaves like that featured in Andy Warhol's *Interview* magazine (1969–present) as well as defiantly low-tech communities like those that formed around magazines like *Punk* (1971–75) and its DIY inheritors of the 1980s and 90s. At the same time, hip-hop artists across the five boroughs were seizing the blank spaces of the physical city as pages upon which to inscribe narrative, commentary, and identity in the late twentieth century. In doing so, they presaged the culture of the present day, in which committing words to paper is only one of a host of possibilities available to those who hope to participate in New York's cultures of print.

NOTES

1. Each of these titles is described in Theodore Peterson, *Magazines in the Twentieth Century* (Urbana: University of Illinois Press, 1956). Their connections to consumer culture are the subject of Richard Ohmann's *Selling Culture: Magazines, Markets, and Class at the Turn of the Century* (New York: Verso, 1996).
2. On little magazines in the teens and twenties, see Frederick Hoffman, Charles Allen, and Carolyn Ulrich, *The Little Magazine: A History and a Bibliography* (Princeton, NJ: Princeton University Press, 1946). On their Beat-era analogues, see Elliott Anderson and Mary Kinzie, eds., *The Little Magazine in America: A Modern Documentary History* (Yonkers, NY: Pushcart Press, 1978).
3. On New York's contributions to the alternative press, see Abe Peck, *Uncovering the 60s: The Life and Times of the Underground Press* (New York: Citadel Books, 1985) and Kevin Michael McAuliffe, *The Great American Newspaper: The Rise and Fall of the "Village Voice"* (New York: Scribner, 1978). On New Directions, see Greg Barnhisel, *James Laughlin, New Directions, and the Remaking of Ezra Pound* (Amherst: University of Massachusetts Press, 2005). Grove Press's tumultuous history is detailed in S. E. Gontarski, *Modernism, Censorship, and the Politics of Publishing: The Grove Press Legacy* (Chapel Hill: University of North Carolina Press, 2000). The newsletters, journals, presses, and stores of the mid-century print underground are exquisitely catalogued in Steven Clay and Rodney Phillips, *A Secret Location on the Lower East Side: Adventures in Writing, 1960–1980* (New York: New York Public Library and Granary Books, 1998). Some institutions (not just magazines) are treated in greater detail in the essays in Anderson and Kinzie's *The Little Magazine*. On the Oscar Wilde Memorial Bookshop and other key institutions of gay print culture, see Felice

Picano, *Art and Sex in Greenwich Village: A Memoir of Gay Literary Life after Stonewall* (New York: Basic Books, 2007).

4. On the Macfadden empire, see Ann Fabian, "Making a Commodity of Truth: Speculations on the Career of Bernarr Macfadden," *American Literary History* (Spring 1993): 51–76. On pulp publishing, see Larry E. Sullivan and Lydia Cushman Schurman, *Pioneers, Passionate Ladies, and Private Eyes: Dime Novels, Series Books, and Paperbacks* (New York: Haworth Press, 1996). On the rise of science-fiction publishing in New York, including its complex overlaps with other pulp genres and markets, see Mike Ashley, *The Time Machines: The Story of the Science-Fiction Pulp Magazines from the Beginning to 1950* (Liverpool: Liverpool University Press, 2000).

5. On the trade in pornography, see Jay Gertzman's carefully researched *Bookleggers and Smuthounds: The Trade in Erotica, 1920–1940* (Philadelphia: University of Pennsylvania Press, 1999) and Bob Adelman, *Tijuana Bibles: Art and Wit in America's Forbidden Funnies, 1930s–1950s* (New York: Simon and Schuster, 1997).

6. Malcolm Cowley, *Exile's Return* (New York: Viking, 1934), p. 48.

7. Thomas Bender, *New York Intellect: A History of Intellectual Life in New York City, from 1750 to the Beginnings of Our Own Time* (New York: Knopf, 1987), p. 319.

8. John Tebbel, *A History of Book Publishing in the United States*, 4 vols. (New York: R. R. Bowker, [1972]–1981), ii, p. 185.

9. *Ibid.*, iii, pp. 43, 42.

10. *Ibid.*, ii, p. 675; *ibid.*, iii, p. 662. Tebbel notes industry surveys at the time relied on self-reporting, and did not necessarily distinguish among books, booklets, and pamphlets when assessing "title" output. These laxities, along with a host of other irregularities, mean statistics about the publishing industry are best seen as suggestive rather than definitive.

11. Alan Trachtenberg, *The Incorporation of America: Culture and Society in the Gilded Age* (New York: Hill and Wang, 1982); Donald Sheehan, *This Was Publishing: A Chronicle of the Book Trade in the Gilded Age* (Bloomington: Indiana University Press, 1952).

12. Quoted in Sheehan, *This Was Publishing*, p. 187.

13. Louis Menand, "Missionary: Edmund Wilson and American Culture," *The New Yorker* (August 8, 2005), www.newyorker.com/archive/2005/08/08/050808crat_ atlarge. Accessed August 28, 2009.

14. Tebbel, *A History of Book Publishing*, iii, p. 32.

15. On the distinctive Eastern European culture of Jews in Hollywood, see Neal Gabler, *An Empire of their Own: How the Jews Invented Hollywood* (New York: Crown Publishing, 1988).

16. On trade publishers' role in this regard, see Catherine Turner, *Marketing Modernism between the Two World Wars* (Amherst: University of Massachusetts Press, 2003).

17. Disputes about the quality of the titles in the series are present in various places in the Council on Books in Wartime Papers, Seeley G. Mudd Manuscript Library, Princeton University. Clear tension on the issue is recorded in the Executive Committee Meeting minutes of 1943–44, Box 3.

18. Kenneth C. Davis, *Two-Bit Culture: The Paperbacking of America* (Boston, MA: Houghton Mifflin, 1984).
19. Louise Robbins, "The Overseas Libraries Controversy and the Freedom to Read: U.S. Libraries and Publishers Confront Joseph McCarthy," *Libraries and Culture* (Winter 2001): 27–39.
20. Quoted in Louise Robbins, "Publishing American Values: The Franklin Book Program as Cold War Cultural Diplomacy," *Library Trends* (Winter 2007): n.p.
21. Al Silverman, *The Time of their Lives: The Golden Age of Great American Publishers, Their Editors, and Authors* (New York: St. Martin's Press, 2008).
22. André Schiffrin, *The Business of Books: How International Conglomerates Took Over Publishing and Changed the Way We Read* (New York: Verso, 2000).

13

DANIEL KANE

From poetry to punk in the East Village

Downtown New York's vibrant poetic community of the 1960s informed the down-at-the-heels though ultimately influential proto-punk scene nurtured during the 1970s in New York's legendary clubs including Max's Kansas City, The Mercer Arts Center, CBGB's, and the Mudd Club. Beloved by early punk pioneers, East Village based poets like Ted Berrigan, Anne Waldman, Lewis Warsh, and Tom Clark referenced rock music in their poems to foreground the kinds of class affiliations and aesthetic tastes that would be picked up on by musicians like Richard Hell and Patti Smith. Ted Berrigan's "Bean Spasms" (1967), for example, referred to rock 'n' roll in part to ground the poem as a vehicle for establishing a specific "underground" community:

> The rock&roll songs of this earth
> commingling absolute joy AND
> incontrovertible joy of intelligence
>
> certainly can warm
> can't they?   YES!
>   and they do.
>   Keeping eternal whisperings around.
>
> (Mr. MacAdams writes in
> the nude: no that's not
> (we want to take the underground   me that: then zips in &
> revolution to Harvard!)   out of the boring taxis, re-
> fusing to join the army
> and yet this girl has   asleep "on the springs"
> so much grace   of red GENEROSITY
> I wonder!
> Were all their praises simply prophecies
> of this
> the time!   NO GREATER THRILL
> my friends[1]

Situating us directly within a contemporary tribal youth culture ("The rock&roll songs of this earth"), Berrigan positioned poets including himself and Lewis MacAdams as participants in an allusively anarchic community. High art here makes way for bass, guitar, and drums, and images of a primarily collective experience (think Monterey Pop Festival, Woodstock, the San Francisco be-ins) work their way into the erudite and friendly pep of New York School poetry.

These simultaneously outlaw and group signals promoted in poetry affected performance culture in New York throughout the 1960s and 1970s. Links developed between poets and punk-folkies including the band The Fugs, and – combined with the interest among young musicians in poetry and poetics from Rimbaud and Baudelaire through to Allen Ginsberg, Berrigan, Waldman, and beyond – resulted in remarkable artistic cross-fertilization. Ultimately, the move from poetry to punk suggests that the period under consideration provided a fascinating challenge to conventional understandings of what constitutes "high culture," "low culture," and the status of the lyric as static, page-bound text.

Of course, not *all* the musicians affiliated with New York's early punk scene were that engaged with poetry. It's unlikely, for example, that The Dictators, the Dead Boys, or the Ramones (with the possible exception of Joey) sat around reading John Ashbery poems to each other. That said, some of the most influential musicians of the period were all very much engaged with poetry and poetics as they related to the music scene. "I was coming [to New York] to do poetry," Lydia Lunch recalled when discussing what motivated her to become a teenage runaway. "But no one would read my poems except [Patti Smith Group guitarist] Lenny Kaye. He always had an ear that was so kind."[2]

Proto-punk musicians looked to Rimbaud's and Verlaine's *poète maudit*, the vatic resonance of the Beat chant, and the wildly sociable collaborative poems affiliated with the second-generation New York School poets to create a kind of literary aura around their variously monotone, ecstatic, whining, frenzied songs. A number of musicians used the Poetry Project at St. Mark's Church in New York's East Village as their early stomping grounds, and, indeed, one is likely to find Richard Hell, Lou Reed, or Patti Smith performing at the Church for special occasions like the New Year's Day marathon readings well into the twenty-first century. (Patti Smith, for one, began her public career on February 10, 1971, when she shared a reading bill at the Poetry Project with poet and Andy Warhol collaborator Gerard Malanga [see *Figure 13*]. It was at the Church that Smith met and befriended writers including William Burroughs and Allen Ginsberg. Burroughs and Ginsberg later ended up reading their work at

.... Reading... February 10... 8:30... 1971
Gerard Malanga: POETRY.
patti smith: WORK —
St. Marks Church-on-the- Bowery... 2nd Ave. + 10th St.

Figure 13: Gerard Malanga and Patti Smith. Flyer for a poetry reading at St. Mark's Church in-the-Bowery, New York City, 1971. Smith described the evening in this way: "On February 10, 1971, I gave my first poetry reading, opening for Gerard Malanga at St. Mark's Church on the Bowery. In desiring to project a raw energy, I recruited Lenny Kaye. We climaxed the reading with his sonic interpretation of a stock car race with electric guitar while I read 'Ballad of a Bad Boy.' It seemed to have a negative effect. I took that as a positive sign."

clubs including the Mudd Club at 77 White Street, The Peppermint Lounge on West 45th Street, and other sites.) Many musicians also published (and in most cases continue to publish) their own poetry. Patti Smith's *Babel* (1978), Lou Reed's publications throughout the 1970s in poetry magazines like *The Coldspring Journal*, Lydia Lunch's and Exene Cervenka's collaborative book *Adulterers Anonymous* (1982), and Richard Hell's poems from the late 1960s through 1971 featured in his journal *Genesis: Grasp* (which he edited from his apartment in the Lower East Side) are just a few early instances of the many examples one could list here.

Musicians looked to poetry not just in terms of what the art had to offer them as a model for their own song-writing, but also as a form that could provide them with ways of thinking about how to make actual lifestyle choices. That is to say, poetry was both something they read and, in one form or another, something they tried to *live*. In an interview with Victor Bockris, for example, Patti Smith provides us with a candid acknowledgment of why she was initially drawn to French poetry and fiction. In response to Bockris's question "Why are your influences mostly European: Rimbaud, Cendrars, Celine, Michaux?" Smith replied, "It's because of biographies. I was mostly attracted to lifestyles, and there just wasn't [sic] any great biographies of genius American lifestyles except the cowboys." Smith went on to explain that she was writing a "poetry of performance" because "of Victorian England, how they crucified Oscar Wilde. Poets became simps, sensitive young men in attics. But it wasn't always like that. It used to be that the poet was a performer and I think the energy of Frank O'Hara started to re-inspire that. I mean in the Sixties there was all that happening stuff. Then Frank O'Hara died and it sort of petered out, and then Dylan and Allen Ginsberg revitalized it."[3] It's worth paying special attention to three things Smith said: her stated appreciation of the poets' lives prior to her even reading them, her tacit approval of cowboys, and her definition of her writing as a "poetry of performance."

Poetry as lifestyle played a very real role in Smith's and other proto-punks' self-fashioning. Smith was enamored of the Beats. She became close friends with William Burroughs, Gregory Corso, and Ginsberg, and promoted them by writing a number of articles on and forewords to their works. Smith was as likely to stress these writers' outrageous antics as she was to refer to their actual poetry. In her foreword to Gregory Corso's *An Accidental Autobiography*, for example, Smith opens with an anecdote that illustrates and celebrates Corso's anti-establishment gestures:

> I first encountered Gregory long ago in front of the Chelsea Hotel. He lifted his overcoat and dropped his trousers, spewing Latin expletives. Seeing my astonished face, he laughed and said, "I'm not mooning you sweetheart, I'm mooning the world." I remember thinking, how fortunate for the world to be privy to the exposed rump of a true poet.[4]

Smith continues to align herself materially with Corso: "My living space was akin to his – piles of papers, books, old shoes, piss in cups – mortal disarray."[5] This raggedy bohemia, in evidence most ideally in the rebellious figure of a poet-outlaw like Corso, would be absorbed and redirected by Smith into what would soon be called punk rock.

Smith did not limit her adoration of underground writers to relatively recent influences, but reached back to the nineteenth century. Smith recalls a particularly momentous lunch break in her young life as a South Jersey factory girl: "I went across the railroad tracks to this little bookstore. I was roaming around there, looking for something to read, and I saw ... the cheap paperback of *Illuminations* by Rimbaud. I mean, every kid has had it. There's that grainy picture of Rimbaud in it and I thought he was so neat looking. Rimbaud looks so genius. I instantly snatched it up. I didn't even know what it was about, I just thought Rimbaud was a neat name ... I thought he was so cool ... I just really fell in love with [*Illuminations*]. It was gracious Son of Pan that I fell in love with, cause it was so sexy."[6] In Smith's narrative, we don't even necessarily have to read poetry before we understand its latent dissident power embodied in a sexy cover photo and a "neat" name. These signs offered Smith an early "out" of the mundane working-class life to which she initially thought she was doomed.

Smith nodded towards the cowboy as a symbol that, standing next to the poet, offered another outsider sign that she could mine in her ongoing efforts to create herself as a poet / singer / icon. For the singer who snarled "Outside of society, that's where I want to be" in her song "Rock 'n' Roll Nigger," it's significant that Rimbaud and the mythic cowboy – defined as much by their willful place on the social margins as they are by the work they do – are conflated in the punk chanteuse's imagination.[7] Indeed, the iconography of the cowboy and his place on the frontier would play a real part in the Lower East Side poetry scene in the 1960s and 70s.

The Lower East Side was an area that was seen throughout the 1960s as a kind of no-man's-land ready to be conquered, especially by those mostly young artists attracted by cheap rents and the historically progressive reputation of the neighborhood. For example, the editor and writer Hettie Jones (Amiri Baraka's wife during the early 1960s) wrote of the Lower East Side, "The real estate broker D. D. Stein offered his twenty-five-dollar bathtub-in-kitchen apartments on Avenue B with the slogan 'Join the Smart Trend,' and the café Les Deux Mégots on Seventh Street advertised 'Come East Young Man.'"[8] Note the inverted Western slogans – "Come East Young Man" replaces the iconic "Go West Young Man," and D. D. Stein's offer hearkens back to pioneer-era posters promising riches to those willing to take a risk by making the move out west.

The cowboy found a place in the poetry and writing coming out of or favored by the Lower East Side scene. George Economou, a poet who wrote modern-day versions of Virgilian Georgics and held a Ph.D. in Medievalism and comparative literature, produced work including "Crazy-Eyed Cowboys," which begins, "Those crazy-eyed cowboys / Lady, who romp you fantastically / have sharp little knee caps / beneath their horse sweat stinky."[9] In Ted Berrigan's *The Sonnets* one finds lines including "my dream a drink with Ira Hayes we discuss the code of the west," "As I am a cowboy and you imaginary / Ripeness," and the aggressive, if ironically, posturing line found throughout *The Sonnets*, "I like to beat people up."[10] Berrigan's novel *Clear The Range* (composed by cutting up, replacing, and rearranging words from a popular Western) further established the "cowboy" as intrinsically related to the avant-garde: "Just down the steep pitch tree The Sleeper heard a hoof – a hoof that rattled stone shoes. He went mad. He was flying. The horse he shot. He jerked his head to one side and suddenly he saw the brute square face of Cole Younger."[11] In their collaborative book *Tonto Lavoris* (1973), Clark Coolidge and Larry Fagin edited word groups from Coolidge's poetry, many of which (title included) suggested surrealist cowboy characters.

Poets didn't just refer to cowboys in their writing – they walked around dressed as cowboys. In the early 1960s, poet Paul Blackburn walked around the Lower East Side in a trademark black cowboy hat. According to poet and former St. Mark's Poetry Project coordinator Bob Holman, this hat was so familiar to fellow poets that "for awhile, [the poet Joel] Oppenheimer affected a white cowboy hat, a self-mocking response to Paul's familiar black hat. The smile widens. In 1961, 'The Great American Desert' opened at Judson Church, with Paul Blackburn playing Doc Holliday, who 'is dressed in black.' Joel wrote the play."[12] The smile widens even further when we consider Smith's debt to this poetry scene, her participation in such events as Sam Shepard's 1971 play "Cowboy Mouth" and her linking of poetry, the figure of the outsider, and the romanticized Western range in some of her most transcendent songs. Take Smith's song "Land," for instance, which introduces us to "Johnny," who "suddenly … gets the feeling he's being sur-rounded by / horses, horses, horses, horses / coming in in all directions / white shining silver studs with their nose in flames." Beautifully, strangely, the song continues to find Johnny lying in a "sperm coffin" only to be resur-rected by an angel. And what does Johnny scream out when he gets up out of his grave? "Go Rimbaud! / Go Rimbaud! Go Rimbaud!"[13]

Poetry performances taking place in the Lower East Side extended the "out there" aura associated with the cowboy's push out into the margins. Prior to the emergence of the Beats in the late 1950s, poetry readings in New York were generally staid affairs taking place at institutions like the 92nd Street Y where elder statesmen and stateswomen of modernism such as W. H. Auden, T. S. Eliot, Marianne Moore, and Wallace Stevens read alongside populist writers like Robert Frost, Langston Hughes, and Dylan Thomas. As accounts and recordings of these readings attest, audience-reader interaction was lim-ited, due in no small part to the formality inherent in the Y's raised stage and the audience's place in rows of fixed chairs. However, the 1960s found poetry readings in the Lower East Side in New York becoming increasingly performance-oriented, raucous events. Especially significant reading series in this area began in 1960 with the opening of Mickey Ruskin's and Ed Kaplan's Tenth Street Coffee House, on a block between Third and Fourth Avenues that was also bursting with art galleries featuring work by Willem de Kooning, Franz Kline, and Alex Katz, among others. It was at Tenth Street where poets including Jackson Mac Low and Diane Wakoski performed their work and set the stage for a variously outrageous, dissident, and collaborative performance aesthetic. In June 1961, the series at Tenth Street shifted to Ruskin's and Bill Mackey's Les Deux Mégots coffeehouse at 64 East 7th Street. While Les Deux Mégots shut down because of a business disagreement between Ruskin and Mackey, the poetry community in the Lower East Side became increasingly vital and strange when Maurice Margules's Le Metro coffeehouse opened at 149 Second Avenue in March 1963.

Here is where the associations between poetry and a kind of outlaw posture verging on nihilism became more apparent. Poet and reading-series participant Jerry Bloedow remembers that "there was a lot of drug dealing going on at Le Metro. I say this for the record. [William] Burroughs showed up back in town. He went off back in the corner, and people were clustered around him. All that was happening was that people were dealing drugs. And the thing is, Le Metro was probably run by the cops. It was part of the shady world of the Lower East Side."[14] In response to being asked why he had a bad reputation among many poets, Margules replied, "I had to kick out the guys shooting up in the bathroom. I was the bad guy."[15] This kind of seedy behavior was reflected in the poetry associated with the neighborhood as it was published in D.I.Y. mimeographed magazines, such as Amiri Baraka's and Diane di Prima's *The Floating Bear*, Ted Berrigan's *C*, and Ed Sanders's notorious *Fuck You/a magazine of the arts*. Indeed, with their mix of poetry, local literary news and gossip, and, in the case of Sanders's *Fuck You*, candid celebrations of (a then-illegal) homosexuality, drug use, "group gropes," and intergenerational sex, poetry mimeos pointed ahead to the willfully sloppy punk 'zines of the seventies like Legs McNeil's, Ged Dunn's, and John Holmstrom's *Punk*, which began in 1976 and featured Lou Reed and Patti Smith on its first two covers.

A trajectory can be traced from the Tenth Street Coffee House to Les Deux Mégots to Le Metro to, in the fall of 1966, the Poetry Project at St. Mark's Church, located on Second Avenue just north of Le Metro. It was here that the growing anarchic aura surrounding the poetry scene exploded as the Church became a social center for poets, friends of poets, junkies, intellectuals, college students, suburban day trippers, Young Lords, and beyond. Art in the Lower East Side during this period expanded beyond literature, jazz, and the visual arts. New sounds like acid rock and La Monte Young's aggressively dissonant Theater of Eternal Music were part of the neighborhood soundtrack. Pop-artist Andy Warhol rented the Polish National Social Hall at 23 St. Mark's Place and transformed it into the Electric Circus. Here Warhol debuted the multimedia Exploding Plastic Inevitable, where poet

Gerard Malanga and "superstar" Mary Woronov danced on stage to the music of the Velvet Underground. In early 1968, Bill Graham opened the Fillmore East, a performance space on Second Avenue where musicians including legendary proto-punk band the MC5 (as well as more pastoral longhairs like Janis Joplin, The Grateful Dead, and Jefferson Airplane) could be heard.

These phenomena suggest that the Poetry Project and St. Mark's Church as a whole should be understood as a radical space, positioning poetry as anti-authoritarian, improvised, and threatening to polite society. One example out of the hundreds of radical poetry-centered events at the Church illustrates this point. In April 1966, a benefit reading for the Committee for Non-Violence was held in the parish hall. A tape of the event indicates that a pretty anarchic spirit prevailed. Ed Sanders's presence at the reading received perhaps the greatest applause, possibly because the audience was familiar with his long-standing role as sex-liberationist, poet, anti-war protester, troublemaker, and lead singer for The Fugs. The first thing Sanders did when he got up on stage was to yell out "O.K. pants down!" After a couple of seconds, Sanders peevishly asked the audience, "This is a church, isn't it, is this a church?" Someone yelled back, "Yes, it is a church!" Then Sanders said, "Pants up, church," which elicited a host of whistling, laughter, and hooting from the audience. Introducing his "Gobble-Gang Poems," Sanders explained how he used to work in a cigar store in Times Square for five years. "I got to know this bull-dyke, who ran a gobble-gang. I was peace-freaking at the time and I managed to convert her towards a peace-position, pacifist cluster. The lady's name is Conzuela."[16]

The scatological and sexual fun in works like the "Gobble-Gang Poems" resonated with Sanders's role in The Fugs. The group (whose name is a euphemism for "The Fucks," borrowed by Sanders from the pages of Norman Mailer's *The Naked and the Dead*) was composed variously and often interchangeably of poets, playwrights, folk artists, and Dionysian political activists. Included in its shifting line-up were such figures as Steve Weber and Pete Stampfel (founders of the terrific anti-hippie hippie band The Holy Modal Rounders), Ken Weaver, Tuli Kupferberg, Szabo, and Al Fowler – who, in his timeless poem "Caroline: An exercise for our Cocksman Leader," wrote, "I saw the hot eyes of my young daughter / rolling in passion / her body writhing naked / groping thru my pants and shorts / feeling for her daddy's prick." This hilarious if ultimately throw-away poetry anticipated in some small part punk's fast and furious aesthetic.[17]

The Fugs's first album (titled initially in 1965 *The Village Fugs – Ballads and Songs of Contemporary Protest, Points of View and General Dissatisfaction*, and, in its second incarnation with ESP Records in 1966, *The Fugs First*

Album) blurred boundaries between high and low culture. *The Fugs First Album* included sung versions of William Blake's poem "Ah Sunflower" next to super-stupid proto-punk anthems like "Boobs a Lot" (with its immortal refrain "Do you like boobs a lot? Yes I like boobs a lot") and nihilistic songs such as "Nothing," which is especially rich, as it were. The song begins despondently: "Monday nothing, Tuesday nothing, Wednesday and Thursday nothing, Friday for a change a little more nothing," then moves on to "poetry nothing, music nothing, painting and dancing nothing ... fucking nothing, sucking nothing flesh and sex nothing" and ends with Sanders shouting: "Nothing! nothing! nothing! NOTHING! NOTHING!" These insistently negative chants resonate with any number of American and English punk refrains from Richard Hell's "Blank Generation" (with its chorus "I belong to the blank generation / And I can take it or leave it each time") to The Sex Pistols' "No future, no future, no future for *you*" (from their song "God Save the Queen") to X-Ray Spex's song "I Can't Do Anything" ("I can't write / And I can't sing / I can't do anything") to Lydia Lunch and 8 Eyed Spy's "Lazy in Love" ("No time for you, yeah, rip roar fandango / lazy in love, i'm just lazy in love / ... lazy in love ugh").[18]

These anecdotes suggest in part why musicians like Lunch, Smith, and Hell were drawn to the poetry scene in the neighborhood. They also suggest why poetry could be an art-form that existed most vibrantly not on the page but on the democratic, anarchic stage, and why it could, at least in some small measure, feed into the growing music culture percolating in the East Village. Poetry was always, after all, traditionally understood as music, as *lyric*. Certainly by the early 1970s, musicians in the Lower East Side were able to see how that lyric aura, combined with a dissident sensibility enacted in the marginal space of an increasingly decrepit neighborhood, might very well point away from a Pollyanna-like post-hippie culture defined by bands like Crosby, Stills, and Nash or the Carpenters toward something *dirtier*. Take an early punk classic like Smith's revision of Van Morrison's "Gloria," for example, which begins with the phrase "Jesus died / for somebody's sins / but not mine."[19] As Lenny Kaye recalls regarding Smith's historic performance at the Poetry Project in 1971, "The first thing we did was 'Mack the Knife,' because it was Bertolt Brecht's birthday, and then Patti read a bunch of poems including 'Oath,' which was 'Jesus died for somebody's sins ...'."[20]

Richard Hell's "Blank Generation" – arguably *the* ultimate American punk anthem – stemmed in part from the collaborative spirit of the late 1960s and early 1970s downtown poetry to which Hell was personally drawn. As Hell remembers, "I was only 17 when I came to New York to be a writer. I was some kind of hayseed. I wanted to know where the poets were, and I guess I looked in most all the wrong places before finally I found the poetry project [at St. Mark's Church]. I got a big crush on Bernadette Mayer right away but I was still too shy to introduce myself to anyone. I liked to buy 'The World' and 'Angel Hair.' Ted Berrigan and Ron Padgett and Tom Veitch knocked me out."[21] The names Hell mentions here are significant given Hell's later work in poetry and music. The Poetry Project at St. Mark's Church during the late 1960s and early 1970s was a kind of Ground Zero for collaborative work, much of which was published in its house organ *The World* and Anne Waldman's and Lewis Warsh's own *Angel Hair* magazine. Bernadette Mayer, for example, ran a series of writing workshops in which collaboration and anonymity were key to composition. As Ed Friedman remembers it, one Mayer workshop devoted itself entirely to producing a magazine called *Unnatural Acts*:

> Towards the end of Bernadette's first workshop at the Poetry Project, which ran from Fall 1971 through Spring 1972, we came up with the writing method which produced *Unnatural Acts*. We were interested in collaboration and *process* ... We decided to have everyone in the workshop writing in the same place for an extended time period. Everyone anonymously contributed a piece of writing, which someone else in the group used as the basis for composing a new work. The "originals" were then discarded and the afternoon proceeded with everyone continuing to write works inspired by the reworkings of reworkings of reworkings. We decided to publish the results as *Unnatural Acts*; since no one could really claim complete ownership of any of the individual works, none of the pieces were credited to a particular writer. The following fall (1972) we repeated the experiment, inviting John Giorno, Anne Waldman, Joe Ceravalo and others to participate. One of the funny things that happened was that we got a set of pieces written in Giorno's "repetition style," only I don't think John wrote any of them. We published the results as *Unnatural Acts 2*.[22]

In light of this community-oriented, collaboratively produced, and pseudonymous and/or anonymous literary culture that Hell was drawn to, it is interesting to note that the first sentence of "Blank Generation" – which opens with the now-iconic stanza "I was saying lemme out of here before I was / even born. It's such a gamble when you get a face. / It's fascinatin' to observe what the mirror does / but when I dine it's for the wall that I set a place" – was cultured initially in the pages of *Wanna Go Out?*, a small-press poetry book dreamed up, edited, and designed by Hell, who collaborated on the book's poems with his then best friend, Television co-founder Tom (Miller) Verlaine under the single pseudonym "Theresa Stern." As Hell recalls, the lyrics of his song "Blank Generation" were drawn in part from the table of contents in *Wanna Go Out?* The book was published in 1973 under Hell's own imprint "Dot Books," a series in which Hell makes the announcement "OTHER BOOKS FROM THE BLANK GENERATION AVAILABLE FROM DOT" on the books' verso pages. Hell explains:

> You want to know what the origin of those lines from "Blank Generation" is? They have a really sneaky origin ... In this book you'll see it's the first time the phrase "Blank Generation" shows up. The table of contents is a poem itself. "Stars I was / Thinkin now I've started a new game / How come no one / As I lounge in my parlor / And the cars wish they had some candy comes / To amplify my eardrums / When I look at the floor foreground / For the scissors on my wrists / And ponder upon that little cut / After all I wasn't even born / When I first said lemme out of here / Marionette mon amour / My ... oh / The light's too dim in here / I'm getting nervous / But I promise / You stranger I'm tight and juicy."[23]

Who was this fictional Theresa Stern? As Hell's biographical note for her in *Wanna Go Out?* reads:

> THERESA STERN was born on October 27, 1949, of a German Jewish father and a Puerto Rican mother in Hoboken, N.J., directly across the Hudson from New York City. She still lives there, alone, where all the poems in this book were written over a four month period in the summer and fall of 1971. She has since devoted that of her time not spent in flipping coins to composing a love story, THIN SKIN. It describes the murder, in ten chapters fired by Theresa, of her closest friend. WANNA GO OUT? is a question often asked on the streets around the cheaper bars in New York and Hoboken.

In the fourth issue of *Punk* magazine, the writer Mary Harron, who later directed films including *Who Shot Andy Warhol* and *American Psycho*, conducted an interview with "Theresa" by providing Hell with a set of questions, who then went on to write the answers. Harron pretended to have elicited the answers herself through a personal visit to "Theresa" in her purported home in Hoboken. In response to the question "What are your literary influences ... how and why did you start writing," we find "Stern" responding, "I started writing because it was so easy. I saw all this writing being praised and I knew I could do better with a splitting headache on the subway at rush hour. Most poets are such bullshitters – they have so many vested interests, whereas I hardly have any interests at all (laughter). As for influences – my favorite poet of the century is Breton. Infinitely passionate, profound and incorruptible and what's more he's the smartest guy I ever came across, and his poetry doesn't make any sense. (laughter)."[24]

A number of poems in *Wanna Go Out?* evoke the conflation of snotty punk attitude and lyric poem that we have been discussing so far. Phrases like "Fuck this whole goddamn apartment," "Of the cunt that was nailed to the cross," and "Close this book I scream and come look me up so we can fuck as long / as I don't have to talk" augur Hell's literate rage in his own music's articulation of urban blight and provocative nihilism.[25] The poem "To Amplify My Eardrums" suggests rock 'n' roll chaos in the lines "They came last night and amplified my eardrums. / It's to glee bay / (TERRIBLE TERRIBLE) / they want to take me away. / Well I don't belong here anyway. I'm the only rock band on earth who's the earth's hernia" (14). The poem "AFTER ALL I WASN'T EVEN BORN" (20), of course, points forward to the first two lines of the song "Blank Generation." The link between poem and song is enhanced further when we get to the next poem, which begins "Lemme out of here / Triangles burst from my flesh / Everything is ending / *Am I my monster's mother?* / I wrap my arms more tightly around me at the approach of love" (21).

As this potted history of the origins of "Blank Generation" attests, poetry informed a music scene that ultimately developed into punk. Again, though, we should be careful not to overstate the case, as any number of proto-punk and post-punk musicians couldn't have cared less about *The World*, who was reading on a given Wednesday night at the Poetry Project, and so on. Additionally, we should refrain from over-exaggerating the influence of the Lower East Side poetry scene even on those musicians mentioned here. Richard Hell, for example, may not have cared much for The Fugs, and he has often described his move from poetry to punk as a conscious decision to abandon poetry in favor of rock 'n' roll. Lydia Lunch may have been drawn more toward the Beat-era poets than the second-generation New York School writers living in and around the Bowery during the early seventies. And yet, looking back at Lydia Lunch, at Patti Smith, at Richard Hell, and at a number of other musicians who made their way to New York to become poets, it behooves us at least to question *why* so many of these artists found a model for life and music in poetry and poetics, and to examine further how New York City's Lower East Side in the 1960s and 1970s generated a vibrant, outlaw, and angry lyric culture that informed and interacted with the burgeoning Blank Generation.

NOTES

1. Ted Berrigan, "Bean Spasms," in *The Angel Hair Anthology*, ed. Anne Waldman and Lewis Warsh (New York: Granary Books, 2001), pp. 42–43.
2. Byron Coley and Thurston Moore, eds., *No Wave: Post-Punk, Underground, New York, 1976–1980* (New York: Abrams Image, 2008), p. 12.
3. Victor Bockris, *Beat Punks: New York's Underground Culture from the Beat Generation to the Punk Explosion* (New York: Da Capo Press, 1998), p. 42.
4. Patti Smith, "Foreword," in *An Accidental Autobiography: The Selected Letters of Gregory Corso*, by Gregory Corso (New York: New Directions, 2003), p. xi.
5. *Ibid.*, p. xi.

6. Legs McNeil and Gillian McCain, *Please Kill Me: The Uncensored Oral History of Punk* (New York: Grove Press, 1996), p. 108.
7. Patti Smith Group, "Rock 'n' Roll Nigger," *Easter* (Arista Records, 1978).
8. Daniel Kane, *All Poets Welcome: The Lower East Side Poetry Scene in the 1960s* (Berkeley: University of California Press, 2003), p. 74.
9. *Ibid.*, p. 81.
10. Ted Berrigan, *The Sonnets* (New York: Grove Press, 1967), pp. 41, 38.
11. Ted Berrigan, *Clear The Range* (New York: Adventures in Poetry, 1977), p. 106.
12. Bob Holman, "History of the Poetry Project," in Poetry Project Archives (New York: St. Mark's Church, 1978), p. 18.
13. Patti Smith Group, "Land," *Horses* (Arista Records, 1975).
14. Kane, *All Poets Welcome*, p. 40.
15. Holman, "History of the Poetry Project," p. 9.
16. Kane, *All Poets Welcome*, p. 127.
17. Al Fowler, "Caroline: An exercise for our Cocksman Leader," *Fuck You/a magazine of the arts* 5:1 (Dec. 1962): n. pag.
18. The Fugs, "Boobs a Lot," *The Fugs First Album* (ESP Records, 1966); Richard Hell and the Voidoids, "Blank Generation," *Blank Generation* (Sire Records, 1977); The Sex Pistols, "God Save the Queen," *Never Mind the Bollocks Here's The Sex Pistols* (Virgin Records, 1977); X-Ray Spex, "I Can't Do Anything," *Germ Free Adolescents* (EMI Records, 1978); 8 Eyed Spy, "Lazy in Love," *8 Eyed Spy* (Fetish Records, 1981).
19. Patti Smith Group, "Gloria," *Horses* (Arista Records, 1975).
20. McNeil and McCain, *Please Kill Me*, p. 106.
21. Anne Waldman, ed., *Out of This World: An Anthology of the St. Mark's Poetry Project, 1966–1991* (New York: Crown Books, 1991), p. 646.
22. Kane, *All Poets Welcome*, pp. 199–200.
23. Richard Hell, Personal Interview (September 25, 2008).
24. Mary Harron, "Theresa Stern," *Punk* 1:4 (July 1976): 15–17.
25. Theresa Stern [Richard Hell and Tom Verlaine], *Wanna Go Out?* (New York: Dot Books, 1973), pp. 25, 31–32. Further references appear in the text.

14

ROBIN BERNSTEIN

Staging lesbian and gay New York

New York, more than any other city, unapologetically names its center for theater and drama: Broadway is the axis surrounded by concentric rings of off-Broadway and off-off-Broadway – marking, respectively, mainstream, margin, and fringe. Anything beyond the shores of Manhattan is designated, sometimes with condescension, "regional theater."

Lesbian and gay drama maps onto this topography. The history of scripted live performances by or about lesbian, gay, bisexual, transgender, and queer people in New York City is the history of a vexed relationship with Broadway, the mainstream visibility it offers, and the politics and aesthetics it polices. Broadway is an object of desire, a longed-for sign of success that can seduce theater practitioners toward conservative aesthetics and politics, away from radical experimentation and social engagement. Broadway spotlights a few extraordinarily talented queer playwrights – often but not always white gay men – while routinely eclipsing equally brilliant people of color, white lesbians, and feminists of all stripes. But theater practitioners who refuse and are refused by Broadway have created other venues, and the syncopation between these sites and Broadway, between the experimental and the established, characterizes New York's theater scene.

Prior to the twentieth century, plays incorporating cross-dressing were common, but a critical mass of plays that included identifiably non-heterosexual characters first emerged in the 1920s.[1] The first of this cluster, Sholem Asch's *God of Vengeance*, was a Yiddish-language play about a Jewish brothel-keeper whose daughter has an affair with a prostitute. *God of Vengeance* opened on the Lower East Side before it was translated into English and moved to the Apollo Theater on Broadway in 1923. The play had received critical acclaim for its downtown production in Yiddish, as well as for international productions in German, Russian, and Italian. The Broadway debut, however, met with a police raid and charges of obscenity.[2] Two other plays featuring same-sex desire, Edouard Bourdet's *The Captive* (1926) and Mae West's *The Drag* (1927), soon followed, and police raided these as well.

Backlash against these early dramas manifested in the passage of the Wales Padlock Act of 1927, which empowered the police to padlock closed, for one full year, any theater showing a play that could "tend to the corruption of youth or others" by including "sex degeneracy or 'perversion.'"[3] This law chilled playwrights and producers, and partly as a result of it, dramas of the mid twentieth century tended either to kill off lesbian or gay characters (as in Lillian Hellman's *The Children's Hour* [1934]) or to subsume same-sex desire to subtext (as in many works by Noel Coward).

Gay male subtext – real or imagined – provoked some critics' homophobic hysteria. At mid-century, a handful of drama critics accused playwrights of installing homosexual – specifically, *degenerate* homosexual – subtext in ostensibly non-gay plays. Richard Schechner criticized Edward Albee's *Who's Afraid of Virginia Woolf?* for its alleged "morbidity and sexual perversity which are there only to titillate an impotent and homosexual theater audience"; Robert Brustein described Albee's *The Zoo Story* as having a "masochistic-homosexual perfume"; and the *New York Review of Books* published Philip Roth's review of Albee's *Tiny Alice* under the title, "The Play that Dare Not Speak its Name."[4] The accusation that gay playwrights disguised naturally depraved gay characters as unnaturally depraved heterosexual characters reached its apex in Stanley Kauffmann's 1966 *New York Times* article, "Homosexual Drama and its Disguises." In this article, Kauffmann argued that social taboos prevented openly gay plays from being staged, and that therefore "the homosexual dramatist … has no choice but to masquerade" homosexual characters as heterosexual ones and thus to "invent a two-sex version of the one-sex experience he really knows."[5] Referring obliquely to Albee, Tennessee Williams, and William Inge, Kauffmann accused gay playwrights, first, of disguising decadent homosexuals as heterosexuals and thus libeling heterosexuals, and, second, of critiquing heterosexuality and "sublimat[ing] social hatreds" into "lurid violence" and "viciousness toward women" (Kauffmann took no issue with non-lesbians such as Frank Marcus or Jean-Paul Sartre writing plays that featured psychopathic lesbians; nor with playwrights who weren't gay men, such as Mae West, depicting suicidally miserable gay male characters).[6] Kauffmann called for "social and theatrical convention" to be "widened so that homosexual life may be as freely dramatized as heterosexual life" – not to improve the lives of gay people, but rather to curb gay playwrights' urge to "vent their feelings in camouflaged form."[7]

Kauffmann's wish was soon realized, although in ways Kauffmann probably never envisioned. In the years immediately before the Stonewall Rebellion of 1969, with which many historians mark the beginning of the modern gay and lesbian rights movement, plays with gay male content began to receive production away from Broadway's glare. Gay playwright Joe Cino's Greenwich Village venue, the Caffe Cino, staged openly gay plays by playwrights such as Lanford Wilson, Doric Wilson, William Hoffman, and Robert Patrick. In 1967, Charles Ludlam founded the Ridiculous Theater Company, whose actors used drag to question, mock, and re-write gender. A watershed moment came in 1968 with the off-Broadway staging of Mart Crowley's *The Boys in the Band*. In this play, set in the East Fifties in Manhattan, a group of gay men gather to celebrate their friend Harold's birthday. The characters bait and taunt each other, and the play climaxes in a game in which each character must telephone someone and tell him he loves him. The one supposedly straight guest, Alan, calls his wife, and the play ends with the implication that Alan wanted to come out, but the flamboyance and bitterness of the other party guests persuaded him back into the closet. Some gay men were repulsed by Crowley's campy and self-pitying characters, but others welcomed the play as either sympathetically realistic or kitschy.[8] Regardless of one's assessment of the play, *The Boys in the Band* "undeniably" constituted "a turning point in the evolution of gay theater," as the critic Don Shewey notes.[9] The play's popularity in and beyond New York brought a new level of visibility to gay theater and to homosexuality in general.

In the same period, lesbian and bisexual women playwrights, both white and of color, reshaped drama in and beyond New York – but often did so without including lesbian content. Lorraine Hansberry's 1959 *A Raisin in the Sun* inaugurated and invigorated a tradition of realism in African American theater; Cuban-American Maria Irene Fornes emerged as a leading force in New York's avant-garde theater of the 1960s (some of her later plays, including the 1977 *Fefu and Her Friends*, included lesbian characters); and Megan Terry arguably invented the rock musical with *Viet Rock*, an anti-war piece that debuted at La Mama in 1966 and whose theatrical progeny include *Hair* (1967), *Rent* (1996), and *Hedwig and the Angry Inch* (1997).

One of the actors in *Viet Rock* was Muriel Miguel, a member of the Kuna and Rappahannock Native American nations and a founding performer of the Open Theater. In 1975, Miguel co-created the feminist Native American company, Spiderwoman Theater, with her heterosexual sisters Gloria Miguel and Lisa Mayo. The troupe, which is today one of the oldest feminist theater troupes still in existence, developed a powerful aesthetic that combines story-weaving with improvisation, a burlesque performance style, and bawdy wit to attack racism and sexism.[10] Much of Spiderwoman Theater's drama reflects the sisters' lives in New York City; for example, *Sun, Moon, and Feather* (1980) was "inspired by their childhood" in Brooklyn's Red Hook neighborhood, and *The Three Sisters from Here to There* (1982) replaced

Chekhov's *The Three Sisters*' dreams of Moscow with three Brooklyn sisters' dreams of Manhattan.[11]

While on tour in Berlin in 1977, Spiderwoman lost its costumes in transit. Faced with this emergency, the troupe contacted Hot Peaches, a New York male drag company that happened also to be in Berlin, to borrow some costumes. When the two troupes connected, Lois Weaver, a non-Native member of Spiderwoman, fell in love with Peggy Shaw, a butch lesbian member of Hot Peaches. Shaw left Hot Peaches to join Spiderwoman for *Cabaret: An Evening of Disgusting Songs and Pukey Images* (1979), but soon Shaw and Weaver both left Spiderwoman to strike out on their own.[12] The ensuing personal and professional partnership between Shaw and Weaver became one of the most fecund in New York's theater history. In 1980, the two collaborated on WOW (Women's One World), an international women's theater festival that was staged in the Electric Circus at St. Mark's Place. The tremendous success of that festival, which included thirty-six performances from eight countries, led to the founding of the WOW Café, a permanent East Village theater space that continues to foster innovative theater.[13]

At WOW, Shaw and Weaver teamed up first with Pam Verge and Naja Beye and later with Deb Margolin to create the troupe Split Britches, which combined a Spiderwoman-inspired sense of free-associative play and raunchy humor with a sexy, campy centering of butch-femme and "eclectic combinations of fastidious attention to realistic detail with bizarre flights of surrealistic fantasy."[14] Split Britches innovated a method of playwriting rooted in fantasy, desire, and improvisation. As Shaw describes the process:

[W]e get together in a room and we list everything that we hate, that we love. And we think, what's our fantasy? "OK, this time, this show, I want to be a girl, and I wanna be bad, and I wanna sing the blues." You just make all your lists of fantasies, and then you practice every morning. We get together for weeks and we just start putting it together, totally from desire, from fantasy, not having any idea what it's going to be.[15]

Through this method, Split Britches has created many shows including *Upwardly Mobile Home* (1984; see *Figure 14*), *Little Women – The Tragedy* (1988), *Lesbians Who Kill* (1992), and most recently *Miss America* (2008).[16] The troupe has earned a cascade of honors, including four OBIE Awards and a Jane Chambers Award, and has energized a generation of feminist scholars and theater critics. Weaver, Shaw, and Margolin have each pursued solo careers: Margolin, who is straight, has written eight full-length performance pieces and won a 1999–2000 OBIE award, and she currently teaches playwriting at Yale University. Lois Weaver, now lecturer in Contemporary Performance at Queen Mary University of London, performs solo as the

Figure 14: A scene from the Split Britches' play *Upwardly Mobile Home*, first staged at the WOW Café on East 11th Street in 1984. The piece depicts a troupe of actors who camp under the Brooklyn Bridge, performing plays and attempting to sell out and get rich in Reagan's America. In this scene, Tammy (Lois Weaver), Mom (Peggy Shaw), and LeVine (Deb Margolin) perform the 1926 melodrama *The Shanghai Gesture*.

character Tammy WhyNot. Shaw's solo pieces include *You're Just Like My Father* (1995), *Menopausal Gentleman* (1999), and most recently *To My Chagrin* (2001), which asks the astonishing question, how can a white, butch grandmother pass on the gift of masculinity to her beloved biracial grandson, across their differences of sex, age, and race?

Another troupe that incubated at WOW is The Five Lesbian Brothers, composed of Lisa Kron, Peg Healey, Moe Angelos, Babs Davy, and Dominique Dibbell, whose *Voyage to Lesbos* launched from WOW in 1989. The Brothers forged a style that collided cabaret and Brechtian modes of performance with moments of understated, often shockingly

Figure 15: The Five Lesbian Brothers performing *Brave Smiles* at the WOW Café in 1992. Left to right: Babe (Peg Healey), Thalia (Maureen Angelos), Frau von Pussenheimer (Dominique Dibbell), Millicent (Babs Davy). In this moment (Act I, scene 2), Millicent has just found Thalia, the "new girl," wandering by the river, and has brought her to school. The scene includes several comments on Thalia's coat, which has been turned inside-out by boys who tormented her. The real reason that the coat is inside-out, however, is that the Brothers were touring and had only one coat available as a costume, and another character needed to wear it in Act II. Director Kate Stafford suggested turning the coat inside-out in the first Act to create the appearance of two coats, and that directorial choice became embedded in the script.

intimate, closely observed realism. Foregrounding sexual desire, irreverence toward all orthodoxies (including lesbian and feminist orthodoxies), and a commitment to explore whatever frightened them most, the Brothers created *Brave Smiles* (1992; see *Figure 15*) and *The Secretaries* (1994), both of which parodied films that stereotype lesbians, and *Brides of the Moon* (1997), which satirized the nuclear family from the vantage point of outer space. The Brothers' most realistic drama, *Oedipus at Palm Springs* (2005), re-imagined the Greek myth through the eyes of Jocasta. Brother Lisa Kron has pursued a solo career as a playwright and performer with works including *101 Humiliating Stories* (1993), *2.5 Minute Ride* (1996), and most recently *Well*, which opened on Broadway in 2006 and received two Tony nominations. Kron has developed a unique mode of drama in which a character, often named "Lisa Kron," steps on stage intending to tell the audience a self-serving story, but circumstances intervene – other actors refuse to cooperate, the set falls apart, the storyteller fails to hit a mark – and a different, messier, and ultimately far more important story erupts.

WOW's most celebrated alumnae also include Alina Troyano and Holly Hughes. Troyano, who often performs under the name Carmelita Tropicana, writes that she came to New York's downtown theater scene in a "search for Kunst" – a pun upon the German word for "art" as well as another Anglo-Saxon term.[17] She found both entities at WOW, where she met, to her delight, "feministas with a sense of humor!" including the members of Split Britches.[18] Troyano became a member of the WOW collective, studied playwriting with Maria Irene Fornes, and developed the persona of Carmelita Tropicana, a performance artist who sports "red lipstick, a beauty mole, an accent," and an evening gown that "disidentifies," as José Esteban Muñoz puts it, with stereotypes of Cuban culture.[19] Troyano performs solo in the alter ego of Tropicana as well as other characters; in *Milk of Amnesia – Leche de Amnesia* (1994), for example, she plays multiple roles including Carmelita Tropicana and a Cuban man named Pingalito (a pun on Cuban slang for penis).

Troyano performed her first role at WOW in Holly Hughes's first play, *The Well of Horniness* (1983). This campy take-off on detective drama (and loose parody of Radclyffe Hall's tortured lesbian novel, *The Well of Loneliness* [1928]) resulted, Hughes said, from "economic desperation and too many Bloody Marys."[20] The original cast included Hughes, Peggy Shaw of Split Britches, and Moe Angelos of The Five Lesbian Brothers; Troyano played a Sapphic sorority sister with hilarious lines such as, "You sit in a puddle, or you just glad to see me?"[21] The playwright, Holly Hughes, was a white lesbian who had recently moved from Michigan to New York in search of a career in the visual arts. Attracted to WOW's anarchy, Hughes launched a career as a playwright and performance artist. She followed *The Well of Horniness* with *Dress Suits for Hire* (1987), which Lois Weaver and Peggy Shaw performed, *World Without End* (1989), an elegy for her mother, and other solo performances at and beyond WOW.

In the late 1980s, Hughes applied for a grant from the National Endowment for the Arts (NEA). The NEA's peer reviewers recommended that she receive this much-needed funding, and made the same recommendation for gay male performance artists Tim Miller (who co-founded New York's avant-garde theater PS 122) and John Fleck, and heterosexual feminist performance artist Karen Finley. But in 1990 John Frohnmayer, chairman of the National Endowment for the Arts (NEA), vetoed these grants solely on the basis of the queer and sexual content of the artists' work; thus he defunded Hughes, Miller, Fleck, and Finley. Under the leadership of Senator Jesse Helms, the NEA then impelled all grant recipients to sign a pledge not to use federal monies for art that some unspecified individual, at some unspecified time, *might* deem obscene or blasphemous. Some theatrical artists refused to sign the pledges and rejected NEA grants; others, including Ellen Stewart of La Mama, continued to accept funding. The four original defunded artists, subsequently dubbed "the NEA four" (or, occasionally, "three queers and Karen Finley"), joined with the American Civil Liberties Union to sue the federal government. The group won a settlement equal to the grants plus court expenses, but the Supreme Court overturned part of that ruling in 1998. Hughes wrote about the fiasco in a solo performance piece, *Preaching to the Perverted* (2000), a cutting meditation on democracy and denigration.

The founding and flourishing of Spiderwoman, Split Britches, and WOW figured in a larger movement in the 1970s and 1980s, as second-wave feminism and gay liberation fostered a new generation of lesbian and gay plays, playwrights, and theatrical companies off- and off-off-Broadway. Magaly Alabau and Ana Maria Simo founded Medusa's Revenge in 1976; and Doric Wilson founded TOSOS (The Other Side of Silence) in 1972.[22] Lesbian theaters and gay theaters such as these opened in close geographical proximity in New York City, but as Don Shewey writes, "they may as well have been on different planets." Separate gay and lesbian theaters "occupied completely distinct social circles and aesthetic realms, with no conscious or unconscious solidarity around any shared notions."[23] In retrospect, however, these separate theaters may have had much in common: Simo commented in 1995 that she now saw "Medusa's Revenge, in a way, as closer to what Doric Wilson was trying to do. That is, it was a community-based thing."[24] One venue that staged both gay and lesbian plays was The Glines, a primarily gay male theater that opened in 1976 and that premiered Jane Chambers's *Last Summer at Bluefish Cove* in 1980.[25] *Last Summer* is a moving portrait of a terminally ill lesbian who, while vacationing with a community of lesbian friends, falls in love with a straight woman. Chambers's exceptionally adept use of realism appealed to lesbians who were eager to see their lives reflected on stage; as a result, Chambers's plays, including *A Late Snow* (1974) and *The Quintessential Image* (1982), continue to be staged thirty years later.

Ellen Stewart, a straight African American woman, founded La Mama Experimental Theater Club (La Mama E.T.C.) in 1961. Since its inception, this East Village theater has fostered and produced drama and performance by and about diverse GLBTQ people. The first production was Andy Milligan's adaptation of Tennessee Williams's short story, "One Arm"; a decade and a half later, La Mama premiered each of Harvey Fierstein's three one-acts that later combined to constitute *Torch Song Trilogy*, a play about a Jewish drag queen and his relationships with his lover, mother, and son.

Torch Song Trilogy played at The Glines in 1981, where it starred Fierstein, Matthew Broderick, and Estelle Getty, and then moved to Broadway in 1982. Other playwrights and performers who have worked at La Mama include Maria Irene Fornes, Remy Charlip, Marga Gomez, Stacy Makishi, Ethyl Eichelberger, and Cino alumni Robert Patrick, William Hoffman, and Jean-Claude Van Itallie. "Eighty percent of what is now considered the American theater," Harvey Fierstein once said, "originated at La Mama."[26]

In the 1980s, AIDS devastated New York, and dramatists responded to the epidemic with activist plays. In 1985, New York's theaters premiered William M. Hoffman's *As Is* and Larry Kramer's *The Normal Heart* – two of the first of what came to be known as the genre of "AIDS plays."[27] No clear line divides AIDS theater from AIDS activism, and it is no accident that Larry Kramer both authored one of the most famous AIDS plays and co-founded the Gay Men's Health Crisis and ACT UP (the AIDS Coalition to Unleash Power), a direct action group that embraces a confrontational style of public demonstration and civil disobedience. ACT UP's theatrical strategies overlap with and influence those of other activist groups, including WHAM (Women's Health Action and Mobilization, with which ACT UP collaborated on the famous "Stop the Church" demonstration at New York's St. Patrick's Cathedral in 1989), the Lesbian Avengers (a group that continues to draw attention to demonstrations through trademark performances of fire-eating), and Queer Nation (whose anonymous manifestos of 1990 and 1991 were probably authored by members of ACT UP).

Two of the most celebrated shows of the 1990s revolved around AIDS, and in each the setting of New York was palpably significant to the point that one could read the city as a character. In Jonathan Larson's rock musical *Rent* (1996), impoverished artists and musicians – many gay, lesbian, or bisexual; many HIV+ – struggle to create art and keep roofs over their heads in the rapidly gentrifying East Village. Larson, who was heterosexual, publicly acknowledged that his musical adapted Giacomo Puccini's nineteenth-century opera *La Bohème*, with AIDS replacing that opera's scourge of tuberculosis. Privately, Larson allegedly acknowledged another, uncredited and uncompensated contemporary source: lesbian fiction writer and playwright Sarah Schulman's 1990 novel, *People in Trouble*.[28] As Schulman puts it, "Basically *Rent* had two plots: the straight half was from Puccini, and the gay half was from me."[29] The musical's engaging and affecting music, and its sympathetic portrayal of queer and HIV+ people, earned *Rent* critical acclaim and numerous accolades, including the 1996 Pulitzer Prize, four Tony Awards, six Drama Desk Awards, and three OBIEs. *Rent* troubles some queer audiences, however, with the way in which it locates heterosexuals at the center of the AIDS crisis, portrays queers as grateful for straights' assistance, and ultimately suggests that queer people deserve sympathy because they are no different from heterosexuals.

Tony Kushner's two-part saga, *Angels in America: A Gay Fantasia on National Themes*, stages gay life in specific locations in New York – Central Park, the Hall of Justice in Brooklyn, an abandoned lot in the South Bronx – but leaps from those real locations to a fantastically imagined Antarctica and a no-place in which one character's pill-induced hallucination merges with another's dream. The characters are at once individuals and sweeping gestures toward desirous dreamers of "America": immigrants, Jews, gay men, people with AIDS, Mormons, and, nightmarishly, the historical figures of closeted homophobe Roy Cohn and his victim, Ethel Rosenberg.

Part One: Millennium Approaches premiered in San Francisco in 1991 and traveled to New York (in a 1993 production directed by George C. Wolfe) via Los Angeles and London, and in all locations it generated unparalleled excitement for its operatic re-imagining of America. Larry Kramer described Kushner's play as "drunk on ideas, on language, on the possibility of changing the world"; John Lahr called *Part Two: Perestroika* a "masterpiece" and declared that "[n]ot since [Tennessee] Williams has a playwright announced his poetic vision with such authority on the Broadway stage."[30] *Part One*'s honors of 1993 alone include the Tony Award for Best Play, the Pulitzer Prize for Drama, the New York Drama Critics' Circle Award for Best Play, and the Drama Desk Award for Best Play; *Part Two: Perestroika* won the Tony Award for Best Play and the Drama Desk Award for Outstanding Play. Critics hailed the saga's "breathtaking scope and intellectual, political, and theatrical daring," but the play often becomes the object of censorship efforts.[31] Among gay scholars, critics, and audiences, Kushner's triumph marked "a turning point in the history of gay drama, the history of American drama, and of American literary culture … remov[ing] from the closet once and for all the enlivening relationship of gay culture and American theater and the centrality of the homosexual gaze in American literature."[32]

The critical and popular acclaim for *Angels in America* was extraordinary but not isolated. During the final decade of the twentieth century, a small coterie of lesbians and gay men including Kushner, Margaret Edson, George C. Wolfe, Jane Wagner, Charles Busch, Terrence McNally, Paula Vogel, Lisa Kron, and Craig Lucas authored plays – some with queer characters, some without – that enjoyed substantial runs in major theaters. The public comings-out of well-known performers such as Rosie O'Donnell, Ellen Degeneres, Sir Ian McKellan, Rupert Everett, and Lily Tomlin suggested to some that the twenty-first century would constitute a "post-gay" period in which sexual identity was irrelevant.

The 2003 Tony Awards Show appeared, to some, to inaugurate this "post-gay" era: in that year, gay men nearly swept the Tony Awards, prompting Frank Rich, critic for the *New York Times*, to call the Awards ceremony the "first live gay network reality show." Open gay men and lesbians had won Tonys before (Cherry Jones, for example, thanked her partner while accepting a Tony for Best Actress in 1995). In 2003, however, the openly gay awardees reached critical mass for the first time. That year, actor and playwright Harvey Fierstein was named Best Leading Actor in a Musical for his drag role in *Hairspray* (which earned the title of Best Musical, as well as six other Awards); and the Tony for Best Play went to *Take Me Out*, the story of a gay ballplayer. It was Marc Shaiman and Scott Wittman, however, who stole the show when they accepted their award for Best Original Score for *Hairspray*. The two men lingered in a loving kiss on the lips. Then Shaiman said to Wittman, his partner of twenty-five years: "I'd like to declare in front of all these people, I love you and I'd like to live with you the rest of my life."[33] The *New York Times* serenely described the Awards show kiss as theatrical "business as usual," and most audience members seemed to agree. Of the eight million people who watched the Tony Awards that year, only ten telephoned CBS to complain about gay visibility at the ceremony, and only sixty-eight emailed the network.

The spectacle of white gay male theater practitioners pledging long-term domesticity apparently delivered little shock value, even if they prefaced that declaration with a tender kiss. As playwright Richard Hall has pointed out, however, gay content on stage generally receives the least censure when sexuality is couched within a larger affirmation of long-term relationships and nuclear families. The 1983 Tony Award-winning musical *La Cage Aux Folles*, for example, challenged audiences to respect and sympathize with gay male protagonists, including a drag queen, but the show's plot revolved around one of the gay men's relationship with his heterosexual son on the occasion of the son's engagement. The popular success of *Torch Song Trilogy*, Hall points out, would seem unlikely, given its "brilliant scene in a backroom bar in which [protagonist] Arnold Beckoff mimes getting fucked while managing, among other things, to light a cigarette" – but the larger arc of the play "tells critics and [the straight] public what they hope to hear: gay people are just like straight people; all they want is a loving spouse, nice in-laws and a kid who gets good grades."[34] In that context, Shaiman's wish to "live with [Wittman] for the rest of my life" may neutralize rather than magnify the political impact of the kiss.

Race and ethnicity, as well as familial configuration, can undermine a gay or lesbian play's chances for mainstream success. Chicana playwright Cherríe Moraga notes that the transgressive sexual and political content of *Angels in America* would play very differently in a Chicana lesbian context:

> Of course, I loved [*Angels in America*], as did ... most of the theater-going public of the United States ... The play is undeniably and unabashedly queer and dangerously "commie" in perspective, which I relish and respect about Kushner's work. But what I anticipated would make the audience uncomfortable was precisely what made the audience hysterical. Every dick joke, even every Jewish dick joke, even every homosexual Jewish dick joke, tore the audience up. They weren't offended. They were entertained ... I look around at this Broadway audience, mostly straight, overwhelmingly White, upper middle class, of course: your typical theater crowd ... [T]o my amazement two guys start to "fuck" on stage (as Kushner describes it in the stage directions: "They fuck.") and everyone is fine with it ... So, I did a little private experiment. Every time I heard the word or a reference to "Jewish dick," I replaced it with "Mexican pussy." Jewish dick ... Mexican pussy. Jewish dick ... Mexican pussy. Jewish dick ... Mexican pussy. And nobody was laughing. That's me on Broadway. That's my people on Broadway. That chilling silence.[35]

Jewish humor, Moraga astutely observes, is "synonymous with New York" and abundant on Broadway and television; therefore the Jewishness of *Angels in America* makes the play seem "translatable" even to "laughing lawyers and stockbrokers in the audience who may very well cry at the *real* news of having a *real* gay son."[36] In other words, the Jewish humor serves as the drama's affective connector that makes the play *feel* familiar and accessible to audiences who do not, in fact, have any meaningful connections to Jews, queers, or Marxists. Because of racism and sexism, however, plays by and about gay men of color and lesbians of all races and ethnicities can feel, to straight white audiences, *more* unfamiliar and inaccessible than they actually may be.

When Moraga imagines one of her plays produced on Broadway, she hears "chilling silence" in response to her jokes about "Mexican pussy." But the most common form that silence takes is the refusal to produce works by gay men of color and lesbians in the first place. Supremely accomplished playwrights who have never been produced on Broadway include white lesbian Paula Vogel, who won a 1998 Pulitzer Prize for *How I Learned to Drive*; Latino gay man Luis Alfaro, who received a MacArthur Fellowship, commonly known as a "genius grant," for his playwriting and performing; Asian American gay man Chay Yew, the winner of the London Fringe Award and the George and Elisabeth Marton Playwriting Award, whose work has "significantly shifted the poetic and political landscape of both Asian American theater and gay theater";[37] and Chicana lesbian Cherríe Moraga, recipient of the 1993 Pen West Award for Drama, the 1993 NEA Theater Playwrights'

Fellowship, the 2001 Scholars Award from the National Association for Chicana and Chicano Studies, Lifetime Achievement Awards from Ellas in Acción, and (with Gloria E. Anzaldúa) the 2001 Bode-Pearson Prize for Outstanding Contributions to American Studies – one of the oldest and most prestigious honors awarded by the national American Studies Association.

Many open lesbians and gay men assume leadership positions in major regional and off-Broadway theaters: Luis Alfaro spent a decade as Associate Producer, Director of New Play Development, and co-director of the Latino Theater Initiative at the Mark Taper Forum in Los Angeles; George C. Wolfe served from 1993 to 2004 as Artistic Director and Producer at the New York Shakespeare Festival and the Public Theater; Brian Freeman, co-founder of the brilliant San Francisco-based performance troupe PomoAfroHomos (postmodern Afro-American homosexuals), recently founded the Playwrights' Lab at the New York Public Theater, where he developed a play based on the life of Bayard Rustin, a gay African American man who organized the 1963 Civil Rights march on Washington, DC; and Megan Terry and her life partner Joanne Schmidman operate the Omaha Magic Theater, which Schmidman founded in 1970 and which Terry has served as a playwright since 1974.

Some lesbian and gay theaters, such as the Alice B. Theater in Seattle, have closed in recent years, but others continue to produce work, often despite breathtaking economic challenges. Primarily or exclusively queer theaters include Theater Rhinoceros in San Francisco; Theater Offensive in Boston; Bailiwick in Chicago; Buddies in Bad Times Theater in Toronto, Canada; TheaterOut in Anaheim, California; Triangle Productions in Portland, Oregon; and many others. As funding for the arts becomes scarcer, colleges and universities become increasingly important to American theater, including lesbian and gay theater. Colleges and universities provide crucial venues for solo actors and small troupes, who often tour with offerings that include linked performances and master classes in playwriting or acting. Theater has also become a key site of community and support for queer youth: in Boston, for example, members of the True Colors Out Youth Theater co-create and perform original shows.

Broadway declares itself the sun around which off-Broadway, off-off-Broadway, and regional theaters orbit, but GLBTQ theater practitioners move in multidirectional trajectories that challenge the primacy of not only Broadway, but also heterosexuality, realism, and normalized configurations of gender and family. When padlocks barred gay and lesbian content from Broadway, some queer people clandestinely picked the locks while others created a downtown scene of unrivaled brilliance and beauty. When AIDS decimated New York's gay communities, GLBTQ people organized, launched street activism, and channeled rage and grief into stunning theatrical works that foundationally changed American theater, including Broadway. When performers and playwrights are repeatedly defunded, GLBTQ theater practitioners find and create unlikely venues for performance. The *New York Times* may yawn at a supposedly "post-gay" moment in which gay men and lesbians are welcome to the extent that they affirm monogamy, parenthood, and typical modes of gender – but radical queers continue to critique, defamiliarize, and explode these norms, and to tell the complex and messy truths of our lives. Against all odds, radical queers, especially lesbians of color, stage "[b]rief flashes of image, word, sound that respond finally to that most censored desire." These moments are, in Cherríe Moraga's words, "ruptures of queer hero-ism." When we witness these ruptures, these world-making glimpses at the world that exists and the world we have the power to create, we are "breathless at the self-recognition."[38]

NOTES

Parts of this chapter are adapted from the introduction to *Cast Out: Queer Lives in Theater*, ed. Robin Bernstein (Ann Arbor, MI: University of Michigan Press, 2006), pp. 1–22.

1. On the history of drag performance, see Laurence Senelick, *The Changing Room: Sex, Drag and Theater* (New York: Routledge, 2000).
2. Kaier Curtin's *"We Can Always Call Them Bulgarians": The Emergence of Lesbians and Gay Men on the American Stage* (Boston, MA: Alyson Publications, 1987) includes respective chapters on *God of Vengeance*, *The Captive*, and *The Drag*. See also Harley Erdman, "Jewish Anxiety in 'Days of Judgment': Community Conflict, Antisemitism, and the *God of Vengeance* Obscenity Case," *Theater Survey* 40:1 (May 1999): 51–74.
3. Curtin, *"We Can Always Call Them Bulgarians,"* p. 100.
4. Richard Schechner, "Who's Afraid of Edward Albee?" *Tulane Drama Review* 7:3 (1963): 7–10; Robert Brustein, *Seasons of Discontent: Dramatic Opinions 1959–1965* (London: Jonathan Cape, 1966), p. 29; Philip Roth, "The Play that Dare Not Speak its Name," *New York Review of Books* 4:2 (February 25, 1965).
5. Stanley Kauffmann, "Homosexual Drama and its Disguises," *New York Times* (January 23, 1966): 93. Howard Taubman forwarded similar claims in "Not What it Seems: Homosexual Motif Gets Heterosexual Guise," *New York Times* (November 5, 1961): II:1.
6. *Ibid.* See also Frank Marcus, *The Killing of Sister George* (1965), in *Gay Plays: The First Collection*, ed. William M. Hoffman (New York: Avon Books, 1979), pp. 337–411; Jean-Paul Sartre, *No Exit*, trans. Paul Bowles (original French edn. [*Huis Clos*] published 1944; New York: Samuel French, 1958); and Lillian Schlissel, ed., *Three Plays by Mae West: "Sex," "The Drag," "The Pleasure Man"* (New York: Routledge, 1997).

7. Kauffmann, "Homosexual Drama and its Disguises," 93.

8. See Alan Sinfield, *Out on Stage: Lesbian and Gay Theater in the Twentieth Century* (New Haven, CT: Yale University Press, 1999), pp. 300–2.

9. Don Shewey, "Pride in the Name of Love: Notes on Contemporary Gay Theater," Introduction to *Out Front: Contemporary Gay and Lesbian Plays*, ed. Don Shewey (New York: Grove Press, 1988), p. xii.

10. Meg Swanson with Robin Murray, *Playwrights of Color* (Yarmouth, ME: Intercultural Press, 1999), pp. 76–89. See also Ann Haugo, "Weaving a Legacy: An Interview with Muriel Miguel of the Spiderwoman Theater," in *The Color of Theater: Race, Culture, and Contemporary Performance*, ed. Roberta Uno with Lucy Mae San Pablo Burns (London and New York: Continuum, 2002), pp. 218–34; and Charlotte Canning, *Feminist Theaters in the U.S.A.: Staging Women's Experience* (London and New York: Routledge, 1996), pp. 82–84, 93–99, 165–69. Spiderwoman maintains an excellent website, containing many production stills, at staff.lib.muohio.edu/nawpa/spdrwmnarchv.html.

11. Ann Haugo, "Native American Drama," in *A Companion to Twentieth-Century Drama*, ed. David Krasner (Malden, MA: Blackwell, 2005), pp. 341, 342.

12. Sue-Ellen Case, ed., *Split Britches: Lesbian Practice/Feminist Performance* (New York: Routledge, 1996), pp. 4–5. As Case notes, "tales told in various critical essays, and in interviews, present various versions" of Weaver and Shaw's exit from Spiderwoman. These tales vary particularly in their assessment of the roles of race and sexuality in the split. See Rebecca Schneider's "See the Big Show: Spiderwoman Theater Doubling Back," in *Acting Out: Feminist Performances*, ed. Lynda Hart and Peggy Phelan (Ann Arbor, MI: University of Michigan Press, 1993), pp. 227–55; Jill Dolan, *The Feminist Spectator as Critic* (Ann Arbor, MI: University of Michigan Research Press, 1988), pp. 71, 136; and Case, ed., *Split Britches*, p. 5.

13. See Alisa Solomon, "The WOW Café," *TDR* 29:1 (Spring 1985): 92–101 for an oral history of the WOW Café. See also Case, ed., *Split Britches*, pp. 7–8.

14. Dolan, *Feminist Spectator*, p. 72.

15. Peggy Shaw, "How I Learned Theater," in *Cast Out*, ed. Bernstein, p. 28.

16. Case collects many of these dramatic scripts in *Split Britches*.

17. Alina Troyano, *I, Carmelita Tropicana: Performing Between Cultures* (Boston, MA: Beacon Press, 2000), p. xiii.

18. *Ibid.*, p. xiv.

19. *Ibid.*, p. xv, and José Esteban Muñoz, *Disidentifications: Queers of Color and the Performance of Politics* (Minneapolis, MN: University of Minneapolis Press, 1999). See especially ch. 5, "Sister Acts: Ela Troyano and Carmelita Tropicana."

20. Holly Hughes, introduction to *The Well of Horniness*, in *Out Front*, ed. Shewey, p. 222.

21. *Ibid.*, p. 228.

22. William M. Hoffman, *Gay Plays: The First Collection* (New York: Avon Books, 1979), pp. xxxi, xxxii. See also "From the Invisible to the Ridiculous: The Emergence of an Out Theater Aesthetic: A Conversation among Moe Angelos, Susan Finque, Lola Pashalinski, Everett Quinton, Ana Maria Simo, and Doric Wilson, Moderated by Don Shewey," in *The Queerest Art: Essays on Lesbian*

and Gay Theater, ed. Alisa Solomon and Framji Minwalla (New York: New York University Press, 2002).

23. Don Shewey, "'Be True to Yearning': Notes on the Pioneers of Queer Theater," in *The Queerest Art*, ed. Solomon and Minwalla, p. 133.

24. *Ibid.*, p. 139.

25. Don Rubin and Carlos Solorzano, eds., *World Encyclopedia of Contemporary Theater: The Americas* (New York: Taylor & Francis, 2000), p. 339.

26. Alvin Eng, "'Some place to be somebody': La Mama's Ellen Stewart," in *The Color of Theater*, ed. Uno and Burns, p. 135.

27. David Román points out that these two plays are sometimes falsely identified as "the earliest responses to AIDS in the theater," an error that "does a grievous disservice to such artists, playwrights, and theater collectives as Robert Chesley, Jeff Hagedorn, Rebecca Ranson, and San Francisco's A.I.D.S. Show collaborators, among others, whose AIDS performances were produced as early as 1983" (*Acts of Intervention: Performance, Gay Culture, and AIDS* [Bloomington, IN: University of Indiana Press, 1998], p. xx). Román devotes a full chapter of his book to theatrical interventions to the AIDS crisis in the early 1980s. John M. Clum also treats AIDS drama in depth in *Still Acting Gay: Male Homosexuality in Modern Drama* (New York: St. Martin's Press, 2000).

28. Sarah Schulman, *Stagestruck: Theater, AIDS, and the Marketing of Gay America* (Durham, NC: Duke University Press, 1998), p. 13.

29. *Ibid.*

30. Kramer quoted in Tony Kushner, *Thinking about the Longstanding Problems of Virtue and Happiness* (New York: Theater Communications Group, 1995), rear cover; John Lahr, "The Theater: Earth Angels," *The New Yorker* (December 13, 1993): 133.

31. Jill Dolan, "Lesbian and Gay Drama," in *A Companion to Twentieth-Century Drama*, ed. Krasner, p. 498. On censorship and *Angels in America*, see John Houchin, *Censorship of the American Theater in the Twentieth Century* (New York: Cambridge University Press, 2003), esp. pp. 250–52 and 263–65.

32. John Clum, *Acting Gay: Male Homosexuality in Modern Drama* (New York: Columbia University Press, 1992), p. 324.

33. Frank Rich, "Gay Kiss: Business as Usual," *New York Times* (June 22, 2003): ii:1.

34. Richard Hall, *Three Plays for a Gay Theater and Three Essays* (San Francisco, CA: Grey Fox Press, 1983), pp. 173–74.

35. Cherríe Moraga, "The Art of Anger in América," in *The Color of Theater*, ed. Uno and Burns, pp. 118–19.

36. *Ibid.*, pp. 118, 119, emphasis in original.

37. David Román, "Los Angeles Intersections: Chay Yew," in *The Color of Theater*, ed. Uno and Burns, p. 237.

38. Cherríe Moraga, "And Frida Looks Back: The Art of Latina/o Queer Heroics," in *Cast Out*, ed. Bernstein, p. 89.

15

CYRUS R. K. PATELL

Emergent ethnic literatures

In the final chapter of Chang-rae Lee's first novel, *Native Speaker* (1995), the protagonist, a Korean American named Henry Park, thinks about the streets of Flushing, Queens, and why he loves them:

> I love these streets lined with big American sedans and livery cars and vans. I love the early morning storefronts opening up one by one, shopkeepers talking as they crank their awnings down. I love how the Spanish disco thumps out from windows, and how the people propped halfway out still jiggle and dance in the sill and frame. I follow the strolling Saturday families of brightly wrapped Hindus and then the black-clad Hasidim, and step into all the old churches that were once German and then Korean and are now Vietnamese. And I love the brief Queens sunlight at the end of the day, the warm lamp always reaching through the westward tops of that magnificent city.[1]

The novel's epigraph comes from Whitman's poem "The Sleepers": "I turn but do not extricate myself, / Confused, a past-reading, another, but with darkness yet." The lines are drawn from a passage in which the poem's narrator has just imagined "a beautiful gigantic swimmer swimming naked through the eddies of the sea," a swimmer who is ultimately dashed to death against the rocks: "Swiftly and out of sight is borne the brave corpse." Lee's novel, like Whitman's poem, is haunted by loss, occurring in the aftermath of the death of the narrator's son, Mitt, who is inadvertently suffocated at the bottom of a "dog pile" of neighborhood boys. Despite the bitter memories that they evoke, the streets of Flushing remain a source of hope and promise for Henry Park.

Lee's novel finds this promise in the constant influx of new immigrants to the city. "They were of all kinds, these streaming and working and dealing, these various platoons of Koreans, Indians, Vietnamese, Haitians, Columbians, Nigerians, these brown and yellow whatevers, whoevers, countless unheard nobodies" (83). This passage echoes Whitman's "Salut au monde!" (1856): "You whoever you are! ... All you continentals of Asia, Africa, Europe, Australia, indifferent of place! ... Health to you! Good will to you all – from me and America sent." Whitman saw in the new arrivals the ongoing revitalization of American democracy, and *Native Speaker* dramatizes one immigrant's attempt to realize Whitman's cosmopolitan, democratic dream: the novel's plot revolves around a mayoral bid by City Councilman John Kwang, who represents the "brown and yellow whatevers [and] whoevers" of Flushing. Kwang's rise and fall, seen through the eyes of Henry Park, encapsulates the continual promise of New York cosmopolitanism, a promise that remains unfulfilled at the novel's end but is no less alluring.

In 2002, an all-white ad hoc committee of bookstore owners, libraries, publishers' groups, and other groups such as the New York Women's Agenda decided that New York should emulate Chicago's successful "One Book, One City" program, which urged Chicago's residents to read and discuss Harper Lee's novel *To Kill a Mockingbird*. The New York committee chose four finalists: *Native Speaker*, James McBride's memoir *The Color of Water: A Black Man's Tribute to His White Mother* (1996), E. L. Doctorow's novel *Ragtime* (1975), and Dennis Smith's 1972 memoir *Report from Engine Co. 82*. Committee members then voted by e-mail, and *Native Speaker* edged out *The Color of Water*.

Controversy immediately ensued.

The contours of the controversy highlight some of the problems with the ways in which late twentieth-century institutional multiculturalism has encouraged us to read literary texts, particularly ethnic literary texts. One problem that became evident from committee members' subsequent comments was the fact that many of them hadn't bothered to read the texts carefully or to finish them before voting. According to the *New York Times*, "John C. Liu, the first Asian-American councilman, said he had not finished [*Native Speaker*] but relished the idea of a book about an Asian-American councilman." In contrast, Barbara Gerard, a representative of the Women's Agenda on the selection committee and a consultant to the Board of Education, also admitted not finishing the book and wanted to reserve judgment until she had seen "if there is anything derogatory toward Korean-Americans or Asians at this point." Gerard, like some other members of the committee, seemed to have a programmatic idea of multicultural reading that verged on socialist realism, assuming that multicultural texts should be celebrations of particular ethnic identities. Members of the committee who had dismissed Doctorow's *Ragtime* as insufficiently multicultural had either not read up to the novel's final pages, in which the rags-to-riches Jewish studio magnate imagines a film featuring "a bunch of children who were pals, white black, fat thin rich poor, all kinds, mischievous little urchins who would have funny adventures in their own neighborhood, a society of ragamuffins, like all of us, a gang, getting into trouble and getting out again," or simply dismissed the novel because it didn't include Asians or Latinos and spent a lot of time describing the lives of white people.[2]

Ultimately, the New York Women's Agenda decided to withdraw from the program and promote the reading of *The Color of Water*, the biracial McBride's paean to his white mother, in part because of its greater attention to issues of gender and because, according to the *Times*, "Members of the group were concerned that *Native Speaker* was not engaging enough for high school students and might offend some Asian-Americans," presumably because two of its central characters are Asian and turn out to be flawed human beings. This controversy suggests that the pursuit of multiculturalism often leads to an essentialism in which the depiction of particular minority characters is assumed to reflect on the character of the minority as a whole.

The assumption that ethnic writing should have this kind of a representative function, that it should make a case to mainstream audiences about the acceptability and even the assimilability of the ethnic culture it is supposed to be representing, was certainly the norm for Jewish American writing, which was the most prominent ethnic American literature at the beginning of the twentieth century. For example, William Dean Howells praised Abraham Cahan as a "master of realism" in a review of Cahan's first novel, *Yekl* (1896), which tells the story of a Jewish immigrant on the Lower East Side who desperately wants to Americanize himself. An extended description of Suffolk Street in the early pages of the novel describes the Jewish denizens of the Lower East Side as part of "a human hodgepodge with its component parts changed but not yet fused into one homogeneous whole," the "yet" implying – as does the entire novel – that the process of assimilation is underway. The subsequent landmarks in Jewish American fiction published before the beginning of the Second World War – for example, Anzia Yezierska's *Bread Givers* (1925) and Mike Gold's *Jews Without Money* (1930) – tend to adopt realist modes of representation and are generally autobiographically inflected. Even Henry Roth's *Call It Sleep* (1934), long viewed as the sole example of a Jewish American text in the modernist tradition, begins in a realistic autobiographical mode before it veers away into formal experimentation.

Roth's novel, however, presages the work of later ethnic writers who sought to free themselves from the shackles of ethnic realism, particularly from the assumption that the primary task of ethnic writing is to represent groups rather than individuals. Indeed, one of the abiding subjects of New York ethnic writing is the impossibility of maintaining the purity of Old World cultural traditions – or even New World cultural traditions – in an urban situation where ethnic neighborhoods impinge as closely on one another as they do in New York.

New York's twentieth-century ethnic literatures are best seen as "emergent literatures" in the cultural critic Raymond Williams's sense of the term: they are the literary expressions of cultural groups that define themselves either as an alternative to or in direct opposition to a dominant mainstream. Williams characterizes culture as a constant struggle for dominance in which a hegemonic mainstream seeks to defuse the challenges posed to it by both residual and emergent cultural forms. What Williams calls "residual culture" consists of those practices that are based on the "residue of ... some previous social and cultural institution or formation," but continue to play a role in the present. This description is not meant to suggest that residual cultures should be considered "unimportant" or "minor." On the contrary, they are major parts of any cultural formation. Emergent cultures, in contrast, exist as sites where "new meanings and values, new practices, new relationships and kinds of relationships are continually being created." In both cases, "definitions of the emergent [and] the residual ... can be made only in relation to a full sense of the dominant," because these forms of culture define themselves in relation to dominant, mainstream culture.[3] It is important to note that what's new in emergent culture is what's new from the standpoint of the dominant: the Native American novel, for example, was an emergent literary formation in the late 1960s, even though it portrayed beliefs and perspectives that were thousands of years old.

Emergent literatures demonstrate the power of what the philosopher Kwame Anthony Appiah calls "cosmopolitan contamination." Cultures, in Appiah's account, never tend toward purity: they tend toward change, toward mixing and miscegenation, toward an "endless process of imitation and revision."[4] To keep a culture "pure" requires the vigilant policing often associated with fundamentalist regimes or xenophobic political parties. Like Williams's account of the interaction of dominant, residual, and emergent cultures, Appiah's description of culture is all about "conversation across boundaries." Such conversations, Appiah writes, "can be delightful, or just vexing: what they mainly are, though, is inevitable."[5]

Multiculturalism, according to Appiah, "often designates the disease it purports to cure," because its approach to the promotion of cultural diversity is often strongly inflected by a pluralism that, as the intellectual historian David Hollinger puts it, "respects inherited boundaries and locates individuals within one or another of a series of ethno-racial groups to be protected and preserved." Hollinger argues that "pluralism differs from cosmopolitanism in the degree to which it endows with privilege particular groups, especially the communities that are well established at whatever time the ideal of pluralism is invoked ... In its extreme form, this conservative concern takes the form of a bargain: 'You keep the acids of your modernity out of my culture, and I'll keep the acids of mine away from yours.'"[6]

Emergent writers realize that such a bargain is not only undesirable but untenable. Contemporary emergent writing thus sets itself against the idea of cultural purity that lies behind contemporary US multiculturalism and identity politics – and behind the objections to the choice of Chang-rae Lee's *Native Speaker*, which depicts Flushing as a place where emergent cultures take root and begin to flourish.

One way of thinking about the history of New York's ethnic literatures in the twentieth century is geographically, seeing a shift in the center of gravity away from the Lower East Side to uptown Manhattan and then to the other boroughs. Cahan's *Yekl* is set in the Lower East Side, but the Schearl family in Henry Roth's *Call It Sleep* settles in Brownsville, Brooklyn. When the Schearls are forced by economic circumstances to move to the Lower East Side, it is represented as a step backward to a place where the novel's narrator, David, comes to experience poverty and hardship. The family portrayed in Lin Yutang's *Chinatown Family* (1948) is not, for most of the novel, a Chinatown family at all: they live on Lexington Avenue on the Upper East Side.

The dynamics of this trajectory are encapsulated by two classic New York films that touch on ethnic experience: Woody Allen's *Manhattan* (1979) and Spike Lee's *Do the Right Thing* (1989). Allen's career itself is an example of cultural contamination, a merger of the traditions of the "New York Intellectual" as exemplified by the journal *Partisan Review* (1934–2003), many of whose early authors were the children of Jewish immigrants; the *New Yorker*, founded by William Ross in 1925 as an alternative to lowbrow humor magazines, eventually becoming a venue for serious journalism and fiction; and the stand-up tradition of Borscht Belt humor.

Manhattan was the follow-up to Allen's successful romantic comedy *Annie Hall* (1977), which used a failing love relationship to explore Allen's sense of the differences not only between Jews and WASPs (the film critic Pauline Kael described the film as "the neurotic's version of *Abie's Irish Rose*"), but also between the cultures of New York and Los Angeles.[7] Annie declares New York "a dying city," but the film suggests that its virtue lies precisely in its connection to the past. *Annie Hall* was a defense of New York in the aftermath of its celebrated fiscal crisis of the 1970s, but in *Manhattan* Allen resists the temptation to romanticize the city. The film begins in a romantic vein with a stunning montage of scenes from the city that shows off the film's widescreen black-and-white cinematography, as Gershwin's "Rhapsody in

Blue" plays on the soundtrack. But the romantic imagery serves only to heighten the contrast between the grandeur of the city and the smallness of the lives that the film goes on to depict. *Manhattan*'s New York is a rarefied place, consisting mostly of midtown Manhattan, from Lincoln Center to the Upper East Side, a reflection of the limited perspective of its protagonist, Isaac Davis. The choice of Gershwin's music not only emphasizes Isaac's propensity for nostalgia, but also serves as an emblem for both Isaac's and Allen's aspirations: Gershwin, after all, was a Jewish popular entertainer from New York who yearned to be accepted as a "serious" artist. Running throughout both *Annie Hall*, which begins with a jokey conversation about anti-Semitism, and *Manhattan* is the worry that Jews remain outsiders in some crucial way.

By the late 1970s, however, Jewish American literature could no longer be considered either marginalized or emergent. Saul Bellow had won a Nobel Prize for Literature in 1976 "for the human understanding and subtle analysis of contemporary culture that are combined in his work," and Allen's *Annie Hall* had received Oscars for Best Picture, Best Director, Best Original Screenplay, and Best Actress. As Robin Bernstein points out earlier in this volume, citing Cherríe Moraga's reaction to Tony Kushner's play *Angels in America*, "Jewish humor ... is 'synonymous with New York' and abundant on Broadway and television," and therefore can serve to make a challenging play like *Angels in America* palatable to audience members who otherwise might resist representations of gay experience.

Although it did not deliberately set itself against *Manhattan*, Spike Lee's third film *Do the Right Thing* (1989) can be read as a rejoinder to Allen's film. It too opens with a vivid and deliberately artificial musical sequence, but Lee substitutes bright colors for Allen's black-and-white; Rosie Perez's in-your-face hip-hop dancing before a photograph of Brooklyn stoops for *Manhattan*'s impersonal camera eye; Public Enemy's "Fight the Power" for Gershwin's "Rhapsody"; and, most significantly, the Bedford-Stuyvesant section of Brooklyn for Manhattan. Responding to a series of racially charged incidents of violence against African Americans in New York during the 1980s, the film depicts a racially diverse neighborhood, primarily African American, in which Puerto Ricans, an Italian American family, a Korean couple who own the local grocery store, a WASP brownstone-owner, and white cops all play important roles. The drama in the film erupts around the question of whether Sal, an Italian American who owns the local pizza joint, should display pictures of African Americans on his "Wall of Fame," which honors famous Italian Americans only. Sal invokes the rights of private property, but he is challenged by Buggin' Out, a young African American who points out that Sal's customers are almost all African Americans. Sal, the movie suggests, has a right to hang what he wants on his walls, but – given that the pizzeria is also an important community space for the neighborhood – is omitting pictures of African Americans the right thing to do?

Part of the neighborhood's problem is that no one can talk about problems like this without resorting to shouting or, even worse, racially charged language. The neighborhood's civil society is impaired because it lacks any sense of civil discourse. Even friends swear at each other and refer to one another as "nigger," and in one of the film's signature set pieces (described in the script as the "racial slur montage") some of the film's characters do "the dozens" – a ritual of "trash talking" that is an element from African American oral tradition – by insulting different ethnic groups; the African American Mookie insults Italians; the Italian Pino insults blacks; the Puerto Rican Stevie insults Koreans; the white police officer insults Puerto Ricans; and the Korean grocery-store owner insults Ed Koch (and by extension New York's Jews).[8] Uncivil discourse is the norm in this neighborhood on a good day, and therefore at a moment of crisis, the neighborhood's residents lack the linguistic resources to stave off violence through conversation and negotiation. Challenged by Buggin' Out and the menacing Radio Raheem, Sal, for most of the film the voice of reason and cross-ethnic and racial sympathy, suddenly spews racist invective, which leads to a riot. The film depicts the failure of cosmopolitan conversation, although the one bright spot is that the Koreans are spared the wrath of the primarily African American crowd, which is persuaded by the grocery-store owner's plea, "Me no white. Me no white. Me Black. Me Black. Me Black."[9] Even more so than Chang-rae Lee's Native Son, Do the Right Thing presents the opportunity for cosmopolitanism, but dramatizes the powerful obstacles that prevent it from being realized.

The genesis and transformation of the category of the "Nuyorican" offers a more hopeful case study in the dynamics of cultural contamination and the history of ethnic literatures in the United States. Its genesis lies in that annus mirabilis of New York history – 1898 – though not in the incorporation of the five boroughs into Greater New York but across the Atlantic in Paris, where commissioners from both the United States and Spain met at the beginning of October to seek a treaty that would end the Spanish-American War. Although the main issue on the table was the disposition of the Philippines, which ultimately became an American territory for which the United States paid Spain $20 million, the treaty that was signed on December 10, 1898 also gave the United States control of Puerto Rico and Guam and required Spain to relinquish its claims to Cuba. On April 2, 1900, President McKinley signed the Foraker Act into law. Officially known as the Organic Act of 1900, the legislation established a civil government in Puerto Rico and free trade between the island and the United States. The new government inaugurated on May 1 was led by an American governor, Charles H. Allen, and five Puerto Rican cabinet members. Fifteen years later, the Jones Act of 1917 amended the Foraker Act: it transformed Puerto Rico into a US "territory"; created a bill of rights; required elections to be held every four years; declared English the official language of the island; and, most significantly for the history of New York City, granted US citizenship to all citizens of Puerto Rico.[10]

As a result of the Jones Act, Puerto Ricans were able to move between the island and the mainland without restriction. Immigration scholars generally identify a first wave of pioneer immigrants arriving from Puerto Rico before 1945 and a "great migration" between 1945 and 1964; after 1965, there is a greater back-and-forth flow between the US and Puerto Rico that immigration scholars have described variously as "circular," "commuting," "returning," and "revolving."[11] In the middle of the twentieth century, the great majority of migrating Puerto Ricans settled in New York City, reaching a high of 81.3% in 1950, then declining as the century continued: 62% in 1970, and 40% in 1989.[12] Mainland Puerto Ricans often refer to themselves as "Boricuas" to stress their connection to the island's native inhabitants, the Taino: the term is adapted from the Taino word *borike'n*, which means "great land of the valiant and noble lord."[13] In contrast, Puerto Ricans on the mainland coined the term "Nuyorican" to describe Puerto Ricans living or born in the US. Many Puerto Ricans disdained the Nuyoricans as non-Boricua, who were likely to contaminate Puerto Rican culture with influences from the mainland.[14]

The Nuyorican writer Esmeralda Santiago, who moved to the US with her family in 1961, attempted to capture "that feeling of Puertoricanness I had before I came here" in her first book, the acclaimed memoir *When I Was Puerto Rican* (1993). Santiago has described the experience of being identified as "Nuyorican" rather than "Boricua":

> I felt as Puerto Rican as when I left the island, but to those who had never left, I was contaminated by Americanisms, and therefore, had become less than Puerto Rican. Yet, in the United States, my darkness, my accented speech, my frequent lapses into the confused silence between English and Spanish identified me as foreign, non-American.

Santiago realizes that the double-bind she describes is an experience shared by many immigrants, who discover that "once they've lived in the U.S. their 'cultural purity' has been compromised."[15] In the case of Puerto Rican immigrants and their children, a complicating factor is race, both because of the island's mixed heritage and because of the blending of African American and Puerto Rican cultures in New York as a result of shared neighborhoods and intermarriage.

The link between African American and Puerto Rican cultures marks the book that became the first classic of Nuyorican literature, Piri Thomas's autobiography, *Down These Mean Streets* (1967), which reviewers have likened to the writings of Malcolm X, James Baldwin, and Eldridge Cleaver. Born Juan Pedro Tomás in 1928 to Puerto Rican and Cuban parents, Thomas was described in a 1967 *New York Times* interview as "a Puerto Rican Negro who grew up in Spanish Harlem."[16] *Down These Mean Streets* is an account of his fall into drugs and gang life, his incarceration for armed robbery, and his eventual redemption. The book was immediately recognized as a landmark text when it was first published in 1967. Daniel Stern, writing on the first page of the *New York Times Book Review*, described the book as a "linguistic event" because of the way in which it blends "gutter language, Spanish imagery and personal poetics."[17] The poetic prologue, which Thomas claims to have written in a moment of inspiration – "I sat down and wrote that out, scratched it out, in five minutes" – begins with a "rooftop" echo of Whitman's "barbaric yawp" in "Song of Myself," but ends by conveying the hatred that arises from living in the shadows of poverty and racism – and of being born dark, the only "black" child in a mixed race family: "when I look down at the streets below, I can't help thinking / It's like a great big dirty Christmas tree with lights but no fuckin' presents."[18] The gritty, no-holds-barred approach of Thomas's book led to its being banned in 1971 by a school district in Flushing, Queens, because of its use of obscenities and its description of heterosexual and homosexual acts. (The ban was reversed in 1975.)[19]

Not all of the writing about *el barrio* is fueled by the sense of rage that marks Thomas's *Mean Streets*. For example, Nicholasa Mohr's first novel, *Nilda* (1973), describes life in the Bronx as seen by a ten-year-old girl and is written in a simple style appropriate to a child's point of view. The daughter of parents who came to the United States from Puerto Rico during the Second World War, Mohr grew up in the Bronx and attended the Art Students League, the Brooklyn Museum Art School, and the Pratt Center for Contemporary Printmaking, eventually becoming a prominent graphic artist. She became a writer after she was asked by her art agent to write about the experience of growing up Puerto Rican and female in the Bronx. *Nilda* was listed by the *New York Times* as one of its Outstanding Books of the Year, and three of Mohr's later works – *Felita* (1979), *Going Home* (1986), and *All for the Better* (1993), a biography of Evelina Antonetty – are in fact intended for an adolescent audience. The stories in *El Bronx Remembered*

(1986) and *In Nueva York* (1988) all emphasize the everyday dilemmas faced by their central characters in order to counter the sensationalistic stereotypes of Puerto Ricans as criminals and gang-members that arose in the aftermath of Thomas's success.

In part, the story of redemption told both by *Down These Mean Streets* and Thomas's subsequent career as a writer of both prose and poetry turns on learning not only to accept but to celebrate his identity as a mixed-race person. Stern, the *Times*'s reviewer, perceptively noted:

> The American Negro has, of course, developed his own argot, partly to put the white man off, partly to put him down. The Puerto Rican living in New York faces an even more complex fate and linguistic adjustment. He shares with the Negro the neologisms of the street, but the Puerto Rican's are mixed with a heavy complement of Spanish.[20]

In the interview that accompanied Stern's review, Thomas cited Harlem as "a whole example for the world to follow": "Harlem is like the whole world rolled into one, with every type of human being that you can find: American Indians, Indians from India, Chinese, Japanese, black men, Polynesians, West Indians, Puerto Ricans, Filipinos, the whole bit."[21] The "contamination" and loss of "cultural purity" that Esmeralda Santiago describes is, for Thomas, a source of hope and redemption.

Marked from the start by the dynamics of cultural contamination, Nuyorican culture quickly became a site for the promotion of multiculturalism. In the aftermath of the success of Thomas's book, Nuyorican writing gained a significant measure of cultural standing. Miguel Piñero's play *Short Eyes* premiered off-Broadway at the Public Theater in February 1974 and moved to the Vivian Beaumont Theatre on Broadway three months later. The play, whose title is prison slang for a pedophile, was written as part of a prisoners' writing workshop during the author's incarceration for armed robbery and explores the racial dynamics and ideas of justice that mark prison life. *Short Eyes* won the OBIE Award and the New York Drama Critics Circle Award for Best Play and was nominated for six Tony Awards. Meanwhile, Piñero and Miguel Algarín, a professor of English at Rutgers University, co-edited an anthology entitled *Nuyorican Poetry* that was published in 1974 by William Morrow, a mainstream press. And the following year, Algarín founded the Nuyorican Poets Cafe along with Piñero and the poet Pedro Pietri.

The poetry salon that Algarín had been convening for the previous two years had begun to outgrow his living room, so he rented the Sunshine Cafe, an Irish bar on East 6th Street. By now the term "Nuyorican," originally used disparagingly by Boricuas to denigrate the Puerto Rican diaspora, had become a badge of honor. In the anthology *Aloud: Voices from the Nuyorican Poets Cafe*, Algarín offers a definition-cum-manifesto:

> **Nuyorican** (nü yòr 'ē kən) (New York + Puerto Rican) 1. Originally Puerto Rican epithet for those of Puerto Rican heritage born in New York: their Spanish was different (Spanglish), their way of dress and look were different. They were a stateless people (like most U.S. poets) until the Cafe became their homeland. 2. After Algarín and Piñero, a proud poet speaking New York Puerto Rican. 3. A denizen of the Nuyorican Poets Cafe. 4. New York's riches.[22]

In 1980, Algarín purchased an "in rem" building at 236 East 3rd Street in order to accommodate the cafe's growing audiences and expand its programs. Two years, later, however, the cafe shut down for renovations and didn't reopen until 1990 when Bob Holman approached Algarín after the death of Miguel Piñero, and said, "Miguel, it's time to reopen the Cafe. This is the moment, you know, and Miky is insisting on it, and we are ready."[23]

When the cafe reopened, the *New York Times* noted that there were a few changes. For one thing, it "has been virtually packed from its small stage to out the door." Perhaps more significantly, "the new Nuyoricans are not necessarily young, angry, or Puerto Rican." According to Holman, a Kentucky native and veteran of the Chicago poetry slam scene, "New York Puerto Rican" is "the narrow definition of Nuyorican ... Anyone who calls himself or herself Nuyorican is a Nuyorican."[24] Holman infused the cafe with new ideas, designed to attract attention and audiences, including the weekly poetry slam, an idea developed by construction worker and poet Marc Smith in 1984. Each Friday night, poets would compete against one another for the grand prize – the princely sum of $10 – reciting poems under three minutes in length and judged by a panel of three usually drawn from the audience. Holman acted as host and always served up his signature line: "The best poet always loses."[25]

If Chicago was the birthplace of the poetry, New York became the place where it came of age and became a national phenomenon, thanks in large part to Holman's showmanship. Holman founded Mouth Almighty, the first record label devoted to poetry; the label sponsored the team that won the 1997 National Poetry Slam, a group of "all-stars" from the Nuyorican Poets Cafe – Regie Cabico, Evert Eden, Taylor Mali, and Beau Sia – coached by Holman. Sia was one of the members of the "novice team" from New York City that had won the previous year's national competition, the subject of the documentary film *SlamNation* (1998), which also featured performances by Holman, Mali, and Marc Smith himself.[26] In 2002, hip-hop entrepreneur Russell Simmons produced the HBO series *Def Poetry Jam*, a spin-off of the successful series *Def Comedy Jam*. The new show, which ran for six seasons, featured a range of spoken-word poets, including established poets, national slam winners, neophytes, and even well-known actors and musicians with a taste for poetry. *Def Poetry* did not adopt the slam format, but was influenced by the slam sensibility. According to the poet John S. Hall, a critic of the slam format:

> *Def Poetry* is still extremely slam-informed, and I think it will probably always be. What they say about *Def Poetry* is that it wants to bring an urban feel. And to me, they don't mean black or Latino, or non-white. What they really mean is, a rhythm of poetry that comes out of the Nuyorican Poets Cafe, that came out of the slams.[27]

In November 2002, a version of the show called *Russell Simmons Def Poetry Jam* opened on Broadway and won a 2003 Tony Award for Best Special Theatrical Event.

Five years later, the life of *el barrio* was the subject of the Broadway musical *In the Heights*, which dramatizes a significant day in the life of a neighborhood in Washington Heights. Conceived by Lin-Manuel Miranda while he was a sophomore at Wesleyan University, *In the Heights* is a cultural hybrid: it is bilingual, with dialogue in both English and Spanish, and it blends a number of musical forms, mixing traditional Broadway show tunes with hip-hop and salsa. As is often the case with cultural hybrids, one side dominates a little bit: the bilingualism is tilted toward English, so a non-Spanish-speaking viewer will never feel ill at ease, though there are Spanish puns and in-jokes for those who get them. Most of the verbal hip-hop is delivered by Usnavi, a bodega-owner who is played by Miranda himself, and the show features a surprisingly large number of traditional Broadway ballads delivered by characters singing alone in the spotlight. The show was designed to build on, rather than challenge, the conventions of the Broadway musical.

In the Heights demonstrates that a Latino neighborhood like Washington Heights is in fact a confluence of different cultural traditions: Puerto Rican, Dominican, Cuban, even Mexican. In contrast to the Bedford-Stuyvesant of *Do the Right Thing*, this Washington Heights is quite civil: there's a little bit of inter-ethnic tension, but not much; and a little more interracial tension, which in the end is not fully resolved, but the residents of this neighborhood have learned how to talk – and sing – to one another. Sad things happen during *In the Heights*, but they are part of the bittersweetness of change. The show, in the end, is all about the idea of home: where it is, what it means, what it owes you, what you owe to it. Asked about the genesis of the musical, Miranda recalled:

> I always tell people Washington Heights is full of music, and they sort of think it's just a line I use to plug the show. But I swear to God when I was writing

the first draft I was walking around and I saw a Chinese delivery guy riding his bike with a boom box strapped to the front of his bike. It wasn't a little radio; it was a two speaker boom box blasting music. It was like Pimp My Ride but with a two wheeler. I always thought that was a classic New York thing: of course the Chinese delivery guy has got a subwoofer on his bike!

This anecdote suggests why thinking of New York's ethnic literatures as emergent literatures is so productive: these literatures, whether produced by Jews, Asians, Latinos, or other groups not explicitly treated here, all value cultural contamination over cultural purity and find inspiration in the city's often contentious, sometimes violent, but always vibrant confluence of cultures.

NOTES

1. Chang-rae Lee, *Native Speaker* (1995; New York: Riverhead, 1996), p. 83. Further references appear in the text.
2. E. L. Doctorow, *Ragtime* (New York: Random House, 1975), pp. 269–70.
3. Raymond Williams, *Marxism and Literature* (Oxford: Oxford University Press, 1977), pp. 121–27.
4. Kwame Anthony Appiah, "The Case for Contamination," *New York Times Magazine* (January 1, 2006): 52.
5. Kwame Anthony Appiah, *Cosmopolitanism: Ethics in a World of Strangers* (New York: Norton, 2006), p. xxi.
6. David A. Hollinger, *Post Ethnic America* (1995; revised edn., New York: Basic Books, 2000), pp. 3, 85.
7. Quoted in Douglas Brode, *The Films of Woody Allen* (New York: Citadel Press, 1991), p. 158.
8. Spike Lee and Lisa Jones, *Do the Right Thing: A Spike Lee Joint* (New York: Simon & Schuster, 1989), pp. 186–87.
9. *Ibid.*, p. 250.
10. See Arturo Morales Carrion, *Puerto Rico: A Political and Cultural History* (New York: Norton, 1983); José Cabranes, *Citizenship and the American Empire* (New Haven, CT: Yale University Press, 1979).
11. José Lorenzo-Hernandez, "The Nuyorican's Dilemma: Categorization of Returning Migrants in Puerto Rico," *International Migration Review* 33 (1999): 989.
12. *Ibid.*, 991.
13. Taino Inter-Tribal Council, "Dictionary of the Spoken Taino Language," members.dandy.net/~orocobix/tedict.html.
14. According to Lorenzo-Hernandez, "Returning migrants, labeled as Nuyoricans, may be wrongly perceived as hybrids who may 'contaminate' the culture with influences from the North" ("The Nuyorican's Dilemma," p. 991).
15. www.randomhouse.com/vintage/read/puerto/santiago.html
16. Christopher Lehmann-Haupt, "A Talk with Piri Thomas," *New York Times Book Review* (May 21, 1967): 47.
17. Daniel Stern, "One Who Got Away," *New York Times Book Review* (May 21, 1967): 44.

18. Piri Thomas, *Down These Mean Streets* (New York: Knopf, 1967), pp. ix–x; Lehmann-Haupt, "A Talk with Piri Thomas," 45.
19. Leonard Buder, "School Ban Ends on Piri Thomas Book," *New York Times* (December 27, 1975): 21.
20. Stern, "One Who Got Away," 1.
21. Lehmann-Haupt, "A Talk with Piri Thomas," 47.
22. Miguel Algarín and Bob Holman, eds., *Aloud: Voices from the Nuyorican Poets Cafe* (New York: Henry Holt, 1994), p. 5.
23. *Ibid.*, p. 8.
24. Evelyn Nieves, "Again, Clubs for Poets to Read and Rage," *New York Times* (November 19, 1990): B1.
25. Eve M. Kahn, "The Word's Turn: Urban Poets Re-emerge," *New York Times* (January 31, 1992): C1.
26. See www.slamnation.com. The film was directed by Paul Devlin.
27. Cristin O'Keefe Aptowicz, *Words in Your Face: A Guided Tour Through Twenty Years of the New York City Poetry Slam* (New York: Soft Skull Press, 2007), p. 288.

BRYAN WATERMAN

Epilogue: Nostalgia and counter-nostalgia in New York City writing

In the mid-1940s, the *New Yorker* writer Joseph Mitchell created a 93-year-old resident of the South Street Seaport named Hugh G. Flood – not quite antediluvian and not quite postdiluvian, either. He was a "tough Scotch-Irishman," a composite of "several old men" Mitchell knew from the Fulton Fish Market. The "truthful rather than factual" sketches Mitchell wrote about Mr. Flood were "stories of fish-eating, whiskey, death, and rebirth."[1] The title character, an inveterate consumer of freshly imported seafood, dispenses wisdom on topics such as the medicinal properties of oysters (including where to find the best ones in lower Manhattan and Brooklyn) and complains that scientists have ruined the most basic foods (he gives Mitchell's narrator the inside scoop on where to find a decent, old-fashioned loaf of bread on Elizabeth Street). Like Mitchell's other writing for the *New Yorker*, these stories featured people and places representative of older, threatened, but persistent remnants of the city's past.

Mitchell's Mr. Flood is a "retired house-wrecking contractor," a participant in the never-ending capitalist ritual of tearing things down to put new things up: "creative destruction," as the economist Joseph Schumpeter, a contemporary of Mitchell's, put it.[2] But like Mitchell, who was a founder of the South Street Seaport Museum and, in part, responsible for landmarking much of the waterfront neighborhood, Mr. Flood is also a preservationist. On the marble mantelpiece of his fifth-floor room in a seaport flophouse on Peck Slip, Mr. Flood displays bits of cast-iron he has rescued from nearby buildings: "a bare-knuckle pug with his fists cocked, a running horse with its mane streaming, and an American eagle." Mitchell explains:

> Mr. Flood is sentimental about the stone and iron ornaments on many buildings down in the old city, and he thinks they should be preserved. He once wrote the Museum of the City of New York suggesting that the owners of [the old *Police Gazette* building on the corner of Dover and Pearl, from which he took these cast-iron specimens] be asked to donate the fire-escape ornaments to the Museum. "Suppose this bldg. is torn down," he wrote. "All that

beautiful iron work will disappear into scrap. If the owners do not see fit to donate, I am a retired house-wrecker and I could go there in the dead of night with a monkey-wrench and blow-torch and use my own discretion."

(414–15)

This guerrilla preservationist manifesto, written by a demolition worker, captures something of the nostalgic strain that runs through much New York City writing, particularly in the twentieth century, when the modern city threatened repeatedly to eclipse its previous incarnations. There's a slight resignation to the fact that old buildings such as the *Police Gazette*'s will come down; but Mr. Flood hopes to live to the age of 115, and one imagines he'll have preserved a lot more cast-iron by then.

The nostalgic strain in New York writing, rooted not just in the fear that the old city will pass away unnoticed, but that it already passed away before one arrived, might be said to have followed on the heels of other broad patterns in New York's literature: an accommodationist mode in the nineteenth century, when writers scrambled (to borrow a phrase from *Leaves of Grass*) simply to "contain multitudes"; and an assimilationist mode – or at least an ambivalent yielding to assimilation – found in much of the writing from immigrant traditions at the turn of the twentieth century. (The writer Pete Hammill has identified the plight of the immigrant, trapped between Old and New worlds, as *the* abiding concern of New York City literature.[3]) But in the late twentieth and early twenty-first centuries, the problem of gentrification, or what one anthology of essays calls "the suburbanization of New York," has brought the nostalgic strain – even its most extreme form, the jeremiad – into the ascendant.[4] At present, some of the most vital acts of literary preservation (writing about what's lost) come in the form of blog posts, on sites with titles that mark their relation to neighborhoods that change faster than their authors feel is warranted: "Lost City," "Jeremiah's Vanishing New York," "EV [East Village] Grieve," "Ephemeral New York," and "Forgotten NY," all of which document the steady progression of closing diners and dive bars, disappearing neon signage, demolition of unlandmarked architecture, and disappearance of grit and edge under the rigorous scrubbing of gentrification and "development."[5]

This chorus in favor of preserving the city's historical character is joined by commentators in the mainstream media. For example, one of Mitchell's most prolific successors at the *New Yorker*, Adam Gopnik, laments the city's transformation into a "monocultural desert of sameness" in the new millennium:

This transformation is one you see on every street corner in Manhattan, and now in Brooklyn, too, where another local toy store or smoked-fish emporium disappears and another bank branch or mall store opens. For the first time in

Manhattan's history, it has no bohemian frontier. Another bookstore closes, another theatre becomes a condo, another soulful place becomes a sealed residence. These are small things, but they are the small things that the city's soul clings to.[6]

But of course the city's literature doesn't fall into tidy periods of accommodation, assimilation, and gentrification-driven nostalgia; these strains overlap, persist, outsound one another depending on where and when you're listening. The complaint that the real soul of Manhattan has already expired is a long-standing one – perhaps as old as nineteenth-century Knickerbocker's pining for a mythological Dutch past – and more often than not it masks class politics. Take an example from Theodore Dreiser's 1923 collection of local-color sketches, *The Color of a Great City*, part of a tradition of urban journalism that helped produce Mitchell. Dreiser wrote these sketches, he explains by way of preface, because the city he discovered when he arrived in the 1890s had now all but vanished:

> For, to begin with, the city, as I see it, was more varied and arresting and, after its fashion, poetic and even idealistic then than it is now. It offered, if I may venture the opinion, greater social and financial contrasts than it does now: the splendor of the purely social Fifth Avenue of the last decade of the last century and the first decade of this, for instance, as opposed to the purely commercial area that now bears that name; the sparkling, personality-dotted Wall Street of 1890–1910 as contrasted with the commonplace and almost bread and butter world that it is to-day. (There were argonauts then.) The astounding areas of poverty and of beggary even, – I refer to the east side and the Bowery of that period – unrelieved as they were by civic betterment and social service ventures of all kinds, as contrasted with the beschooled and beserviced east side of to-day.[7]

Dreiser's implicit wish to prevent the education of immigrants in the name of preserving the Lower East Side's "poetic" atmosphere betrays something of the romantic condescension that characterized relations between Village bohemians and their immigrant neighbors. Gopnik, of course, is not romanticizing the sunshine and shadow of the nineteenth century (or the 1970s) to the degree that he would wish some city residents back into poverty and a lack of social services. Many readers today would cringe at Dreiser's move to enshrine robber barons as Argonauts; if anything, banks and bankers bear the brunt of the blame heaped by anti-gentrification bloggers and critics like Gopnik, and the fiction that treats Wall Street in the 1980s and 90s – most notably, Tom Wolfe's *The Bonfire of the Vanities* and Brett Easton Ellis's *American Psycho* – indicts an extreme form of narcissism that threatens the city's cosmopolitan character.

The cycle of attraction, transformation, mourning, and renewed attraction is an old one in New York City writing. In 1916, writing in *Pearson's Magazine*, Djuna Barnes responded to the first wave of complaints that the Village was dying, and this only a year after the founding of the Provincetown Players. Like Dreiser, who also spent time as a city-beat journalist, Barnes anticipates the nostalgic strain in New York writing: it's always already over, she seems to say. (Interestingly, Barnes defends the Village against the charge that it is not "of the real Manhattan," when within a few decades its partisans would be arguing that it was, in fact, the last bastion of authenticity in an ever-changing, commercially overrun urban landscape.) But Barnes also mounts a defense of the Village against those who say its time has come and gone. And though she spends the better part of her piece redirecting visitors from sites that are no longer there, reproducing for her readers the sense that they have already missed the party, she also resists the impulse toward nostalgia by arguing that her neighborhood has a vitality not visible to outsiders' eyes:

> And so you of the outer world be not so hard on us, and above all forbear to pity us – good people. We have all that the rest of the world has in common commodities and we have the better part: men and women with a new light flickering in their eyes, or on their foreheads the radiance of some unseen splendor.[8]

Marked by the beast, apparently, and wearing it proudly – a sign, perhaps, of Barnes's conflicting impulses to let her readers in (as a good tour guide) and to keep them at arm's length (directing them away from things she holds dearest).

Barnes's overall point, though, is that it's too easy to indulge in New York nostalgia. (As Melissa Bradshaw suggests in this volume, such self-indulgence, and the certainty that the city's glory has already faded, is an enduring hallmark of the bohemian legacy.) But Barnes's invocation of secret knowledge also suggests how hard it is to preserve the mystery – and difficulty – of the past, even while acknowledging nostalgia's seductive pull. This is work of another strain of New York writing, one typified by novels as diverse as Edith Wharton's *The Age of Innocence* (1920), E. L. Doctorow's *Ragtime* (1975), and Michael Chabon's *The Amazing Adventures of Kavalier & Clay* (2000). The first and last novel in this trio, both Pulitzer Prize-winners, are very different looks backward at very different periods: the Gilded Age of the 1870s and the Golden Age of Comic Books in the 1940s, respectively. The two books share an unlikely trope: the figure of an unopened envelope – a figure I take to represent the dispatches from the past that remain possibilities only, potentialities whose history is eventually buried under the rubble or covered over with the sheen of a new façade.

In Wharton's novel, the envelope contains a key sent by the repressed protagonist Newland Archer to the scandalous Countess Olenska, who has returned to her native New York after separating from her disreputable and probably abusive husband, a European nobleman. The key could facilitate the long-suppressed love affair between her and Newland, but she returns it to him unopened. In Martin Scorsese's 1993 adaptation of the novel, the key is enclosed in Newland's pocket in a series of unopened papers – almost like Chinese boxes or Russian dolls, one tucked inside the next. Countess Olenska refuses to allow Newland to violate the codes of high society in the Gilded Age: she will not jeopardize Newland's marriage to her cousin by remaining in New York when most of its claustrophobic society – which he thinks of as "a band of dumb conspirators" and which the narrator refers to as a "tribe" – already thinks she is Newland's mistress. Their effort to expel Olenska, Newland realizes,

> was the old New York way of taking life "without effusion of blood": the way of people who dreaded scandal more than disease, who placed decency above courage, and who considered that nothing was more ill-bred than "scenes," except the behaviour of those who gave rise to them.[9]

Rather than taking a nostalgic view of the world Wharton grew up in, this nod toward tribal behavior suggests a premodern society more violent and much less pleasant than its would-be inheritors (in and out of the novel) would like to think.

In Chabon's *The Amazing Adventures of Kavalier & Clay*, the unopened envelope contains a letter from Joseph Kavalier's mother, fatally trapped in Nazi-occupied Prague, to her son, who came to America in the first of the novel's many daring escapes. Though the novel reproduces the text of the letter from Joe's mother – complete with words and phrases marked out by Nazi censors – the narrator makes it plain that Joe (unlike the novel's readers) never laid eyes on these pages. Instead, he tucks the unopened envelope into a pocket and, eventually, loses it, try as he might to retrace his steps and recover it. Years later, we're told,

> Joe would sometimes find himself thinking about the pale-blue envelope from Prague. He would try to imagine its contents, wondering what news or sentiments or instructions it might have contained. It was at these times that he began to understand, after all those years of study and performance [of magic and escape tricks], of feats of wonder and surprises, the nature of magic. The magician seemed to promise that something torn to bits might be mended without a seam, that what had vanished might reappear, that a scattered handful of

doves or dust might be reunited by a word, that a paper rose consumed by fire could be made to bloom from a pile of ash. But everyone knew it was only an illusion. The true magic of this broken world lay in the ability of the things it contained to vanish, to become so thoroughly lost, that they might never have existed in the first place.[10]

The unopened envelopes in Wharton's and Chabon's novels are perfect emblems for the counter-nostalgic strain in New York writing: the recognition that the past had faults we'd best let go. The novel ends, after all, with Joe's gay cousin Sammy, who'd heroically married to be a father to Joe's son, vanishing without a trace once Joe returns from a self-imposed exile. The novel heaves a sigh of relief to let the homophobic past – if not the Holocaust – pass away. Similarly, in Wharton's book, Newland Archer seems relieved, in the end, by his son's freedom to marry one of "Beaufort's bastards" – a freedom to love that he had not enjoyed in his youth. There's a violence in both portraits of bygone eras, something conspiring against identity and imagination. They are reminders that nostalgia too easily papers over portions of the past that might be too painful to preserve.

Perhaps the best fictional statement of this counter-nostalgic strain in New York writing comes in the opening paragraph of Doctorow's *Ragtime*. The narrative identifies itself in this passage with the perspective of Mother's Younger Brother, "a lonely, withdrawn young man with blond moustaches, … thought to be having difficulty finding himself." As it progresses, though, the sequence makes a gradual transition from Mother's Younger Brother's blindspots to the more complicated consciousness of the Lower East Side: "Patriotism," we're told, "was a reliable sentiment in the early 1900's":

> Teddy Roosevelt was President. The population customarily gathered in great numbers either out of doors for parades, public concerts, fish fries, political picnics, social outings, or indoors in meeting halls, vaudeville theatres, operas, ballrooms. There seemed to be no entertainment that did not involve great swarms of people. Trains and steamers and trolleys moved them from one place to another. That was the style, that was the way people lived. Women were stouter then. They visited the fleet carrying white parasols. Everyone wore white in summer. Tennis racquets were hefty and the racquet faces elliptical. There was a lot of sexual fainting. There were no Negroes. There were no immigrants. On Sunday afternoon, after dinner, Father and Mother went upstairs and closed the bedroom door.[11]

Near the end of the paragraph, the narrator introduces the newspaper sensation surrounding the murder of the architect Stanford White by the husband of his mistress Evelyn Nesbit, a "celebrated beauty," on whom Mother's Younger Brother has an intense crush. In response to the shooting,

> Evelyn fainted. She had been a well-known artist's model at the age of fifteen. Her underclothes were white. Her husband habitually whipped her. She happened once to meet Emma Goldman, the revolutionary. Goldman lashed her with her tongue. Apparently there *were* Negroes. There *were* immigrants. And though the newspapers called the shooting the Crime of the Century, Goldman knew it was only 1906 and there were ninety-four years to go.[12]

Goldman's revolutionary consciousness functions to undercut the nostalgia of the suburban pastoral; someone pining for a simpler time is forced to acknowledge that the times were only simpler for some.

"All that is solid melts into air," Karl Marx wrote in *The Communist Manifesto* of modern capitalism's tendency to destroy its own creations in order to build anew. The phrase anticipates Schumpeter's "creative destruction" by almost a century. The political philosopher Marshall Berman – one of New York's most optimistic defenders and relentless critics – borrowed the phrase for the title of his 1982 book on the pressures of modernization and modernity. In the book's final chapters, Berman bears witness to the creative destruction of the great urban planner Robert Moses – "probably the greatest creator of symbolic forms in twentieth-century New York" – under whose expansive and at times tyrannical authority slums were cleared, freeways built, parks and pools and beaches developed, and the city disciplined to meet what he saw as the demands of modern commerce.[13] Berman positions himself, along with the Village writer and community activist Jane Jacobs, as Moses's antagonist. A Bronx native, Berman witnessed his childhood world fall victim to one of Moses's endless projects, the Cross-Bronx Expressway, which Berman credits with destroying traditional neighborhood life in the borough as he transformed "our ordinary nice neighborhood … into sublime, spectacular ruins" (293).

Using Moses's career as a backdrop, Berman recounts the movement from New York's centrality to the invention of modernism to its ironic embrace of an anti-urban modernity, which "conceived of cities principally as obstructions to the flow of traffic, and as junkyards of substandard housing and decaying neighborhoods from which Americans should be given every chance to escape" (307). And so entire blocks were razed, "modern" high-rise public housing erected, roads expanded, all to meet the demands of an imagined future more than the needs of the present inhabitants. These actions mobilized Jacobs and others to resist, sometimes successfully (as in their prevention of the Lower Manhattan Expressway, which would have obliterated the heart of present-day SoHo), but just as often not (as in the Bronx). In the 1970s, Berman argues, when the slowing economy brought traffic, city bureaucracies, and real-estate development to a standstill, forward-thinking moderns began to create by remembering, by returning to history and ethnic memory, by creatively preserving their surroundings, by "com[ing] to terms with the world they had, and work[ing] from there" (332). The neighborhood Moses had wanted to raze became a haven for artists in low-rent lofts. Modern art promised to transform society by turning its critique on modernity itself. Berman ends his book on an optimistic note: "I believe that we and those who come after us will go on fighting to make ourselves at home in this world, even as the homes we have made, the modern street, the modern spirit, go on melting into air" (348).

From where we stand – on the other side of a quarter-century's economic growth (dotted by downturns, some more extreme than others), after seeing Berman's SoHo utopia transformed into a high-end, open-air shopping mall, with artists' lofts selling for multiple millions of dollars, after witnessing development-oriented administrations disregard neighborhood character in favor of luxury high-rises – it might be tempting to say that the low points in the cycle Berman outlines perhaps overshadow the moments of creative imagination. Much New York writing of the new millennium already reflects this outlook, from the scathing representation of Lower East Side hipsters in Richard Price's *Lush Life* to Michael Cunningham's suggestion in his post-9/11 novel *Specimen Days* that once New York has completely transformed itself into a theme park, there will be nowhere left for the utopians to go except for outer space. And yet Berman, at least, hangs on to hope: he concludes a more recent meditation on New York with an echo of his earlier optimism: our "city of ruins," he writes, "turned out to be a place where people coming from a hundred different places started to talk together and work together in ways people had never quite done before."[14] In his refusal to stop loving the city, Berman marries the nostalgic and counter-nostalgic strains in New York writing in a way that keeps alive the memory of ordinary people whose lives are lost to history, while at the same time celebrating the power of art to keep us focused on what's worth carrying forward from our collective pasts. Fish-eating, whiskey, death, and rebirth: the city remains new to those newly arrived; it needs to be preserved by those long-since settled; it will be mourned and then rebuilt by those with imaginations that are up to the task.

NOTES

1. Joseph Mitchell, *Old Mr. Flood* (1948), rpt. in *Up in the Old Hotel* (New York: Vintage Books, 1993), pp. 373–436, quotes on pp. 375 and 373. Further references appear in the text.
2. The architectural historian Max Page borrows the term for the title of his history of New York's development in this period: *The Creative Destruction of Manhattan, 1900–1940* (Chicago, IL: University of Chicago Press, 2001).

3. Comments made at the 50th Anniversary of Fales Library and Special Collections at NYU, April 17, 2007, author's notes.
4. Jerilou Hammett and Kingsley Hammett, eds., *The Suburbanization of New York: Is the World's Greatest City Becoming Just Another Town?* (New York: Princeton Architectural Press, 2007).
5. At time of going to press, these websites can be found at the following addresses: Lost City (lostnewyorkcity.blogspot.com), Jeremiah's Vanishing New York (vanishingnewyork.blogspot.com), EV Grieve (evgrieve.com), Ephemeral New York (ephemeralnewyork.wordpress.com), and Forgotten NY (www.forgotten-ny.com), which is a companion site to Kevin Walsh, *Forgotten New York* (New York: HarperCollins, 2006).
6. Adam Gopnik, "Gothamitis," *New Yorker* (January 8, 2007).
7. Theodore Dreiser, *The Color of a Great City* (New York: Boni and Liveright, 1923), p. v.
8. Djuna Barnes, "Greenwich Village As It Is," *Pearson's Magazine* (Oct. 1916), collected in *Greenwich Village As It Is* (New York: Phoenix Bookshop, 1978), n.p.
9. Edith Wharton, *The Age of Innocence* (1920; New York: Library of America, 1985), p. 1282.
10. Michael Chabon, *The Amazing Adventures of Kavalier & Clay* (New York: Random House, 2000), p. 339.
11. E. L. Doctorow, *Ragtime* (1975; New York: Plume, 1997), pp. 3–4.
12. *Ibid.*, pp. 4–5.
13. Marshall Berman, *All That Is Solid Melts into Air: The Experience of Modernity* (1982; New York: Penguin, 1988), p. 289. Further references appear in the text.
14. Marshall Berman, "Introduction" to *New York Calling: From Blackout to Bloomberg*, ed. Berman and Brian Berger (New York: Reaktion Books, 2007), p. 38.

FURTHER READING

Website

- Patell and Waterman's History of New York: www.ahistoryofnewyork.com.

General histories

- Bender, Thomas, *New York Intellect: A History of Intellectual Life in New York City from 1750 to the Beginnings of Our Own Time*, New York: The New Press, 1988.
- Bergmann, Hans, *God in the Street: New York Writing from Penny Press to Melville*, Philadelphia, PA: Temple University Press, 1995.
- Burrows, Edwin G. and Mike Wallace, *Gotham: A History of New York City to 1898*, New York: Oxford University Press, 1999.
- Homberger, Eric, *The Historical Atlas of New York City: A Visual Celebration of Nearly 400 Years of New York City's History*, New York: Holt Paperbacks, 1998.
- Jackson, Kenneth T., *The Encyclopedia of New York City*, New Haven, CT: Yale University Press, 1995.
- O'Connell, Shaun, *Remarkable, Unspeakable New York: A Literary History*, Boston, MA: Beacon, 1995.
- Sante, Luc, *Low Life: Lures and Snares of Old New York*, New York: Farrar, Straus, & Giroux, 1991.
- Sharpe, William Chapman, *New York Nocturne: The City after Dark in Literature, Painting, and Photography, 1850–1950*, Princeton, NJ: Princeton University Press, 2008.

Anthologies

- Algarín, Miguel and Bob Holman, *Aloud: Voices from the Nuyorican Poets Cafe*, New York: Henry Holt, 1994.
- Baer, Ulrich, ed., *110 Stories: New York Writes after September 11*, New York: New York University Press, 2002.
- Berman, Marshall and Brian Berger, *New York Calling: From Blackout to Bloomberg*, New York: Reaktion Books, 2007.
- Fishman, Steve, John Homans, and Adam Moss, *New York Stories: Landmark Stories from* New York *Magazine*, New York: Random House, 2008.

- Jackson, Kenneth T. and David S. Dunbar, eds., *Empire City: New York through the Centuries*, New York: Columbia University Press, 2002.
- Locke, Alain, ed., *The New Negro*, 1925; rpt. New York: Atheneum, 1999.
- Lopate, Philip, ed., *Writing New York: A Literary Anthology*, New York: Library of America, 1998.
- Remnick, David, *Wonderful Town: New York Stories from "The New Yorker"*, New York: Random House, 2000.
- Richards, Jeffrey H., ed. *Early American Drama*, New York: Penguin, 1997.
- Sawyers, June, ed., *The Greenwich Village Reader: Fiction, Poetry, and Reminiscences*, New York: Cooper Square Press, 2001.

Specialized studies

- Adickes, Sandra E., *To Be Young Was Very Heaven: Women in New York Before the First World War*, New York: St. Martin's Press, 1997.
- Augst, Thomas, *Young Men and Moral Life in Nineteenth-Century America*, Chicago, IL: University of Chicago Press, 2003.
- Berman, Marshall, *On the Town: One Hundred Years of Spectacle in Times Square*, New York: Random House, 2006.
- Bradley, Elizabeth, *Knickerbocker: The Myth behind New York*, New Brunswick, NJ: Rutgers University Press, 2009.
- Chauncey, George, *Gay New York: Gender, Urban Culture, and the Making of the Gay Male World, 1890–1940*, New York: Basic Books, 1994.
- Douglas, Ann, *Terrible Honesty: Mongrel Manhattan in the 1920s*, New York: Farrar, Straus, & Giroux, 1995.
- Hajdu, David, *Positively 4th Street: The Lives and Times of Joan Baez, Bob Dylan, Mimi Baez Farina, and Richard Farina*, New York: Farrar, Straus, & Giroux, 2001.
- Henderson, Mary C., *The City and the Theatre: The History of New York Playhouses*, revised edn., New York: Back Stage Books, 2004.
- Howe, Irving, *World of Our Fathers: The Journey of the East European Jews to America and the Life They Found and Made There*, New York: Harcourt Brace Jovanovich, 1976.
- Hutchinson, George, *The Harlem Renaissance in Black and White*, Cambridge, MA: Harvard University Press, 1995.
- Kane, Daniel, *All Poets Welcome: The Lower East Side Poetry Scene in the 1960s*, Berkeley, CA: University of California Press, 2003.
- Lehman, David, *The Last Avant-Garde: The Making of the New York School of Poets*, New York: Doubleday, 1998.
- McNamara, Brooks, *The New York Concert Saloon: The Devil's Own Nights*, Cambridge, UK: Cambridge University Press, 2002.
- Murphy, Brenda, *The Provincetown Players and the Culture of Modernity*, Cambridge, UK: Cambridge University Press, 2005.
- Nadell, Martha, *Enter the New Negroes: Images of Race in American Culture*, Cambridge, MA: Harvard University Press, 2004.
- Sanders, James, *Celluloid Skyline: New York and the Movies*, New York: Knopf, 2001.
- Scott, William B. and Peter M. Rutkoff, *New York Modern: The Arts and the City*, Baltimore, MD: Johns Hopkins University Press, 1999.

- Stansell, Christine, *American Moderns: Bohemian New York and the Creation of a New Century*, 2000; rpt. Princeton, NJ: Princeton University Press, 2009.
- Tchen, John Kuo Wei, *New York before Chinatown: Orientalism and the Shaping of American Culture*, Baltimore, MD: Johns Hopkins University Press, 1999.
- Waterman, Bryan, *Republic of Intellect: The Friendly Club of New York City and the Making of American Literature*, Baltimore, MD: Johns Hopkins University Press, 2007.
- Wetzsteon, Ross, *Republic of Dreams: Greenwich Village: The American Bohemia, 1910–1960*, New York: Simon & Schuster, 2002.
- White, Shane, *Stories of Freedom in Black New York*, Cambridge, MA: Harvard University Press, 2002.
- Widmer, Edward L., *Young America: The Flowering of Democracy in New York City*, New York: Oxford University Press, 1999.

INDEX

9/11 xxiv, 1, 8, 23, 239
92nd Street Y 194

Abie's Irish Rose 134–44, 222
ACT UP 210
Addison and Steele *see Spectator, The*
Africa
  in Blackstone 15–16
  influence on New York 160
  as a place 172
  as a trope 166
African Americans 160
  and anti-abolition riots xvii
  and baseball xxii
  in Brooklyn 112
  in *Do the Right Thing* 223–24
  and food 14
  and migration 130
  as mythologized 171
  oral traditions 224
  protest march xx
  and Puerto Rican culture 226
  and segregation 161
  writing 7, 160
Agee, James 112, 119
AIDS 210–11, 214, 217
Alabau, Magaly 209
Albee, Edward 203–11
Alfaro, Luis 213, 214
Algarín, Miguel 227–28
Alger, Horatio xix, 1–2
Algonquin Round Table xx
Allen, Woody xxiii, 222–23
American Company 44
American Dream, the 21, 138
American Hotel, the 14, 17, 19
American identity 115, 140–42
American mythology 180–81
  New York's role in 1, 3, 5

American Renaissance 176
American Revolution 11, 29, 44
Americanization 129, 137–38, 139, 140–42
anarchy
  and East Village poetry 190, 195, 196
  and Greenwich Village bohemia 146, 147, 150, 157
Anburey, Thomas 20
Angels in America see Kushner, Tony
Angelos, Moe 206, 208
Annie Hall (film) 223–24
anonymity
  and literary authorship 72, 198
  and the urban experience 59, 61, 64, 71, 72
anti-Semitism 124, 136, 143, 193–95
Appiah, Kwame Anthony 4, 221
  see also cosmopolitan contamination
Asch, Sholem 202
Ashbery, John 190
aspiring servants 16
assimilation 114–15, 116, 129–30, 134, 137, 139–40, 161, 220
Astor, John Jacob 13, 90
Astor Place Riot xvii, 51, 74
Auchincloss, Louis xxii
Auden, W. H. 194
Austen, Jane 121
Auster, Paul xxiii, xxiv, 116
avant-garde xxii, 7, 146, 158, 177, 194, 204, 208

Baker, Benjamin A. xvii, 43–48, 92
  A Glance at New York 48, 50, 92
Baldwin, James 170, 171–72, 173
Baraka, Amiri 173–74, 193, 195
Barlow, Joel 32
Barnes, Djuna xx, xxi, 7, 147, 148, 235
Barnum, P. T. xvii, xviii, 47

Baudelaire, Charles 101, 190
Beat writing 88, 173, 176, 186, 194
  and punk music 190–94, 192, 200
Beckert, Sven 103
Bender, Thomas 3–4
Bercovici, Konrad 122
Berman, Marshall 238–39
Berrigan, Ted 79, 189, 195
Beye, Naja 205
Black Arts Movement 167, 170, 174
Blackburn, Paul 194
Blackstone, Sir William 15–16
Blake, William 197
Bloedow, Jerry 195
blogs 233
Boas, Franz 168
Bobo, William M. 94
Bodenheim, Maxwell 153
bohemianism 7, 8, 69, 146–58, 176, 234–35
  Patti Smith's 192
Book-of-the-Month Club 181
boroughs, consolidation of the 109
Borscht Belt humor 222
Boston 3–5 *see also* Puritan New England
Boucicault, Dion: xviii, 43–55, 52, 53
boundaries 114, 124, 127, 131
Bourdet, Edouard 202
bourgeois, rejection of the 147
Bourne, Randolph 143–44, 147
Bowery, The 43–55
Bowery B'hoy 50–51, 66
Bowery Theater xvi, 42, 43, 46, 48
Boyce, Neith 147
Boys in the Band, The (play) 204
Bradford, William 28
Brace, Charles Loring 94
branding *see* publishing and branding
Brevoort, Henry 30
Bristed, Charles Astor xviii, 6, 35–36, 90–91, 94, 95, 99, 100, 101, 102
British view of America 11, 17
Broadway 17, 18, 36, 60, 64, 69, 71, 76, 78, 80, 81–84, 94
  and theater xv, 134, 137, 151, 158, 173, 202, 204, 211, 213, 214 *see also* off-Broadway
Broadway Tabernacle 48, 98
Brodhead, John Romeyn 34
Brook, Stephen 23
Brooks, Van Wyck 147
Brooklyn xiv, xviii, xx, xxii, 30, 76, 81, 204, 232
  Bedford-Stuyvesant 223–24, 229

Bridge xix, 110–12
  Dodgers xx, 112, 116
  writing xvii, xix, 6, 109–19, 172
Bronx, The xiv, xix, 119, 149, 157, 211, 226–27, 238–39
Brustein, Robert 203
Bryant, William Cullen 14, 34, 143
Bullard, Arthur 126
Buntline, Ned xvii, 93, 94
Burroughs, William xxii, 190, 192, 195
Busch, Charles 211

Cahan, Abraham xx, 122, 128, 137, 138, 141, 220, 222
Caribbeans, influence of the 166, 172
carpe diem 153
capitalism
  and cosmopolitanism 3
  and power 185
Capote, Truman xxii, xxiv, 119
CBGB xxiii
Céline, Louis-Ferdinand 192
Cendrars, Blaise 192
censorship 15, 211, 215, 236
  resistance to 183
Central Park xviii, xix, 1, 2, 81
Ceravalo, Joe 198
Cervenka, Exene 191
Chabon, Michael xxiv, 235–37
Chambers, Jane 209
Chanfrau, F. S. 50
change, quickness to 7, 8
Charlip, Remy 210
Chekhov, Anton 151
Chesnutt, Charles 161
Chesterfield, Lord 18
Chinese Exclusion Act xix
Chu, Louis xxii
Cino, Joe 204, 210
City College xvii, 166
City University of New York (CUNY) xxii
city versus country 23
Clark, Tom 189
class anxiety 48–49, 51, 53, 90, 151–52, 168
Cobbett, William 17
coffee house, the 14
Cogswell, Joseph Green 13–14
Cohn, Roy 203–11
Cold War, the 85
Cole, Bob 162
Columbia University xv
coming-of-age novel, the 110, 115, 116
Commissioners' Plan of 1811 xvi

Committee for Non-Violence 196
commodity culture
    and Greenwich Village 157, 235
    nineteenth-century 53
    and publishing industry 179
common table 90
Communist Party, the 170, 171
community and East Village Poetry 190
commuters 110, 113
conduct books 18–19
Coney Island xvi, 112, 113
confidence men 94
conservatism 92, 95, 98
consumerism 16, 156
contact 76
Coolidge, Clark 194
Cooper, James Fenimore xvi, 11–14, 16, 21
copyright law 135
corrupt, New York as 130
Corso, Gregory 192
cosmopolitan contamination 4–8, 221, 227
cosmopolitanism 3, 4–5, 28, 113, 122, 123,
    124, 131, 169, 224, 234
    and capitalism 3
    and conversation 224
    and democracy 65
    in Moby-Dick 65–66
    and multiculturalism 221–22
    in Native Speaker 219
    and nativism 35
    and pluralism 221–22
    in publishing 181, 184, 185
    and Whitman 219
coterie culture 5, 85
Council on Books in Wartime (CBW) 182
counterculture 79, 85, 86, 147
cowboy
    and Lower East Side poetry scene 193–94
Coward Noel 203
Cowley, Malcolm 156–57, 177, 180
Crane, Hart xxi, 79, 110, 147
Crane, Stephen xix, 118, 127
criminal life, 93, 94, 110, 117, 122
Crowley, Mart 204
Cullen, Countee xxi, 165, 166
culture
    high v. low 190
Cunningham, Michael 239
Curtis, George William 103

Daly, Augustin xviii, 43–55
dance 99–102
dandy, the 82

Danticat, Edwige 116
Davy, Babs 206
Dead Boys, The 190
DeLillo, Don xxiii
Dell, Floyd xx, 147
democracy 92, 98, 134
    and cosmopolitanism 65
    and Ginsberg 86
    the failure of 171, 209
    Jacksonian 13
    and Moby-Dick 65–66, 67
    and Native Speaker 219
    and Pierre 60
    and publishing 178, 180–85
    and the theater 42–43, 197
    and Whitman's poetics 76, 79, 82–84, 86,
        87, 219
Democratic Review 66
Denton, Daniel xv, 11, 23
Depression years, the xxi, 169, 182
detectives 92
Dewey, John 143–44
dialect and vernacular speech 167, 169
Dibbell, Dominique 206
Dickens, Charles xvii, 92, 93
Dictators, The 190
difference, the appreciation of 3, 4
    the erasure of 114, 115, 118, 134
    the inescapability of 121, 122, 131
di Prima, Diane 176, 195
diversity 109, 115, 122, 142
Do the Right Thing 222, 223–24, 229
Doctorow, E. L. xxiii, 219, 235, 237–38
Dodge, Mabel 147, 157
Donne, John 18
Dos Passos, John 110
doughnuts 32, 40, 51
Douglass, Frederick 161
downtown scenes 176–77, 208, 214
Dreiser, Theodore xix, xxi, 122, 130, 138,
    234
Drunkard, The (play) see Smith, William
    Henry
Du Bois, W. E. B. xix, 161, 162, 163, 165,
    168
Dunbar, Paul Laurence xix, 122, 130, 161
Dunn, Ged 195
Dutch past, New York's xiv, 3, 31–32, 38,
    234
    lack of literary materials concerning 5–6, 30
Dutch surrender 10
Duyckinck, Evert 64, 66, 68
Dylan, Bob 192

East Village xxiii, 177, 189–200, 205, 210, 233
Eastman, Crystal 147
Eastman, Max xx, 165
Ebdus, Dylan 119
Eichelberger, Ethyl 210
Eliot, T. S. 61, 171, 194
elite 6, 90–91, 94–103, 161
Ellis, Bret Easton xxiii, 234
Ellis Island xix
Ellison, Ralph xxii, 170–71
Ellsworth, Williams 179–80
emergent literatures
   African American literature as emergent 162
   American literature as emergent 13, 14, 21
   defined 221
   ethnic 7
Emerson, Ralph Waldo 62, 103, 178
Empire State Building xxi
Erie Canal xvi
ethnic literature 136
Evers, Medgar 173
exceptionalism 28
excess 13, 18, 83
exclusion 90, 143
   see also Chinese Exclusion Act
existentialism 171

Fagin, Larry 194
failure, literary 146
Famine, Irish xvii
Fanon, Frantz 173
fashion 44, 97–98
femininity 169
feminism 153
Fern, Fanny 97
Fiddler on the Roof 138
Fierstein, Harvey 209, 210, 212
Fifth Avenue 43–55, 54, 163, 164, 234
financial ruin 124
Finley, Karen 208
Finney, Charles Grandison 48
First World War *see* World War I
Fitch, Clyde xix, 43, 54–55
Fitzgerald, F. Scott xxi, 131, 138, 181
Five Lesbian Brothers, The 206–8, 207
Five Points 35, 47, 62, 92, 160
flâneur 92
Fleck, John 208
Flushing xxi, 218–19, 222
"Flushing Remonstrance" xiv
Foer, Jonathan Safran xxiv

Foraker Act 224–25
Fornes, Maria Irene 204, 208, 210
Forrest, Edwin 47, 51
Forty-Second Street 43–55
Foster, George G. xvii, xviii, 34–35, 93, 94
founding mythology 28, 91
Fox, Paula 119
Franklin, Benjamin 22
Free Love 155
Freeman, Brian 214
Friedman, Ed 198
Frohmayer, John 208
Frost, Robert 194
Fuchs, Daniel xxi, 112–13
Fugs, The xxii, 190, 196–97
Fuller, Margaret 67
Funk, Elisabeth Paling 30

Garvey, Marcus 163, 164, 165, 166
gastronomy 6, 11–13, 14–15, 17–18
gay and lesbian cultures 147, 192, 226
   booksellers 177
   Ginsberg and 84
   GLBTQ 209, 214–15
   in Harlem 162
   "post-gay" culture 211–12, 215
   representations of 172
   Whitman and 84–85, 88
Gehring, Charles 5
generational change 121, 123, 134, 139, 173
genteel traditions 33, 37, 43–48, 51, 60, 63, 68, 70, 73, 92, 126, 147, 178–80
gentrification 8, 119, 210, 233
Gershwin, George 222, 223
Gilded Age 235
Ginsberg, Allen xxii, 6, 79, 81, 84–87, 190, 192
   and democracy 86
   "Howl" 78
   photograph of 80
   and Whitman 81–87
Giorno, John 198
Glaspell, Susan 147, 151
Glines, The 209
Gold, Michael xxi, 139, 220
Goldman, Emma xx, 147, 238
Gomez, Marga 210
Gopnik, Adam 8, 233–34
Gotham 22–23
Grace Church 69
Grateful Dead, The 196
Great Migration 165, 169, 170
Greeley, Horace xvii

Greenwich Village xx, xxi, 235
  see also bohemianism
Gunn, Bill 172
Gunn, Thomas Butler 94

Hair (musical) 204
Haley, Alex 174
Hall, Basil 11–13, 14–15, 17–19
Hall, Margaret 18–19
Hall, Richard 212
Halleck, Fitz-Greene 14, 34
Hammill, Pete 233
Hansberry, Lorraine 173, 214
Hapgood, Hutchins 122
Harlem xix, 7, 43–55, 160
Harlem Renaissance xx, 162
  silent protest parade begins 163, 164
Harlem Riot of 1935 169, 174
Hamilton, Andrew 16
Harron, Mary 199
Hawthorne, Nathaniel xvii, 14, 66, 178
Haywood, Big Bill 150, 157
Healey, Peg 206
Hearst, William Randolph 122
hedonism 18, 147
Hedwig and the Angry Inch 204
hell, New York as 21, 23
Hell, Richard xxiii, 189, 190–91
  "Blank Generation" 197–200
Hellman, Lillian 203
Helms, Jesse 208
Hemingway, Ernest 180
high-life see elite
Hijuelos, Oscar xxiii
Himes, Chester 172
hip-hop 186, 223, 228, 229
hipsters 239
Hoffman, Charles Fenno 14, 34
Hoffman, Dustin 238
Hoffman, William 204, 210
Hollinger, David 221
Hollywood, as rival cultural center 144, 181,
  185, 222
Holman, Bob xxiv, 194, 228
Holmstrom, John 195
homophobia 203–211
homosexuality see gay and lesbian cultures
Hone, Philip xvi
Horsmanden, Daniel xv
Hot Peaches 205
Howells, William Dean xix, 122, 126–27,
  138, 220
Hudson, Henry xiv

Hudson River 30, 64
Hughes, Holly 208–09
Hughes, Langston xxi, 78, 167, 168, 171,
  194
humor
  Jewish 213, 222, 223
  in Washington Irving 27
Hurston, Zora Neale xxi, 168–69
Hutchinson, Anne xiv

Ibsen, Henrik 151
ideology of New York 185
immigrant cultures 4, 6, 112, 114, 115,
  134–44, 148, 233
immigration xx
  and Ellis Island xix
  Irish xvii, 128, 135
  Jewish xiv, 112–13, 141, 142–43,
    148, 181
  and poverty 115
  and publishing 181
  Puerto Rican 225–26
In the Heights (musical) 229–30
incorporation of the five boroughs xix, 224
individualism 62, 65
Inge, William 203
interracial marriage 136
intimacy 113
investigative journalism 92
Irish, portrayals of 35, 116, 127–28, 134–35,
  136, 139, 148
Irving, Washington xvi, 5, 6, 14, 22, 27
  History of New York 27–33, 35,
    37, 39
  as humorist 27
  Letters of Jonathan Oldstyle 46
IWW see Wobblies

Jackson and Dunbar, Empire City 3
Jackson, Andrew 13
Jacobs, Jane 238
Jaher, Frederic Cople 91
James, Henry xix, 6, 13, 91, 102, 121, 122,
  123–24
jazz 161, 170, 195
Jazz Age 181
Jazz Singer, The (film) xxi
Jefferson Airplane 196
Jeffersonianism 3–4, 5
Jews, as immigrants xiv, 112–13, 135, 141,
  142–43, 148, 181
  portrayals of xiv, 112–13, 114, 116–17,
    124, 128–30, 134, 135, 137–40, 141,

181, 199, 202, 211, 213, 219, 220–21, 222–23, 224
Jim Crow laws 169–70
John Street Theater xv, 44, 45, 46
Johns, Orrick 153
Johnson, James Weldon xx, 130, 162, 165
Johnson, Samuel 15, 19
Johnson-Reed Act 139–40
Jones Act 226–25
Jones, Gayl 168, 173
Jones, Hettie 193
Jones, LeRoi *see* Baraka, Amiri
Joplin, Janis 196
Judson, Edward Z. C. *see* Buntline, Ned

Kallen, Horace 143–44
Kaplan, Justin 79–80
Katz, Alex 195
Kauffmann, Stanley 203
Kazin, Alfred xxii, 116
Kennedy, Adrienne 173
Kerouac, Jack xxii, 111
King's College *see* Columbia University
Kline, Franz 195
Knickerbocker
    Diedrich 28, 234
    the trope of the 6
Knickerbocker Magazine xvi, 14, 27, 66, 92
Koch, Ed 224
Kramer, Larry xxiii, 210
Kron, Lisa 206–08, 211
Kushner, Tony 211, 213, 223
    Angels in America xxiii, 211, 213, 223

labor conditions 150, 151
labor novels 126
La Mama Experimental Theater Club
    209–10
Lambert, John 17, 22
Lambert, Marchioness 19
Larsen, Nella xxi, 168
Larson, Jonathan 210 *see also Rent* (musical)
Lazarus, Emma 143, 220
Lee, Chang-rae xxiv, 7, 218–20, 222, 224
Lee, Spike xxiii, 222, 223–24, 229
Lennox, Charlotte xv, 19–20
Les Deux Mégots 195
Lesbian Avengers, The 210
Lethem, Jonathan xxiv, 112, 118
Lewis, Sinclair 181
LGBT 7
Lin Yutang xxii, 222
Lippard, George xviii

Literary World 66
"Little Africa" 160
little magazines 147, 181
local color sketches 148
local knowledge 2–3, 7
Locke, Alain xxi, 162, 165, 171
Locke, John 16
Lopate, Philip 3, 110
Lorca, Federico García 79, 110
Lovecraft, H. P. 117–18
Loving v. *Virginia* 136
Lowell, Amy 146
Lowell, James Russell 178
Lower East Side, the 7, 79, 139, 143–95,
    191, 202, 220, 234, 237, 238–39
    poetry scene 193, 194
Lucas, Craig 211
Ludlam, Charles 204
Lunch, Lydia 191, 200

MacAdams, Lewis 190
Mackey, Bill 195
Mac Low, Jackson 195
Makishi, Stacy 210
Malanga, Gerard 190, 191, 196
Malkiel, Theresa 126
Manifest Destiny 66
Manhattan
    1851 map of 59
    and Brooklyn, contrasted 111–12, 114,
        116–17, 119, 204–05
    and consumerism 16
    and food 11–13
    bustling nature of 29
    and class 35–36, 90
    fires in 29–31
    gentrification of 8
    incorporation xix
    Ginsberg's view of 81–87
    lower 32, 58, 73, 81–87, 85, 232, 238–39
    and masculinity 51, 66, 128
    and *Moby-Dick* 58–59, 65–66
    Native Americans in 31
    neighborhoods 2–3
    during Revolutionary War xv
    and transportation xix, 64, 113–14, 116
    and Whitman 76–78, 85
    Woody Allen's 222–23
Manhattan (film) *see* Allen, Woody
manhood 51, 84, 128, 161, 164, 168, 173
manners 45, 84, 85
    American lack of 95; *see also* novel of
        manners

Margolin, Deb 205
Margules, Maurice 195
Marshall, Paule xxii, 115–16, 172
mass media and publishing industry see print
 cultures
Mathews, Cornelius 66
Matthews, Brander 122
Mattison, Alice 114
du Maurier, George 147
Mayer, Bernadette 79
Mayo, Lisa 204
McBride, James 220
McCabe, James Dabney xix, 94
McHenry, Elizabeth 161
McKay, Claude xx, 112, 163–64, 165, 168
McNally, Terrence 211
McNeil, Legs 195
Medusa's Revenge 209
melodrama 128
melting pot, the trope of the 141–42
Melville, Herman xvi, xvii, xviii, 5, 6, 91,
 94, 171
 "Bartleby, the Scrivener" 60–64, 65, 70, 71
 "Hawthorne and His Mosses" 66, 67
 "Jimmy Rose" 60, 74
 Mardi 64
 Moby-Dick 58–59, 60, 62, 64–66, 67,
  71–73
 Pierre 60, 67–72
 Redburn 60, 63, 64
 Typee 63, 67, 69
 White-Jacket 64
metanarrative 157
metatheatricality 6
Metro, Le 195
Mayakovsky, Vladimir 110
Michaëlius, Rev. Jonas xiv
Michaux, Henri 192
microcosms 101
middle class, the
 and Greenwich Village 157
 and publishing 176–78
middlebrow 7, 155, 177
Miguel, Gloria 204
Miguel, Muriel 204
Millay, Edna St. Vincent xx, 7, 147, 151, 154
Miller, Arthur xxii, 117
Miller, Nina 156
Miller, Tim 208
Milligan, Andy 209
Milton, John 14
Minerva Room xvii, 80, 82
minstrelsy 161, 169

Miranda, Lin-Manuel xxiv, 229–30
Mitchell, Donald G. 99, 100, 101
Mitchell, Joseph 232–33
Mitchill, Samuel Latham 30–31, 34–41
modernism 110, 112, 147, 154, 167, 194,
 238
 and the city 178, 185
 and publishing 181
Mohr, Nicholasa xxiii, 226–27
Monroe, Harriet 153
Moore, Marianne 111, 194
Moraga, Cherríe 212–14, 215, 223
mortality, awareness of 8
Mose, the character of 50–51, 92, 103
Mowatt, Anna Cora xvii, 43–55
Mullholland, Inez 147
multiculturalism 4, 114, 116, 130, 219,
 221–22, 227
multilingualism 115
multiracialism and biracialism 168
Mumford, Louis xxii, xxiii, 112
Muñoz, José Esteban 208

National Association for the Advancement
 of Colored People (NAACP) xx, 162
national consciousness 6
nationalism 87, 170
Native Americans, in New York 30, 31
nativism 33, 35
naturalism 118, 122, 128, 152, 170, 173
neighborhoods 2–3, 4, 118
New Amsterdam xiv, 30–41
New Negro movement see Harlem
 Renaissance
New Netherland Project see Gehring,
 Charles
New Woman, the 147, 153
New York as un-American 3
New York City Draft Riots xviii
New-York Historical Society xvi, 5, 29–31
New York Intellectuals 222
New York Knickerbocker Group 14
New York Public Library 14, 163
New York School see poetry; New York
 School of
New York Society Library 14
New York University xvi, 66
New Yorker, The (magazine) xxi, 4–8, 135,
 176, 222, 232
Nichols, Anne xxi, 7, 134–140
Norris, Frank 118
North American Review 66
nostalgia in New York writing 233, 235

and counter-nostalgia 239
novel of manners 6, 121
Nuyorican 7
  as category 224–28
  definition 225, 228
  Poets Cafe xxiii, 227–28
  v. Boricua 225

O'Callaghan, Edmund 34
O'Hara, Frank xxii, 79, 84–81, 192
O'Keefe, John 45
off-Broadway 172, 202, 204, 209, 214,
  221–22
Old New York 123–25
Olmsted, Frederick Law xviii
Olympic Theater 48
Omaha Magic Theater 214
"One Book, One City" 219–20
O'Neill, Eugene xx, 7, 147, 151–52
Open Theater, The 204
Oppen, George 79
Oppenheimer, Joel 194
O'Sullivan, Louis 66
Outcault, R. F. 122

Park Theater xvi, xvii, 43–45, 46, 47–48
Parker, Dorothy xx
Partisan Review 222
"passing" 162
Paterson Strike Pageant 151
Patrick, Robert 204, 210
patriotism 152, 156
Paulding, James Kirke xvi, 10–13, 22, 33
penny press 92
Pessen, Edward 91
Petry, Ann 165, 170
Picabia, Francis 12
Piñero, Miguel xxiii, 227
plantations 163, 171
Playwright's Lab 214
pluralism
  and censorship 183
  and cosmopolitanism 221–22
  cultural 143–44
  and *Moby-Dick* 65
  and multiculturalism 221–22
  and publishing 177–78, 185
Poe, Edgar Allan xvii, 14, 49, 67, 92, 93
poetry
  and collective experience 190
  as lifestyle 192
  lyric 190
  New York School of 190

slam 228–29
  threatening to polite society 196
Poetry Project *see* St. Mark's Church
politeness 13, 17–19, 20, 45, 97, 196
population increase 11
populism 167
pornography 177
postmodernism 186
poverty 142
prejudice 140, 142
preservationism 233
  and blogs 233
Price, Richard xxiv, 239
print cultures 5, 7, 164–65, 174
private/public divide 124, 131
propaganda 140, 183
protest xx, 86, 163, 170
Provincetown Players, the xx, 7, 151, 235
provincialism 112
PS 122 208
psychoanalysis 156
publishing and branding 179, 185
  dime novels 177
  and the middle class 176–78
  and modernism 181
  paperbacks 180, 182–83
  pulp 33, 34, 36, 177
  satirized by Melville 68–69
  trade 178–80, 184–86
Puccini, Giacomo 147
Puerto Rican
  and African American culture 226
  character in *Do the Right Thing* 224
  immigration 225–26
  see also Nuyorican
Pulitzer, Joseph 122
punk
  rock 7, 192
  subcultures 186
Punk (magazine) 195, 199
Puritanism xiv, 3–5, 28, 35

Queens xix, 30, 119
  see also Flushing
queer sexuality *see* gay and lesbian cultures

race consciousness 166
racism 171, 173
radio 135, 156, 164, 179–180, 182, 230
rags to riches *see* upward mobility
ragtime 162
Ramones, The 190
Rauh, Ida 147

realism 6, 127, 151, 220
  ethnic 220
  socialist 219
rebirth 169
"Red Summer" 163
Reed, John 147, 150
Reed, Lou 190–91, 195
reform 127, 146
Rent (musical) 204, 210
Reznikoff, Charles 110
Rice, T. D. xvi
Richardson, Dorothy 122
Ridiculous Theater Company 204
Riis, Jacob xix
Rimbaud, Arthur 190, 192, 194
  Patti Smith on 192–93
Riordan, Wiliam and Plunkitt, George
  Washington 122
riots 163
Robinson, Jackie xxii
Robinson, Solon 94
Rodman, Henrietta 147
Roosevelt, Theodore 140–42, 144, 237
Rosenberg, Ethel 211
Ross, Harold xx, xxi
Ross, Joel H. 94
Ross, William 222
Roth, Henry xxi, 112, 134, 220
  Call It Sleep xxi, 112, 115, 134
Roth, Philip 135, 203
Rothstein, Arnold 137, 139
Rowson, Susannah xvi, 19–20
Ruskin, Mickey 194

St. Mark's Church 190, 191, 194–95, 196,
  200
Salinger, J. D. xxii
Sandeau, Jules 102
Sanders, Ed xxii, 79, 176, 195, 196–97
Santiago, Esmeralda 225, 227
Sartre, Jean-Paul 72
Saturday Night Fever (film) 111
Schechner, Richard 203–11
Schmidman, Joanne 214
Schulman, Sarah 210
Schumpeter, Joseph 232
Scorsese, Martin 94
Second World War *see* World War II
segregation 161, 174
Selby, Hubert xxii, 118
self-destruction 85
self-invention 131
self-making 62

Selyns, Henricus 5–6
Shaiman, Mark 212
Shakespeare, William 14, 44, 46, 74
Shaw, George Bernard 151
Shaw, Peggy 205–06, 208
Shepard, Sam 194
Sheridan, Richard Brinsley 44
Shewey, Don 204, 209
shiksa 141–42
shtetl 138–39
Simms, William Gilmore 67
Simo, Ana Maria 209
slang 78, 129
slave narrative 161
slavery xvi, xv, 160, 162, 169, 173
slum and tenement life 122, 126, 127, 129,
  138, 139, 148, 170, 173
small towns as "America" 3
Smith, Bessie 162
Smith, Betty xxi, 114–16
Smith, Matthew Hale 94, 96
Smith, Patti xxiii, 189, 190–93, 195, 200
  and cowboy as symbol 193
  and Gerard Malanga 191
  and punk rock 192
  on Rimbaud 192–93
Smith, Sydney 11
Smith, William Henry. xviii, 43–55, 47
social change 121, 127, 130, 147, 149
social mobility 62
social laboratory 126
social theatricality 45, 49, 53, 54, 130–31,
  147, 151, 157
socialism 103, 126, 141, 146, 147, 148, 150,
  151, 156
SoHo 226
Sorrentino, Gilbert 176
South, the (rural) 166, 168–69, 172, 173
  see also Jeffersonianism
South Street Seaport Museum 232
Spanish-American War 224
spectacle 6
Spectator, The 15, 22
Spiegelman, Art xxiv
Spiderwoman Theater 204–05, 209
Split Britches 205, 206, 209
Stansell, Christine 148
Staten Island xix, 85
Statue of Liberty xix
steamboats 64
Steendam, Jacob xiv, 5
Stein, D. D. 193
Stephens, Ann S. 99

stereotypes 135, 161, 168
Stern, Theresa 198–200
Stevens, Wallace 194
Stewart, Ellen 209
    see also La Mama Experimental Theater
    Club
Stonewall Riots xxiii
Stowe, Harriet Beecher xviii, 178
strikes 126, 127, 151
Strong, George Templeton xvii, 99, 100,
    102–03
Stuyvesant, Peter xiv
subway xix, 113–14, 116
Swift, Jonathan 22, 28

temperance xviii, 43, 47, 52, 56
Tenderloin, the 160
Terry, Megan 204, 214
Theater of Eternal Music 195
theatricality 45, 49, 53, 54, 130, 133, 151
Thomas, Dylan 194
Thomas, Piri xxiii, 226–25
Thompson, George F. xvii
Thoreau, Henry David 62, 103, 178
Thurman, Wallace 168
Times Square xix
Tin Pan Alley xix
Tocqueville, Alexis de xvii, 13, 42–43, 51, 91
tolerance 134, 140–44
Tony Awards 212
Toomer, Jean 165–66
topoi 110, 112
TOSOS (The Other Side of Silence) 209
tour guides, the trope of 2–3, 8
Townsend, Edward 130
Trachtenberg, Alan and Haw, Richard 110
transatlanticism 19–20, 102
Transcendentalism xviii, 103, 176–78
Triangle Shirtwaist factory xx
Trilling, Lionel 122
Trinity Church xv
Trobriand, Regis de 98, 101–02
Trollope, Frances 14, 23
Tropicana, Carmelita see Troyano, Alina
Troyano, Alina 208
turn-of-the-century city 123
Twain, Mark 171
Tyler, Royall xv, 22, 43–46, 48–49

Uncle Tom's Cabin xviii
Universal Negro Improvement Assocciation
    164
Untermeyer 153

Uplift era 164
upper ten thousand 90, 95
upward mobility 1–2, 16, 138
urban childhood 94
urbanism 6, 85, 110, 155

Valentine, David 34
Van der Donck, Adrian xiv
Van Itallie, Jean-Claude 210
van Vechten, Carl 167
van Wassenaer, Nicolaes xiv, 3
vaudeville 137, 160, 179, 237
Vaux, Calvert xviii
Velvet Underground, The xxii, 196
Verge, Pam 205
Verlaine, Paul 190
Verlaine, Tom xxiii, 198
Verplanck, Giulian 14
Verrazano, Giovanni da xiv
Victorian ideals 169
Vielé, Herman Knickerbocker xix, 36–37
Village Voice (newspaper) xxii, 173, 177
Virginia 3–4, 5
Vogel, Paula 211, 213
Vorse, Mary Heaton 147, 150
Vose, John D. 36

Wagne, Jane 211
Wakoski, Diane 195
Waldman, Anne 79, 189, 190, 198
Wales Padlock Act 203
Walker, Alice 168, 173
Wall Street xv, 10, 43–55, 61, 85, 234
Walrond, Eric 165, 166
Warhol, Andy xxii, 186, 190, 195
Warsh, Lewis 189, 198
Washington, Booker T. 161
Washington Square xx, 123–24, 132
wasteland, the trope of the 11, 73
Weaver, Lois 205, 208
Wells, Ida B. 161, 162, 164, 165
West, Dorothy 165
West, Mae 202
Wharton, Edith xix, xx, xxi, 6, 37–39, 121,
    124–26, 127
White, E. B. xxii, 2–3, 7
white supremacists 161, 169, 174
Whitehead, Colson xxiv, 112
Whitman, Walt xvi, xvii, xviii, 5, 6, 12, 29,
    46, 48, 93, 109–10, 113, 153, 218–19,
    226
    "Calamus" 84
    "Crossing Brooklyn Ferry" 77–78

Whitman, Walt (*cont.*)
  and democracy 76, 79, 82–84, 86, 87
  "Democratic Vistas" 81, 87, 89
  and *Down These Mean Streets* 226
  engraving of 77
  and Ginsberg 81–87
  Leaves of Grass xviii, 76, 78, 87, 233
  and *Native Speaker* 218–19
  "Salut au monde!" 218
  "Song of Myself" 76, 79, 81, 82–83, 88,
    89
  "Specimen Days" 78
Whittier, John Greenleaf 14, 67
widening audience 15
Wigglesworth, Michael 11
Wilde, Oscar 192
wilderness, New York as 10, 19
Williams, John A. 172
Williams, Raymond 221
Williams, Tennessee 203, 209, 211
Williams, William Carlos 147
Willis, Nathaniel Parker 14, 34, 91, 95–99,
  100
Wilson, Doric 204, 209
Wilson, Lanford 204
Winthrop, Theodore xviii
Wittman, Scott 212
Wobblies, the 150, 152
Wolfe, George C. 211, 214
Wolfe, Tom xxiii, 222

women, portrayals of 19–22, 48–49, 51,
  53, 54, 99–101, 116, 123–24, 126–28,
  148–50, 155, 166, 168–169, 170, 173,
  196, 199, 204–05, 207–08, 220
Wolfe, Thomas 113, 181
Woollcott, Alexander xx
working class, the 167
World Trade Center xxiii
  see also 9/11
World War I xx, 139–40, 156, 162, 163,
  168, 169
World War II, and the atomic bomb xxi, 8,
  114, 181–82, 220
Woronov, Mary 196
WOW (Women's One World) 205–8, 209
Wright, Richard 165, 169, 171, 181

X, Malcolm 174
xenophobia 4, 156

Yew, Chay 213
Yentl 138
Yezierska, Anzia xx, xxi, 131, 139, 220
Yiddish 110–12, 134, 141
Young America Movement xvii, 6, 66–68
Young, LaMonte 195
Yurick, Sol xxii, 113

Zangwill, Israel 141–42, 143
Zenger, John Peter xv, 16

Cambridge Companions To...

AUTHORS

Edward Albee edited by Stephen J. Bottoms

Margaret Atwood edited by Coral Ann Howells

W. H. Auden edited by Stan Smith

Jane Austen edited by Edward Copeland and Juliet McMaster

Beckett edited by John Pilling

Aphra Behn edited by Derek Hughes and Janet Todd

Walter Benjamin edited by David S. Ferris

William Blake edited by Morris Eaves

Brecht edited by Peter Thomson and Glendyr Sacks (second edition)

The Brontës edited by Heather Glen

Frances Burney edited by Peter Sabor

Byron edited by Drummond Bone

Albert Camus edited by Edward J. Hughes

Willa Cather edited by Marilee Lindemann

Cervantes edited by Anthony J. Cascardi

Chaucer, second edition edited by Piero Boitani and Jill Mann

Chekhov edited by Vera Gottlieb and Paul Allain

Kate Chopin edited by Janet Beer

Caryl Churchill edited by Elaine Aston and Elin Diamond

Coleridge edited by Lucy Newlyn

Wilkie Collins edited by Jenny Bourne Taylor

Joseph Conrad edited by J. H. Stape

Dante edited by Rachel Jacoff (second edition)

Daniel Defoe edited by John Richetti

Don DeLillo edited by John N. Duvall

Charles Dickens edited by John O. Jordan

Emily Dickinson edited by Wendy Martin

John Donne edited by Achsah Guibbory

Dostoevskii edited by W. J. Leatherbarrow

Theodore Dreiser edited by Leonard Cassuto and Claire Virginia Eby

John Dryden edited by Steven N. Zwicker

W. E. B. Du Bois edited by Shamoon Zamir

George Eliot edited by George Levine

T. S. Eliot edited by A. David Moody

Ralph Ellison edited by Ross Posnock

Ralph Waldo Emerson edited by Joel Porte and Saundra Morris

William Faulkner edited by Philip M. Weinstein

Henry Fielding edited by Claude Rawson

F. Scott Fitzgerald edited by Ruth Prigozy

Flaubert edited by Timothy Unwin

E. M. Forster edited by David Bradshaw

Benjamin Franklin edited by Carla Mulford

Brian Friel edited by Anthony Roche

Robert Frost edited by Robert Faggen

Elizabeth Gaskell edited by Jill L. Matus

Goethe edited by Lesley Sharpe

Günter Grass edited by Stuart Taberner

Thomas Hardy edited by Dale Kramer

David Hare edited by Richard Boon

Nathaniel Hawthorne edited by Richard Millington

Seamus Heaney edited by Bernard O'Donoghue

Ernest Hemingway edited by Scott Donaldson

Homer edited by Robert Fowler

Horace edited by Stephen Harrison

Ibsen edited by James McFarlane

Henry James edited by Jonathan Freedman

Samuel Johnson edited by Greg Clingham

Ben Jonson edited by Richard Harp and Stanley Stewart

James Joyce edited by Derek Attridge (second edition)

Kafka edited by Julian Preece

Keats edited by Susan J. Wolfson

Lacan edited by Jean-Michel Rabaté

D. H. Lawrence edited by Anne Fernihough

Primo Levi edited by Robert Gordon

Lucretius edited by Stuart Gillespie and Philip Hardie

David Mamet edited by Christopher Bigsby

Thomas Mann edited by Ritchie Robertson

Christopher Marlowe edited by Patrick Cheney

Herman Melville edited by Robert S. Levine

Arthur Miller edited by Christopher Bigsby
(second edition)

Milton edited by Dennis Danielson
(second edition)

Molière edited by David Bradby and Andrew
Calder

Toni Morrison edited by Justine Tally

Nabokov edited by Julian W. Connolly

Eugene O'Neill edited by Michael Manheim

George Orwell edited by John Rodden

Ovid edited by Philip Hardie

Harold Pinter edited by Peter Raby
(second edition)

Sylvia Plath edited by Jo Gill

Edgar Allan Poe edited by Kevin J. Hayes

Alexander Pope edited by Pat Rogers

Ezra Pound edited by Ira B. Nadel

Proust edited by Richard Bales

Pushkin edited by Andrew Kahn

Rilke edited by Karen Leeder and
Robert Vilain

Philip Roth edited by Timothy Parrish

Salman Rushdie edited by Abdulrazak
Gurnah

Shakespeare edited by Margareta de Grazia
and Stanley Wells

Shakespearean Comedy edited by
Alexander Leggatt

Shakespeare on Film edited by Russell
Jackson (second edition)

Shakespeare's History Plays edited by
Michael Hattaway

Shakespeare's Last Plays edited by
Catherine M. S. Alexander

Shakespeare's Poetry edited by
Patrick Cheney

Shakespeare and Popular Culture edited by
Robert Shaughnessy

Shakespeare on Stage edited by Stanley Wells
and Sarah Stanton

Shakespearean Tragedy edited by
Claire McEachern

George Bernard Shaw edited by
Christopher Innes

Shelley edited by Timothy Morton

Mary Shelley edited by Esther Schor

Sam Shepard edited by Matthew C. Roudané

Spenser edited by Andrew Hadfield

Laurence Sterne edited by Thomas Keymer

Wallace Stevens edited by John N. Serio

Tom Stoppard edited by Katherine E. Kelly

Harriet Beecher Stowe edited by
Cindy Weinstein

August Strindberg edited by
Michael Robinson

Jonathan Swift edited by Christopher Fox

J. M. Synge edited by P. J. Mathews

Tacitus edited by A. J. Woodman

Henry David Thoreau edited by Joel
Myerson

Tolstoy edited by Donna Tussing Orwin

Mark Twain edited by Forrest G. Robinson

Virgil edited by Charles Martindale

Voltaire edited by Nicholas Cronk

Edith Wharton edited by Millicent Bell

Walt Whitman edited by Ezra Greenspan

Oscar Wilde edited by Peter Raby

Tennessee Williams edited by
Matthew C. Roudané

August Wilson edited by
Christopher Bigsby

Mary Wollstonecraft edited by
Claudia L. Johnson

Virginia Woolf edited by Susan Sellers
(second edition)

Wordsworth edited by Stephen Gill

W. B. Yeats edited by Marjorie Howes and
John Kelly

Zola edited by Brian Nelson

TOPICS

The Actress edited by Maggie B. Gale and
John Stokes

The African American Novel edited by
Maryemma Graham

The African American Slave Narrative
edited by Audrey A. Fisch

Allegory edited by Rita Copeland and
Peter Struck

American Modernism edited by Walter
Kalaidjian

American Realism and Naturalism edited by
Donald Pizer

American Travel Writing edited by
Alfred Bendixen and Judith Hamera

American Women Playwrights edited by
Brenda Murphy

Ancient Rhetoric edited by Erik Gunderson

Arthurian Legend edited by
Elizabeth Archibald and Ad Putter

Australian Literature edited by
Elizabeth Webby

British Romanticism edited by Stuart Curran

British Romantic Poetry edited by James
Chandler and Maureen N. McLane

British Theatre, 1730–1830 edited by
Jane Moody and Daniel O'Quinn

Canadian Literature edited by Eva-Marie
Kröller

Children's Literature edited by M. O. Grenby
and Andrea Immel

The Classic Russian Novel edited by
Malcolm V. Jones and Robin Feuer Miller

Contemporary Irish Poetry edited by
Matthew Campbell

Crime Fiction edited by Martin Priestman

Early Modern Women's Writing edited by
Laura Lunger Knoppers

The Eighteenth-Century Novel edited by
John Richetti

Eighteenth-Century Poetry edited by
John Sitter

English Literature, 1500–1600 edited by
Arthur F. Kinney

English Literature, 1650–1740 edited by
Steven N. Zwicker

English Literature, 1740–1830 edited by
Thomas Keymer and Jon Mee

English Literature, 1830–1914 edited by
Joanne Shattock

English Novelists edited by Adrian Poole

English Poets edited by Claude Rawson

English Poetry, Donne to Marvell edited by
Thomas N. Corns

English Renaissance Drama, second edition
edited by A. R. Braunmuller and Michael
Hattaway

English Restoration Theatre edited by
Deborah C. Payne Fisk

Feminist Literary Theory edited by
Ellen Rooney

Fiction in the Romantic Period edited by
Richard Maxwell and Katie Trumpener

The Fin de Siècle edited by Gail Marshall

The French Novel: from 1800 to the Present
edited by Timothy Unwin

German Romanticism edited by
Nicholas Saul

Gothic Fiction edited by Jerrold E. Hogle

The Greek and Roman Novel edited by
Tim Whitmarsh

Greek and Roman Theatre edited by
Marianne McDonald and J. Michael Walton

Greek Lyric edited by Felix Budelmann

Greek Mythology edited by
Roger D. Woodard

Greek Tragedy edited by P. E. Easterling

The Harlem Renaissance edited by
George Hutchinson

The Irish Novel edited by
John Wilson Foster

The Italian Novel edited by Peter Bondanella
and Andrea Ciccarelli

Jewish American Literature edited by Hana
Wirth-Nesher and Michael P. Kramer

The Latin American Novel edited by
Efraín Kristal

The Literature of Los Angeles edited by
Kevin R. McNamara

The Literature of New York edited by
Cyrus Patell and Bryan Waterman

The Literature of the First World War
edited by Vincent Sherry

The Literature of World War II edited by
Marina MacKay

Literature on Screen edited by Deborah
Cartmell and Imelda Whelehan

Medieval English Literature edited by
Larry Scanlon

Medieval English Theatre edited by Richard
Beadle and Alan J. Fletcher (second edition)

Medieval French Literature edited by Simon
Gaunt and Sarah Kay

Medieval Romance edited by
Roberta L. Krueger

Medieval Women's Writing edited by
Carolyn Dinshaw and David Wallace

Modern American Culture edited by
Christopher Bigsby

Modern British Women Playwrights
edited by Elaine Aston and Janelle Reinelt

Modern French Culture edited by
Nicholas Hewitt

Modern German Culture edited by Eva Kolinsky and Wilfried van der Will

The Modern German Novel edited by Graham Bartram

Modern Irish Culture edited by Joe Cleary and Claire Connolly

Modernism edited by Michael Levenson

The Modernist Novel edited by Morag Shiach

Modernist Poetry edited by Alex Davis and Lee M. Jenkins

Modern Italian Culture edited by Zygmunt G. Baranski and Rebecca J. West

Modern Latin American Culture edited by John King

Modern Russian Culture edited by Nicholas Rzhevsky

Modern Spanish Culture edited by David T. Gies

Narrative edited by David Herman

Native American Literature edited by Joy Porter and Kenneth M. Roemer

Nineteenth-Century American Women's Writing edited by Dale M. Bauer and Philip Gould

Old English Literature edited by Malcolm Godden and Michael Lapidge

Performance Studies edited by Tracy C. Davis

Postcolonial Literary Studies edited by Neil Lazarus

Postmodernism edited by Steven Connor

Renaissance Humanism edited by Jill Kraye

Roman Satire edited by Kirk Freudenburg

The Roman Historians edited by Andrew Feldherr

The Spanish Novel: from 1600 to the Present edited by Harriet Turner and Adelaida López de Martínez

Travel Writing edited by Peter Hulme and Tim Youngs

Twentieth-Century Irish Drama edited by Shaun Richards

The Twentieth-Century English Novel edited by Robert L. Caserio

Twentieth-Century English Poetry edited by Neil Corcoran

Victorian and Edwardian Theatre edited by Kerry Powell

The Victorian Novel edited by Deirdre David

Victorian Poetry edited by Joseph Bristow

War Writing edited by Kate McLoughlin

Writing of the English Revolution edited by N. H. Keeble